**Street & Smith's
Guide to Baseball 1996**

Street & Smith's Guide to Baseball 1996

By the Editors of
Street & Smith's

★ ★ ★

Consulting Editor
Scott Gray

BALLANTINE BOOKS • NEW YORK

Copyright © 1995 by
Condé Nast Publications, Inc.

All rights reserved under International and
Pan-American Copyright Conventions.
Published in the United States of America by
Ballantine Books, a division of Random
House, Inc., New York, and simultaneously
in Canada by Random House of Canada
Limited, Toronto.

Library of Congress Catalog Card Number:
95-94961

ISBN 0-345-40250-2

Manufactured in the United States of America

Cover Photo of Greg Maddux
© Duomo Pictures

Player photos appear courtesy of the
individual teams and/or MLB Photos.

First Edition: March 1996

10 9 8 7 6 5 4 3 2

Table of Contents

Historical Section

Acknowledgments

First and foremost, thanks to the fans who remember that underneath the business of baseball there remains the simple pleasure of our national pastime.

We appreciate the patient assistance afforded us by the league offices and the departments of media relations of all 28 major-league teams, who answered our queries and requests quickly and helpfully.

The professionals at Creative Graphics are appreciated for their work with the photographs and their contribution to the production of this book.

Ballantine Books provides an all-star lineup. Cathy Repetti is currently batting 1.000 in clutch situations, while Mark Rifkin is the ultimate cleanup hitter. The table setters are Carlos Beltrán, George Davidson, Betsy Elias, Betsy Flagler, Caron Harris, Alix Krijgsman, Nora Reichard, and Darren Schillace.

Gioia Di Biase designed the cover and the internal layout.

Lefty pinch hitters and one-batter relief specialists include: Paul Bratt, Chris Beightel, Parker Cross, Dondi DeMarco, Sim Denton, Chris Haven, Bruce, Steve, and Matthew Hoffacker, Kendall Lee, David Slade, Paul and Aidan Stone, and Gene Taback.

Those who went deep in the bottom of the ninth include John Richard Gray, Tom Helberg, Cliff Phillips, and David Seidemann.

Roberto Alomar

Introduction

Welcome back—let's talk a little baseball. Most of what you'll find in this guide is self-explanatory, but here are some notes that might come in handy:

• We go to press in December, so free agency and trades will render some of the rosters and lineup cards partially inaccurate. To avoid confusion regarding players who change teams before press time and those who move after the book goes to print, every player bio is located with the player's 1995 team.

• If a player switched leagues in midseason, we've shown his combined numbers in his player bio (if he has one) and left them separate on the Statistics pages.

• You'll recognize most of the statistical abbreviations we use, but in case these two are unfamiliar: **WHIP** is the ratio of walks plus hits divided by innings pitched, and **OBA** is the aggregate batting average of opponents when facing the pitcher in question.

Whether you're gearing up for a fantasy-league draft or getting up to speed on your home team's prospects, we're thrilled that you've decided to start your season with Street & Smith's. If you have questions, comments, or opinions to express, just e-mail us at the following address:

StreetBase@aol.com

Larry Walker

Fantasy Rankings

For readers who aren't accustomed to the non–reality based realities of fantasy-league baseball, this section of the book may not be particularly useful. Most fantasy leagues base their scoring on the necessarily simplistic concept that each statistical category carries equal weight, that all things being equal it's better to win the strikeouts category than to finish third in wins, for example—a patently false concept in real baseball, where wins are all that matter. We won't risk losing your attention by laying out the technical aspects of the rating system, but there are two things you'll need to know. First, the ratings are based on a mythical seven-team league, which causes extreme percentage variations based on small actual differences. In a larger league, Greg Maddux would be the number-one starting pitcher on the board, but in this league it's Randy Johnson. The calculations are formulated using the following categories: hitters—runs scored, runs batted in, batting average, home runs, and stolen bases minus caught stealings; pitchers—wins minus losses, earned run average, walks plus hits divided by innings pitched, saves, and strikeouts. Zero represents the average player at that position of the worst team in the fantasy league.

First Basemen

Mo Vaughn	1.776
Frank Thomas	1.462
Rafael Palmeiro	1.287
Andres Galarraga	1.266
Mark Grace	0.968
Tino Martinez	0.966
Eric Karros	0.858
Jeff Bagwell	0.753
Mark McGwire	0.586
J.T. Snow	0.577

Second Basemen

Craig Biggio	2.149
Chuck Knoblauch	1.917
Roberto Alomar	1.188
Quilvio Veras	1.002
Carlos Baerga	0.937
Eric Young	0.545
Delino DeShields	0.335
Mike Lansing	0.239
Jeff Kent	−0.205
Bret Boone	−0.208

Third Basemen

Ken Caminiti	0.850
Tony Phillips	0.684
Jim Thome	0.638
Robin Ventura	0.558
Vinny Castilla	0.490
Gary Gaetti	0.464
Chipper Jones	0.461
Travis Fryman	0.096
Mike Blowers	−0.013
Jeff King	−0.041

Shortstops

Barry Larkin	2.648
John Valentin	1.768
Omar Vizquel	0.463
Shawon Dunston	−0.041
Cal Ripken	−0.149
Royce Clayton	−0.269

Wil Cordero	−0.349
Jose Vizcaino	−0.365
Pat Meares	−0.416
Kurt Abbott	−0.482

Catchers

Mike Piazza	1.039
Mike Stanley	−0.172
Ivan Rodriguez	−0.417
Brad Ausmus	−0.540
Chris Hoiles	−0.556
Joe Girardi	−0.713
Terry Steinbach	−0.724
Javier Lopez	−0.739
Todd Hundley	−0.762
Darren Daulton	−0.847

Outfielders

Albert Belle	2.289
Sammy Sosa	2.227
Barry Bonds	2.197
Dante Bichette	2.070
Reggie Sanders	2.007
Kenny Lofton	1.862
Lance Johnson	1.826
Larry Walker	1.756
Raul Mondesi	1.672
Tim Salmon	1.530

Designated Hitters

Edgar Martinez	1.843
Geronimo Berroa	0.507

Designated Hitters (continued)

Eddie Murray	0.490
Chili Davis	0.451
Jose Canseco	0.372
Paul Molitor	0.124
Mickey Tettleton	0.102
Juan Gonzalez	0.088
Harold Baines	−0.183
Greg Vaughn	−0.320

Starting Pitchers

Randy Johnson	3.968
Greg Maddux	3.719
Hideo Nomo	2.169
Pete Schourek	1.848
Mike Mussina	1.545
David Cone	1.464
Kenny Rogers	1.110
John Smoltz	1.068
Ramon Martinez	1.064
Tom Glavine	1.045

Relief Pitchers

Jose Mesa	1.065
Mark Wohlers	1.062
Julian Tavarez	1.031
Stan Belinda	0.890
Jeff Nelson	0.810
Todd Worrell	0.786
Dave Veres	0.671
Brad Clontz	0.640
Greg McMichael	0.617
Darren Holmes	0.612

Top Ten Prospects

Paul Wilson, SP, Mets: The top pick overall in the 1994 draft, Wilson is the number-one prospect in a system that is brimming with talented arms.

Alex Rodriguez, SS, Mariners: The number-one pick in the 1993 draft, Rodriguez has been celebrated since high school as a five-tool talent.

Alan Benes, SP, Cardinals: Benes flashed overpowering stuff in a big-league trial last season.

Todd Greene, C, Angels: Greene is a slugging backstop who could emerge as a star if his glovework improves.

Billy Wagner, SP, Astros: He isn't physically imposing, but Wagner's fastball is the best in the minor leagues.

Ruben Rivera, OF, Yankees: The Yankees haven't had a Rookie of the Year since 1991, but Rivera can be a force if given the opportunity.

Karim Garcia, OF, Dodgers: The Dodgers seem to have a lock on the NL's rookie award, and young Garcia has the raw talent to carry on that legacy.

Steve Gibralter, OF, Reds: Gibralter led the American Association in home runs last year before a thumb injury ended his season.

Jim Pittsley, SP, Royals: Pittsley possesses the stuff and makeup of a number-one starter.

Chris Snopek, 3B, White Sox: Snopek batted .323 at triple-A last year, then hit .324 in a late-season call-up.

Hideo Nomo

National League

1995 Review

Simply put, the best team won. The NL's trio of division winners—Atlanta, Cincinnati, and Los Angeles—lived up to their respective talent levels in the regular season, and unstoppable Atlanta rampaged through the postseason.

Like a T. Rex after feeding, the Braves were sluggish at times, yet there was never a shadow of doubt about who would win the East. The Mets traded the fat contracts of Bonilla and Saberhagen, put the team's fortunes in the hands of young players, and finished in a second-place tie with the stumbling Phillies. Florida continued to endure the growing pains of an expansion team, while the Expos held a fire sale and devolved back to an expansion level themselves.

It looked as if Houston and Cincy might be pitted in a dogfight at the top of the Central, but Jeff Bagwell's third broken hand in three years sent the Astros spinning out of orbit as the streaking Reds buried them in second place. The Cubs, paced by Sammy Sosa's bat and a fine young starting staff, won eight of their final ten games and were closing in on second place when the short season ended. The league's two weakest clubs, St. Louis and Pittsburgh, were never in contention.

Los Angeles won the West on the last day of September, but the Rockies took advantage of slugger-friendly Coors Field and gave the Dodgers all they could handle before settling for second. The Padres played well enough to linger on the fringe of the wild-card race, thanks to a deal with Houston that brought veterans Ken Caminiti and Steve Finley to San Diego. Up the coast in San Francisco, poor pitching and weak hitting put the Giants in the cellar.

1995 Final Standings

EASTERN DIVISION

Team	Won	Lost	Pct	GB
Atlanta	90	54	.625	—
New York	69	75	.479	21.0
Philadelphia	69	75	.479	21.0
Florida	67	76	.469	22.5
Montreal	66	78	.458	24.0

CENTRAL DIVISION

Team	Won	Lost	Pct	GB
Cincinnati	85	59	.590	—
Houston	76	68	.528	9.0
Chicago	73	71	.507	12.0
St. Louis	62	81	.434	22.5
Pittsburgh	58	86	.403	27.0

WESTERN DIVISION

Team	Won	Lost	Pct	GB
Los Angeles	78	66	.542	—
Colorado	77	67	.535	1.0
San Diego	70	74	.486	8.0
San Francisco	67	77	.465	11.0

First-Round Playoffs: Atlanta 3, Colorado 1; Cincinnati 3, Los Angeles 0

League Championship: Atlanta 4, Cincinnati 0

World Series: Atlanta 4, Cleveland 2

Team Statistics

BATTING

TEAM	BA	G	RS	H	2B	3B	HR	RBI	BB	SB	SLG
Colorado	.282	144	785	1406	259	43	200	749	484	125	.471
Houston	.275	144	747	1403	260	22	109	694	566	176	.399
San Diego	.272	144	668	1345	231	20	116	618	447	124	.397
Cincinnati	.270	144	747	1326	277	35	161	694	519	190	.440
New York	.267	144	657	1323	218	34	125	617	446	58	.400
Chicago	.265	144	693	1315	267	39	158	648	440	105	.430
Los Angeles	.264	144	634	1303	191	31	140	593	468	127	.400
Florida	.262	143	673	1278	214	29	144	636	517	131	.406
Philadelphia	.262	144	615	1296	263	30	94	576	497	72	.384
Montreal	.259	144	621	1268	265	24	118	572	400	120	.394
Pittsburgh	.259	144	629	1281	245	27	125	587	456	84	.396
San Francisco	.253	144	652	1256	229	33	152	610	472	138	.404
Atlanta	.250	144	645	1202	210	27	168	618	520	73	.409
St. Louis	.247	143	563	1182	238	24	107	533	436	79	.374

PITCHING

TEAM	W	L	ERA	G	SV	H	ER	HR	BB	SO	OBA
Atlanta	90	54	3.44	144	34	1184	494	107	436	1087	.244
Los Angeles	78	66	3.66	144	37	1188	526	125	462	1060	.243
New York	69	75	3.88	144	36	1296	556	133	401	901	.262
Cincinnati	85	59	4.03	144	38	1270	578	131	424	903	.260
Houston	76	68	4.06	144	32	1357	596	118	460	1056	.266
St. Louis	62	81	4.09	143	38	1290	575	135	416	842	.268
Montreal	66	78	4.11	144	42	1286	586	128	416	950	.262
Chicago	73	71	4.13	144	45	1313	597	162	518	926	.262
San Diego	70	74	4.13	144	35	1242	590	142	512	1047	.255
Philadelphia	69	75	4.21	144	41	1241	603	134	538	980	.254
Florida	67	76	4.27	143	29	1299	610	139	562	994	.264
Pittsburgh	58	86	4.70	144	29	1407	666	130	477	871	.283
San Francisco	67	77	4.86	144	34	1368	699	173	505	801	.275
Colorado	77	67	4.97	144	43	1443	711	160	512	891	.286

Craig Biggio

Departmental Leaders

HITTING

Batting Average
Tony Gwynn, SD	.368
Mike Piazza, LA	.346
Dante Bichette, COL	.340
Derek Bell, HOU	.334
Mark Grace, CHI	.326
Barry Larkin, CIN	.319
Vinny Castilla, COL	.309
David Segui, MON	.309
Gregg Jefferies, PHI	.306
Reggie Sanders, CIN	.306
Larry Walker, COL	.306

Hits
Dante Bichette, COL	197
Tony Gwynn, SD	197
Mark Grace, CHI	180
Craig Biggio, HOU	167
Steve Finley, SD	167
Brian McRae, CHI	167
Eric Karros, LA	164
Vinny Castilla, COL	163
Ken Caminiti, SD	159
Barry Larkin, CIN	158

Runs Scored
Craig Biggio, HOU	123
Barry Bonds, SF	109
Steve Finley, SD	104
Dante Bichette, COL	102
Barry Larkin, CIN	98
Mark Grace, CHI	97
Larry Walker, COL	96
Brian McRae, CHI	92
Raul Mondesi, LA	91
Reggie Sanders, CIN	91

Runs Batted In
Dante Bichette, COL	128
Sammy Sosa, CHI	119
Andres Galarraga, COL	106
Jeff Conine, FLO	105
Eric Karros, LA	105
Barry Bonds, SF	104
Larry Walker, COL	101
Reggie Sanders, CIN	99
Ken Caminiti, SD	94
Fred McGriff, ATL	93
Mike Piazza, LA	93

At-Bats Per RBI
Dante Bichette, COL	4.5
Jeff Conine, FLO	4.6
Ron Gant	4.7
Mike Piazza, LA	4.7
Sammy Sosa, CHI	4.7
Barry Bonds, SF	4.9
Reggie Sanders, CIN	4.9
Larry Walker, COL	4.9
Jeff Bagwell, HOU	5.1
Jeff King, PIT	5.1

Doubles
Mark Grace, CHI	51
Dante Bichette, COL	38
Brian McRae, CHI	38
Reggie Sanders, CIN	36
Wil Cordero, MON	35
Ray Lankford, STL	35
Bret Boone, CIN	34
Vinny Castilla, COL	34
Mickey Morandini, PHI	34
Ken Caminiti, SD	33
Bernard Gilkey, STL	33
Tony Gwynn, SD	33
Rondell White, MON	33

Triples
Brett Butler, LA	9
Eric Young, COL	9
Steve Finley, SD	8
Luis Gonzalez, CHI	8
Deion Sanders, SF	8
Kurt Abbott, FLO	7
Barry Bonds, SF	7
Scott Bullett, CHI	7

Triples (continued)

Brian McRae, CHI	7
Mickey Morandini, PHI	7
Quilvio Veras, FLO	7

Home Runs

Dante Bichette, COL	40
Sammy Sosa, CHI	36
Larry Walker, COL	36
Barry Bonds, SF	33
Vinny Castilla, COL	32
Eric Karros, LA	32
Mike Piazza, LA	32
Andres Galarraga, COL	31
Ron Gant, CIN	29
Reggie Sanders, CIN	28

At-Bats Per Home Run

Mike Piazza, LA	13.6
Larry Walker, COL	13.7
Ron Gant, CIN	14.1
Dante Bichette, COL	14.5
Barry Bonds, SF	15.3
Sammy Sosa, CHI	15.7
Vinny Castilla, COL	16.5
David Justice, ATL	17.1
Eric Karros, LA	17.2
Reggie Sanders, CIN	17.3

On-Base Percentage

Barry Bonds, SF	.431
Craig Biggio, HOU	.406
Tony Gwynn, SD	.404
Walt Weiss, COL	.403
Mike Piazza, LA	.400
Jeff Bagwell, HOU	.399
Reggie Sanders, CIN	.397
Mark Grace, CHI	.395
Barry Larkin, CIN	.394
Jose Offerman, LA	.389

Slugging Percentage

Dante Bichette, COL	.620
Larry Walker, COL	.607
Mike Piazza, LA	.606
Reggie Sanders, CIN	.579
Barry Bonds, SF	.577
Vinny Castilla, COL	.564
Ron Gant, CIN	.554
Eric Karros, LA	.535
Jeff Conine, FLO	.520
Mark Grace, CHI	.516

Total Bases

Dante Bichette, COL	359
Larry Walker, COL	300
Vinny Castilla, COL	297
Eric Karros, LA	295
Barry Bonds, SF	292
Mark Grace, CHI	285
Andres Galarraga, COL	283
Sammy Sosa, CHI	282
Reggie Sanders, CIN	280
Ken Caminiti, SD	270

Walks

Barry Bonds, SF	120
Walt Weiss, COL	98
Craig Biggio, HOU	80
Quilvio Veras, FLO	80
Jeff Bagwell, HOU	79
Ron Gant, CIN	74
Chipper Jones, ATL	73
David Justice, ATL	73
Dave Magadan, HOU	71
Ken Caminiti, SD	69
Jose Offerman, LA	69
Reggie Sanders, CIN	69

Strikeouts

Andres Galarraga, COL	146
Sammy Sosa, CHI	134
Reggie Sanders, CIN	122
Eric Karros, LA	115
Rico Brogna, NY	111
Jay Bell, PIT	110
Kurt Abbott, FLO	110
Ray Lankford, STL	110
Royce Clayton, SF	109
Ron Gant, CIN	108

Stolen Bases

Quilvio Veras, FLO	56
Barry Larkin, CIN	51
Delino DeShields, LA	39

Steve Finley, SD	36
Reggie Sanders, CIN	36
Eric Young, COL	35
Sammy Sosa, CHI	34
Craig Biggio, HOU	33
Brett Butler, LA	32
Darren Lewis, CIN	32

Caught Stealing

Quilvio Veras, FLO	21
Darren Lewis	18
Delino DeShields, LA	14
Jacob Brumfield, PIT	12
Steve Finley, SD	12
Reggie Sanders, CIN	12
Eric Young, COL	12
Chuck Carr, FLO	11
Al Martin, PIT	11
Barry Bonds, SF	10
Roberto Kelly, LA	10

PITCHING

Earned Run Average

Greg Maddux, ATL	1.63
Hideo Nomo, LA	2.54
Andy Ashby, SD	2.94
Ismael Valdes, LA	3.05
Tom Glavine, ATL	3.08
Joey Hamilton, SD	3.08
John Smoltz, ATL	3.18
Frank Castillo, CHI	3.21
Pete Schourek, CIN	3.22
Jaime Navarro, CHI	3.28

Innings Pitched

Greg Maddux, ATL	209.2
Denny Neagle, PIT	209.2
Ramon Martinez, LA	206.1
Joey Hamilton, SD	204.1
Jaime Navarro, CHI	200.1
Tom Glavine, ATL	198.2
Ismael Valdes, LA	197.2
Bobby Jones, NY	195.2
Mark Leiter, SF	195.2
Pedro J. Martinez, MON	194.2

Complete Games

Greg Maddux, ATL	10
Mark Leiter, SF	7
Ismael Valdes, LA	6
Denny Neagle, PIT	5
John Burkett, FLO	4
Tyler Green, PHI	4
Ramon Martinez, LA	4
Hideo Nomo, LA	4
Steve Avery, ATL	3
Tom Glavine, ATL	3
Chris Hammond, FLO	3
Bobby Jones, NY	3
Pat Rapp, FLO	3
Shane Reynolds, HOU	3
Bret Saberhagen, COL	3
Paul Wagner, PIT	3
David Wells, CIN	3

Wins

Greg Maddux, ATL	19
Pete Schourek, CIN	18
Ramon Martinez, LA	17
Tom Glavine, ATL	16
John Burkett, FLO	14
Pedro J. Martinez, MON	14
Jaime Navarro, CHI	14
Pat Rapp, FLO	14
Jeff Fassero, MON	13
Denny Neagle, PIT	13
Hideo Nomo, LA	13
Ismael Valdes, LA	13

Winning Percentage

Greg Maddux, ATL	.905
Pete Schourek, CIN	.720
Dave Burba, CIN	.714
Ramon Martinez, LA	.708
John Smiley, CIN	.706
Jaime Navarro, CHI	.700
Tom Glavine, ATL	.696
Hideo Nomo, LA	.684
Pat Rapp, FLO	.667
John Smoltz, ATL	.632

Losses

Paul Wagner, PIT	16
John Burkett, FLO	14

Losses (continued)

Tom Candiotti, LA	14
Jeff Fassero, MON	14
Steve Avery, ATL	13
Terry Mulholland, SF	13
Steve Trachsel, CHI	13
Danny Jackson, STL	12
Darryl Kile, HOU	12
Mark Leiter, SF	12
Paul Quantrill, PHI	12

Saves

Randy Myers, CHI	38
Tom Henke, STL	36
Rod Beck, SF	33
Heathcliff Slocumb, PHI	32
Todd Worrell, LA	32
Trevor Hoffman, SD	31
Mel Rojas, MON	30
John Franco, NY	29
Jeff Brantley, CIN	28
Mark Wohlers, ATL	25

Strikeouts

Hideo Nomo, LA	236
John Smoltz, ATL	193
Greg Maddux, ATL	181
Shane Reynolds, HOU	175
Pedro J. Martinez, MON	174
Jeff Fassero, MON	164
Pete Schourek, CIN	160
Andy Ashby, SD	150
Denny Neagle, PIT	150
Ismael Valdes, LA	150

Strikeouts Per Nine Innings

Hideo Nomo, LA	11.1
John Smoltz, ATL	9.0
Shane Reynolds, HOU	8.3
Pedro J. Martinez, MON	8.0
Jeff Fassero, MON	7.8
Kevin Foster, CHI	7.8
Greg Maddux, ATL	7.8
Pete Schourek, CIN	7.6
Steve Avery, ATL	7.3
Chris Hammond, FLO	7.0

Walks

Ramon Martinez, LA	81
Hideo Nomo, LA	78
Pat Rapp, FLO	76
Steve Trachsel, CHI	76
Mike Mimbs, PHI	75
Jeff Fassero, MON	74
Darryl Kile, HOU	73
John Smoltz, ATL	72
Paul Wagner, PIT	72
Tom Glavine, ATL	66
Tyler Green, PHI	66
Pedro J. Martinez, MON	66

Walks Per Nine Innings

Greg Maddux, ATL	1.0
Shane Reynolds, HOU	1.8
Denny Neagle, PIT	1.9
Bret Saberhagen, COL	1.9
John Smiley, CIN	2.0
Pete Schourek, CIN	2.1
Paul Quantrill, PHI	2.2
Terry Mulholland, SF	2.3
Greg Swindell, HOU	2.3
Ismael Valdes, LA	2.3

Hits

Denny Neagle, PIT	221
Paul Quantrill, PHI	212
Bobby Jones, NY	209
John Burkett, FLO	208
Jeff Fassero, MON	207
Doug Drabek, HOU	205
Estaban Loaiza, PIT	205
Shane Reynolds, HOU	196
Jaime Navarro, CHI	194
Terry Mulholland, SF	190

Hits Per Nine Innings

Hideo Nomo, LA	5.83
Greg Maddux, ATL	6.31
Pedro J. Martinez, MON	7.30
Pete Schourek, CIN	7.47
Ismael Valdes, LA	7.65
Ramon Martinez, LA	7.68
John Smoltz, ATL	7.75
Kevin Foster, CHI	8.00

Tom Glavine, ATL	8.24
Joey Hamilton, SD	8.32

Opponents Batting Average

Hideo Nomo, LA	.182
Greg Maddux, ATL	.197
Pedro J. Martinez, MON	.227
Pete Schourek, CIN	.228
Ismael Valdes, LA	.228
Ramon Martinez, LA	.231
John Smoltz, ATL	.232
Kevin Foster, CHI	.240
Tom Glavine, ATL	.246
Joey Hamilton, SD	.246

Home Runs

Kevin Foster, CHI	32
Terry Mulholland, SF	25
Steve Trachsel, CHI	25
Jose Bautista, SF	24
Dave Mlicki, NY	23
Steve Avery, ATL	22
John Burkett, FLO	22
Frank Castillo, CHI	22
Esteban Loaiza, PIT	21
Pedro J. Martinez, MON	21
Bret Saberhagen, COL	21
Greg Swindell, HOU	21

Wild Pitches

Hideo Nomo, LA	19
Hector Carrasco, CIN	15
John Smoltz, ATL	13
Toby Borland, PHI	12
John Ericks, PIT	11
Darryl Kile, HOU	11
Willie Banks, FLO	9
Tyler Green, PHI	9
Mark Leiter, SF	9
Mike Mimbs, PHI	9

1996 Preview

Free agency, fire sales, and the youth movement—not to mention potential franchise relocations—continue to alter the complexion of the league, but the division races could be classics.

The Braves boast the NL's deepest starting rotation, not to mention a loaded batting order. With young talents like Jones, Lopez, and Klesko set to develop even further, the road to a championship runs through Atlanta. Look for the Mets to take a quantum leap forward on the strength of three strong-armed pitching prospects who could lead New York to a wild-card berth. Florida is slowly building toward respectability, while the Expos are on their way to expansion status. Philadelphia has maintained the veteran nucleus of its 1993 pennant winner, but the franchise has been hit hard by injuries the past two seasons.

Pittsburgh and Houston could be making big moves in the Central, but not on the field. There's a high probability that one or both of the financially strapped franchises will have vacated their current cities by the time you read this. The Astros underachieved last season and don't figure to improve, so the Reds will be heavy favorites to repeat as division champs. The Cubs have a stellar yet unheralded starting staff and should be a factor in the wild-card race, while the Cards and Bucs still have rebuilding to do.

The West is harder to read than a Nomo fastball, but San Francisco appears to have no pitching at press time, and there is only so much that Bonds and Williams can do to compensate. The Padres may be the most fundamentally sound team in the division, though they'll need to take one more step forward to challenge the slugging Rockies and pitching-rich Dodgers.

1996 Projected Standings

EASTERN DIVISION

Team	Won	Lost	Pct	GB
Atlanta	98	64	.605	—
New York	88	74	.543	10
Florida	76	86	.469	22
Montreal	73	89	.451	25
Philadelphia	72	90	.444	26

CENTRAL DIVISION

Team	Won	Lost	Pct	GB
Cincinnati	93	69	.574	—
Houston	83	79	.512	10
Chicago	82	80	.506	11
St. Louis	71	91	.438	22
Pittsburgh	68	94	.420	25

WESTERN DIVISION

Team	Won	Lost	Pct	GB
Los Angeles	87	75	.537	—
Colorado	85	77	.525	2
San Diego	81	81	.500	6
San Francisco	77	85	.475	10

First-Round Playoffs: Atlanta 3, Los Angeles 2; Cincinnati 3, New York 1

League Championship: Atlanta 4, Cincinnati 2

World Series: Atlanta 4, New York 3

Projected Statistical Leaders

BATTING

Batting Average
Tony Gwynn   .356
Barry Bonds   .348
Jeff Bagwell   .344

Home Runs
Matt Williams   47
Mike Piazza   42
Dante Bichette   41

Runs Batted In
Dante Bichette   136
Mike Piazza   133
Barry Bonds   122

PITCHING

Wins
Greg Maddux   24
Jason Isringhausen 21
Ismael Valdes   20

Earned Run Average
Greg Maddux   1.81
Ismael Valdes   2.48
Shane Reynolds   2.49

Strikeouts
Hideo Nomo   244
John Smoltz   224
Shane Reynolds   218

Projected All-Stars

First Team
First Base: Jeff Bagwell
Second Base: Bret Boone
Shortstop: Barry Larkin
Third Base: Matt Williams
Catcher: Mike Piazza
Outfield: Barry Bonds
Outfield: Sammy Sosa
Outfield: Dante Bichette
Starting Pitcher: Greg Maddux
Relief Pitcher: Mark Wohlers

Second Team
First Base: Gregg Jefferies
Second Base: Jeff Kent
Shortstop: Jose Vizcaino
Third Base: Chipper Jones
Catcher: Darren Daulton
Outfield: Tony Gwynn
Outfield: Larry Walker
Outfield: Raul Mondesi
Starting Pitcher: Jason Isringhausen
Relief Pitcher: Trevor Hoffman

Greg Maddux

Atlanta
BRAVES

Scouting Report

Outfielders: Gold Glove center fielder Marquis Grissom, who signed a four-year contract in the offseason, is one of the league's most talented all-around players. His power numbers should get a lift from the Launching Pad, and he's a brilliant basestealer. Right fielder David Justice no longer swings for the fences and has matured as a hitter. A shoulder injury limited his 1995 production. Powerful slugger Ryan Klesko will return in left field.

Infielders: Hotlanta's Chipper Jones is a hot property at the hot corner, with a converted shortstop's fielding skills and a third baseman's hitting abilities. The Braves wisely re-upped Fred McGriff to play first base. He has a perfect home-run stroke and is one of the league's silkiest glovemen. The Braves get grit to spare from their middle infielders, Jeff Blauser at shortstop and Mark Lemke at second base. Don't expect Blauser to duplicate his career year, 1993, in which he scored 110 runs, stole 16 bases, and batted .305. He positions himself well in the field and bops 10 to 15 homers per year. Lemke is money on the double play and clutch at the plate, but his overall talents are strictly complementary.

Catchers: Javier Lopez has turned into a quiet star, both at the plate and behind it. Eddie Perez, a 27-year-old rookie, has a reputation for strong defense but probably won't do much hitting in the backup role.

Starting Pitchers: Greg Maddux has flawless command of a deadly arsenal of offerings, and his artfully simple pitching philosophy is ultraeffective. He's baseball's best starter on baseball's best staff. Tom Glavine has a knack for winning games, and any speculation concerning his statistical demise appears to have been premature. John Smoltz has the nastiest stuff in the Atlanta rotation, and though he's never posted a 20-win season it could happen anytime. Steve Avery is blessed with a rare blend of youth and experience, but he seems to have regressed drastically and is no longer considered a safe bet for stardom. Terrell Wade, a rookie southpaw who signed his first pro contract in a pool hall, has a mid-90s heater and a nasty slider.

Relief Pitchers: Mark Wohlers, who has blossomed into a dominant closer, throws hard and throws strikes. Greg McMichael is an underrated setup man. Sidewinder Brad Clontz was 8–1 in middle relief last season, and the rookie prospects just keep pouring out of triple-A Richmond. Lefty finesse pitcher Brad Woodall, fireballer Jason Schmidt, and postseason contributor Pedro Borbon will comprise a youthful but potentially unbeatable middle-relief crew.

Outlook

The Braves' primary assets are organizational stability and on-field balance. With a productive farm system and inspired free-agent signings, the team has few appreciable weaknesses. There are rarely any clubhouse controversies in Atlanta, and despite down years from several stars, the Braves overwhelmed the competition on their way to the 1995 World Series title. They should be at least as tough this season because once again the starting pitching is phenomenal, the pen is reliable, the defense is seamless, and the batting order is well balanced.

Fungoes

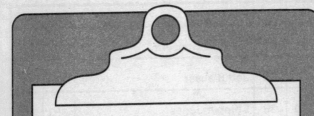

Quick Quiz: Which outfielder became the only player to ever pinch hit for Hank Aaron?

Franchise Milestone: The 1914 Boston Braves won a championship, and the franchise also won a World Series, for Milwaukee in 1957, but the 1995 title was the first major sports championship in Atlanta history.

Top Pitcher: Greg Maddux, 1993–

Top Player: Hank Aaron, 1954–76

Top Manager: Bobby Cox, 1978–81 and 1990–

Wacky Nickname: Road Runner (Ralph Allen Garr)

Quick Quiz Answer: Mike Lum

Lineup Card

NO	POS	PLAYER	OBP	SLG
9	CF	Marquis Grissom	.317	.376
4	SS	Jeff Blauser	.319	.341
10	3B	Chipper Jones	.353	.450
27	1B	Fred McGriff	.361	.489
23	RF	David Justice	.365	.479
18	LF	Ryan Klesko	.396	.608
8	C	Javier Lopez	.344	.498
20	2B	Mark Lemke	.325	.356

In a Nutshell: The Braves registered one of the league's worst batting averages last season, but they made up for it by drawing walks, belting home runs, and delivering in the clutch. The heart of the order offers not only the threat of the home run but table-setting patience as well, which benefits the bottom third of the lineup. In fact, the Atlanta sluggers—Jones, McGriff, and Justice—are more likely to get on base than impatient leadoff hitter Grissom. Few batting orders could have weathered substandard seasons from both their leadoff and cleanup hitters, but the Braves proved to be an exception last season because their lineup is so well rounded. Jeff Blauser has struggled through two consecutive injury-hampered, subpar seasons. It won't be a shock if utility infielder Mike Mordecai sees plenty of action at shortstop. His 1995 slugging percentage (.480 in 69 games) was just nine points below Fred McGriff's.

Atlanta–Fulton County Stadium

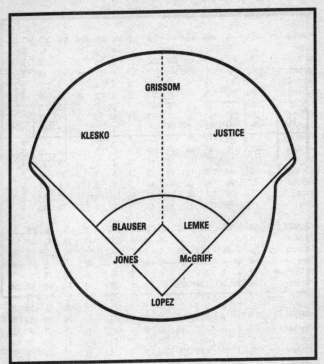

Capacity: 52,710
Turf: Natural

LF Line: 330
RF Line: 330
Center: 402
Left CF: 385
Right CF: 385

Tickets:
404-522-7630

The Launching Pad owes its rep for being a hitter's paradise to three factors: high altitude, hot weather, and a history of famous sluggers. The Atlanta pitchers are actually even better than their fine stats show—their ERAs are inflated at home. The infield grass is well kept and fast, so you'll see fewer errors and more double plays at Fulton than in most natural-turf stadiums.

Statistics

Minimum 25 at-bats or 10.0 innings pitched

PLAYER	BA	G	AB	RS	H	TB	2B	3B	HR	RBI	BB	SO	SB	CS
Lopez	.315	100	333	37	105	166	11	4	14	51	14	57	0	1
Klesko	.310	107	329	48	102	200	25	2	23	70	47	72	5	4
McGriff	.280	144	528	85	148	258	27	1	27	93	65	99	3	6
Mordecai	.280	69	75	10	21	36	6	0	3	11	9	16	0	0
Jones	.265	140	524	87	139	236	22	3	23	86	73	99	8	4
Polonia	.264	28	53	6	14	21	7	0	0	2	3	9	2	0
Grissom	.258	139	551	80	142	207	23	3	12	42	47	61	29	9
Devereaux	.255	29	55	7	14	20	3	0	1	8	2	11	2	0
Justice	.253	120	411	73	104	197	17	2	24	78	73	68	4	2
Lemke	.253	116	399	42	101	142	16	5	5	38	44	40	2	2
Smith	.252	103	131	16	33	54	8	2	3	21	13	35	0	3
O'Brien	.227	67	198	18	45	79	7	0	9	23	29	40	0	1
Belliard	.222	75	180	12	40	44	2	1	0	7	6	28	2	2
Blauser	.211	115	431	60	91	147	16	2	12	31	57	107	8	5
Kelly	.190	96	137	26	26	43	6	1	3	17	11	49	7	3

PITCHER	W	L	SV	ERA	G	GS	CG	SH	IP	H	R	ER	BB	SO
Maddux	19	2	0	1.63	28	28	10	3	209.2	147	39	38	23	181
Wohlers	7	3	25	2.09	65	0	0	0	64.2	51	16	15	24	90
Pena	2	0	0	2.61	27	0	0	0	31.0	22	9	9	7	39
McMichael	7	2	2	2.79	67	0	0	0	80.2	64	27	25	32	74
Glavine	16	7	0	3.08	29	29	3	1	198.2	182	76	68	66	127
Borbon	2	2	2	3.09	41	0	0	0	32.0	29	12	11	17	33
Smoltz	12	7	0	3.18	29	29	2	1	192.2	166	76	68	72	193
Clontz	8	1	4	3.65	59	0	0	0	69.0	71	29	28	22	55
Mercker	7	8	0	4.15	29	26	0	0	143.0	140	73	66	61	102
Avery	7	13	0	4.67	29	29	3	1	173.1	165	92	90	52	141
Stanton	1	1	1	5.59	26	0	0	0	19.1	31	14	12	6	13
Schmidt	2	2	0	5.76	9	2	0	0	25.0	27	17	16	18	19
Woodall	1	1	0	6.10	9	0	0	0	10.1	13	10	7	8	5
Bedrosian	1	2	0	6.11	29	0	0	0	28.0	40	21	19	12	22
Murray	0	2	0	6.75	4	1	0	0	10.2	10	8	8	5	3

Roster

MANAGER: Bobby Cox
COACHES: Jim Beauchamp, Pat Corrales, Clarence Jones, Leo Mazzone, Jimy Williams, Ned Yost

NO	PITCHERS	B	T	HT	WT	DOB
33	Steve Avery	L	L	6-4	205	4/14/70
51	Pedro Borbon	L	L	6-1	205	11/15/67
52	Brad Clontz	R	R	6-1	180	4/25/71
47	Tom Glavine	L	L	6-1	185	3/25/66
31	Greg Maddux	R	R	6-0	175	4/14/66
38	Greg McMichael	R	R	6-3	215	12/1/66
50	Kent Mercker	L	L	6-2	195	2/1/68
60	Matt Murray	L	R	6-6	235	9/26/70
40	Rod Nichols	R	R	6-2	220	12/29/64
46	Jason Schmidt	R	R	6-5	185	1/29/73
29	John Smoltz	R	R	6-3	185	5/15/67
36	Terrell Wade	L	L	6-3	205	1/25/73
43	Mark Wohlers	R	R	6-4	207	1/23/70
48	Brad Woodall	S	L	6-0	175	6/25/69
	CATCHERS					
8	Javier Lopez	R	R	6-3	185	11/5/70
12	Eddie Perez	R	R	6-1	175	5/4/68
	INFIELDERS					
2	Rafael Belliard	R	R	5-6	160	10/24/61
4	Jeff Blauser	R	R	6-1	180	11/8/65
30	Ed Giovanola	L	R	5-10	170	3/4/69
10	Chipper Jones	S	R	6-3	195	4/24/72
20	Mark Lemke	S	R	5-9	167	8/13/65
27	Fred McGriff	L	L	6-3	215	10/31/63
16	Mike Mordecai	S	R	5-11	175	12/13/67
	OUTFIELDERS					
9	Marquis Grissom	R	R	5-11	190	4/17/67
23	David Justice	L	L	6-3	200	4/14/66
25	Mike Kelly	R	R	6-4	195	6/2/70
18	Ryan Klesko	L	L	6-3	220	6/12/71

FREE AGENTS: Mike Devereaux, Fred McGriff, Charlie O'Brien, Alejandro Pena, Luis Polonia, Dwight Smith

Steve Avery   P

Age: 26   **Seasons:** 6
Height: 6' 4"   **Weight:** 205
Bats: Left   **Throws:** Left
1995 OBA: .252   **1995 WHIP:** 1.25

Avery still features plus stuff, but his downfall has been a tendency toward wildness within the strikezone. He was throwing very hard late last season and overpowered the Rockies in his lone NLCS start, so don't count him out for 1996.

	G	GS	IP	ER	ERA	H	BB	SO	W	L	SV
1995	29	29	173.1	90	4.67	165	52	141	7	13	0
Career	179	178	1091.1	455	3.75	1034	331	729	65	52	0
Projected	31	31	209.2	84	3.61	191	55	165	15	9	0

Jeff Blauser   SS

Age: 30   **Seasons:** 9
Height: 6' 1"   **Weight:** 180
Bats: Right   **Throws:** Right
1995 OBP: .319   **1995 SLG:** .341

Blauser has nose-dived from a career year in 1993 to injury-prone (and possibly replacement-level) status, but he still has good pop for a shortstop and discipline at the plate (despite the high whiff rate). His defense is solid but unspectacular.

	G	AB	H	2B	3B	HR	RS	RBI	BB	SB	CS	BA
1995	115	431	91	16	2	12	60	31	57	8	5	.211
Career	950	3177	835	156	23	82	463	356	373	50	36	.263
Projected	128	472	129	19	2	15	71	66	61	6	5	.273

Tom Glavine P

Age: 30 | **Seasons:** 9
Height: 6' 1" | **Weight:** 185
Bats: Left | **Throws:** Left
1995 OBA: .246 | **1995 WHIP:** 1.25

It appeared that Glavine might begin to slip from the ranks of baseball's best pitchers—he'd taken to nibbling with little margin for error—but he put together a stellar 1995 season and an MVP performance in the World Series. He's a bulldog.

	G	GS	IP	ER	ERA	H	BB	SO	W	L	SV
1995	29	29	198.2	68	3.08	182	66	127	16	7	0
Career	262	262	1721.0	674	3.52	1649	579	1031	124	82	0
Projected	34	34	220.1	83	3.39	209	70	137	18	9	0

Marquis Grissom OF

Age: 29 | **Seasons:** 7
Height: 5' 11" | **Weight:** 190
Bats: Right | **Throws:** Right
1995 OBP: .317 | **1995 SLG:** .376

Having established himself as a top power/speed threat in Montreal, the fleet-footed Grissom took a giant step backward as a Brave in 1994. His OBPs have never been great, but last season—phew! He's a Gold Glove center fielder.

	G	AB	H	2B	3B	HR	RS	RBI	BB	SB	CS	BA
1995	139	551	142	23	3	12	80	42	47	29	9	.258
Career	837	3229	889	153	26	66	510	318	255	295	57	.275
Projected	157	622	180	26	5	21	109	55	53	41	10	.289

Chipper Jones   3B

Age: 23   **Seasons:** 1
Height: 6' 3"   **Weight:** 195
Bats: Switch   **Throws:** Right
1995 OBP: .353   **1995 SLG:** .450

A balanced, disciplined hitter who has linedrive pop to all fields, Jones is second only to Matt Williams as the NL's most complete third baseman. Like Williams, Jones is a converted shortstop with great range and reflexes at the hot corner.

	G	AB	H	2B	3B	HR	RS	RBI	BB	SB	CS	BA
1995	140	524	139	22	3	23	87	86	73	8	4	.265
Career	148	527	141	23	3	23	89	86	74	8	4	.268
Projected	161	597	166	30	5	26	100	99	80	9	5	.278

David Justice   OF

Age: 30   **Seasons:** 7
Height: 6' 3"   **Weight:** 200
Bats: Left   **Throws:** Left
1995 OBP: .365   **1995 SLG:** .479

Justice has matured as a hitter, which shows in his improved walks-to-whiffs ratio. He's a steady run producer with low-ball power, but he's nothing special with the glove and arguably has the least speed of the NL's upper-echelon outfielders.

	G	AB	H	2B	3B	HR	RS	RBI	BB	SB	CS	BA
1995	120	411	104	17	2	24	73	78	73	4	2	.253
Career	777	2718	741	118	16	154	452	497	431	32	30	.273
Projected	160	580	152	16	3	30	93	105	80	2	3	.262

Ryan Klesko   OF/1B

Age: 24   **Seasons:** 4
Height: 6' 3"   **Weight:** 220
Bats: Left   **Throws:** Left
1995 OBP: .396   **1995 SLG:** .608

A classic low-ball-loving lefty slugger, Klesko feasts on righthanders and isn't crippled by southpaws. His bat is electric and he can turn around a fastball quicker than you can say "gopher hunt." He'll be at first base, his natural position, this year.

	G	AB	H	2B	3B	HR	RS	RBI	BB	SB	CS	BA
1995	107	329	102	25	2	23	48	70	47	5	4	.310
Career	234	605	176	39	5	42	93	123	76	6	4	.291
Projected	134	433	129	21	3	36	94	101	58	4	4	.298

Mark Lemke   2B

Age: 30   **Seasons:** 8
Height: 5' 9"   **Weight:** 167
Bats: Switch   **Throws:** Right
1995 OBP: .325   **1995 SLG:** .356

Lemke has limited range in the field, but he made just five errors last season while turning the double play brilliantly as always. He walks more than he whiffs and has been a clutch hitter in World Series play.

	G	AB	H	2B	3B	HR	RS	RBI	BB	SB	CS	BA
1995	116	399	101	16	5	5	42	38	44	2	2	.253
Career	794	2290	565	87	14	25	242	200	256	4	16	.247
Projected	145	418	111	15	2	4	49	40	50	1	3	.266

Javier Lopez C

Age: 25 **Seasons:** 4
Height: 6' 3" **Weight:** 185
Bats: Right **Throws:** Right
1995 OBP: .344 **1995 SLG:** .498

Though he didn't draw many walks or throw out even an average number of basestealers (22 percent) last season, Lopez did a veteran's job with the Braves' starting staff and led the club in batting average.

	G	AB	H	2B	3B	HR	RS	RBI	BB	SB	CS	BA
1995	100	333	105	11	4	14	37	51	14	0	1	.315
Career	197	642	185	23	5	28	68	90	31	0	3	.288
Projected	134	440	124	21	2	19	48	55	21	0	3	.282

Greg Maddux P

Age: 30 **Seasons:** 10
Height: 6' 0" **Weight:** 175
Bats: Right **Throws:** Right
1995 OBA: .197 **1995 WHIP:** 0.81

Mad Dog has won an unprecedented four straight Cy Youngs and is the first pitcher since Walter Johnson to post back-to-back sub-1.80 ERAs. His control is uncanny, his movement is baffling, and his glove is golden.

	G	GS	IP	ER	ERA	H	BB	SO	W	L	SV
1995	28	28	209.2	38	1.63	147	23	181	19	2	0
Career	301	297	2120.2	679	2.84	1877	561	1471	150	93	0
Projected	36	36	258.0	49	1.81	200	29	216	24	5	0

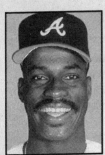

Fred McGriff 1B

Age: 32　　　　**Seasons:** 10
Height: 6' 3"　　**Weight:** 215
Bats: Left　　　**Throws:** Left
1995 OBP: .361　**1995 SLG:** .489

McGriff has been baseball's steadiest slugger for nearly a decade, but last season was not one of his best as he posted a career-worst on-base percentage. He'll be back in Atlanta, having re-signed in the offseason.

	G	AB	H	2B	3B	HR	RS	RBI	BB	SB	CS	BA
1995	144	528	148	27	1	27	85	93	65	3	6	.280
Career	1291	4512	1284	229	17	289	788	803	744	48	29	.285
Projected	154	529	155	24	1	35	98	105	77	5	3	.293

Kent Mercker P

Age: 28　　　　**Seasons:** 7
Height: 6' 2"　　**Weight:** 195
Bats: Left　　　**Throws:** Left
1995 OBA: .258　**1995 WHIP:** 1.41

With wicked breaking stuff and killer heat, Mercker is equipped to be a dominant southpaw, but bouts of wildness have stunted his development. There's a strong possibility that he'll be traded for financial reasons after press time.

	G	GS	IP	ER	ERA	H	BB	SO	W	L	SV
1995	29	26	143.0	66	4.15	140	61	102	7	8	0
Career	233	54	515.2	200	3.49	440	242	426	31	25	19
Projected	33	33	217.1	79	3.27	213	70	163	12	9	0

John Smoltz   P

Age: 28   **Seasons:** 8
Height: 6' 3"   **Weight:** 185
Bats: Right   **Throws:** Right
1995 OBA: .232   **1995 WHIP:** 1.24

Scouts have been anticipating a Cy Young–quality season from Smoltz for years. His fastball-slider combo is extremely nasty to righty batters, but he's prone to digging holes for himself and he's had bad luck in terms of run support.

	G	GS	IP	ER	ERA	H	BB	SO	W	L	SV
1995	29	29	192.2	68	3.18	166	72	193	12	7	0
Career	231	231	1550.2	610	3.54	1346	572	1252	90	82	0
Projected	34	34	232.1	72	2.79	199	76	224	17	9	0

Mark Wohlers   P

Age: 26   **Seasons:** 5
Height: 6' 4"   **Weight:** 207
Bats: Right   **Throws:** Right
1995 OBA: .211   **1995 WHIP:** 1.16

Once a reliever with myriad pluses but few successes, Wohlers finally put together a season in keeping with his mid-90s stuff. The key, of course, was better command of the strikezone and a concurrent increase in aggressiveness.

	G	GS	IP	ER	ERA	H	BB	SO	W	L	SV
1995	65	0	64.2	15	2.09	51	24	90	7	3	25
Career	211	0	218.2	82	3.38	184	106	223	24	10	32
Projected	72	0	70.0	14	1.80	54	20	101	5	1	37

Chicago CUBS

Scouting Report

Outfielders: Sammy Sosa was one of only two 30/30 men in the majors last season, the other being Barry Bonds. A streak hitter with an electric bat, notorious for his erratic work in all facets of the game, he seems to have (at least in part) harnessed his raw talents. As dynamic as Sosa was in right field, some observers considered Brian McRae to be the Cubs' MVP. He led all NL center fielders in chances but committed just three miscues, and his performance in the leadoff slot was credible. While all was warm and cozy in center and right, there was tumult in left field. The Cubs used no fewer than seven different starters in the pasture behind third base, but Luis Gonzalez figures to rate the starting nod over Ozzie Timmons and Scott Bullett.

Infielders: Smooth veteran Mark Grace is unsigned at press time, but the Cubs have indicated they'd like to reenlist his services at first base. Ryne Sandberg has put his inevitable entry into the Hall of Fame on hold for now. He'll be back at second base after a season of retirement. If money were no object, free-agent Shawon Dunston would be re-signed to play shortstop, with Rey Sanchez backing up both middle-infield spots. In more realistic scenarios, Dunston will leave Chicago or be re-upped and moved to third base in place of Todd Zeile. Sanchez would move to shortstop in either case. Zeile struggled through a down year in 1995—he drew the same number of walks (34) in 426 at-bats as sub–Mendoza hitting Howard Johnson had in 169. Zeile's future is hazy at press time.

Catchers: Scott Servais belted 13 homers in just 264 at-bats last season, but he also was charged with 12 errors, more than any other NL catcher. His platoon mate, Mark Parent, rang up 18 dingers but will probably sign elsewhere for 1996. Look for rookie Mike Hubbard to be the backup.

Starting Pitchers: Chicago has five quality starters who performed in inverse proportion to what was expected. Steve Trachsel entered 1995 as the staff ace after his 9–7, 3.21 rookie campaign, but he wound up with the worst ERA on the staff. Kevin Foster was overpowering at times, but he also was touched for a league-high 32 longballs. Jim Bullinger pitched well enough to win 60 percent of his decisions, which is all that can be asked of a fifth starter. Frank Castillo led the starting staff with two shutouts and a 3.21 ERA. Veteran workhorse Jaime Navarro ranked fifth in the league in innings pitched, despite not being among the top 13 in games started.

Relief Pitchers: Veteran closer Randy Myers is a free agent at press time, and the Cubs don't have a clear successor if the 1995 NL saves champ doesn't re-sign.

Outlook

Chicago has had no home-field advantage for three straight seasons, a situation that must change if the Cubbies are to contend for a wild-card berth. The problem is as simple as this: Cubs pitchers ranked twelfth in the NL in walks allowed, Cubs batters ranked twelfth in walks drawn. This is the mirror opposite of a recipe for success at Wrigley, where creating (and avoiding) big innings is paramount. Whether the Cubs make a leap forward or take a step back this year, their ratio of walks taken to walks given will be the key.

Fungoes

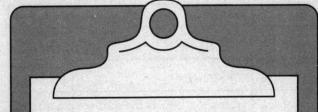

Quick Quiz: Prior to 1920, when the park was renamed for owner William Wrigley Jr., what was the name of the Cubs' home field?

Franchise Milestone: The Cubs won back-to-back World Series titles—in 1907 and 1908—defeating the Tigers both times behind the perfect pitching of Mordecai Brown and Orvall Overall.

Top Pitcher: Mordecai Brown, 1904–13 and 1916

Top Player: Ernie Banks, 1953–71

Top Manager: Cap Anson, 1879–97

Wacky Nickname: Hippo (James Leslie Vaughn)

Quick Quiz Answer: Weeghman Park

Lineup Card

NO	POS	PLAYER	OBP	SLG
56	CF	Brian McRae	.348	.440
23	2B	Ryne Sandberg	.000	.000
17	1B	Mark Grace	.395	.516
21	RF	Sammy Sosa	.340	.500
25	LF	Luis Gonzalez	.357	.454
27	3B	Todd Zeile	.305	.397
9	C	Scott Servais	.348	.496
11	SS	Rey Sanchez	.301	.360

In a Nutshell: Assuming that Sandberg is something like his old self, the Cubs will have an often- and well-set table from which to feast. Grace may not reach the half-century mark in doubles again, but he might not have to if Zeile carries his own weight in the power department. The Cubs have contract decisions to make regarding Dunston, Grace, and Zeile, so this batting order may undergo major alterations after press time. The departure of Dunston might diminish the Cubs' ability to plate runners, but it would raise the team's on-base percentage and remove the concern of what to do when Shawon's chronically bad back isn't up to snuff. Last year's lineup finished fourth in the league in runs scored, despite a slumping Zeile and a retired Sandberg, so the Cubbies should have no trouble generating enough offense to win games if they bunch their runs efficiently.

Wrigley Field

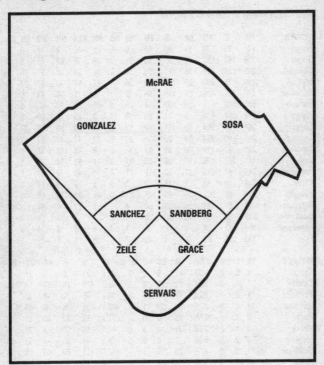

Capacity: 38,765
Turf: Natural

LF Line: 355
RF Line: 353
Center: 400
Left CF: 368
Right CF: 368

Tickets:
312-831-2827

Before the lights were installed (1988), this was a fantastic park for offense of all types—100-percent day games meant good visibility and warmth, every hitter's two best friends—and it's still "the friendly confines" for visiting teams. The out-blowing wind creates gift taters and the small foul territory gives second chances, but the Cubs have not played well here of late.

Statistics

Minimum 25 at-bats or 10.0 innings pitched

PLAYER	BA	G	AB	RS	H	TB	2B	3B	HR	RBI	BB	SO	SB	CS
Haney	.411	25	73	11	30	44	8	0	2	6	7	11	0	0
Grace	.326	143	552	97	180	285	51	3	16	92	65	46	6	3
Dunston	.296	127	477	58	141	225	30	6	14	69	10	75	10	5
McRae	.288	137	580	92	167	255	38	7	12	48	47	92	27	9
Sanchez	.278	114	428	57	119	154	22	2	3	27	14	48	6	4
Gonzalez	.276	133	471	69	130	214	29	8	13	69	57	63	6	9
Bullett	.273	104	150	19	41	69	5	7	3	22	12	30	8	3
Sosa	.268	144	564	89	151	282	17	3	36	119	58	134	33	7
Servais	.265	80	264	38	70	131	22	0	13	47	32	52	2	2
Timmons	.263	77	171	30	45	81	10	1	8	28	13	32	3	0
Zeile	.246	113	426	50	105	169	22	0	14	52	34	76	1	0
Hernandez	.245	93	245	37	60	118	11	4	13	40	13	69	1	0
Kmak	.245	19	53	7	13	19	3	0	1	6	6	12	0	0
Parent	.238	81	261	30	62	127	11	0	18	38	26	69	0	0
Johnson	.195	87	169	26	33	60	4	1	7	22	34	46	1	1
Buechele	.189	32	106	10	20	25	2	0	1	9	11	19	0	0
Roberson	.184	32	38	5	7	20	1	0	4	6	6	14	0	1
Pratt	.133	25	60	3	8	10	2	0	0	4	6	21	0	0

PITCHER	W	L	SV	ERA	G	GS	CG	SH	IP	H	R	ER	BB	SO
Casian	1	0	0	1.93	42	0	0	0	23.1	23	6	5	15	11
Castillo	11	10	0	3.21	29	29	2	2	188.0	179	75	67	52	135
Walker	1	3	1	3.22	42	0	0	0	44.2	45	22	16	24	20
Navarro	14	6	0	3.28	29	29	1	1	200.1	194	79	73	56	128
Perez	2	6	1	3.66	68	0	0	0	71.1	72	30	29	27	49
Young	3	4	2	3.70	32	1	0	0	41.1	47	20	17	14	15
Myers	1	2	38	3.88	57	0	0	0	55.2	49	25	24	28	59
Bullinger	12	8	0	4.14	25	24	1	1	150.0	151	80	69	66	93
Foster	12	11	0	4.51	33	28	0	0	167.2	149	90	84	65	146
Wendell	3	1	0	4.92	43	0	0	0	60.1	71	35	33	24	50
Trachsel	7	13	0	5.15	30	29	2	0	160.2	174	104	92	76	117
Nabholz	0	1	0	5.40	34	0	0	0	23.1	22	15	14	14	21
Adams	1	1	1	6.50	18	0	0	0	18.0	22	15	13	10	15

Roster

MANAGER: Jim Riggleman
COACHES: Dave Bialas, Fergie Jenkins, Tony Muser, Mako Oliveras, Dan Radison, Billy Williams

NO	PITCHERS	B	T	HT	WT	DOB
51	Terry Adams	R	R	6-3	205	3/6/73
52	Jim Bullinger	R	R	6-2	185	8/21/65
55	Larry Casian	R	L	6-0	170	10/28/65
49	Frank Castillo	R	R	6-1	190	4/1/69
32	Kevin Foster	R	R	6-1	170	1/13/69
29	Jose Guzman	R	R	6-3	195	4/9/63
—	Scott Moten	R	R	6-1	195	4/12/72
47	Mike Perez	R	R	6-0	185	10/19/64
41	Roberto Rivera	L	L	6-0	200	1/1/69
50	Ottis Smith	R	L	6-1	170	1/28/71
34	Tanyon Sturtze	R	R	6-5	205	10/12/70
36	Dave Swartzbaugh	R	R	6-2	210	2/11/68
44	Amaury Telemaco	R	R	6-3	210	1/19/74
46	Steve Trachsel	R	R	6-4	205	10/31/70
39	Wade Walker	R	R	6-1	190	9/18/71
13	Turk Wendell	S	R	6-2	190	5/19/67
16	Anthony Young	R	R	6-2	215	1/19/66
	CATCHERS					
6	Mike Hubbard	R	R	6-1	195	2/16/71
9	Scott Servais	R	R	6-2	195	6/4/67
	INFIELDERS					
37	Brant Brown	L	L	6-3	205	6/22/71
15	Matt Franco	L	R	6-2	200	8/19/69
24	Todd Haney	R	R	5-9	165	7/30/65
18	Jose Hernandez	R	R	6-1	180	7/14/69
—	Jason Maxwell	R	R	6-1	170	3/26/72
—	Bobby Morris	L	R	6-0	190	11/22/72
—	Kevin Orie	R	R	6-4	210	9/1/72
11	Rey Sanchez	R	R	5-9	170	10/5/67
23	Ryne Sandberg	R	R	6-2	190	9/18/59
27	Todd Zeile	R	R	6-1	190	9/9/65
	OUTFIELDERS					
10	Scott Bullett	L	L	6-2	190	12/25/68
—	Darren Burton	S	R	6-1	185	9/16/72
1	Doug Glanville	R	R	6-2	170	8/25/70
25	Luis Gonzalez	L	R	6-2	180	9/3/67
—	Brooks Kieschnick	L	R	6-4	228	6/6/72
56	Brian McRae	S	R	6-0	185	8/27/67
21	Sammy Sosa	R	R	6-0	185	11/12/68
30	Ozzie Timmons	R	R	6-2	205	9/18/70

FREE AGENTS: Shawon Dunston, Mark Grace, Howard Johnson, Randy Myers, Jaime Navarro, Mark Parent

Jim Bullinger   P

Age: 30   **Seasons:** 4
Height: 6' 2"   **Weight:** 185
Bats: Right   **Throws:** Right
1995 OBA: .265   **1995 WHIP:** 1.45

Bullinger posted the worst whiffs-to-walks ratio on the team last season, but he also allowed a team-low 14 dingers, which is how he wound up winning despite mediocre stuff. He's been a swingman in the past and probably will reprise that role.

	G	GS	IP	ER	ERA	H	BB	SO	W	L	SV
1995	24	24	150.0	69	4.14	152	65	93	12	8	0
Career	111	43	351.2	161	4.12	329	162	211	21	18	10
Projected	29	29	171.2	58	3.04	169	60	111	12	10	0

Frank Castillo   P

Age: 27   **Seasons:** 5
Height: 6' 1"   **Weight:** 190
Bats: Right   **Throws:** Right
1995 OBA: .248   **1995 WHIP:** 1.23

A superb pitcher for Wrigley, Castillo walked fewer than 2.5 batters per nine innings last year. He features a varied repertoire that's effective against righties and lefties, but his best pitch is a hard-breaking slider.

	G	GS	IP	ER	ERA	H	BB	SO	W	L	SV
1995	29	29	188.0	67	3.21	179	52	135	11	10	0
Career	113	109	669.1	287	3.86	652	192	446	34	37	0
Projected	32	32	210.2	79	3.38	199	58	142	12	8	0

Shawon Dunston   SS

Age: 33   **Seasons:** 11
Height: 6' 1"   **Weight:** 180
Bats: Right   **Throws:** Right
1995 OBP: .317   **1995 SLG:** .472

It's hard to believe that a veteran at Wrigley could draw just ten walks in over 400 at-bats. He finishes rallies well for a shortstop but doesn't set the table for the hitters behind him, which somewhat lessens his usefulness.

	G	AB	H	2B	3B	HR	RS	RBI	BB	SB	CS	BA
1995	127	477	141	30	6	14	58	69	10	10	5	.296
Career	1140	4151	1100	207	44	98	506	448	163	146	64	.265
Projected	135	491	134	23	3	11	60	66	16	12	7	.273

Kevin Foster   P

Age: 27   **Seasons:** 3
Height: 6' 1"   **Weight:** 170
Bats: Right   **Throws:** Right
1995 OBA: .240   **1995 WHIP:** 1.28

A converted third baseman (he hit like a pitcher) with little experience as a big-league hurler, Foster has an excellent fastball and a decent change-up, but his repertoire is limited and his control wasn't always sharp last season.

	G	GS	IP	ER	ERA	H	BB	SO	W	L	SV
1995	30	28	167.2	84	4.51	149	65	146	12	11	0
Career	45	42	255.1	121	4.27	232	107	227	15	16	0
Projected	32	32	183.0	100	4.92	176	70	153	10	13	0

Luis Gonzalez   OF

Age: 28   **Seasons:** 6
Height: 6' 2"   **Weight:** 180
Bats: Left   **Throws:** Right
1995 OBP: .357   **1995 SLG:** .454

Gonzalez has the skills to be a fine player at Wrigley, but the first thing he needs to do is stop trying to steal bases. He did set a career best in walks, a very good sign, and he could easily bust out with a 20-homer season in 1996.

	G	AB	H	2B	3B	HR	RS	RBI	BB	SB	CS	BA
1995	133	471	130	29	8	13	69	69	57	6	8	.276
Career	670	2284	617	141	27	59	300	332	219	58	44	.270
Projected	149	522	155	26	6	19	74	71	54	7	6	.297

Mark Grace   1B

Age: 31   **Seasons:** 8
Height: 6' 2"   **Weight:** 190
Bats: Left   **Throws:** Left
1995 OBP: .395   **1995 SLG:** .516

Grace's batting eye and stickwork are impeccable, but until last season his power production was below average for a first sacker. A three-time Gold Glover, he sparkles when starting the double play and is a master of positioning.

	G	AB	H	2B	3B	HR	RS	RBI	BB	SB	CS	BA
1995	143	552	180	51	3	16	97	92	65	6	2	.326
Career	1155	4356	1333	261	28	82	608	589	525	55	28	.306
Projected	157	604	188	40	3	15	88	94	71	7	3	.311

Brian McRae — OF

Age: 28 **Seasons:** 6
Height: 6' 0" **Weight:** 185
Bats: Switch **Throws:** Right
1995 OBP: .348 **1995 SLG:** .440

Though he closed out the year in an injury-induced slump, McRae's overall 1995 numbers were the best of his career. He isn't a great offensive player in any single area, but he also has few substantial weaknesses.

	G	AB	H	2B	3B	HR	RS	RBI	BB	SB	CS	BA
1995	137	580	167	38	7	12	92	48	47	27	8	.288
Career	751	2973	794	147	39	42	411	296	213	120	49	.267
Projected	154	622	174	33	6	13	99	53	52	25	11	.279

Randy Myers — P

Age: 33 **Seasons:** 11
Height: 6' 1" **Weight:** 230
Bats: Left **Throws:** Left
1995 OBA: .237 **1995 WHIP:** 1.38

An up-and-down season for the Cubs' gritty closer was capped by a bizarre on-field assault by a disgruntled fan. Myers still has very good stuff—lefties hit just .130 off him—but he's had some control problems over the past year and a half.

	G	GS	IP	ER	ERA	H	BB	SO	W	L	SV
1995	57	0	55.2	24	3.88	49	28	59	1	2	38
Career	543	12	709.2	192	2.43	592	319	713	34	49	243
Projected	68	0	74.2	30	3.62	67	35	79	1	3	43

Jaime Navarro P

Age: 29   **Seasons:** 7
Height: 6' 4"   **Weight:** 225
Bats: Right   **Throws:** Right
1995 OBA: .251   **1995 WHIP:** 1.25

Rebounding from a 1994 performance (4–9, 6.62) that could easily have been the last of his career, Navarro signed a one-year deal with the Cubs, made adjustments (he was tipping his pitches), and had his best year since 1992 (17–11, 3.33).

	G	GS	IP	ER	ERA	H	BB	SO	W	L	SV
1995	29	29	200.1	73	3.28	194	56	128	14	6	0
Career	212	180	1243.1	571	4.13	1319	374	652	76	65	0
Projected	33	33	241.1	101	3.77	344	63	140	11	10	0

Ryne Sandberg 2B

Age: 36   **Seasons:** 14
Height: 6' 2"   **Weight:** 190
Bats: Right   **Throws:** Right
1995 OBP: .000   **1995 SLG:** .000

Players who leave the game for an extended period usually lose some of their skills during the absence, but Sandberg, who's in the Cubs' top ten in virtually every category, still figures to be an above-average middle infielder.

	G	AB	H	2B	3B	HR	RS	RBI	BB	SB	CS	BA
1995	0	0	0	0	0	0	0	0	0	0	0	.000
Career	1879	7384	2133	349	72	245	1179	905	679	325	95	.289
Projected	121	459	121	21	2	14	75	63	44	12	3	.264

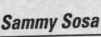

Sammy Sosa OF

Age: 27
Height: 6' 0"
Bats: Right
1995 OBP: .340

Seasons: 7
Weight: 185
Throws: Right
1995 SLG: .500

Topping his previous career high in walks by 20, Sosa lifted his OBP out of the subpar range while also cranking his power stats to a personal-best level last season. No longer Sammy So-So, he's finally matured as a ballplayer.

	G	AB	H	2B	3B	HR	RS	RBI	BB	SB	CS	BA
1995	144	564	151	17	3	36	89	119	58	34	7	.268
Career	802	2881	738	110	27	131	419	423	198	159	65	.256
Projected	155	589	161	20	5	30	90	94	42	35	10	.273

Todd Zeile 3B

Age: 30
Height: 6' 1"
Bats: Right
1995 OBP: .305

Seasons: 7
Weight: 190
Throws: Right
1995 SLG: .397

If the Cubs hang on to Zeile, he's more than capable of putting up solid stats at Wrigley. He usually walks almost as often as he strikes out, though last season was an exception, and he's sure to lift his slugging percentage back toward .450.

	G	AB	H	2B	3B	HR	RS	RBI	BB	SB	CS	BA
1995	113	426	105	22	0	14	50	52	34	1	0	.246
Career	836	2993	787	165	13	84	390	424	362	33	32	.263
Projected	154	566	151	31	1	19	65	72	60	1	3	.267

John Smiley

Cincinnati
REDS

Scouting Report

Outfielders: If the Reds aren't able to re-sign left fielder Ron Gant, they might install a platoon made up of utility outfielder Thomas Howard, who stole 17 bases last year and hit .313 versus righthanders, and rookie Nigel Wilson, who slugged .589 in 304 at-bats at triple-A Indianapolis. Ex-Giant Darren Lewis rarely makes an error in center field, but he's a liability as a hitter. The fulltime job could fall to Steve Gibralter, a hard-nosed rookie who slugged .616 at Indianapolis last season. Right field is set, with Reggie Sanders coming off a career year.

Infielders: Free agent Hal Morris isn't likely to return at first base. Brian R. Hunter, who was on the disabled list for much of last season, has shown flashes of ability but probably isn't an everyday player. The organization's top first-base prospect is Tim Belk, a Hal Morris–type in terms of hitting skills. The Reds' double-play combo is perhaps the best in baseball. National League MVP Barry Larkin is a Gold Glove shortstop, a phenomenal basestealer, and a complete hitter. Bret Boone, known more for his stick than his glove, was tops in the league in fielding percentage among second basemen (.994). Willie Greene's stock as a top prospect has dropped a tad, but he'll have another shot at the third-base assignment. Eric Owens, whose natural position at second base is blocked by Boone, will also see action at the hot corner. Jeff Branson, a surehanded fielder who chips in with the bat, provides flexibility and insurance in the infield.

Catchers: Benito Santiago is a free agent who isn't likely to re-up with Cincy, so look for Eddie Taubensee to be the first-string receiver, with Damon Berryhill in the role of backup.

Starting Pitchers: Former ace Jose Rijo isn't expected to return from elbow surgery until July. Pete Schourek, by all accounts the club's new ace, was 13–2 in 15 starts at home last season. Big John Smiley made the All-Star team but pitched poorly in his final eight starts. The third southpaw on the Reds' starting staff is late-1995 addition David Wells, a veteran workhorse who racked up nine straight wins for Detroit before his arrival in Cincinnati. The Reds traded for reliever Dave Burba, put him in the rotation, and watched him go 4–1, 2.41 as a starter. Mark Portugal didn't have a great season, but he finished the year 6–2, 2.57 in his final ten starts.

Relief Pitchers: Jeff Brantley, one of the best-kept bullpen secrets in baseball, is a solid closer. Mike Jackson figures to depart via free agency, so the bulk of the setup work will be in the hands of fireballer Hector Carrasco.

Outlook

The Reds are clearly the class of the Central Division, but free-agent losses could drag them a little closer to their closest competitors, Chicago and Houston. Cincy's overall team defense, the league's best in 1995, is almost certain to be diminished by the transition from Benito Santiago to Eddie Taubensee and the loss of Hal Morris. The bullpen has no proven replacement for Mike Jackson, but that may not matter because new manager Ray Knight plans to milk every possible inning from his starting rotation, which must remain effective for the Reds to stay on top.

Fungoes

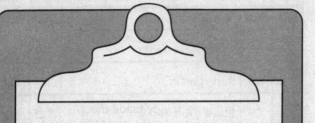

Quick Quiz: Which two catchers won batting titles?

Franchise Milestone: The Reds won the 1990 World Series, a 4–0 sweep over the heavily favored A's. The Big Red Machine won back-to-back titles in 1975 and 1976 . The Reds were champs in 1940 despite being outplayed, and they won the fixed 1919 Series against the Black Sox.

Top Pitcher: Eppa Rixey, 1921–33

Top Player: Johnny Bench, 1967–83

Top Manager: Sparky Anderson, 1970–78

Wacky Nickname: Greasy (Alfred Earle Neale)

Quick Quiz Answer: Bubbles Hargrave and Ernie Lombardi

Lineup Card

NO	POS	PLAYER	OBP	SLG
22	LF	Thomas Howard	.350	.402
11	SS	Barry Larkin	.394	.492
61	CF	Steve Gibralter	.333	.333
16	RF	Reggie Sanders	.397	.579
29	2B	Bret Boone	.326	.429
10	C	Eddie Taubensee	.354	.491
00	1B	Tim Belk	.000	.000
20	3B	Jeff Branson	.345	.435

In a Nutshell: Ray Knight has never managed at any level of pro ball, so his lineup strategies are a little bit tough to predict. Will he be guided primarily by stereotypes (small, speedy type in the leadoff spot, bat-control type in the two-hole, etc.) or will he analyze? Does he have the courage and patience to let rookies play a crucial role, or does he play it safe with familiar faces? The organization is brimming with blue-chip hitting prospects ready to recharge the Cincinnati batting order. It's time for Willie Greene to step up and lock down the third-base job, but if he struggles the Reds can turn to valuable utility man Jeff Branson or 1995 American Association (triple-A) MVP Eric Owens, who is expected to be 100 percent recovered following August knee surgery. Steve Gibralter, who also endured a season-ending injury (thumb), is the number-one outfield prospect in the system.

Riverfront Stadium

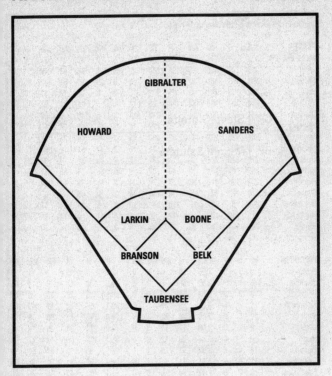

Capacity: 52,952
Turf: Artificial

LF Line: 330
RF Line: 330
Center: 404
Left CF: 375
Right CF: 375

Tickets:
513-421-4510

The two words most often used to describe the Reds' home stadium are *featureless* and *neutral*. Most of the current Cincy hitters don't fair as well here as on the road, but home runs are slightly easier to come by. The essential fairness of the place encourages the Reds to build balanced ballclubs, emphasizing power, speed, pitching, and defense in equal measure.

Statistics

Minimum 25 at-bats or 10.0 innings pitched

PLAYER	BA	G	AB	RS	H	TB	2B	3B	HR	RBI	BB	SO	SB	CS
M. Lewis	.339	81	171	25	58	82	13	1	3	30	21	33	0	4
Larkin	.319	131	496	98	158	244	29	6	15	66	61	49	51	6
Sanders	.306	133	484	91	148	280	36	6	28	99	69	122	36	12
Howard	.302	113	281	42	85	113	15	2	3	26	19	37	17	8
Walton	.290	102	162	32	47	85	12	1	8	22	17	25	10	7
Duncan	.287	81	265	36	76	112	14	2	6	36	5	62	1	3
Santiago	.286	81	266	40	76	129	20	0	11	44	24	48	2	2
Taubensee	.284	80	218	32	62	107	14	2	9	44	22	52	2	2
Morris	.279	101	359	53	100	162	25	2	11	51	29	58	1	1
Gant	.276	119	410	79	113	227	19	4	29	88	74	108	23	8
Anthony	.269	47	134	19	36	57	6	0	5	24	13	30	2	1
Boone	.267	138	513	63	137	220	34	2	15	68	41	84	5	1
Branson	.260	121	331	43	86	144	18	2	12	45	44	69	2	1
D. Lewis	.250	132	472	66	118	140	13	3	1	24	34	57	32	18
Hunter	.215	40	79	9	17	26	6	0	1	9	11	21	2	1
Harris	.208	101	197	32	41	61	8	3	2	16	14	20	10	1
Berryhill	.183	34	82	6	15	24	3	0	2	11	10	19	0	0

PITCHING	W	L	SV	ERA	G	GS	CG	SH	IP	H	R	ER	BB	SO
Ruffin	0	0	0	1.35	10	0	0	0	13.1	4	3	2	11	11
Jackson	6	1	2	2.39	40	0	0	0	49.0	38	13	13	19	41
Brantley	3	2	28	2.82	56	0	0	0	70.1	53	22	22	20	62
Schourek	18	7	0	3.22	29	29	3	1	190.1	158	72	68	45	160
Smiley	12	5	0	3.46	28	27	1	0	176.2	173	72	68	39	124
Wells	6	5	0	3.59	11	11	3	0	72.2	74	34	29	16	50
Pugh	6	5	0	3.84	29	12	0	0	98.1	100	46	42	32	38
Burba	10	4	0	3.97	52	9	1	1	106.2	90	50	47	51	96
Portugal	11	10	0	4.01	31	31	1	0	181.2	185	91	81	56	96
Carrasco	2	7	5	4.12	64	0	0	0	87.1	86	45	40	46	63
Rijo	5	4	0	4.17	14	14	0	0	69.0	76	33	32	22	62
Hernandez	7	2	3	4.60	59	0	0	0	90.0	95	47	46	31	84
Jarvis	3	4	0	5.70	19	11	1	1	79.0	91	56	50	32	33
Reed	0	0	0	5.82	4	3	0	0	17.0	18	12	11	3	10
McElroy	3	4	0	6.02	44	0	0	0	40.1	46	29	27	15	27
Nitkowski	1	3	0	6.12	9	7	0	0	32.1	41	25	22	15	18
Viola	0	1	0	6.28	3	3	0	0	14.1	20	11	10	3	4
Smith	1	2	0	6.66	11	2	0	0	24.1	30	19	18	7	14

Roster

MANAGER: Ray Knight
COACHES: Don Gullett, Grant Jackson, Hal McRae, Joel Youngblood

NO	PITCHERS	B	T	HT	WT	DOB
45	Jeff Brantley	R	R	5-10	189	9/5/63
34	Dave Burba	R	R	6-4	240	7/7/66
58	Hector Carrasco	R	R	6-2	175	10/22/69
—	Chad Fox	R	R	6-3	175	9/3/70
37	Xavier Hernandez	L	R	6-2	195	8/16/65
32	Kevin Jarvis	L	R	6-2	200	8/1/69
—	Domingo Jean	R	R	6-2	175	1/9/69
31	Chuck McElroy	L	L	6-0	195	10/1/67
21	Mark Portugal	R	R	6-0	190	10/30/62
—	Tim Pugh	R	R	6-6	230	1/26/67
27	Jose Rijo	R	R	6-2	215	5/13/65
42	John Roper	R	R	6-0	175	11/21/71
26	Johnny Ruffin	R	R	6-3	170	7/29/71
—	Roger Salkeld	R	R	6-5	215	3/6/71
46	Pete Schourek	L	L	6-5	205	5/10/69
57	John Smiley	L	L	6-4	212	3/17/65
47	Scott Sullivan	R	R	6-3	210	3/13/71
36	David Wells	L	L	6-3	225	5/20/63
	CATCHERS					
8	Damon Berryhill	S	R	6-0	205	12/3/63
10	Eddie Taubensee	L	R	6-4	205	10/31/68
	INFIELDERS					
—	Tim Belk	R	R	6-3	200	4/6/70
29	Bret Boone	R	R	5-10	180	4/6/69
20	Jeff Branson	L	R	6-0	180	1/26/67
12	Willie Greene	L	R	5-11	184	9/23/71
28	Lenny Harris	L	R	5-10	212	10/28/64
30	Brian R. Hunter	R	L	6-0	195	3/4/68
11	Barry Larkin	R	R	6-0	185	4/28/64
51	Eric Owens	R	R	6-1	185	2/3/71
—	Pokey Reese	R	R	5-11	180	6/10/73
	OUTFIELDERS					
9	Eric Anthony	L	L	6-2	195	11/8/67
61	Steve Gibralter	R	R	6-0	185	10/9/72
22	Thomas Howard	S	R	6-2	205	12/11/64
7	Darren Lewis	R	R	6-0	189	8/28/67
—	Chad Mottola	R	R	6-3	220	10/15/71
16	Reggie Sanders	R	R	6-1	186	12/1/67
19	Jerome Walton	R	R	6-1	185	7/8/65
49	Nigel Wilson	L	L	6-1	170	1/12/70

FREE AGENTS: Mariano Duncan, Ron Gant, Mike Jackson, Hal Morris, Benito Santiago, Frank Viola

Bret Boone 2B

Age: 27   **Seasons:** 4
Height: 5' 10"   **Weight:** 180
Bats: Right   **Throws:** Right
1995 OBP: .326   **1995 SLG:** .429

Boone put together a streak of 400 total chances without a boot between July 1994 and July 1995. His batting average sank 50 points last season from 1994, but he has 20-HR potential and is a good bet for a career year in 1996.

	G	AB	H	2B	3B	HR	RS	RBI	BB	SB	CS	BA
1995	138	513	137	34	2	15	63	68	41	5	1	.267
Career	355	1294	352	75	6	43	168	189	86	11	9	.272
Projected	147	531	153	26	1	18	78	84	49	7	3	.288

Jeff Brantley P

Age: 32   **Seasons:** 8
Height: 5' 10"   **Weight:** 189
Bats: Right   **Throws:** Right
1995 OBA: .206   **1995 WHIP:** 1.04

Brantley doesn't blow hitters out of the box with 90-plus heat, but he's no finesse type either. He mixes his offerings, holds runners near the bag, fields his position well, and uses a superb forkball as an out pitch.

	G	GS	IP	ER	ERA	H	BB	SO	W	L	SV
1995	56	0	70.1	22	2.82	53	20	62	3	2	28
Career	405	18	641.0	222	3.12	556	267	509	38	25	85
Projected	62	0	77.2	21	2.43	50	19	71	4	2	32

Dave Burba P

Age: 29	**Seasons:** 6
Height: 6' 4"	**Weight:** 240
Bats: Right	**Throws:** Right
1995 OBA: .228	**1995 WHIP:** 1.32

A nondescript, hard-throwing middle reliever in San Francisco, Burba came to Cincy and went 4–1, 2.41 in nine starts for the Reds. He put together a streak of 37.2 innings without allowing an earned run at Riverfront.

	G	GS	IP	ER	ERA	H	BB	SO	W	L	SV
1995	52	9	106.2	47	3.97	90	51	96	10	4	0
Career	214	27	391.1	186	4.28	366	180	335	27	22	1
Projected	27	27	173.2	75	3.89	159	65	160	14	11	0

Ron Gant OF

Age: 30	**Seasons:** 8
Height: 6' 0"	**Weight:** 200
Bats: Right	**Throws:** Right
1995 OBP: .386	**1995 SLG:** .554

Having missed the strike-spoiled 1994 season (with a multiple compound fracture of his right leg), Gant came back to show he's lost none of his power and little of his speed. He's no great shakes in left field, but he's a force on offense.

	G	AB	H	2B	3B	HR	RS	RBI	BB	SB	CS	BA
1995	119	410	113	19	4	29	79	88	74	23	8	.276
Career	977	3602	949	177	31	176	594	568	374	180	76	.263
Projected	155	530	148	21	5	30	84	89	81	20	10	.279

Barry Larkin   SS

Age: 32   **Seasons:** 10
Height: 6' 0"   **Weight:** 185
Bats: Right   **Throws:** Right
1995 OBP: .394   **1995 SLG:** .492

The league's top all-around shortstop had an MVP season in 1995. He's a phenomenal basestealer; last season he became the 28th player in history to achieve a 91-percent single-season success ratio (minimum 20 steals).

	G	AB	H	2B	3B	HR	RS	RBI	BB	SB	CS	BA
1995	131	496	158	29	6	15	98	66	61	51	5	.319
Career	1176	4429	1322	222	44	102	711	537	449	239	41	.298
Projected	143	528	160	31	4	13	101	60	62	38	3	.303

Darren Lewis   OF

Age: 28   **Seasons:** 6
Height: 6' 0"   **Weight:** 189
Bats: Right   **Throws:** Right
1995 OBP: .311   **1995 SLG:** .297

Lewis is blessed with superior speed and instincts in center field—he won a Gold Glove in 1994—but his inability to get on base as a leadoff hitter led to his being dealt from San Francisco and then to his release in Cincinnati.

	G	AB	H	2B	3B	HR	RS	RBI	BB	SB	CS	BA
1995	132	472	118	13	3	1	66	24	34	32	18	.250
Career	579	2022	503	58	23	9	303	135	189	151	61	.249
Projected	109	312	82	9	4	2	43	21	24	14	7	.263

Hal Morris   1B

Age: 31   **Seasons:** 8
Height: 6' 3"   **Weight:** 200
Bats: Left   **Throws:** Left
1995 OBP: .333   **1995 SLG:** .451

Somewhat underrated as a fielder but probably not the offensive asset his lifetime average suggests, Morris has below-average power and strikes out almost twice as often as he walks. He hit .309 in 249 second-half at-bats.

	G	AB	H	2B	3B	HR	RS	RBI	BB	SB	CS	BA
1995	101	359	100	25	2	11	53	51	29	1	1	.279
Career	702	2394	737	149	13	55	327	330	210	34	18	.308
Projected	135	458	146	23	1	9	71	59	32	3	1	.319

Jose Rijo   P

Age: 30   **Seasons:** 12
Height: 6' 2"   **Weight:** 215
Bats: Right   **Throws:** Right
1995 OBA: .285   **1995 WHIP:** 1.42

One of the five best starters in baseball from 1988 through 1994, Rijo was pitching in pain last season before going under the knife in August. He's expected to be ready by midseason, but it will take time for his arm strength to return.

	G	GS	IP	ER	ERA	H	BB	SO	W	L	SV
1995	14	14	69.0	32	4.17	76	22	62	5	4	0
Career	332	260	1786.0	627	3.16	1602	634	1556	111	87	3
Projected	17	17	111.2	46	3.71	115	31	102	7	3	0

Reggie Sanders   OF

Age: 28   **Seasons:** 5
Height: 6' 1"   **Weight:** 180
Bats: Right   **Throws:** Right
1995 OBP: .397   **1995 SLG:** .579

Sanders has as much pure talent as any player in the NL. His bat is ultra-quick, he has blazing speed, and his throwing arm is strong and accurate. He still strikes out too often, but he's also drawing more walks.

	G	AB	H	2B	3B	HR	RS	RBI	BB	SB	CS	BA
1995	133	484	148	36	6	28	91	99	69	36	12	.306
Career	503	1805	501	98	24	78	315	283	209	101	39	.278
Projected	150	534	159	32	5	25	93	104	58	31	10	.298

Benito Santiago   C

Age: 31   **Seasons:** 10
Height: 6' 1"   **Weight:** 185
Bats: Right   **Throws:** Right
1995 OBP: .351   **1995 SLG:** .485

Santiago was on the disabled list for two months last year (elbow surgery) but was productive at the plate when healthy. A free agent at press time, he'll probably be on the move during the offseason to his fourth team in five years.

	G	AB	H	2B	3B	HR	RS	RBI	BB	SB	CS	BA
1995	81	266	76	20	0	11	40	44	24	2	2	.286
Career	1110	3944	1034	177	23	120	436	510	225	75	57	.262
Projected	141	532	137	15	2	12	49	50	30	1	4	.258

Pete Schourek P

Age: 26   **Seasons:** 5
Height: 6' 5"   **Weight:** 205
Bats: Left   **Throws:** Left
1995 OBA: .228   **1995 WHIP:** 1.06

Released by the Mets after logging a 5–12 record in 1993, Schourek made some mechanical adjustments and blossomed into the Reds' staff ace last season. He's vulnerable to the long-ball, but his fine control minimizes the damage.

	G	GS	IP	ER	ERA	H	BB	SO	W	L	SV
1995	29	29	190.1	68	3.22	158	45	160	18	7	0
Career	149	86	622.1	286	4.14	635	206	428	41	33	0
Projected	34	34	241.0	77	2.88	202	51	211	22	8	0

John Smiley P

Age: 31   **Seasons:** 10
Height: 6' 4"   **Weight:** 212
Bats: Left   **Throws:** Left
1995 OBA: .263   **1995 WHIP:** 1.20

Smiley posted stellar first-half stats in 1995 and was an NL All-Star for the second time in his career. He allowed more than four runs in only three of his starts, and he seems to have put his past arm troubles behind him.

	G	GS	IP	ER	ERA	H	BB	SO	W	L	SV
1995	28	27	176.2	68	3.46	173	39	124	12	5	0
Career	300	220	1536.0	627	3.67	1451	401	993	102	75	4
Projected	32	32	191.2	71	3.33	188	32	137	16	6	0

Eddie Taubensee C

Age: 27   **Seasons:** 5
Height: 6' 4"   **Weight:** 205
Bats: Left   **Throws:** Right
1995 OBP: .354   **1995 SLG:** .491

Taubensee has developed into a solid major-league hitter, but he tossed out just 21 percent of enemy thieves and was charged with three times the number of errors as Santiago in just 10 fewer games at catcher.

	G	AB	H	2B	3B	HR	RS	RBI	BB	SB	CS	BA
1995	80	218	62	14	2	9	32	44	22	2	2	.284
Career	370	1056	269	50	6	31	115	143	105	7	3	.255
Projected	110	318	91	18	1	15	61	55	29	1	2	.286

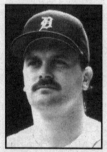

David Wells P

Age: 32   **Seasons:** 9
Height: 6' 3"   **Weight:** 225
Bats: Left   **Throws:** Left
1995 OBA: N/A   **1995 WHIP:** 1.22

Wells doesn't have an excess of star-quality stuff, but he spots his pitches beautifully and usually keeps games close. His transition to the National League was fairly smooth, as he hurled consecutive complete games in August.

	G	GS	IP	ER	ERA	H	BB	SO	W	L	SV
1995	29	29	203.0	73	3.24	194	53	133	16	8	0
Career	314	144	1188.2	498	3.77	1149	320	792	79	61	13
Projected	33	33	241.0	91	3.40	235	59	152	15	10	0

Colorado
ROCKIES

Scouting Report

Outfielders: Ellis Burks has plus skills in center field and dangerous power at the plate, but he's rarely healthy for a full season. Trenidad Hubbard, a "rookie" who toiled in the minors for eight years before his first cup of coffee in 1994, has hit .301 in 83 big-league at-bats. But the Rockies are hoping that 26-year-old Quinton McCracken will make a bid for the starting job in center field this season. Larry Walker has the total package: a golden glove and a deadly arm in right field, plus speed and power on offense. He finished second in the NL in slugging last season. The Rockies have re-signed left fielder Dante Bichette, who topped the league in homers and RBIs in 1995.

Infielders: Andres Galarraga, who became the Rockies' fourth 30-home-run slugger of 1995 (launching the Blake Street Bombers into the history books alongside the 1977 Dodgers), is super smooth at first base. Eric Young, whose batting average was under .200 for the first three months of last season, stormed back to hit .355 after the break. But young Jason Bates flashed good power and clutch hitting (.370 in 73 at-bats with runners in scoring position) in his major-league debut. Bates provides a more reliable glove than Young at second base. Colorado received an expansion-draft gift from the Braves, as Vinny Castilla morphed from a utility infielder into an All-Star third baseman. The Rockies weren't ready to give rookie Craig Counsell the starting job at shortstop; they've re-signed veteran Walt Weiss to anchor the infield.

Catchers: Rookie backstop Jayhawk Owens slugged .561 at triple-A Colorado Springs last season, then cracked a pair of homers in his first outing after being called to the big club. He nailed five of eight would-be thieves in ten starts behind the plate.

Starting Pitchers: Two big-name free agents, Bill Swift and Bret Saberhagen, haven't lived up to expectations in Colorado, but both are still capable of having ace-type seasons. Except for a very poor showing in August, Kevin Ritz was the club's most reliable starter last season. Marvin Freeman and Armando Reynoso are both quality starters who have battled elbow injuries in recent seasons. Young-sters who could have an impact on the Colorado rotation include Bryan Rekar (1.49 in seven triple-A starts), Roger Bailey, and Juan Acevedo.

Relief Pitchers: The Rockies have one of baseball's most underrated setup crews but lack a fulltime closer at press time. Last year's bullpen by committee blew a whopping 23 save chances, although Steve Reed, Darren Holmes, Curt Leskanic, and Bruce Ruffin are serviceable pitchers.

Outlook

Thanks to free agency and record-setting attendance fig-ures, Colorado has never fit the mold of an expansion team. Though loaded with veteran stars—Bichette, Swift, Walker, Saberhagen, Galarraga—the organization has also poured resources into player development. Colorado Springs, the club's triple-A affiliate, won the Pacific Coast League championship last year, and kids like Quinton McCracken and Bryan Rekar could give the Rox a boost beyond 1995's wild-card success. Parity rules in the NL West, but Colorado may tip the balance of power in 1996.

Fungoes

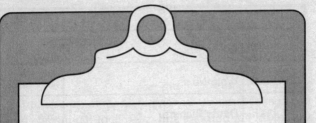

Quick Quiz: Which two hitters set the major-league marks for homers by a Mexican- and Canadian-born player, respectively, in 1995?

Franchise Milestone: The Rockies made the playoffs as a wild card in 1995, their third year of existence.

Top Pitcher: Bruce Ruffin, 1993–

Top Player: Andres Galarraga, 1993–

Top Manager: Don Baylor, 1993–

Wacky Nickname: Blake Street Bombers (Dante Bichette, Vinny Castilla, Andres Galarraga, Larry Walker)

Quick Quiz Answer: Vinny Castilla and Larry Walker

Lineup Card

NO	POS	PLAYER	OBP	SLG
21	2B	Eric Young	.404	.473
22	SS	Walt Weiss	.403	.321
10	LF	Dante Bichette	.364	.620
33	RF	Larry Walker	.381	.607
26	CF	Ellis Burks	.359	.496
14	1B	Andres Galarraga	.331	.511
9	3B	Vinny Castilla	.347	.564
34	C	Jayhawk Owens	.286	.556

In a Nutshell: The 1995 Rockies topped the National League in batting (.282), runs scored (785), triples (43), home runs (200), and several other offensive categories. That's due in part to their home park, but this would still be an explosive lineup if the Rox played at Busch rather than Coors. Colorado has stockpiled sluggers, and no other team outside of Cleveland has such firepower in spots three through eight, yet none of the Rockies' big boppers are slow-footed types who are prone to grounding into double plays. It's useless to quibble with the results of Don Baylor's batting order, but the Blake Street Bombers would be even more productive if Walt Weiss were kept out of the eight-hole and inserted permanently near the top. Why not have your two best on-base percentages in spots one and two? Expect newcomers Jason Bates and Quinton McCracken to eventually join the starting nine.

Coors Field

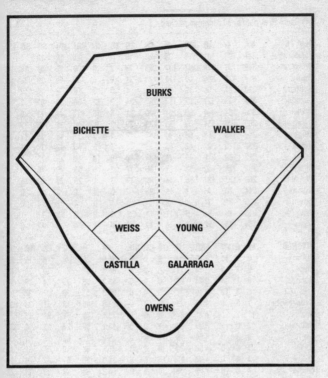

BURKS

BICHETTE WALKER

WEISS YOUNG

CASTILLA GALARRAGA

OWENS

Capacity: 50,000
Turf: Natural

LF Line: 347
RF Line: 350
Center: 415
Left CF: 390
Right CF: 375

Tickets:
303-762-5437

Most fans know about the altitude-aided longballs at Coors Field, but the park also increases triples—by as much as 300 percent! Errors of all types are way up, too. Because runs are far easier to come by here than at any other National League venue, it's imperative that pitchers not issue walks that can lead to big innings. Larry Walker hit .343 at home in 1995, just .268 on the road.

Statistics

Minimum 25 at-bats or 10.0 innings pitched

PLAYER	BA	G	AB	RS	H	TB	2B	3B	HR	RBI	BB	SO	SB	CS
Vander Wal	.347	105	101	15	35	60	8	1	5	21	16	23	1	1
Bichette	.340	139	579	102	197	359	38	2	40	128	22	96	13	9
Young	.317	120	366	68	116	173	21	9	6	36	49	29	35	12
Hubbard	.310	24	58	13	18	31	4	0	3	9	8	6	2	1
Castilla	.309	139	527	82	163	297	34	3	32	90	30	87	2	8
Walker	.306	131	494	96	151	300	31	5	36	101	49	73	16	3
Galarraga	.280	143	554	89	155	283	29	3	31	106	32	145	12	2
Kingery	.269	119	350	66	94	144	18	4	8	37	45	39	13	5
Bates	.267	116	322	42	86	135	17	4	8	46	42	70	3	6
Burks	.266	103	278	41	74	138	10	6	14	49	39	72	7	3
Girardi	.262	125	462	63	121	166	17	2	8	55	29	76	3	3
Weiss	.260	137	427	65	111	137	17	3	1	25	98	57	15	3
Owens	.244	18	45	7	11	25	2	0	4	12	2	15	0	0
Tatum	.235	34	34	4	8	11	1	1	0	4	1	7	0	0
Brito	.216	18	51	5	11	14	3	0	0	7	2	17	1	0
Mejia	.154	23	52	5	8	12	1	0	1	4	0	17	0	1

PITCHER	W	L	SV	ERA	G	GS	CG	SH	IP	H	R	ER	BB	SO
Ruffin	0	1	11	2.12	37	0	0	0	34.0	26	8	8	19	23
Reed	5	2	3	2.14	71	0	0	0	84.0	61	24	20	21	79
Holmes	6	1	14	3.24	68	0	0	0	66.2	59	26	24	28	61
Leskanic	6	3	10	3.40	76	0	0	0	98.0	83	38	37	33	107
Saberhagen	7	6	0	4.18	25	25	3	0	153.0	165	78	71	33	100
Ritz	11	11	2	4.21	31	28	0	0	173.1	171	91	81	65	120
Painter	3	0	1	4.37	33	1	0	0	45.1	55	23	22	10	36
Swift	9	3	0	4.94	19	19	0	0	105.2	122	62	58	43	68
Bailey	7	6	0	4.98	39	6	0	0	81.1	88	49	45	39	33
Rekar	4	6	0	4.98	15	14	1	0	85.0	95	51	47	24	60
Grahe	4	3	0	5.08	18	10	0	0	56.2	69	42	32	27	27
Reynoso	7	7	0	5.32	20	18	0	0	93.0	116	61	55	36	40
Freeman	3	7	0	5.89	22	18	0	0	94.2	122	64	62	41	61
Acevedo	4	6	0	6.44	17	11	0	0	65.2	82	53	47	20	40
Thompson	2	3	0	6.53	21	5	0	0	51.0	73	42	37	22	30
Sager	0	0	0	7.36	10	0	0	0	14.2	19	16	12	7	10
Munoz	2	4	2	7.42	64	0	0	0	43.2	53	38	36	27	37
Hickerson	3	3	1	8.57	56	0	0	0	48.1	69	52	46	28	40

Roster

MANAGER: Don Baylor
COACHES: Larry Bearnarth, Gene Glynn, Ron Hassey, Rick Mathews

NO	PITCHERS	B	T	HT	WT	DOB
—	Garvin Alston	R	R	6-1	175	12/8/71
—	Ivan Arteaga	L	R	6-2	220	7/20/72
—	Roger Bailey	R	R	6-1	180	10/3/70
—	John Burke	S	R	6-4	215	2/9/70
44	Marvin Freeman	R	R	6-7	222	4/10/63
40	Darren Holmes	R	R	6-0	203	4/25/66
16	Curtis Leskanic	R	R	6-0	188	4/2/68
43	Mike Munoz	L	L	6-2	196	7/12/65
17	David Nied	R	R	6-2	188	12/22/68
28	Lance Painter	L	L	6-1	194	7/21/67
39	Steve Reed	R	R	6-2	202	3/11/66
56	Bryan Rekar	R	R	6-3	208	6/3/72
42	Armando Reynoso	R	R	6-0	196	5/1/66
30	Kevin Ritz	R	R	6-4	220	6/8/65
18	Bruce Ruffin	S	L	6-2	212	10/4/63
—	Bret Saberhagen	R	R	6-1	200	4/11/64
20	Bill Swift	R	R	6-0	191	10/27/61
32	Mark Thompson	R	R	6-2	205	4/7/71
	CATCHERS					
34	Jayhawk Owens	R	R	6-1	200	2/10/69
	INFIELDERS					
6	Jason Bates	S	R	5-11	170	1/5/71
9	Vinny Castilla	R	R	6-1	185	7/4/67
—	Craig Counsell	L	R	6-0	177	8/21/70
14	Andres Galarraga	R	R	6-3	245	6/18/61
—	Roberto Mejia	R	R	5-11	165	4/14/72
—	Tom Schmidt	R	R	6-3	200	2/12/73
35	John Vander Wal	L	L	6-2	190	4/29/66
22	Walt Weiss	S	R	6-0	175	11/28/63
21	Eric Young	R	R	5-9	170	5/18/67
	OUTFIELDERS					
10	Dante Bichette	R	R	6-3	225	11/18/63
26	Ellis Burks	R	R	6-2	205	9/11/64
1	Trenidad Hubbard	R	R	5-8	180	5/11/66
—	Quinton McCracken	S	R	5-7	170	3/16/70
33	Larry Walker	L	R	6-3	215	12/1/66

FREE AGENTS: Mike Kingery

Dante Bichette OF

Age: 32   **Seasons:** 8
Height: 6' 3"   **Weight:** 215
Bats: Right   **Throws:** Right
1995 OBP: .364   **1995 SLG:** .620

Bichette was a late bloomer—in 1992 he hit just five homers in 387 at-bats. Last season he became the only National League hitter to log 20 homers, 80 RBIs, and a .300 batting average in each of the past three seasons.

	G	AB	H	2B	3B	HR	RS	RBI	BB	SB	CS	BA
1995	139	579	197	38	2	40	102	128	22	13	9	.340
Career	820	2966	858	183	15	126	413	488	129	88	42	.289
Projected	153	602	184	33	3	41	95	136	30	13	8	.306

Ellis Burks OF

Age: 31   **Seasons:** 9
Height: 6' 2"   **Weight:** 205
Bats: Right   **Throws:** Right
1995 OBP: .359   **1995 SLG:** .496

Burks, a player whose talents have always exceeded his stats, has played his entire career in hitters' parks, posting mild lifetime numbers. If he could stay off the disabled list, it wouldn't be a shock if he suddenly had a late-career career year.

	G	AB	H	2B	3B	HR	RS	RBI	BB	SB	CS	BA
1995	103	278	74	10	6	14	41	49	39	7	3	.266
Career	1013	3720	1044	202	40	137	589	534	366	109	57	.281
Projected	115	311	89	15	6	16	58	61	43	12	2	.286

Vinny Castilla 3B

Age: 28   **Seasons:** 5
Height: 6' 1"   **Weight:** 175
Bats: Right   **Throws:** Right
1995 OBP: .347   **1995 SLG:** .564

A great pickup from Atlanta in the 1992 expansion draft, Castilla bashed 20 more homers last season than he'd hit in his previous four seasons combined. His batting average was 154 points higher at Coors (.383) than on the road (.229).

	G	AB	H	2B	3B	HR	RS	RBI	BB	SB	CS	BA
1995	139	527	163	34	3	32	82	90	30	2	8	.309
Career	317	1015	297	55	10	44	136	139	51	6	14	.293
Projected	158	578	163	30	4	25	80	88	34	2	6	.282

Andres Galarraga 1B

Age: 34   **Seasons:** 11
Height: 6' 3"   **Weight:** 245
Bats: Right   **Throws:** Right
1995 OBP: .331   **1995 SLG:** .511

It's surprising that more of the league's struggling hitters aren't imitating the Big Cat's wide-open stance. Galarraga has parlayed a change in mechanics, a hitter-friendly park, and a quick bat into one of the most impressive career revivals ever.

	G	AB	H	2B	3B	HR	RS	RBI	BB	SB	CS	BA
1995	143	554	155	29	3	31	89	106	32	12	2	.280
Career	1308	4848	1372	267	23	200	669	761	310	81	46	.283
Projected	156	589	171	25	2	31	95	100	30	8	4	.290

Joe Girardi C

Age: 31   **Seasons:** 7
Height: 5' 11"   **Weight:** 195
Bats: Right   **Throws:** Right
1995 OBP: .308   **1995 SLG:** .359

Girardi has little to offer as a hitter, and his new home, Yankee Stadium, isn't going to help his numbers. But his catching skills are extremely valuable. He blocks the plate like a brick house and handles the pitching staff like an on-field coach.

	G	AB	H	2B	3B	HR	RS	RBI	BB	SB	CS	BA
1995	125	462	121	17	2	8	63	55	29	3	3	.262
Career	608	1995	536	79	14	18	218	190	127	22	18	.269
Projected	137	457	114	15	0	4	45	40	31	2	4	.249

Steve Reed P

Age: 30   **Seasons:** 4
Height: 6' 2"   **Weight:** 202
Bats: Right   **Throws:** Right
1995 OBA: .203   **1995 WHIP:** 0.98

Last season was a breakthrough for the sidearming Reed. He was equally effective versus righties (.195 OBA) and lefties (.218 OBA), which hasn't always been the case, and he was extremely tough with runners on base.

	G	GS	IP	ER	ERA	H	BB	SO	W	L	SV
1995	71	0	84.0	20	2.14	61	21	79	5	2	3
Career	214	0	248.0	94	3.41	233	80	192	18	9	9
Projected	74	0	88.0	26	2.66	64	30	82	6	3	5

Armando Reynoso   P

Age: 29   **Seasons:** 4
Height: 6' 0"   **Weight:** 196
Bats: Right   **Throws:** Right
1995 OBA: .316   **1995 WHIP:** 1.63

Reynoso began 1995 on the disabled list, recovering from reconstructive elbow surgery, and he never really got rolling. A prototype finesse pitcher, he keeps his offerings around the knees, moves the ball around the zone, and varies speeds.

	G	GS	IP	ER	ERA	H	BB	SO	W	L	SV
1995	20	18	93.0	55	5.32	116	36	40	7	7	0
Career	68	63	365.1	187	4.61	413	133	194	25	23	1
Projected	30	30	194.2	86	3.98	211	45	112	11	9	0

Kevin Ritz   P

Age: 30   **Seasons:** 6
Height: 6' 4"   **Weight:** 220
Bats: Right   **Throws:** Right
1995 OBA: .259   **1995 WHIP:** 1.36

Even after Tommy John–type elbow surgery, Ritz has an electric fastball. His 1995 numbers were easily the best of his career, and they would have been even better if not for an 0–5, 6.12 August. He recovered nicely in September (2–1, 2.94).

	G	GS	IP	ER	ERA	H	BB	SO	W	L	SV
1995	31	28	173.1	81	4.21	171	65	120	11	11	2
Career	96	75	424.0	242	5.14	453	224	298	22	35	2
Projected	33	33	199.1	81	3.66	179	71	145	15	11	0

Bruce Ruffin   P

Age: 32   **Seasons:** 10
Height: 6' 2"   **Weight:** 212
Bats: Switch   **Throws:** Left
1995 OBA: .222   **1995 WHIP:** 1.32

Ruffin has matured as a pitcher, and he's now one of the league's better lefty relievers. He throws hard, throws strikes, and has converted 27 of his last 30 save chances, including 11 of 12 last year (despite nagging elbow soreness).

	G	GS	IP	ER	ERA	H	BB	SO	W	L	SV
1995	37	0	34.0	8	2.12	26	19	23	0	1	11
Career	375	152	1176.1	547	4.19	1272	518	738	53	75	32
Projected	46	0	51.2	15	2.61	44	32	41	2	3	19

Bret Saberhagen   P

Age: 32   **Seasons:** 12
Height: 6' 1"   **Weight:** 200
Bats: Right   **Throws:** Right
1995 OBA: .273   **1995 WHIP:** 1.29

As has often been the case in his Bela Lugosi–inspired career, Saberhagen followed a dominant season with an inconsistent one. He's a fine pitcher, but trying to forecast what his yearly stats will be is just an entertaining folly.

	G	GS	IP	ER	ERA	H	BB	SO	W	L	SV
1995	25	25	153.0	71	4.18	165	33	100	7	6	0
Career	337	309	2227.2	807	3.19	2100	421	1510	141	100	1
Projected	30	30	220.1	81	3.31	216	22	179	17	8	0

Bill Swift   P

Age: 34   **Seasons:** 10
Height: 6' 0"   **Weight:** 191
Bats: Right   **Throws:** Right
1995 OBA: .296   **1995 WHIP:** 1.56

Shoulder soreness led to a couple of stints on the DL and some subpar starts, but Swifty was 5–0, 2.41 in five midseason outings. When he's healthy, Swift's sinker is perhaps the league's best, inducing buckets of whiffs and groundball outs.

	G	GS	IP	ER	ERA	H	BB	SO	W	L	SV
1995	19	19	105.2	58	4.94	122	43	68	9	3	0
Career	353	178	1371.1	551	3.62	1397	425	656	78	62	25
Projected	25	25	165.1	63	3.43	170	31	113	14	5	0

Larry Walker   OF

Age: 29   **Seasons:** 7
Height: 6' 3"   **Weight:** 215
Bats: Left   **Throws:** Right
1995 OBP: .381   **1995 SLG:** .607

Walker is the Rockies' most complete player. He's a textbook basestealer, a dangerous slugger whose quick uppercut is ideal for Coors Field, and a former Gold Glove right fielder. He tied for second in the league in outfield assists (13).

	G	AB	H	2B	3B	HR	RS	RBI	BB	SB	CS	BA
1995	131	494	151	31	5	36	96	101	49	16	3	.306
Career	805	2860	817	178	21	135	464	485	313	114	38	.286
Projected	140	521	166	26	4	31	99	95	52	17	5	.319

Walt Weiss   **SS**

Age: 32   **Seasons:** 9
Height: 6' 0"   **Weight:** 175
Bats: Switch   **Throws:** Right
1995 OBP: .403   **1995 SLG:** .321

Weiss ranked second in the league (to Barry Bonds) in walks last season and fourth in on-base percentage. He even snapped his 750-at-bat homerless streak. Eight of his 15 steals came in the first 19 games of the year.

	G	AB	H	2B	3B	HR	RS	RBI	BB	SB	CS	BA
1995	137	427	111	17	3	1	65	25	98	15	3	.260
Career	933	2958	745	102	16	11	351	226	392	66	26	.252
Projected	148	471	127	15	3	1	74	27	80	13	4	.270

Eric Young   **2B**

Age: 28   **Seasons:** 4
Height: 5' 9"   **Weight:** 180
Bats: Right   **Throws:** Right
1995 OBP: .404   **1995 SLG:** .473

Young isn't a very good fielder—he does make some slick picks, but his overall skills are of the minus variety. His value lies in his ability to get on base and use his speed, two things he did very well in the second half of last season.

	G	AB	H	2B	3B	HR	RS	RBI	BB	SB	CS	BA
1995	120	366	116	21	9	6	68	36	49	35	12	.317
Career	403	1216	344	51	18	17	196	119	158	101	39	.283
Projected	141	461	141	18	13	5	81	40	57	44	16	.306

Florida **MARLINS**

Scouting Report

Outfielders: The Marlins landed a free-agent catch of the day in center fielder Devon White, who brings a Gold Glove to glisten in the Florida sunshine. Jesus Tavarez's debut in center field last season was far from a bust, but his role will be greatly reduced by the presence of Devo. Gary Sheffield, the team's most explosive hitter when healthy, was shot in a carjacking incident in the offseason, but he should be ready to play right field by spring. Left fielder Jeff Conine has had plus-.500 slugging percentages for the past two years and was the National League's All-Star MVP in 1995.

Infielders: Quilvio Veras, formerly a top prospect in the Mets' minor-league system, was sensational at second base and in the leadoff spot last year. Greg Colbrunn, who is just entering his prime, is capable of hitting 25 homers while keeping his batting average near .300. His defense at first base is steady. Young shortstop Kurt Abbott smashed 17 round-trippers last season. (He also fanned 110 times.) The Marlins were happy with third baseman Terry Pendleton's leadership and production, though he no longer approaches the MVP standard he set back in 1991.

Catchers: Rookie receiver Charles Johnson appeared in less than 100 games last season but walked away with a Gold Glove. His 11 home runs provide evidence that he can develop into an everyday backstop.

Starting Pitchers: Pat Rapp, who had offseason surgery to repair a herniated disk in his back, was one of the league's five most effective starters over the second half of 1995. He's expected to be ready by opening day. Chris Hammond is a reliable lefthanded starter, which is nothing to sneeze at, and the the closest thing the Florida rotation has to a legit strikeout pitcher—that is, unless Ryan Bowen comes back from his knee and shoulder injuries and locates the strikezone on a consistent basis. Control specialist John Burkett eats up innings and was a 22-game winner in 1993. At press time the Marlins are searching the free-agent market for at least one more quality starter.

Relief Pitchers: Bryan Harvey is recovering from elbow surgery and may be ready to pitch in April, but he's a free agent at press time and has reportedly turned down the Marlins' offers. Florida's closer last season, Robb Nen, was an unlucky 0–7 with six blown saves, but he's got an upper-90s fastball and decent control. Look for setup and long relief to come from prospects like Aaron Small and Jay Powell and veterans like Terry Mathews and Richie Lewis.

Outlook

The Marlins are doing good work, having put together an intriguing and downright likable ballclub in a short time; in fact, folks in southern Florida are talking wild card, if not this season then soon. What the team lacks in marquee names it makes up for in balance and efficiency, and the acquisition of Devo White is a statement of organizational commitment that will surely trickle down to the field in tangible manifestations. In other words, Fish fans have good reason to be talking wild card...if not this season then soon.

Fungoes

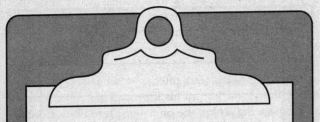

Quick Quiz: Which catcher charged San Francisco's Kevin Rogers in April 1994, setting off the first on-field brawl in Marlins history?

Franchise Milestone: Last season the Marlins escaped the cellar for the first time in the club's three-year history, just a game and a half from a three-way tie for second place.

Top Pitcher: Pat Rapp, 1993–

Top Player: Jeff Conine, 1993–

Top Manager: Rene Lachemann, 1993–

Wacky Nickname: The Guv'nor (Jerome Austin Browne)

Quick Quiz Answer: Benito Santiago

Lineup Card

NO	POS	PLAYER	OBP	SLG
3	2B	Quilvio Veras	.384	.373
00	CF	Devon White	.334	.431
10	RF	Gary Sheffield	.467	.587
19	LF	Jeff Conine	.379	.520
9	3B	Terry Pendleton	.339	.439
4	1B	Greg Colbrunn	.311	.453
7	SS	Kurt Abbott	.318	.452
23	C	Charles Johnson	.351	.410

In a Nutshell: The Marlins have balance and pop from top to bottom, ranking fifth and fourth respectively in slugging and on-base percentage last season. The addition of Devo isn't likely to have tremendous impact if he's inserted into the two-spot. He doesn't get on base more frequently than the man he's replacing, Jesus Tavarez, and he makes a lot less contact. The Marlins would probably be better off if Charles Johnson were batting second and White seventh, but that isn't likely to happen. In any case, young Quilvio Veras may turn out to be the National League's best leadoff man, and he should certainly score 100-plus runs this year, especially if Sheffield is healthy. Jeff Conine doesn't really rank with baseball's top cleanup hitters, but he's certainly the next best thing. Terry Pendleton has always been a good RBI guy and is productive in the five-hole despite marginal home-run power.

Joe Robbie Stadium

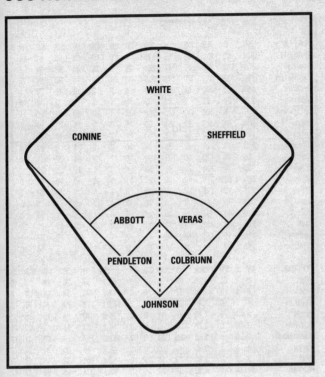

Capacity: 47,226
Turf: Natural

LF Line: 335
RF Line: 345
Center: 410
Left CF: 380
Right CF: 380

Tickets:
305-626-7426

The conversion from football-only to dual-purpose created a quirky gap in center field, which makes for some tricky hops. The stadium gives no pronounced advantage to hitters or pitchers, but several of the Marlins' batters enjoyed better batting averages at home in 1995. Jeff Conine, for example, hit .350 at JRS, .254 on the road. Florida went 37–34 at home last year.

Statistics

Minimum 25 at-bats or 10.0 innings pitched

PLAYER	BA	G	AB	RS	H	TB	2B	3B	HR	RBI	BB	SO	SB	CS
Sheffield	.324	63	213	46	69	125	8	0	16	46	55	45	19	4
Conine	.302	133	483	72	146	251	26	2	25	105	66	94	2	0
Pendleton	.290	133	513	70	149	225	32	1	14	78	38	84	1	2
Tavarez	.289	63	190	31	55	71	6	2	2	13	16	27	7	5
Morman	.278	34	72	9	20	33	2	1	3	7	2	11	0	0
Colbrunn	.277	138	528	70	146	239	22	1	23	89	22	69	11	4
Arias	.269	94	216	22	58	80	9	2	3	26	22	20	1	0
Veras	.261	124	440	86	115	164	20	7	5	32	80	68	56	21
Dawson	.257	79	226	30	58	98	10	3	8	38	9	44	0	0
Abbott	.255	120	420	60	107	190	18	7	17	60	36	111	4	3
Browne	.255	77	184	21	47	54	4	0	1	17	25	20	1	1
Johnson	.251	97	315	40	79	129	15	1	11	40	46	71	0	2
Gregg	.237	72	156	20	37	60	5	0	6	20	16	33	3	1
Natal	.233	16	43	2	10	20	2	1	2	6	1	9	0	0
Diaz	.230	49	87	5	20	26	3	0	1	6	1	12	0	0
Carr	.227	105	308	54	70	96	20	0	2	20	46	49	25	11
Decker	.226	51	133	12	30	43	2	1	3	13	19	22	1	0
Whitmore	.190	27	58	6	11	16	2	0	1	2	5	15	0	0

PITCHER	W	L	SV	ERA	G	GS	CG	SH	IP	H	R	ER	BB	SO
Nen	0	7	23	3.29	62	0	0	0	65.2	62	26	24	23	68
Mathews	4	4	3	3.38	57	0	0	0	82.2	70	32	31	27	72
Rapp	14	7	0	3.44	28	28	3	2	167.1	158	72	64	76	102
Lewis	0	1	0	3.75	21	1	0	0	36.0	30	15	15	15	32
Bowen	2	0	0	3.78	4	3	0	0	16.2	23	11	7	12	15
Hammond	9	6	0	3.80	25	24	3	2	161.0	157	73	68	47	126
Veres	4	4	1	3.88	47	0	0	0	48.2	46	25	21	22	31
Witt	2	7	0	3.90	19	19	1	0	110.2	104	52	48	47	95
Burkett	14	14	0	4.30	31	30	4	0	188.1	208	95	90	57	126
Garces	0	2	0	4.44	18	0	0	0	24.1	25	15	12	11	22
Gardner	5	5	1	4.49	39	11	1	1	102.1	109	60	51	43	87
Mantei	0	1	0	4.73	12	0	0	0	13.1	12	8	7	13	15
Perez	2	6	1	5.21	69	0	0	0	46.2	35	29	27	27	47
Banks	2	6	0	5.66	28	15	0	0	90.2	107	71	57	58	62
Weathers	4	5	0	5.98	28	15	0	0	90.1	104	68	60	52	60
Scheid	0	0	0	6.10	6	0	0	0	10.1	14	7	7	7	10
Groom	1	2	0	7.20	14	0	0	0	15.0	26	12	12	6	12

Roster

MANAGER: Rene Lachemann
COACHES: Rusty Kuntz, Jose Morales, Cookie Rojas, Larry Rothschild, Rick Williams

NO	PITCHERS	B	T	HT	WT	DOB
32	Miguel Batista	R	R	6-0	160	2/19/71
46	Ryan Bowen	R	R	6-0	185	2/10/68
33	John Burkett	R	R	6-3	211	11/28/64
54	Vic Darensbourg	L	L	5-10	165	11/13/70
11	Chris Hammond	L	L	6-1	195	1/21/66
24	Wilson Heredia	R	R	6-0	175	3/30/72
40	John Johnstone	R	R	6-3	195	11/28/68
18	Matt Mantei	R	R	6-1	181	7/7/73
51	Terry Mathews	L	R	6-2	225	10/5/64
53	Kurt Miller	R	R	6-5	205	8/24/72
31	Robb Nen	R	R	6-4	200	11/28/69
58	Yorkis Perez	L	L	6-0	180	9/30/67
59	Jay Powell	R	R	6-4	225	1/19/72
48	Pat Rapp	R	R	6-3	215	7/13/67
41	Chris Seelbach	R	R	6-4	180	12/18/72
37	Aaron Small	R	R	6-5	208	11/23/71
44	Marc Valdes	R	R	6-0	170	12/20/71
52	Randy Veres	R	R	6-3	210	11/26/65
35	Dave Weathers	R	R	6-3	205	9/25/69
30	Matt Whisenant	R	L	6-3	215	6/8/71
	CATCHERS					
23	Charles Johnson	R	R	6-2	215	7/20/71
13	Bob Natal	R	R	5-11	190	11/13/65
	INFIELDERS					
7	Kurt Abbott	R	R	6-0	185	6/2/69
4	Greg Colbrunn	R	R	6-0	200	7/26/69
9	Terry Pendleton	S	R	5-9	180	7/16/60
3	Quilvio Veras	S	R	5-9	166	4/3/71
	OUTFIELDERS					
19	Jeff Conine	R	R	6-1	220	6/27/66
—	Joe Orsulak	L	L	6-1	205	5/31/62
10	Gary Sheffield	R	R	5-11	190	11/18/68
20	Jesus Tavares	R	R	6-0	170	3/26/71
—	Devon White	S	R	6-2	190	12/29/62

FREE AGENTS: Jerry Browne, Andre Dawson, Bryan Harvey

Kurt Abbott   SS

Age: 26   **Seasons:** 3
Height: 6' 0"   **Weight:** 185
Bats: Right   **Throws:** Right
1995 OBP: .318   **1995 SLG:** .452

Abbott's best season so far, which looks vaguely like Cal Ripken's worst (1992), is either a career year or a sign of things to come. He's been prone to whiffs since triple-A, but acceptable glovework and double-figure homers make him valuable.

	G	AB	H	2B	3B	HR	RS	RBI	BB	SB	CS	BA
1995	120	420	107	18	7	17	60	60	36	4	3	.255
Career	241	826	208	36	10	29	112	102	55	9	3	.252
Projected	148	502	126	19	10	14	69	68	43	6	2	.251

Greg Colbrunn   1B

Age: 26   **Seasons:** 4
Height: 6' 0"   **Weight:** 200
Bats: Right   **Throws:** Right
1995 OBP: .311   **1995 SLG:** .453

Colbrunn is a fastball hitter whose power stats took a leap forward last season. Many scouts have compared his swing to Jeff Bagwell's, though Bags never posted a sub-.320 on-base percentage in his life.

	G	AB	H	2B	3B	HR	RS	RBI	BB	SB	CS	BA
1995	138	528	146	22	1	23	70	89	22	11	3	.277
Career	307	1004	277	49	1	35	114	161	43	19	8	.276
Projected	140	536	147	18	0	16	65	74	24	6	3	.274

Jeff Conine   **OF**

Age: 29   **Seasons:** 5
Height: 6' 1"   **Weight:** 220
Bats: Right   **Throws:** Right
1995 OBP: .379   **1995 SLG:** .520

Mechanical adjustments have made Conine a legitimate power threat, and though he isn't likely to slug .500, he is one of the most consistently productive hitters in the league. He's just an average gloveman in left field.

	G	AB	H	2B	3B	HR	RS	RBI	BB	SB	CS	BA
1995	133	483	146	26	2	25	72	105	66	2	0	.302
Career	447	1640	492	84	13	55	220	277	168	5	4	.300
Projected	155	550	171	25	3	22	87	94	57	1	1	.311

Chris Hammond   **P**

Age: 30   **Seasons:** 6
Height: 6' 1"   **Weight:** 195
Bats: Left   **Throws:** Left
1995 OBA: .256   **1995 WHIP:** 1.27

When southpaw Hammond was in the minors, he was often mentioned in the same breath with young K-machines like Smoltz and Wetteland. He hasn't fulfilled that promise, but he's a quality starter when his command doesn't desert him.

	G	GS	IP	ER	ERA	H	BB	SO	W	L	SV
1995	25	24	161.0	68	3.80	157	47	126	9	6	0
Career	121	116	683.2	314	4.13	697	251	407	38	41	0
Projected	30	30	192.1	81	3.79	190	44	135	10	9	0

Charles Johnson   C

Age: 24   **Seasons:** 2
Height: 6' 2"   **Weight:** 215
Bats: Right   **Throws:** Right
1995 OBP: .351   **1995 SLG:** .410

Johnson hit 28 homers at double-A Portland in 1994, yet was still touted more for his defense than his hitting. He didn't disappoint the Marlins last season, nailing 43 percent of would-be thieves while showing discipline and punch at the plate.

	G	AB	H	2B	3B	HR	RS	RBI	BB	SB	CS	BA
1995	97	315	79	15	1	11	40	39	46	0	2	.251
Career	101	326	84	16	1	12	45	43	47	0	2	.258
Projected	136	428	113	16	1	10	51	44	52	1	3	.264

Robb Nen   P

Age: 26   **Seasons:** 3
Height: 6' 4"   **Weight:** 200
Bats: Right   **Throws:** Right
1995 OBA: .244   **1995 WHIP:** 1.29

Robb bblew his share of save chances last season, and his record reflects that fact, but he can be an overpowering closer when his control is sharp. He probably doesn't deserve to lose his job, but it could happen if Bryan Harvey re-signs.

	G	GS	IP	ER	ERA	H	BB	SO	W	L	SV
1995	62	0	65.2	24	3.29	62	23	68	0	7	23
Career	130	4	179.2	85	4.26	171	86	167	7	13	38
Projected	65	0	69.1	21	2.73	60	19	74	1	5	28

Terry Pendleton 3B

Age: 35   **Seasons:** 12
Height: 5' 9"   **Weight:** 180
Bats: Switch   **Throws:** Right
1995 OBP: .339   **1995 SLG:** .439

A classy veteran with championship experience and an MVP trophy on the mantel, Pendleton hit .318 at home last season and .336 versus southpaws. Though no longer a Gold Glover at the hot corner, he has been one of the best of his era.

	G	AB	H	2B	3B	HR	RS	RBI	BB	SB	CS	BA
1995	133	513	149	32	1	14	70	78	38	1	2	.290
Career	1611	6114	1673	311	38	125	772	825	418	122	55	.274
Projected	150	532	141	24	2	11	73	81	44	1	1	.265

Pat Rapp P

Age: 28   **Seasons:** 4
Height: 6' 3"   **Weight:** 215
Bats: Right   **Throws:** Right
1995 OBA: .253   **1995 WHIP:** 1.40

Rapp won his final nine decisions of 1995, topped off by a nifty 24.2-inning scoreless streak, and his second-half ERA was a puny 2.28. He hurt his back in July and wound up having surgery in the offseason.

	G	GS	IP	ER	ERA	H	BB	SO	W	L	SV
1995	28	28	167.1	64	3.44	158	76	102	14	7	0
Career	71	69	404.2	171	0.00	399	190	237	25	23	0
Projected	34	34	224.1	77	3.09	209	77	138	15	10	0

Gary Sheffield OF

Age: 27   **Seasons:** 8
Height: 5' 11"   **Weight:** 190
Bats: Right   **Throws:** Right
1995 OBP: .467   **1995 SLG:** .587

It seems like Sheff has been around forever, but his best seasons could still be ahead if he's able to stay healthy. Ounce for ounce he has the quickest bat in the majors, but his work in right field still needs refinement.

	G	AB	H	2B	3B	HR	RS	RBI	BB	SB	CS	BA
1995	63	213	69	8	0	16	46	46	55	19	4	.324
Career	730	2696	774	139	12	117	399	430	298	96	43	.287
Projected	98	310	91	12	1	15	50	54	62	21	7	.294

Quilvio Veras 2B

Age: 24   **Seasons:** 1
Height: 5' 9"   **Weight:** 166
Bats: Switch   **Throws:** Right
1995 OBP: .384   **1995 SLG:** .373

It's uncommon for a first-time major-league leadoff hitter to do his job so well so quickly, but Veras is a special player. Expect his batting average and stolen-base percentages to improve as he gains experience.

	G	AB	H	2B	3B	HR	RS	RBI	BB	SB	CS	BA
1995	124	440	115	20	7	5	86	32	80	56	21	.261
Career	124	440	115	20	7	5	86	32	80	56	21	.261
Projected	142	505	146	17	12	6	100	35	85	72	27	.289

Houston ASTROS

Scouting Report

Outfielders: Derek Bell, who converted from center to right field after his arrival from San Diego, adjusted to the spacious Astrodome by stroking liners for a .334 batting average and stealing 27 bases. Derrick May wore out his welcome in Chicago but should fit in well as the lefthanded half of a left-field platoon with young speedster James Mouton. Highly-touted center fielder Brian L. Hunter needs only to improve his strikezone judgment to be a superior offensive player. The organization is anticipating the arrival of another top prospect, Bob Abreu, who is an extra-base machine.

Infielders: When 28-year-old Dave Hajek finally made it to the Show, on the strength of a .327 season at triple-A Tucson, he was given a less-than-warm welcome from teammates who were miffed about his having appeared in several spring-training games during the strike. The departure of Craig Biggio puts Hajek in line for the job at second base. His pivot mate will be Orlando Miller, a slick-fielding shortstop who does little to contribute on offense. Third base isn't set at press time, but Craig Shipley could win the starting role by default. First base is in good hands, so to speak, when Jeff Bagwell's aren't broken.

Catchers: This should be an Astros strength, but it hasn't turned out that way. Tony Eusebio does his part with the bat and is not nearly as poor a receiver as he's reputed to be. Rick Wilkins is trying to locate the stroke that produced

30 homers for the Cubs in 1993. Wilkins is actually a good defensive backstop, though he hasn't had a chance to show it in Houston.

Starting Pitchers: Doug Drabek and Greg Swindell have been free-agent flops, but the Astros can't unload their hefty salaries. Drabek could yet bounce back, but Swindell probably won't. Darryl Kile has dropped off the table, much like his renowned curveball, and may not return. The Astros are counting on still further brilliance from Shane Reynolds, who has assumed the role of staff ace, and live-armed Mike Hampton, who emerged as a stellar number-two starter. Donne Wall topped the Pacific Coast League (triple-A) in ERA and wins last year before a late-season call-up, and super prospect Billy Wagner should be ready soon.

Relief Pitchers: Todd Jones and Dave Veres are a tough tandem, either closing or in setup work. John Hudek is attempting to return from arm surgery and reclaim his job as door slammer. Dean Hartgraves and Jeff Tabaka do the dirty work in middle relief and mop-up work.

Outlook

The Astros would have cruised into the playoffs last year had it not been for Jeff Bagwell's thrice-broken hand. This is still the second-best team in the Central Division, even without offensive catalyst Craig Biggio, but the 'Stros will have to get the most from their talented pitching staff if they're to keep distance between themselves and Chicago while closing the gap between themselves and the Reds. If Bagwell stays healthy, don't be surprised to see Houston winning a lot of close games and at least staying in the same stratosphere as their rivals in Cincinnati.

Fungoes

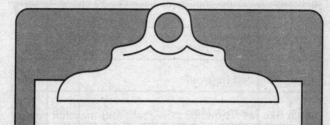

Quick Quiz: Which relief pitcher homered at the Astrodome in his first big-league at-bat, becoming the first Astro ever to do so?

Franchise Milestone: Since entering the National League as the Colt 45s in 1962, the Houston franchise has played in two NLCS series, losing to Philadelphia (3–2) in 1980 and to New York (4–2) in 1986.

Top Pitcher: Nolan Ryan, 1980–88

Top Player: Jose Cruz, 1975–87

Top Manager: Bill Virdon, 1975–82

Wacky Nickname: The Red Rooster (Douglas Lee Rader)

Quick Quiz Answer: Jose Sosa

Lineup Card

NO	POS	PLAYER	OBP	SLG
19	CF	Brian L. Hunter	.346	.396
5	1B	Jeff Bagwell	.399	.496
16	LF	Derrick May	.358	.500
14	RF	Derek Bell	.385	.442
3	C	Rick Wilkins	.351	.322
24	SS	Orlando Miller	.319	.377
21	2B	Dave Hajek	.333	.000
18	3B	Craig Shipley	.291	.345

In a Nutshell: The Astros didn't have much flash in their batting order last year, especially after Jeff Bagwell broke his hand (is there an echo in here?)—they ranked ninth in the NL in slugging, and now-departed free agent Craig Biggio led the team in home runs with a modest 22—but the heart of the order isn't exactly made up of slap hitters. Besides, this is perhaps the only stadium in baseball where the longball takes a seat on the bench in favor of long-sequence strategies like the hit-and-run, the bunt, and the stolen base. And, of course, the base on balls. Leading the league in walks last year helped Houston to finish second in runs scored, despite the lack of extra-base punch. As of press time the Astros still haven't found a permanent replacement for Ken Caminiti at third base, and the gulf that Biggio has left in his wake isn't likely to be filled anytime soon.

The Astrodome

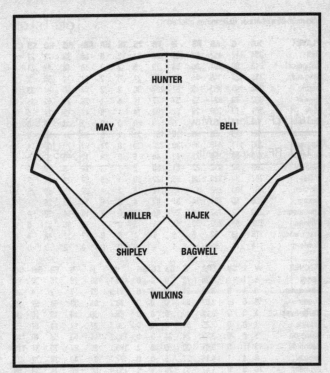

Capacity: 54,350
Turf: Artificial

LF Line: 325
RF Line: 325
Center: 400
Left CF: 375
Right CF: 375

Tickets:
713-799-9555

The Astrodome is a pitcher's park in every respect. The visibility is poor (strikeouts are increased by about 10 percent) and the still air keeps the ball from carrying. Home runs don't come cheaply in the Dome, but neither do other types of offense; it takes teamwork to create runs here. The carpet is fairly fast, and errors are generally cut by about 20 percent.

Statistics

Minimum 25 at-bats or 10.0 innings pitched

PLAYER	BA	G	AB	RS	H	TB	2B	3B	HR	RBI	BB	SO	SB	CS
Bell	.334	112	452	63	151	200	21	2	8	86	33	71	27	9
Cangelosi	.318	90	201	46	64	79	5	2	2	18	48	42	21	5
Magadan	.313	127	348	44	109	139	24	0	2	51	71	56	1	1
Biggio	.302	141	553	123	167	267	30	2	22	77	80	84	33	8
Hunter	.302	78	321	52	97	127	14	5	2	28	21	52	25	6
May	.301	77	206	29	62	102	14	1	8	41	19	24	5	0
Donnels	.300	19	30	4	9	9	0	0	0	2	3	6	0	0
Eusebio	.299	113	368	46	110	151	21	1	6	59	31	59	0	2
Bagwell	.290	114	448	88	130	222	29	0	21	87	79	102	11	6
Gutierrez	.276	52	156	22	43	49	6	0	0	12	10	33	5	0
Shipley	.263	92	232	23	61	80	8	1	3	24	8	28	6	1
Miller	.262	92	324	36	85	122	20	1	5	36	22	71	3	4
Mouton	.262	103	298	42	78	112	18	2	4	27	25	59	25	9
Simms	.256	50	121	14	31	62	4	0	9	24	13	28	1	2
Thompson	.220	92	132	14	29	44	9	0	2	19	14	36	4	2
Wilkins	.203	65	202	30	41	65	3	0	7	19	46	61	0	0
Stankiewicz	.115	43	52	5	6	7	1	0	0	7	12	18	4	3
Borders	.114	11	35	1	4	4	0	0	0	0	2	7	0	0

PITCHER	W	L	SV	ERA	G	GS	CG	SH	IP	H	R	ER	BB	SO
Veres	5	1	1	2.26	72	0	0	0	103.1	89	29	26	30	94
Henneman	0	1	8	3.00	21	0	0	0	21.0	21	7	7	4	19
Jones	6	5	15	3.07	68	0	0	0	99.2	89	38	34	52	96
Hartgraves	2	0	0	3.22	40	0	0	0	36.1	30	14	13	16	24
Tabaka	1	0	0	3.23	34	0	0	0	30.2	27	11	11	17	25
Hampton	9	8	0	3.35	24	24	0	0	150.2	141	73	56	49	115
Reynolds	10	11	0	3.47	30	30	3	2	189.1	196	87	73	37	175
Brocail	6	4	1	4.19	37	6	0	0	77.1	87	40	36	22	39
Swindell	10	9	0	4.47	33	26	1	1	153.0	180	86	76	39	96
Drabek	10	9	0	4.77	31	31	2	1	185.0	205	104	98	54	143
Dougherty	8	4	0	4.92	56	0	0	0	67.2	76	37	37	25	48
Kile	4	12	0	4.96	25	21	0	0	127.0	114	81	70	73	113
Hudek	2	2	7	5.40	19	0	0	0	20.0	19	12	12	5	29
Wall	3	1	0	5.55	6	5	0	0	24.1	33	19	15	5	16
Martinez	0	0	0	7.40	25	0	0	0	20.2	29	18	17	16	17
McMurtry	0	1	0	7.84	11	0	0	0	10.1	15	11	9	9	4

Roster

MANAGER: Terry Collins
COACHES: Matt Galante, Steve Henderson, Julio Linares

NO	PITCHERS	B	T	HT	WT	DOB
46	Doug Brocail	L	R	6-5	230	5/16/67
49	Jim Dougherty	R	R	6-0	210	3/8/68
15	Doug Drabek	R	R	6-1	185	7/25/62
10	Mike Hampton	R	L	5-10	180	9/9/72
58	Dean Hartgraves	R	L	6-0	185	8/12/66
35	John Hudek	S	R	6-1	200	8/8/66
59	Todd Jones	L	R	6-3	200	4/24/68
37	Shane Reynolds	R	R	6-3	210	3/26/68
21	Greg Swindell	R	L	6-3	225	1/2/65
31	Jeff Tabaka	R	L	6-2	195	1/17/64
43	Dave Veres	R	R	6-2	195	10/19/66
13	Billy Wagner	L	L	5-10	180	7/25/71
56	Donne Wall	R	R	6-1	180	7/11/67
	CATCHERS					
20	Tony Eusebio	R	R	6-2	180	4/27/67
3	Rick Wilkins	L	R	6-2	210	6/4/67
	INFIELDERS					
5	Jeff Bagwell	R	R	6-0	195	5/27/68
12	Ricky Gutierrez	R	R	6-1	175	5/23/70
21	Dave Hajek	R	R	5-10	165	10/14/67
—	Ray Holbert	R	R	6-0	165	9/25/70
24	Orlando Miller	R	R	6-1	180	1/13/69
18	Craig Shipley	R	R	6-1	190	1/7/63
4	Andy Stankiewicz	R	R	5-9	165	8/10/64
	OUTFIELDERS					
14	Derek Bell	R	R	6-2	210	12/11/68
36	Mike Brumley	S	R	5-10	155	4/9/63
19	Brian L. Hunter	R	R	6-4	180	3/5/71
16	Derrick May	L	R	6-4	225	7/14/68
6	James Mouton	R	R	5-9	175	12/29/68
23	Mike Simms	R	R	6-4	185	1/12/67

FREE AGENTS: Craig Biggio, Pat Borders, John Cangelosi, Mike Henneman, Dave Magadan, Milt Thompson

Jeff Bagwell   1B

Age: 27   **Seasons:** 5
Height: 6' 0"   **Weight:** 195
Bats: Right   **Throws:** Right
1995 OBP: .399   **1995 SLG:** .496

Just as he was getting up to speed... Bagwell entered June hitting .195, missed the stretch run with his third busted hand in as many seasons, and still led the Astros in runs batted in. He is the NL's best first baseman in every respect.

	G	AB	H	2B	3B	HR	RS	RBI	BB	SB	CS	BA
1995	114	448	130	29	0	21	88	87	79	12	5	.290
Career	684	2523	771	158	16	113	434	469	365	57	23	.306
Projected	127	521	179	41	2	33	105	111	87	14	6	.344

Derek Bell   OF

Age: 27   **Seasons:** 5
Height: 6' 2"   **Weight:** 210
Bats: Right   **Throws:** Right
1995 OBP: .385   **1995 SLG:** .442

Bell is far from perfect—he whiffs twice as often as he walks, his power is inconsistent, and he's prone to mistakes in the field— but for all his faults he's a valuable player, both at the plate and on the basepaths.

	G	AB	H	2B	3B	HR	RS	RBI	BB	SB	CS	BA
1995	112	452	151	21	2	8	63	86	33	27	9	.334
Career	449	1617	471	66	6	45	218	228	106	87	26	.291
Projected	152	539	163	24	2	16	75	93	44	29	10	.302

Craig Biggio 2B

Age: 30   **Seasons:** 8
Height: 5' 11"   **Weight:** 180
Bats: Right   **Throws:** Right
1995 OBP: .406   **1995 SLG:** .483

Biggio adapted his skills perfectly to his home park, but that doesn't mean he won't be incredibly productive anywhere he signs. He's a vastly more valuable player than Roberto Alomar, and that's no knock on Alomar.

	G	AB	H	2B	3B	HR	RS	RBI	BB	SB	CS	BA
1995	141	553	167	30	2	22	123	77	80	33	8	.302
Career	1055	3880	1105	221	24	79	615	389	475	196	65	.285
Projected	156	605	189	34	4	19	116	65	74	35	6	.312

Doug Drabek P

Age: 33   **Seasons:** 10
Height: 6' 1"   **Weight:** 185
Bats: Right   **Throws:** Right
1995 OBA: .282   **1995 WHIP:** 1.40

Drabek has been up and down the past three seasons and hasn't lived up to his fat paycheck, but he's an intelligent veteran with elusive stuff, and another comeback campaign wouldn't come as a shock.

	G	GS	IP	ER	ERA	H	BB	SO	W	L	SV
1995	31	31	185.0	98	4.77	205	54	143	10	9	0
Career	314	305	2081.2	766	3.31	1932	546	1317	130	103	0
Projected	34	34	226.2	107	4.25	241	62	165	13	10	0

Tony Eusebio   C

Age: 29   **Seasons:** 3
Height: 6' 2"   **Weight:** 180
Bats: Right   **Throws:** Right
1995 OBP: .354   **1995 SLG:** .410

Once considered a defensive liability, Eusebio languished in the minors in spite of his bat, but he tossed out an acceptable 30 percent of basestealers last year and made just five errors in 821 innings. He and Wilkins should make a solid platoon.

	G	AB	H	2B	3B	HR	RS	RBI	BB	SB	CS	BA
1995	113	368	110	21	1	6	46	58	31	0	2	.299
Career	178	546	159	31	2	11	68	88	45	0	3	.291
Projected	125	405	121	20	0	7	47	54	35	0	1	.299

Mike Hampton   P

Age: 23   **Seasons:** 3
Height: 5' 10"   **Weight:** 180
Bats: Right   **Throws:** Left
1995 OBA: .247   **1995 WHIP:** 1.26

In 1994, Hampton struggled to locate his fastball and was unable to shut down lefthanders, but last season he walked fewer than three batters per nine innings and held lefties to a livable .272 batting average.

	G	GS	IP	ER	ERA	H	BB	SO	W	L	SV
1995	24	24	150.2	56	3.35	141	49	115	9	8	0
Career	81	27	209.0	91	3.92	215	82	147	12	12	1
Projected	31	31	192.0	62	2.91	177	57	142	14	7	0

Brian L. Hunter OF

Age: 25   **Seasons:** 2
Height: 6' 4"   **Weight:** 180
Bats: Right   **Throws:** Right
1995 OBP: .346   **1995 SLG:** .396

Entering the majors as perhaps the NL's number-one outfield prospect in 1995, Hunter couldn't help but fall a step short of all the lofty expectations. His team-high nine outfield errors and so-so walks total are areas for improvement this season.

	G	AB	H	2B	3B	HR	RS	RBI	BB	SB	CS	BA
1995	78	321	97	14	5	2	52	28	21	24	7	.302
Career	84	345	103	15	5	2	54	28	22	26	8	.299
Projected	142	577	173	22	9	5	81	44	41	37	13	.300

Todd Jones P

Age: 28   **Seasons:** 3
Height: 6' 3"   **Weight:** 200
Bats: Left   **Throws:** Right
1995 OBA: .237   **1995 WHIP:** 1.41

Jones is the type of high-and-hard fireballer who could parlay a raised strikezone into unhittability. Righthanders batted just .213 against him last year, but his control occasionally went missing (4.7 walks per nine innings).

	G	GS	IP	ER	ERA	H	BB	SO	W	L	SV
1995	68	0	99.2	34	3.07	89	52	96	6	5	15
Career	143	0	209.2	69	2.96	169	93	184	12	9	22
Projected	75	0	113.1	29	2.30	100	55	108	6	2	22

Shane Reynolds   P

Age: 28   **Seasons:** 4
Height: 6' 3"   **Weight:** 210
Bats: Right   **Throws:** Right
1995 OBA: .263   **1995 WHIP:** 1.23

He doesn't sport the overpowering repertoire that typically rockets young hurlers to stardom, but Reynolds does feature masterful command (1.76 walks per nine innings), and he ranked in the league's top five in strikeouts last year.

	G	GS	IP	ER	ERA	H	BB	SO	W	L	SV
1995	30	30	189.1	73	3.47	196	37	175	10	11	0
Career	76	50	349.2	136	3.50	377	70	305	19	19	0
Projected	34	34	231.0	64	2.49	220	42	218	17	10	0

Dave Veres   P

Age: 29   **Seasons:** 2
Height: 6' 2"   **Weight:** 195
Bats: Right   **Throws:** Right
1995 OBA: .241   **1995 WHIP:** 1.15

Verily we say unto thee, Veres toiled in the minors for eight weary years, searching for a means by which to harness his superior stuff. Well, he found it and has blossomed into the NL's most effective setup reliever.

	G	GS	IP	ER	ERA	H	BB	SO	W	L	SV
1995	72	0	103.1	26	2.26	89	30	94	5	1	1
Career	104	0	144.1	37	2.31	128	37	122	8	4	2
Projected	80	0	112.2	24	1.92	94	27	104	7	0	9

Los Angeles
DODGERS

Scouting Report

Outfielders: Brett Butler has re-upped for one year at $2 million, so the Dodgers will have no worries in center field or the leadoff spot. In right field, Raul Mondesi's cannon arm is already legendary, though he's also somewhat error prone. What he lacks in discipline at the plate he compensates for with bat speed. Todd Hollandsworth, a 22-year-old lefthander, will enter spring training slated to start in left field. He was hampered by hand injuries last season but demonstrated a nice blend of speed and power at triple-A Albuquerque in 1994. Neophyte speed demon Roger Cedeno may still be a year away from the majors. Dodger fans are drooling in anticipation of 20-year-old lefty slugger Karim Garcia's forthcoming debut.

Infielders: Eric Karros exploded at the plate last season, posting career-best numbers in nearly every category. The Dodgers will either re-sign Delino DeShields and hope he stays healthy enough to play second base, with young Chad Fonville in a utility role, or Fonville will take over at second. Free-agent acquisition Greg Gagne provides a reliable glove at shortstop and mild punch at the plate. Mike Blowers, coming off a career year in Seattle, is the hired gun at the hot corner.

Catchers: Mike Piazza handles the pitching staff well but is a below-average receiver otherwise. His stickwork is MVP quality; in fact he's the only player in Dodgers history to collect at least 20 homers in his first three seasons.

Starting Pitchers: Don't expect to see Kevin Tapani or Tom Candiotti wearing Dodger blue this season. Ramon Martinez is now solidly entrenched as L.A.'s veteran ace, despite not having the best pure stuff on the staff. That distinction belongs to Japanese sensation Hideo Nomo, who was the NL's starting pitcher in the All-Star game. Most members of the national media haven't "discovered" Ismael Valdes, but he's soon to be an All-Star himself. It's not inconceivable that the next Rookie of the Year will be Chan Ho Park, a raw talent with superior stuff and a well-developed repertoire. We'll take this moment to mention an article that appeared in the 1983 edition of the Bill James Baseball Abstract. It suggested that a.) the Dodgers were responsible for the current popularity of five-man rotations and b.) it's foolish to take 32 starts from your four best pitchers and give them to your fifth best pitcher (be he John Cummings, Pedro Astacio, or whomever).

Relief Pitchers: Todd Worrell rose from pitching oblivion to become L.A.'s all-time single-season saves leader. Look for prospects Joey Eischen and Felix Rodriguez to make waves in the bullpen.

Outlook

The defending Western Division champs are trimming the fat in the offseason, dumping high-priced underachievers and gearing up for what is probably Tommy Lasorda's swan song. The Dodgers are dynamic at the core, with three potential 18-game winners—Martinez, Nomo, and Valdes—in the starting rotation and three potential 30-homer sluggers—Piazza, Karros, and Mondesi—in the batting order. The overall team defense is shaky and the middle-relief corps is unproven, but the Dodgers have to like their chances of repeating in the West.

Fungoes

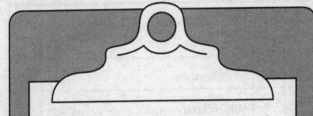

Quick Quiz: Which player unloaded two pinch-hit home runs in the 1959 World Series?

Franchise Milestone: The franchise has won six of its 18 World Series appearances.

Top Pitcher: Sandy Koufax, 1955–66

Top Player: Roy Campanella, 1948–57

Top Manager: Tom Lasorda, 1976–

Wacky Nickname: Some of the wackiest nicknames in franchise history belonged to the team itself. Before becoming the Dodgers, the club was known at various times as the Bridegrooms, the Superbas, the Infants, and the Robins.

Quick Quiz Answer: Chuck Essegian

Lineup Card

NO	POS	PLAYER	OBP	SLG
22	CF	Brett Butler	.377	.376
3	2B	Chad Fonville	.328	.303
31	C	Mike Piazza	.400	.606
23	1B	Eric Karros	.369	.535
43	RF	Raul Mondesi	.328	.496
00	3B	Mike Blowers	.335	.474
28	LF	Todd Hollandsworth	.304	.398
00	SS	Greg Gagne	.316	.374

In a Nutshell: At press time the Dodgers are reportedly thinking of letting Delino DeShields depart and inserting Chad Fonville at second base. It's true that DeShields has not lived up to his salary in his two years in L.A., but he's only 27 and as an all-around player is far superior to the slap-hitting Fonville. If Double-D goes elsewhere, Fonville will probably hit in the nine- or two-hole. The Dodgers' batting order is designed to generate runs in a ballpark that stifles long-sequence offense. The idea is for Butler and DeShields/Fonville to bunt or slap-hit their way on base, distract the pitcher as much as possible, and wait for the big bats—Piazza, Karros, and Mondesi—to deliver the longball. The organization owns two of the best outfield prospects in the Pacific Coast League, Karim Garcia and Roger Cedeno. Either could make an impact if young Todd Hollandsworth doesn't distinguish himself.

Dodger Stadium

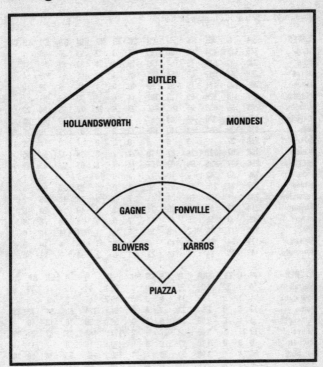

Capacity: 56,000
Turf: Natural

LF Line: 330
RF Line: 330
Center: 404
Left CF: 375
Right CF: 375

Tickets:
213-224-1448

The stadium at Chavez Ravine is known as a pitcher's park, in part because of the Dodgers' legacy of great power pitchers. The mound may or may not be higher than it's supposed to be, and the foul territory is certainly huge, but whatever the reasons there's no doubt that all types of offense, especially triples (by as much as 50 percent), are suppressed here.

Statistics

Minimum 25 at-bats or 10.0 innings pitched

PLAYER	BA	G	AB	RS	H	TB	2B	3B	HR	RBI	BB	SO	SB	CS
Piazza	.346	112	434	82	150	263	17	0	32	93	39	80	1	0
Butler	.300	129	513	78	154	193	18	9	1	38	67	51	32	8
Karros	.298	143	551	83	164	295	29	3	32	105	61	115	4	4
Hansen	.287	100	181	19	52	65	10	0	1	14	28	28	0	0
Offerman	.287	119	429	69	123	161	14	6	4	33	69	67	2	7
Mondesi	.285	139	536	91	153	266	23	6	26	88	33	96	27	4
Fonville	.278	102	320	43	89	97	6	1	0	16	23	42	20	7
Kelly	.278	136	504	58	140	188	23	2	7	57	23	79	19	10
Parker	.276	27	29	3	8	8	0	0	0	4	2	4	1	1
Wallach	.266	97	327	24	87	140	22	2	9	38	27	69	0	0
DeShields	.256	127	425	66	109	157	18	3	8	37	63	83	39	14
Cedeno	.238	40	42	4	10	12	2	0	0	3	3	10	1	0
Ashley	.237	81	215	17	51	80	5	0	8	27	25	88	0	0
Hollandsworth	.233	41	103	16	24	41	2	0	5	13	10	29	2	1
Gwynn	.214	67	84	8	18	28	3	2	1	10	6	23	0	0
Ingram	.200	43	55	5	11	13	2	0	0	3	9	8	3	0
Prince	.200	17	40	3	8	15	2	1	1	4	4	10	0	0
Webster	.179	54	56	6	10	16	1	1	1	3	4	14	0	0
Hernandez	.149	45	94	3	14	21	1	0	2	8	7	25	0	0

PITCHER	W	L	SV	ERA	G	GS	CG	SH	IP	H	R	ER	BB	SO
Worrell	4	1	32	2.02	59	0	0	0	62.1	49	15	14	19	61
Rodriguez	1	1	0	2.53	11	0	0	0	10.2	11	3	3	5	5
Nomo	13	6	0	2.54	28	28	4	3	191.1	124	63	54	78	236
Cummings	3	1	0	3.00	37	0	0	0	39.0	38	16	13	10	21
Valdes	13	11	1	3.05	33	27	6	2	197.2	168	76	67	51	150
Eischen	0	0	0	3.10	17	0	0	0	20.1	19	9	7	11	15
Candiotti	7	14	0	3.50	30	30	1	1	190.1	187	93	74	58	141
Guthrie	0	2	0	3.66	24	0	0	0	19.2	19	11	8	9	19
Martinez	17	7	0	3.66	30	30	4	2	206.1	176	95	84	81	138
Astacio	7	8	0	4.24	48	11	1	1	104.0	103	53	49	29	80
Parra	0	0	0	4.35	8	0	0	0	10.1	10	8	5	6	7
Osuna	2	4	0	4.43	39	0	0	0	44.2	39	22	22	20	46
Bruske	0	0	1	4.50	9	0	0	0	10.0	12	7	5	4	5
Tapani	4	2	0	5.05	13	11	0	0	57.0	72	37	32	14	43
Williams	2	2	0	5.12	16	0	0	0	19.1	19	11	11	7	8
Seanez	1	3	3	6.75	37	0	0	0	34.2	39	27	26	18	29
Daal	4	0	0	7.20	28	0	0	0	20.0	29	16	16	15	11
Hansell	0	1	0	7.45	20	0	0	0	19.1	29	17	16	6	13

Roster

MANAGER: Tom Lasorda
COACHES: Joe Amalfitano, Mark Cresse, Manny Mota, Bill Russell,
Reggie Smith, Dave Wallace

NO	PITCHERS	B	T	HT	WT	DOB
56	Pedro Astacio	R	R	6-2	195	11/28/69
41	John Cummings	L	L	6-3	200	5/10/69
48	Ramon Martinez	L	R	6-4	176	3/22/68
16	Hideo Nomo	R	R	6-2	210	8/31/68
50	Antonio Osuna	R	R	5-11	160	4/12/73
61	Chan Ho Park	R	R	6-2	185	6/30/73
46	Kevin Tapani	R	R	6-0	189	2/18/64
59	Ismael Valdes	R	R	6-3	207	8/21/73
38	Todd Worrell	R	R	6-5	230	9/28/59
	CATCHERS					
26	Carlos Hernandez	R	R	5-11	215	5/24/67
31	Mike Piazza	R	R	6-3	210	9/4/68
	INFIELDERS					
—	Mike Blowers	R	R	6-2	210	4/24/65
25	Mike Busch	R	R	6-5	222	7/7/68
60	Juan Castro	R	R	5-10	163	6/20/72
14	Delino DeShields	L	R	6-1	175	1/15/69
3	Chad Fonville	S	R	5-6	155	3/5/71
—	Greg Gagne	R	R	5-11	180	11/12/61
5	Dave Hansen	L	R	6-0	195	11/24/68
33	Garey Ingram	R	R	5-11	180	7/25/70
23	Eric Karros	R	R	6-4	216	11/4/67
3	Eddie Pye	R	R	5-10	170	2/13/67
	OUTFIELDERS					
7	Billy Ashley	R	R	6-7	230	7/11/70
22	Brett Butler	L	L	5-10	161	6/15/57
27	Roger Cedeno	R	R	6-1	165	8/16/74
12	Karim Garcia	L	L	6-0	200	10/29/75
28	Todd Hollandsworth	L	L	6-2	193	4/20/73
43	Raul Mondesi	R	R	5-11	210	3/12/71
41	Reggie Williams	S	R	6-2	180	5/5/66

FREE AGENTS: Tom Candiotti, Roberto Kelly, Tim Wallach

Raul Mondesi

Brett Butler   *OF*

Age: 38   **Seasons:** 15
Height: 5' 10"   **Weight:** 161
Bats: Left   **Throws:** Left
1995 OBP: .377   **1995 SLG:** .376

Back for one more year with L.A., the pro's pro remains a reliable gloveman in center field (he was charged with only two miscues in his 1,106 innings played last season), and a master at getting on base (he led the NL in bunt singles and infield hits.)

	G	AB	H	2B	3B	HR	RS	RBI	BB	SB	CS	BA
1995	129	513	154	18	9	1	78	38	67	32	8	.300
Career	2074	7706	2243	268	127	54	1285	552	1078	535	244	.291
Projected	143	564	172	15	10	2	90	41	74	30	10	.305

Delino DeShields   *2B*

Age: 27   **Seasons:** 6
Height: 6' 1"   **Weight:** 175
Bats: Left   **Throws:** Right
1995 OBP: .353   **1995 SLG:** .369

The talented but oft-injured DeShields may not have lived up to expectations in his two years as a Dodger, but he's nevertheless a fine player. His range and hands are both well above average, and he's extremely disruptive on the basepaths.

	G	AB	H	2B	3B	HR	RS	RBI	BB	SB	CS	BA
1995	127	425	109	18	3	8	66	37	63	39	14	.250
Career	754	2818	764	46	28	33	422	251	404	253	91	.265
Projected	140	489	134	16	5	7	81	40	55	42	10	.274

Chad Fonville   2B/SS

Age: 25   **Seasons:** 1
Height: 5' 6"   **Weight:** 155
Bats: Switch   **Throws:** Right
1995 OBP: .328   **1995 SLG:** .303

Fonville sprang directly from class-A to the majors last year and is likely to see regular action at shortstop or second base, depending on the contract status of Delino DeShields. Fonville is a slap hitter with plus speed and a steady glove.

	G	AB	H	2B	3B	HR	RS	RBI	BB	SB	CS	BA
1995	102	320	89	6	1	0	43	16	23	20	7	.278
Career	102	320	89	6	1	0	43	16	23	20	7	.278
Projected	135	440	117	13	3	0	55	21	36	24	6	.266

Chan Ho Park   P

Age: 22   **Seasons:** R
Height: 6' 2"   **Weight:** 185
Bats: Right   **Throws:** Right
1995 OBA: .143   **1995 WHIP:** 1.00

The Korean-born Park features a funky delivery and fantastic stuff. Sound familiar? He has a varied repertoire but lacks experience and command. In 110.0 triple-A innings last season he whiffed 101 batters while walking 76.

	G	GS	IP	ER	ERA	H	BB	SO	W	L	SV
1995	2	1	4.0	2	4.50	2	2	7	0	0	0
Career	4	1	8.0	7	7.88	7	7	13	0	0	0
Projected	27	23	158.1	88	5.00	159	84	147	7	10	0

Eric Karros   1B

Age: 28   **Seasons:** 5
Height: 6' 4"   **Weight:** 216
Bats: Right   **Throws:** Right
1995 OBP: .369   **1995 SLG:** .535

Was it a career year fueled by a hot start, or has Karros emerged as one of the league's most productive hitters? Remarkably, he became the first L.A. first sacker to smash the 30-tater barrier since Steve Garvey in 1977.

	G	AB	H	2B	3B	HR	RS	RBI	BB	SB	CS	BA
1995	143	551	164	29	3	32	83	105	61	4	4	.298
Career	575	2134	566	108	7	89	271	320	162	8	9	.265
Projected	157	598	172	24	1	25	86	93	50	3	4	.288

Ramon Martinez   P

Age: 28   **Seasons:** 8
Height: 6' 4"   **Weight:** 176
Bats: Left   **Throws:** Right
1995 OBA: .231   **1995 WHIP:** 1.25

Though he doesn't overpower batters the way he once did (8.56 whiffs per nine innings in 1990), Martinez is pitching the best ball of his career. He went 9–1, 2.66 after the All-Star break last year, including 6–0, 1.89 in his final six decisions.

	G	GS	IP	ER	ERA	H	BB	SO	W	L	SV
1995	30	30	206.1	84	3.66	176	81	138	17	7	0
Career	201	198	1327.2	513	3.48	1166	509	970	91	63	0
Projected	33	33	221.1	75	3.05	185	72	155	16	8	0

Raul Mondesi   OF

Age: 25   **Seasons:** 3
Height: 5' 11"   **Weight:** 210
Bats: Right   **Throws:** Right
1995 OBP: .328   **1995 SLG:** .496

In 1994, Mondesi was an ineffective 58-percent basestealer, but last year he improved dramatically, sliding in safe at a sparkling 87-percent rate. He topped the majors in outfield assists for the second straight year with 16.

	G	AB	H	2B	3B	HR	RS	RBI	BB	SB	CS	BA
1995	139	536	153	23	6	26	91	88	33	27	4	.285
Career	293	1056	311	53	15	46	167	154	53	42	13	.295
Projected	152	547	148	22	7	24	89	94	39	16	6	.271

Hideo Nomo   P

Age: 27   **Seasons:** 1
Height: 6' 2"   **Weight:** 210
Bats: Right   **Throws:** Right
1995 OBA: .182   **1995 WHIP:** 1.06

The former Kintetsu Buffaloes all-star topped the NL in whiffs and OBA on his way to Rookie of the Year honors. Elbow stiffness and a broken fingernail took some of the luster off a dream season, but he was 6–0, 0.89 in June.

	G	GS	IP	ER	ERA	H	BB	SO	W	L	SV
1995	28	28	191.1	54	2.54	124	78	236	13	6	0
Career	28	28	191.1	54	2.54	124	78	236	13	6	0
Projected	32	32	219.2	66	2.70	141	65	244	16	6	0

Mike Piazza C

Age: 27 **Seasons:** 4
Height: 6' 3" **Weight:** 210
Bats: Right **Throws:** Right
1995 OBP: .400 **1995 SLG:** .606

A torn thumb ligament kept the mighty Piazza out of MVP contention, but he should be the early favorite to win the 1996 award. He's committed an atrocious 19 errors over the past two shortened seasons, but he makes up for it at the plate.

	G	AB	H	2B	3B	HR	RS	RBI	BB	SB	CS	BA
1995	112	434	150	17	0	32	82	93	39	1	0	.346
Career	389	1455	469	62	2	92	232	304	122	5	7	.322
Projected	138	504	171	25	1	42	96	133	49	1	2	.339

Kevin Tapani P

Age: 32 **Seasons:** 7
Height: 6' 0" **Weight:** 189
Bats: Right **Throws:** Right
1995 OBA: N/A **1995 WHIP:** 1.44

Tapani struggled at Chavez Ravine, allowing 20 earned runs in 19 innings pitched in L.A., but the Dodgers were 8–3 in his 11 starts. His ERAs have been on the rise every year since 1991, but he still has top-notch control and a rubber arm.

	G	GS	IP	ER	ERA	H	BB	SO	W	L	SV
1995	32	30	185.2	102	4.94	221	47	128	10	13	0
Career	193	190	1223.1	557	4.10	1294	268	764	79	65	0
Projected	34	34	225.1	100	3.99	235	32	164	12	11	0

Ismael Valdes   P

Age: 22   **Seasons:** 2
Height: 6' 3"   **Weight:** 207
Bats: Right   **Throws:** Right
1995 OBA: .228   **1995 WHIP:** 1.11

Considering his age, Valdes has the poise and command to be one of the league's best starters for years to come. Except for a pair of four-game losing streaks in which he was treated like his *Moby-Dick* namesake, he was brilliant in 1995.

	G	GS	IP	ER	ERA	H	BB	SO	W	L	S
1995	33	27	197.2	67	3.05	168	51	150	13	11	
Career	54	28	226.0	77	3.07	189	61	178	16	12	
Projected	33	33	221.1	61	2.48	192	58	191	20	9	

Todd Worrell   P

Age: 36   **Seasons:** 9
Height: 6' 5"   **Weight:** 230
Bats: Right   **Throws:** Right
1995 OBA: .221   **1995 WHIP:** 1.11

Worrell shot out of the gate last year, allowing zero earned runs in his first 25 appearances, and wound up posting his best numbers since the mid-1980s. Three of his four blown saves came in a one-week span in late July.

	G	GS	IP	ER	ERA	H	BB	SO	W	L	S
1995	59	0	62.1	14	2.02	50	19	61	4	1	3.
Career	480	0	568.2	181	2.86	478	209	501	44	40	17.
Projected	64	0	66.1	19	2.58	55	26	63	2	3	3'

Montreal
EXPOS

Scouting Report

Outfielders: Oft-injured left fielder Moises Alou, Montreal's best hitter, is rumored to be on the trading block at press time. If Alou is dealt, Frank-Paul Santangelo, a rookie with excellent on-base ability, will battle Cliff Floyd for the full-time job. The Expos are all smiles about the emergence of Rondell White, whose offensive skills have been compared to those of Andre Dawson, as a potential superstar in center field. Another young outfielder who has only begun to tap his power/speed talents is hard-nosed right fielder Tony Tarasco, who tied Jeff Bagwell for fourth in the NL with 12 intentional walks. The Expos will have to make room for 22-year-old Yamil Benitez, who posted eye-popping stats (.400 OBP, .641 SLG) in his first 39 big-league at-bats.

Infielders: David Segui is a slick-fielding first baseman who hit 52 points better in 1995 than his previous career average. Second baseman Mike Lansing is also a superior defensive player, but unlike Segui, he offers above-average power and speed for his position. The Expos don't respect Wil Cordero's defensive skills at shortstop—they moved him to left field for the final 26 games of last season—but he's a younger Barry Larkin at the plate. Cordero's shift to the outfield created an opening for rookie shortstop Mark Grudzielanek, the 1994 Eastern League (triple-A) MVP, who is actually several months older than Cordero. There's a chance that Cordero will be traded at some point after press time. At the hot corner, the Expos hope that rookie slugger Shane Andrews will eventually cut down on his frequency of whiffs and errors. In the meantime, Sean Berry is a solid all-around third baseman.

Catchers: Darrin Fletcher is a quality defensive backstop who improves his hitting every year. His platoon mate is Tim Laker, who hit .323 with runners in scoring position last season but threw out just 25 percent of opposing thieves.

Starting Pitchers: Pedro J. Martinez is tabbed as the new staff ace, especially if last season's ace, Jeff Fassero, is traded. Rookie righty Ugueth U. Urbina (6–1, 2.90 at triple-A Ottawa) could be a factor in the rotation. Kirk Reuter is an underrated finesse type who didn't allow a run in his final three starts last year. Montreal will probably try to make a trade to round out the staff.

Relief Pitchers: Control specialist Gil Heredia posted a 0.68 ERA in his last 21 long-relief appearances. Mel Rojas rang up 30 saves but was inconsistent in the role of closer. Lefthander Dave Leiper was a bright spot in the bullpen after coming to Montreal from Oakland.

Outlook

The Expos have used up four general managers in five years, dismantled one of baseball's most talented teams, and spiraled from first place in 1994 to the cellar last year. More salary dumping is expected, with Moises Alou, Jeff Fassero, and Wil Cordero rumored to be on the block. But no matter, the farm system keeps cranking out prospects (next up, Yamil Benitez), and the starting rotation won't be any worse than average, so Montreal figures to rebound from last season's collapse to become a middle-of-the-pack wild-card contender.

Fungoes

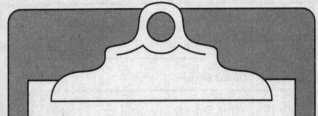

Quick Quiz: Which infielder was hit by pitches an unbelievable 50 times in 1971, his first season as an Expo?

Franchise Milestone: Montreal qualified for the NL playoffs in 1981's strike-split season and gained a hard-fought 3–2 win over Philadelphia. The Expos were eliminated 3–2 by Los Angeles in the NLCS, scoring just one run in each of their losses.

Top Pitcher: Steve Rogers, 1973–85

Top Player: Gary Carter, 1974–84

Top Manager: Dick Williams, 1977–81

Wacky Nickname: Boots (Charles Frederick Day)

Quick Quiz Answer: Ron Hunt

Lineup Card

NO	POS	PLAYER	OBP	SLG
22	CF	Rondell White	.356	.464
25	1B	David Segui	.367	.461
1	RF	Yamil Benitez	.400	.641
5	3B	Sean Berry	.367	.529
30	LF	Cliff Floyd	.221	.188
3	2B	Mike Lansing	.299	.392
24	C	Darrin Fletcher	.351	.446
4	SS	Mark Grudzielanek	.300	.316

In a Nutshell: The Montreal batting order was rarely set for an extended period last season, for reasons including the fire sale that jettisoned Larry Walker and Marquis Grissom, injuries to Cliff Floyd and Moises Alou, and manager Felipe Alou's sometimes-questionable decisions. Case in point: Tony Tarasco—1995 OBP, .329—made 41 starts in the leadoff spot. The potential shape of the 1996 lineup is difficult to gauge before the season starts because three excellent players—Alou, Fletcher, and Wil Cordero—are on the trading block at press time. If they stay in Montreal, Cordero would be in the two- or three-hole, while Alou would bat third or fourth. The Expos' farm system does a great job of developing power/speed types, and players like White, Lansing, and Tarasco fit that tradition. Speaking of Tarasco, he'll battle Benitez and Floyd for a starting spot in the outfield.

Olympic Stadium

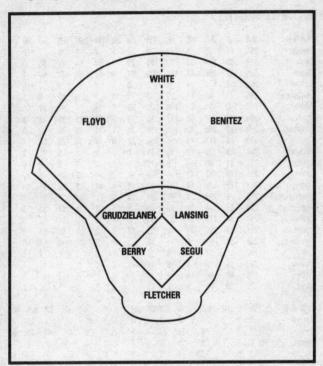

Capacity: 46,500
Turf: Artificial

LF Line: 325
RF Line: 325
Center: 404
Left CF: 375
Right CF: 375

Tickets:
514-846-3976

Before the roof was completed in 1987, the Big O was a poor place for hitters. Now that the chilly air is kept out, the stadium is more of a neutral park, though home runs are still suppressed, in part because the visibility isn't very good. The carpet keeps errors to a minimum and encourages aggressive base-running. The Expos do a fine job of shaping their team to their park.

Statistics

Minimum 25 at-bats or 10.0 innings pitched

PLAYER	BA	G	AB	RS	H	TB	2B	3B	HR	RBI	BB	SO	SB	CS
Benitez	.385	14	39	8	15	25	2	1	2	7	1	7	0	2
Berry	.318	103	314	38	100	166	22	1	14	55	25	53	3	8
Segui	.309	130	456	68	141	209	24	4	12	68	40	47	2	7
Siddall	.300	7	10	4	3	3	0	0	0	1	3	3	0	0
Santangelo	.296	35	98	11	29	39	5	1	1	9	12	9	1	1
White	.295	130	474	87	140	220	33	4	13	57	41	87	25	5
Cordero	.286	131	514	64	147	216	35	2	10	49	36	88	9	5
Fletcher	.286	110	350	42	100	156	21	1	11	45	32	23	0	1
Alou	.273	93	344	48	94	158	22	0	14	58	29	56	4	3
Silvestri	.264	39	72	12	19	31	6	0	2	7	9	27	2	0
Spehr	.257	41	35	4	9	17	5	0	1	3	6	7	0	0
Lansing	.255	127	467	47	119	183	30	2	10	62	28	65	27	4
Tarasco	.249	126	438	64	109	177	18	4	14	40	51	78	24	3
Grudzielanek	.245	78	269	27	66	85	12	2	1	20	14	47	8	3
Rodriguez	.239	45	138	13	33	45	4	1	2	15	11	28	0	1
Laker	.234	64	141	17	33	52	8	1	3	20	14	38	0	1
Andrews	.214	84	220	27	47	83	10	1	8	31	17	68	1	1
Treadway	.209	58	67	6	14	18	2	1	0	13	5	4	0	1
Foley	.208	11	24	2	5	7	2	0	0	2	2	4	1	0
Frazier	.190	35	63	6	12	14	2	0	0	3	8	12	4	0
Pride	.175	46	63	10	11	12	1	0	0	2	5	16	3	2
Floyd	.130	29	69	6	9	13	1	0	1	8	7	22	3	0

PITCHER	W	L	SV	ERA	G	GS	CG	SH	IP	H	R	ER	BB	SO
Harris	2	3	0	2.61	45	0	0	0	48.1	45	18	14	16	47
Henry	7	9	0	2.84	21	21	1	1	126.2	133	47	40	28	60
Leiper	0	2	2	2.86	26	0	0	0	22.0	16	8	7	6	12
Rueter	5	3	0	3.23	9	9	1	1	47.1	38	17	17	9	28
Martinez	14	10	0	3.51	30	30	2	2	194.2	158	79	76	66	174
Perez	10	8	0	3.69	28	23	2	1	141.1	142	61	58	28	106
Scott	2	0	2	3.98	62	0	0	0	63.1	52	30	28	23	57
Rojas	1	4	30	4.12	59	0	0	0	67.2	69	32	31	29	61
Heredia	5	6	1	4.31	40	18	0	0	119.0	137	60	57	21	74
Fassero	13	14	0	4.33	30	30	1	0	189.0	207	102	91	74	164
Shaw	1	6	3	4.62	50	0	0	0	62.1	58	35	32	26	45
Eversgerd	0	0	0	5.14	25	0	0	0	21.0	22	13	12	9	8
Fraser	2	1	2	5.61	22	0	0	0	25.2	25	17	16	9	12
Urbina	2	2	0	6.17	7	4	0	0	23.1	26	17	16	14	15
Alvarez	1	5	0	6.75	8	8	0	0	37.1	46	30	28	14	17
Schmidt	0	0	0	6.97	11	0	0	0	10.1	15	8	8	9	7
White	1	2	0	7.01	19	1	0	0	25.2	26	21	20	9	25

Roster

MANAGER: Felipe Alou
COACHES: Pierre Arsenault, Tommy Harper, Joe Kerrigan,
Jerry Manuel, Luis Pujols, Jim Tracy

NO	PITCHERS	B	T	HT	WT	DOB
48	Tavo Alvarez	R	R	6-3	245	11/25/71
—	Derek Aucoin	R	R	6-7	245	3/27/70
26	Bryan Eversgerd	R	L	6-1	190	2/11/69
13	Jeff Fassero	L	L	6-1	195	1/5/63
—	Scott Gentile	R	R	5-10	205	12/12/70
20	Rodney Henderson	R	R	6-4	193	3/11/71
34	Gil Heredia	R	R	6-1	205	10/26/65
52	Dave Leiper	L	L	6-1	175	6/18/62
37	Pedro J. Martinez	R	L	5-11	170	7/25/71
—	Jose Paniagua	L	L	6-2	185	8/20/73
50	Carlos Perez	L	L	6-3	195	1/14/71
51	Mel Rojas	R	R	5-11	195	12/10/66
42	Kirk Rueter	L	L	6-3	195	12/1/70
43	Curt Schmidt	R	R	6-5	200	3/16/70
54	Tim Scott	R	R	6-2	205	11/16/66
—	Everett Stull	R	R	6-3	200	8/24/71
41	Ugueth Urbina	R	R	6-2	185	2/15/74
47	Gabe White	L	L	6-2	200	11/20/71
—	Esteban Yan	R	R	6-4	180	8/22/74
	CATCHERS					
24	Darrin Fletcher	L	R	6-1	205	10/3/66
19	Tim Laker	R	R	6-3	200	11/27/69
2	Tim Spehr	R	R	6-2	200	7/2/66
	INFIELDERS					
—	Israel Alcantara	R	R	6-2	180	5/6/73
11	Shane Andrews	R	R	6-1	215	8/28/71
5	Sean Berry	R	R	5-11	200	3/22/66
12	Wil Cordero	R	R	6-2	195	10/3/71
30	Cliff Floyd	L	R	6-4	230	12/5/72
4	Mark Grudzielanek	R	R	6-1	185	6/30/70
3	Mike Lansing	R	R	6-0	180	4/3/68
7	F.P. Santangelo	S	R	5-10	168	10/24/67
25	David Segui	S	L	6-1	202	7/19/66
	OUTFIELDERS					
18	Moises Alou	R	R	6-3	195	7/3/66
1	Yamil Benitez	R	R	6-2	195	10/5/72
40	Henry Rodriguez	L	L	6-1	210	11/8/67
—	Darond Stovall	S	L	6-1	185	1/3/73
44	Tony Tarasco	L	R	6-1	205	12/9/70
22	Rondell White	R	R	6-1	205	2/23/72

FREE AGENTS: None

Moises Alou   OF

Age: 29   **Seasons:** 5
Height: 6' 3"   **Weight:** 195
Bats: Right   **Throws:** Right
1995 OBP: .342   **1995 SLG:** .459

Making a bid to become the new Eric Davis, Alou suffered another serious injury in 1995, the third of his career. When he's not on the DL, he's cracking linedrives both all over and out of the park while playing spectacular defense in left field.

	G	AB	H	2B	3B	HR	RS	RBI	BB	SB	CS	BA
1995	93	344	94	22	0	14	48	58	29	4	3	.273
Career	467	1609	475	110	14	63	256	277	134	44	17	.295
Projected	138	443	125	27	3	18	59	69	35	11	5	.282

Sean Berry   3B

Age: 30   **Seasons:** 6
Height: 5' 11"   **Weight:** 200
Bats: Right   **Throws:** Right
1995 OBP: .367   **1995 SLG:** .529

The Expos inexplicably used Berry on a noneveryday basis last season, but he deserves the fulltime job in 1996. Though he's not a pure slugger, he flashes good power, and he's usually a much better basestealer than he showed last year.

	G	AB	H	2B	3B	HR	RS	RBI	BB	SB	CS	BA
1995	103	314	100	22	1	14	38	55	25	3	8	.318
Career	391	1073	299	61	6	40	143	154	106	31	11	.279
Projected	133	510	157	23	1	25	77	81	43	9	4	.308

Wil Cordero SS

Age: 24	**Seasons:** 4
Height: 6' 2"	**Weight:** 195
Bats: Right	**Throws:** Right
1995 OBP: .341	**1995 SLG:** .420

Cordero, who has been playing pro ball since the age of 17, endured a horrendous slump after being moved to left field for the the final month of the 1995 season. His upward potential as a hitter is sky high, but his fielding remains erratic.

	G	AB	H	2B	3B	HR	RS	RBI	BB	SB	CS	BA
1995	131	514	147	35	2	10	64	49	36	9	5	.286
Career	424	1530	425	101	8	37	202	178	120	37	11	.278
Projected	152	590	166	31	3	13	71	51	44	14	4	.281

Jeff Fassero P

Age: 33	**Seasons:** 5
Height: 6' 1"	**Weight:** 195
Bats: Left	**Throws:** Left
1995 OBA: .283	**1995 WHIP:** 1.49

Fassero took a great leap forward in 1993 when he suddenly emerged as a top-flight starter at age 30. The hard-throwing southpaw was 7–1 going into June last season, but he staggered to a 6–13 mark in his final 22 starts.

	G	GS	IP	ER	ERA	H	BB	SO	W	L	SV
1995	30	30	189.0	91	4.33	207	74	164	13	14	0
Career	228	66	618.1	217	3.16	565	219	528	43	37	10
Projected	33	33	222.1	90	3.64	210	63	179	12	12	0

Darrin Fletcher   C

Age: 29   **Seasons:** 7
Height: 6' 1"   **Weight:** 205
Bats: Left   **Throws:** Right
1995 OBP: .351   **1995 SLG:** .446

Fletcher improves his all-around skills a little bit each year. He threw out 33 percent of opposition thieves last season, a far cry from 1993's 12 percent and 1994's 23 percent. He can't handle southpaws but has otherwise become a solid hitter.

	G	AB	H	2B	3B	HR	RS	RBI	BB	SB	CS	BA
1995	110	350	100	21	1	11	42	45	32	0	1	.286
Career	482	1420	367	78	5	34	125	203	112	0	4	.258
Projected	117	364	98	18	0	9	40	47	35	0	2	.269

Greg A. Harris   P

Age: 40   **Seasons:** 15
Height: 6' 0"   **Weight:** 175
Bats: Switch   **Throws:** Switch
1995 OBA: .245   **1995 WHIP:** 1.26

Harris entered Cooperstown through the chimney last season, becoming the first pitcher since Elton "Ice Box" Chamberlain in 1888 to pitch ambidextrously in a game. He's still a serviceable middle reliever and should latch on somewhere for 1996.

	G	GS	IP	ER	ERA	H	BB	SO	W	L	SV
1995	45	0	48.1	14	2.61	45	16	47	2	3	0
Career	703	98	1467.1	600	3.68	1329	652	1141	74	90	54
Projected	51	0	67.0	22	2.95	69	19	58	1	3	0

Mike Lansing 2B

Age: 28   **Seasons:** 3
Height: 6' 0"   **Weight:** 180
Bats: Right   **Throws:** Right
1995 OBP: .299   **1995 SLG:** .392

Lansing endured an injury-induced slump that caused his batting average to sink to .214 in mid-July, yet he still managed to set career highs in homers and steals. He ranked third in fielding percentage among NL second sackers (.991).

	G	AB	H	2B	3B	HR	RS	RBI	BB	SB	CS	BA
1995	127	467	119	30	2	10	47	62	28	27	4	.255
Career	374	1352	365	80	5	18	155	142	104	62	17	.267
Projected	146	508	135	26	3	7	45	58	32	24	5	.266

Pedro J. Martinez P

Age: 24   **Seasons:** 4
Height: 5' 11"   **Weight:** 170
Bats: Right   **Throws:** Left
1995 OBA: .227   **1995 WHIP:** 1.15

Martinez keeps batters from getting comfortable (11 hit batsmen in both 1994 and 1995), and when his stuff is right he flirts with perfection. His peripheral numbers are Cy Young quality, but he isn't likely to win 20 games with the Expos.

	G	GS	IP	ER	ERA	H	BB	SO	W	L	SV
1995	30	30	194.2	76	3.51	158	66	174	14	10	0
Career	121	56	454.1	164	3.25	355	169	443	35	21	3
Projected	32	32	208.1	77	3.33	164	59	181	13	8	0

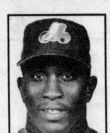

Carlos Perez P

Age: 24   **Seasons:** 1
Height: 6' 3"   **Weight:** 195
Bats: Left   **Throws:** Left
1995 OBA: .257   **1995 WHIP:** 1.20

The younger brother of Pascual and Melido earned a spot on the All-Star team with a 7–2 first half. Second-half lowlights included being knocked unconscious by a batted ball, going 0–5 in his last seven starts, and being arrested for rape.

	G	GS	IP	ER	ERA	H	BB	SO	W	L	SV
1995	28	23	141.1	58	3.69	142	28	106	10	8	0
Career	28	23	141.1	58	3.69	142	28	106	10	8	0
Projected	31	31	211.2	74	3.15	207	35	148	13	9	0

Kirk Reuter P

Age: 25   **Seasons:** 3
Height: 6' 3"   **Weight:** 195
Bats: Left   **Throws:** Left
1995 OBA: .224   **1995 WHIP:** 0.99

The beneficiary of generous run support in previous years, Reuter's luck turned a bit last season. He got rocked then demoted early in the year, returned to post a 1.82 ERA in seven late-season starts, then underwent offseason knee surgery.

	G	GS	IP	ER	ERA	H	BB	SO	W	L	SV
1995	9	9	47.1	17	3.23	38	9	28	5	3	0
Career	43	43	225.1	96	3.83	229	50	109	20	6	0
Projected	32	32	193.1	64	2.98	180	43	101	10	9	0

Mel Rojas   **P**

Age: 29   **Seasons:** 6
Height: 5' 11"   **Weight:** 195
Bats: Right   **Throws:** Right
1995 OBA: .262   **1995 WHIP:** 1.45

Rojas flailed in the role of fulltime closer last season, blowing nine saves (including four against the Giants), but he has the stuff to do the job if his demeanor is right. He's the fourth pitcher in franchise history to rack up 30 saves in a season.

	G	GS	IP	ER	ERA	H	BB	SO	W	L	SV
1995	59	0	67.2	31	4.12	69	29	61	1	4	30
Career	311	0	428.2	143	3.00	367	151	326	22	19	73
Projected	65	0	71.2	29	3.64	65	25	64	2	3	33

David Segui   **1B/OF**

Age: 29   **Seasons:** 6
Height: 6' 1"   **Weight:** 202
Bats: Switch   **Throws:** Left
1995 OBP: .367   **1995 SLG:** .461

Segui's glovework at first base is smooth and consistent (.997 fielding percentage last year), but he's a contact hitter with below-average power for his position, and his newfound status as a go-to player says a lot about the Expos' situation.

	G	AB	H	2B	3B	HR	RS	RBI	BB	SB	CS	BA
1995	130	456	141	25	4	12	68	68	40	2	7	.309
Career	609	1766	478	92	5	37	218	225	174	6	9	.271
Projected	145	512	148	21	2	10	54	60	45	1	4	.289

Tony Tarasco　　OF

Age: 25	**Seasons:** 3
Height: 6' 1"	**Weight:** 205
Bats: Left	**Throws:** Right
1995 OBP: .329	**1995 SLG:** .404

A tough, talented young player who couldn't crack the starting lineup in Atlanta, Tarasco swipes bases with great success, rarely grounds into a double play (once every 219 at-bats last year), and has a potent power stroke.

	G	AB	H	2B	3B	HR	RS	RBI	BB	SB	CS	BA
1995	126	438	109	18	4	14	64	40	51	24	3	.249
Career	237	605	153	26	4	19	86	61	60	29	4	.253
Projected	145	477	124	21	6	19	66	51	63	19	5	.260

Rondell White　　OF

Age: 24	**Seasons:** 3
Height: 6' 1"	**Weight:** 205
Bats: Right	**Throws:** Right
1995 OBP: .356	**1995 SLG:** .464

With speed to spare and an ultraquick bat, White has the talent to be a star. In June he became the fourth player in Expos annals to hit for the cycle, and he hit .343 over the final two months of the season. His work in center field was also inspiring.

	G	AB	H	2B	3B	HR	RS	RBI	BB	SB	CS	BA
1995	130	474	140	33	4	13	87	57	41	25	5	.295
Career	193	644	186	46	6	17	112	85	57	27	8	.289
Projected	155	541	173	30	7	23	99	71	50	34	7	.320

New York
METS

Scouting Report

Outfielders: Carl Everett got off to a cold start last year and was shuttled back to the minors, but he was ultra-productive after being recalled. He's got a center fielder's wheels but a right fielder's cannon. Alex Ochoa, a five-tool prospect acquired in the Bobby Bonilla trade, wields a superior throwing arm, good speed, and an electric bat. Damon Buford, the other outfield prospect obtained in exchange for Bobby Bo, flashed decent power, great speed, and spectacular defense. Ryan Thompson has failed to convert his exceptional talent into consistent production. Joe Orsulak, who hit .348 with runners in scoring position last season, is a valuable utility outfielder. Chris Jones hit .400 in 25 at-bats as a pinch hitter while adding a dose of power in 35 starts.

Infielders: Rico Brogna hit for average and power while topping all NL first sackers in fielding percentage (.998). Jose Vizcaino posted the best fielding percentage among league shortstops (.984) and set a new career high in RBIs. Incumbent second baseman Jeff Kent is a streaky but very productive hitter, especially for a middle infielder. His oft-maligned defense has improved, but some observers have advocated shifting him to third and inserting promising prospect Edgardo Alfonzo at second. If the Mets elect not to move Kent, then either Alfonzo or unpolished young slugger Butch Huskey will play the hot corner.

Catchers: Todd Hundley sports major-league pop in his bat, but he's had trouble staying injury free. Kelly Stinnett is an adequate substitute, but he's shown more grit than talent. Neither catcher has had any success at controlling opposition baserunners.

Starting Pitchers: Jason Isringhausen has the stuff and makeup to become one of the top hurlers in team history. Amazingly, he isn't the highest-rated prospect in the Mets' system. That honor goes to Paul Wilson, unanimously considered a can't-miss star. That one-two punch will be followed by young Bill Pulsipher, one of baseball's most promising southpaw prospects. Two other blue-chip minor leaguers who will have a shot at making the rotation are Jimmy Williams and Reid Cornelius. Crafty control artist Bobby Jones will be a key element of the rotation, and don't forget about veteran Pete Harnisch, who's coming off shoulder surgery.

Relief Pitchers: John Franco returns for another season as the Mets' closer. Doug Henry is a reliable setup man and backup closer.

Outlook

The neophyte Mets enter 1996 brimming with talent and burdened by lofty expectations. Fans and media alike are projecting future all-stars, but ask Ryan Thompson how much the tag "unlimited potential" is worth on a baseball diamond. New York has placed its hopes squarely on the shoulders of two pitchers, Wilson and Isringhausen, who have made a combined total of 14 major-league starts. Most of the position players are equally raw, so wisdom dictates allowing the wunderkinds time to develop, if they need it, before expecting a World Series title.

Fungoes

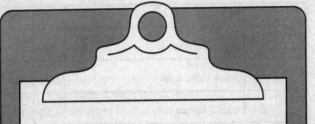

Quick Quiz: Which outfielder blasted two of his season's-total nine homers to beat Steve Carlton in a game in which Lefty whiffed a then-record 19 batters?

Franchise Milestone: The Miracle Mets outpitched Baltimore to win the 1969 World Series. In 1986, New York beat Boston in a dramatic seven-game Series.

Top Pitcher: Tom Seaver, 1967–77 and 1983

Top Player: Darryl Strawberry, 1983–90

Top Manager: Davey Johnson, 1984–90

Wacky Nickname: Pumpsie (Jerry Elijah Green)

Quick Quiz Answer: Ron Swoboda

Lineup Card

NO	POS	PLAYER	OBP	SLG
22	RF	Alex Ochoa	.333	.324
15	SS	Jose Vizcaino	.332	.365
3	CF	Carl Everett	.352	.436
12	2B	Jeff Kent	.327	.464
26	1B	Rico Brogna	.342	.485
42	3B	Butch Huskey	.267	.300
9	C	Todd Hundley	.382	.484
20	LF	Ryan Thompson	.306	.378

In a Nutshell: The Mets are putting together a balanced and deep hitting attack, though much is contingent on how well the youngsters develop. Faced with the pleasant problem of having too many prospects for too few open positions, New York will need to find an infield spot for Edgardo Alfonzo, who hit .300 in his final 223 at-bats last year, and an outfield spot (probably left field) for Damon Buford, who has a spectacular glove and leadoff-type hitting talents. Butch Huskey, 1995's International League (triple–A) MVP, is the wild card in the batting order. If he provides prodigious power at the major-league level, Jeff Kent could become trade bait and Alfonzo may be inserted at second base. The Mets are currently lacking a proven bat at the top of the lineup and a 30-homer slugger in the heart of the order, but they do have the prospects who are capable of filling those gaps.

Shea Stadium

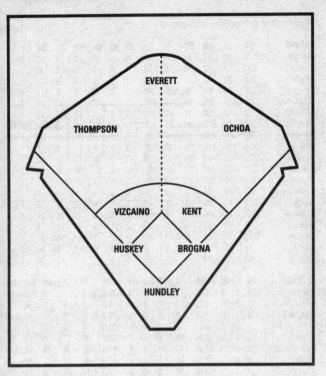

Capacity: 55,601
Turf: Natural

LF Line: 338
RF Line: 338
Center: 410
Left CF: 371
Right CF: 371

Tickets:
718-507-8499

It's no coincidence that the Mets' top hurlers have been strikeout artists. This is a power pitcher's park, and to the extent that, in a typical season, Shea cuts batting averages but has a neutral effect on home runs, it is a power hitter's park as well. Also, Shea joins Coors, Fenway, and the 'Stick as the most error-inducing fields in the major leagues.

Statistics

Minimum 25 at-bats or 10.0 innings pitched

PLAYER	BA	G	AB	RS	H	TB	2B	3B	HR	RBI	BB	SO	SB	CS
Bonilla	.325	80	317	49	103	190	25	4	18	53	31	48	0	3
Ochoa	.297	11	37	7	11	12	1	0	0	0	2	10	1	0
Bogar	.290	76	145	17	42	52	7	0	1	9	9	25	1	0
Brogna	.289	134	495	72	143	240	27	2	22	76	39	111	0	0
Vizcaino	.287	135	509	66	146	186	21	5	3	56	35	77	8	3
Orsulak	.283	108	290	41	82	108	19	2	1	37	19	35	1	3
Hundley	.280	90	275	39	77	133	11	0	15	51	42	64	1	0
Jones	.280	79	182	33	51	85	6	2	8	31	13	45	2	1
Alfonzo	.278	101	335	26	93	128	13	5	4	41	12	37	1	1
Kent	.278	125	472	65	131	219	22	3	20	65	29	89	3	3
Everett	.260	79	289	48	75	126	13	1	12	54	39	67	2	5
Thompson	.251	75	267	39	67	101	13	0	7	31	19	77	3	1
Ledesma	.242	21	33	4	8	8	0	0	0	3	6	7	0	0
Buford	.235	44	136	24	32	49	5	0	4	12	19	28	7	7
Stinnett	.219	77	196	23	43	65	8	1	4	17	29	64	2	0
Spiers	.208	63	72	5	15	19	2	1	0	11	12	15	0	1
Huskey	.189	28	90	8	17	27	1	0	3	11	10	16	1	0
Otero	.137	35	51	5	7	9	2	0	0	1	3	10	2	1
Castillo	.103	13	29	2	3	3	0	0	0	0	3	9	1	0

PITCHER	W	L	SV	ERA	G	GS	CG	SH	IP	H	R	ER	BB	SO
Person	1	0	0	0.75	3	1	0	0	12.0	5	1	1	2	10
Florence	3	0	0	1.50	14	0	0	0	12.0	17	3	2	6	5
Birkbeck	0	1	0	1.63	4	4	0	0	27.2	22	5	5	2	14
Byrd	2	0	0	2.05	17	0	0	0	22.0	18	6	5	7	26
Franco	5	3	29	2.44	48	0	0	0	51.2	48	17	14	17	41
Isringhausen	9	2	0	2.81	14	14	1	0	93.0	88	29	29	31	55
Henry	3	6	4	2.96	51	0	0	0	67.0	48	23	22	25	62
Minor	4	2	1	3.66	35	0	0	0	46.2	44	21	19	13	43
Harnisch	2	8	0	3.68	18	18	0	0	110.0	111	55	45	24	82
Gunderson	1	1	0	3.70	30	0	0	0	24.1	25	10	10	8	19
DiPoto	4	6	2	3.78	58	0	0	0	78.2	77	41	33	29	49
Pulsipher	5	7	0	3.98	17	17	2	0	126.2	122	58	56	45	81
Jones	10	10	0	4.19	30	30	3	1	195.2	209	107	91	53	127
Mlicki	9	7	0	4.26	29	25	0	0	160.2	160	82	76	54	123
Walker	1	0	0	4.58	13	0	0	0	17.2	24	9	9	5	5
Cornelius	3	7	0	5.54	18	10	0	0	66.2	75	44	41	30	39
Telgheder	1	2	0	5.61	7	4	0	0	25.2	34	18	16	7	16
Manzanillo	1	2	0	7.88	12	0	0	0	16.0	18	15	14	6	14
Jacome	0	4	0	10.29	5	5	0	0	21.0	33	24	24	15	11

Roster

MANAGER: Dallas Green
COACHES: Mike Cubbage, Frank Howard, Tom McCraw, Greg Pavlick, Steve Swisher, Bobby Wine

NO	PITCHERS	B	T	HT	WT	DOB
—	Juan Acevedo	R	R	6-2	195	5/5/70
43	Paul Byrd	R	R	6-1	185	12/3/70
47	Reid Cornelius	R	R	6-0	200	6/2/70
45	Jerry DiPoto	R	R	6-2	200	5/24/68
—	Brian Edmondson	R	R	6-2	185	1/29/73
31	John Franco	L	L	5-10	185	9/17/60
27	Pete Harnisch	R	R	6-0	207	9/23/66
35	Doug Henry	R	R	6-4	205	12/10/63
29	Jason Isringhausen	R	R	6-3	196	9/7/72
28	Bobby Jones	R	R	6-4	210	2/10/70
34	Blas Minor	R	R	6-3	203	3/20/66
38	Dave Mlicki	R	R	6-4	190	6/8/68
—	Chris Nabholz	L	L	6-5	210	1/5/67
29	Robert Person	R	R	5-11	180	10/6/69
21	Bill Pulsipher	L	L	6-4	195	10/9/73
—	Hector Ramirez	R	R	6-3	218	12/15/71
—	Bryan Rogers	R	R	5-11	170	10/30/67
49	Pete Walker	R	R	6-2	185	4/8/69
—	Derek Wallace	R	R	6-3	185	9/1/71
	CATCHERS					
30	Alberto Castillo	R	R	6-0	184	2/10/70
9	Todd Hundley	S	R	5-11	185	5/27/69
33	Kelly Stinnett	R	R	5-11	195	2/14/70
	INFIELDERS					
13	Edgardo Alfonzo	R	R	5-11	187	8/11/73
23	Tim Bogar	R	R	6-2	198	10/28/66
26	Rico Brogna	L	L	6-2	200	4/18/70
42	Butch Huskey	R	R	6-3	244	11/10/71
12	Jeff Kent	R	R	6-1	185	3/7/68
11	Aaron Ledesma	R	R	6-2	200	6/3/71
—	Luis Rivera	R	R	5-9	170	1/3/64
15	Jose Vizcaino	S	R	6-1	180	3/26/68
	OUTFIELDERS					
2	Damon Buford	R	R	5-10	170	6/12/70
3	Carl Everett	S	R	6-0	190	6/3/71
5	Chris Jones	R	R	6-2	205	12/16/65
22	Alex Ochoa	R	R	6-0	185	3/29/72
1	Ricky Otero	S	R	5-5	150	4/15/72
20	Ryan Thompson	R	R	6-3	200	11/4/67

FREE AGENTS: Bill Spiers

Edgardo Alfonzo   3B/2B

Age: 22

Height: 5' 11"

Bats: Right

1995 OBP: .301

Seasons: 1

Weight: 187

Throws: Right

1995 SLG: .382

Alfonzo skipped directly to the majors without spending day-one in triple-A. He needs to reassert the strikezone judgment he showed in the minors, and his glovework still needs refinement. Look for his power numbers to increase as he matures.

	G	AB	H	2B	3B	HR	RS	RBI	BB	SB	CS	BA
1995	101	335	93	13	5	4	26	41	12	1	1	.278
Career	101	335	93	13	5	4	26	41	12	1	1	.278
Projected	134	451	134	16	6	8	48	49	25	7	2	.297

Rico Brogna   1B

Age: 26

Height: 6' 2"

Bats: Left

1995 OBP: .342

Seasons: 3

Weight: 200

Throws: Left

1995 SLG: .485

A sure-handed gloveman who does some nice work with the stick, too, Brogna has blossomed into a much better pro than was expected when he was in the minors. He knocked in 19 runs in his final 19 games last season.

	G	AB	H	2B	3B	HR	RS	RBI	BB	SB	CS	BA
1995	134	495	143	27	2	22	72	76	39	0	0	.289
Career	182	652	194	39	4	30	91	99	48	1	0	.298
Projected	155	557	166	24	1	21	77	79	48	0	1	.298

Carl Everett OF

Age: 25   **Seasons:** 3
Height: 6' 0"   **Weight:** 190
Bats: Switch   **Throws:** Right
1995 OBP: .352   **1995 SLG:** .436

Everett hit just .197 in 17 games to start 1995 and was sent back to triple-A, but he finished the year by driving in 34 runs in his final 39 games for New York. His speed translates into fantastic range in center field, but he hasn't used it to steal bases.

	G	AB	H	2B	3B	HR	RS	RBI	BB	SB	CS	BA
1995	79	289	75	13	1	12	48	54	39	2	5	.260
Career	106	359	88	14	1	14	55	60	43	7	5	.245
Projected	135	501	143	24	3	14	86	63	51	5	6	.285

John Franco P

Age: 35   **Seasons:** 12
Height: 5' 10"   **Weight:** 185
Bats: Left   **Throws:** Left
1995 OBA: .251   **1995 WHIP:** 1.26

The all-time saves leader among left-handers, Franco converted 17 of his final 19 chances in 1995. His masterful change-up is an effective weapon, but he is vulnerable to lefty hitters and injuries at this juncture of his career.

	G	GS	IP	ER	ERA	H	BB	SO	W	L	SV
1995	48	0	51.2	14	2.44	48	17	41	5	3	29
Career	661	0	822.0	239	2.62	752	315	600	68	54	295
Projected	51	0	52.2	18	3.08	54	22	44	4	2	33

Pete Harnisch   P

Age: 29   **Seasons:** 8
Height: 6' 0"   **Weight:** 207
Bats: Right   **Throws:** Right
1995 OBA: .261   **1995 WHIP:** 1.23

Last year was a bust for Harnisch, due to his poor won-lost record and season-ending shoulder surgery, but his peripheral stats are actually not half bad. His first four starts resulted in four no-decisions and a 1.73 ERA.

	G	GS	IP	ER	ERA	H	BB	SO	W	L	SV
1995	18	18	110.0	45	3.68	111	24	82	2	8	0
Career	186	185	1151.0	476	3.72	1032	448	867	63	63	0
Projected	26	26	150.1	55	3.29	144	33	124	9	6	0

Doug Henry   P

Age: 32   **Seasons:** 5
Height: 6' 4"   **Weight:** 205
Bats: Right   **Throws:** Right
1995 OBA: .198   **1995 WHIP:** 1.09

Henry's ERA had ballooned to 5.89 by mid-June last year, but he gave up a mere three earned runs in his final 21 appearances (0.92). He's a much better pitcher now than he was in 1992, when he saved 29 games for Milwaukee.

	G	GS	IP	ER	ERA	H	BB	SO	W	L	SV
1995	51	0	67.0	22	2.96	48	25	62	3	6	4
Career	230	0	254.1	105	3.72	227	111	200	12	18	65
Projected	56	0	69.1	21	2.73	44	23	64	3	4	3

Todd Hundley C

Age: 26   **Seasons:** 6
Height: 5' 11"   **Weight:** 185
Bats: Switch   **Throws:** Right
1995 OBP: .382   **1995 SLG:** .484

Hundley had surgery in the offseason to repair his left wrist, which was hurt in a home-plate collision. He has plus bat speed from the left side and can turn around inside heat in a hurry. He calls a good game but has trouble throwing out runners.

	G	AB	H	2B	3B	HR	RS	RBI	BB	SB	CS	BA
1995	90	275	77	11	0	15	39	51	42	1	0	.280
Career	491	1468	338	61	4	50	169	187	121	7	2	.230
Projected	122	387	94	13	1	18	46	58	40	2	1	.243

Jason Isringhausen P

Age: 23   **Seasons:** 1
Height: 6' 3"   **Weight:** 196
Bats: Right   **Throws:** Right
1995 OBA: .254   **1995 WHIP:** 1.28

After going 9–1, 1.55 in 12 starts at triple-A Norfolk, Isringhausen took the National League by storm in the second half of 1995. He throws a very hard fastball and a late-breaking curve, and scouts project him as a future 20-game winner.

	G	GS	IP	ER	ERA	H	BB	SO	W	L	SV
1995	14	14	93.0	29	2.81	88	31	55	9	2	0
Career	14	14	93.0	29	2.81	88	31	55	9	2	0
Projected	33	33	242.1	76	2.82	231	54	131	21	6	0

Bobby Jones   P

Age: 26   **Seasons:** 3
Height: 6' 4"   **Weight:** 210
Bats: Right   **Throws:** Right
1995 OBA: .274   **1995 WHIP:** 1.34

Jones is beating the odds by being a finesse righthander who pitches up in the strikezone. He has pinpoint control and doesn't rattle when the pressure rises, and he helps himself at the plate by being a good bunter.

	G	GS	IP	ER	ERA	H	BB	SO	W	L	SV
1995	30	30	195.2	91	4.19	209	53	127	10	10	0
Career	63	63	417.1	172	3.71	427	131	242	24	21	0
Projected	32	32	205.1	90	3.94	211	55	130	13	10	0

Jeff Kent   2B

Age: 28   **Seasons:** 4
Height: 6' 1"   **Weight:** 185
Bats: Right   **Throws:** Right
1995 OBP: .327   **1995 SLG:** .464

When he's in a zone Kent is one of the majors' most devastating middle-infield sluggers. His fielding isn't bad, but his reputation for making untimely boots precedes his improvement. He hit .297 in his final 84 games.

	G	AB	H	2B	3B	HR	RS	RBI	BB	SB	CS	BA
1995	125	472	131	22	3	20	65	65	29	3	3	.278
Career	474	1688	459	91	10	66	235	263	109	10	14	.272
Projected	137	488	137	19	4	22	68	73	35	2	3	.281

Joe Orsulak **OF**

Age: 33   **Seasons:** 12
Height: 6' 1"   **Weight:** 205
Bats: Left   **Throws:** Left
1995 OBP: .323   **1995 SLG:** .372

Orsulak can't be an everyday player because he performs so poorly against portsiders, but his clutch hitting and wily veteran ways are not-to-be-scoffed-at assets. He'll be a solid backup in Florida this season.

	G	AB	H	2B	3B	HR	RS	RBI	BB	SB	CS	BA
1995	108	290	82	19	2	1	41	37	19	1	3	.283
Career	1268	3926	1091	168	35	54	523	379	284	92	58	.278
Projected	86	101	29	7	1	5	15	17	8	0	0	.287

Bill Pulsipher **P**

Age: 22   **Seasons:** 1
Height: 6' 4"   **Weight:** 195
Bats: Left   **Throws:** Left
1995 OBA: .255   **1995 WHIP:** 1.32

Pulsipher worked seven innings or more in 14 of his starts, including back-to-back complete games, not to mention 13 starts at Norfolk. The talented southpaw had elbow surgery in the offseason but is expected to be ready for 1996.

	G	GS	IP	ER	ERA	H	BB	SO	W	L	SV
1995	17	17	126.2	56	3.98	122	45	81	5	7	0
Career	17	17	126.2	56	3.98	122	45	81	5	7	0
Projected	31	31	211.1	71	3.02	203	66	142	13	8	0

Ryan Thompson OF

Age: 28   **Seasons:** 4
Height: 6' 3"   **Weight:** 200
Bats: Right   **Throws:** Right
1995 OBP: .306   **1995 SLG:** .378

The "tremendous potential" tag has worn thin, and it's perhaps past time for Thompson to justify the numerous chances he's been given to carve out a place in the Mets' outfield. His power and speed have been neutralized by poor judgment.

	G	AB	H	2B	3B	HR	RS	RBI	BB	SB	CS	BA
1995	75	267	67	13	0	7	39	31	19	3	1	.251
Career	283	997	238	53	4	39	127	126	74	8	11	.239
Projected	110	341	86	19	2	15	49	52	26	2	3	.252

Jose Vizcaino SS

Age: 28   **Seasons:** 7
Height: 6' 1"   **Weight:** 180
Bats: Switch   **Throws:** Right
1995 OBP: .332   **1995 SLG:** .365

A silky fielder with superb range and a strong arm, Vizcaino (pronounced Vis-kah-ee-no) would be valuable even without setting career highs in doubles and triples. His 13 sac bunts were the third-best total in the league.

	G	AB	H	2B	3B	HR	RS	RBI	BB	SB	CS	BA
1995	135	509	146	21	5	.3	66	56	35	8	3	.287
Career	612	1961	527	69	17	11	224	172	137	27	25	.269
Projected	152	544	148	17	3	4	69	45	45	6	4	.272

Philadelphia
PHILLIES

Scouting Report

Outfielders: Center fielder Lenny "Nails" Dykstra has been clobbered by injuries since his MVP-caliber 1993 season, but when healthy he provides on-base ability, a dash of power, speed to burn, and the heart of a champion. Right fielder Mark Whiten may not be offered a contract by the December deadline, but Philly would certainly benefit from having his powerful bat in the lineup. Jim Eisenreich has filed for free agency and is unsigned at press time, but the gutsy veteran is coming off a banner season. The farm system is comparatively thin on outfield prospects, so the club will either look to pick up a cheap free agent or hold open tryouts for rookies in the spring.

Infielders: Gregg Jefferies was slotted to play left field in 1995, but after 55 games he was shifted to first base. He lacks a cornerman's power but does his share of good things with the bat. Mickey Morandini has developed into a clutch hitter who lashes doubles and triples into the gaps on a regular basis. He's also an outstanding second baseman. The Phillies, particularly third-base coach Larry Bowa, thought that Kevin Stocker would become one of the league's better shortstops, but it hasn't happened and probably won't. It's unlikely that Charlie Hayes will be wearing a Phillies uniform this year, so third base is an open question at press time. Raw rookie Kevin Sefcik saw action in five games last year as a defensive replacement.

Catchers: An intense, rugged individual at a physically demanding position, Darren Daulton personifies Philly baseball. Rookie backstop Mike Lieberthal built a minor-league reputation for strong defense but isn't likely to do much for the offense.

Starting Pitchers: The Phillies have offseason decisions to make regarding which starters to retain. Curt Schilling is a magnificent hurler when his arm isn't injured, but he's been collecting big paychecks for rehab assignments the past couple of years. First-half sensations Michael Mimbs and Tyler Green were second-half flameouts in 1995. Sid Fernandez was this close to the end of his career, but he suddenly caught fire after joining the Phillies in July. Paul Quantrill led the club in both wins and losses last year. Rookie righty Mike Grace pitched well in two starts before experiencing some shoulder discomfort.

Relief Pitchers: Toby Borland was awful before the All-Star break last season but closed with a 2.28 ERA and six saves in his final 29 appearances. Heathcliff Slocumb made the All-Star team but was ineffective in the second half.

Outlook

The 1993 NL champs have morphed into an aging, injury-riddled ballclub, but if team leaders Dykstra and Daulton can stay healthy for a full season, the Phillies could be a darkhorse in the wild-card race. As with most teams in the poststrike era, financial concerns will partially dictate the look and quality of the pitching staff, and, as always with the Phillies, injury rehab (Abbott, Munoz, Schilling, West) will be a factor, too. Nevertheless, Philly may have the raw materials to build a playoff-quality pitching corps, even if the fates appear to be against them.

Fungoes

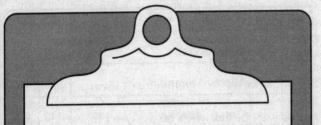

Quick Quiz: Which member of the 500-homer club closed out his career in Philadelphia—as a pitcher!?

Franchise Milestone: In more than a century of major-league existence, the Phillies have won just one World Series, beating Kansas City 4–2 in 1980. The franchise also won NL pennants in 1915, 1950, 1983, and 1993.

Top Pitcher: Steve Carlton, 1972–86

Top Player: Mike Schmidt, 1972–89

Top Manager: Danny Ozark, 1973–79

Wacky Nickname: Possum (George Bostic Whitted)

Quick Quiz Answer: Jimmie Foxx

Lineup Card

NO	POS	PLAYER	OBP	SLG
4	CF	Lenny Dykstra	.353	.354
12	2B	Mickey Morandini	.350	.417
25	1B	Gregg Jefferies	.349	.448
10	C	Darren Daulton	.359	.401
6	LF	Gene Schall	.306	.262
8	RF	Jim Eisenreich	.375	.464
31	3B	Kevin Sefcik	.000	.000
19	SS	Kevin Stocker	.304	.274

In a Nutshell: The Phillies are on a narrow edge between having a rather poor offense and a pretty explosive one, depending first on whether Daulton and Dykstra stay off the disabled list and second on whether the club retains Mark Whiten or Charlie Hayes. The latter appears unlikely at press time, so it may be up to unproven Gene Schall to provide protection for Daulton. Philadelphia's 1–4 hitters stack up with the NL's best when everyone is healthy, but the bottom half of the order is proportionately less potent. Schall, who slugged .528 at triple-A last year, was converted to left field after playing first base for his entire career. If he isn't ready for the Show, one scenario has Jefferies in left field, where he didn't make one error in 55 games last season, Daulton at first base, where he's less likely to reinjure his knees, and defense-minded Mike Lieberthal starting fulltime at catcher.

Veterans Stadium

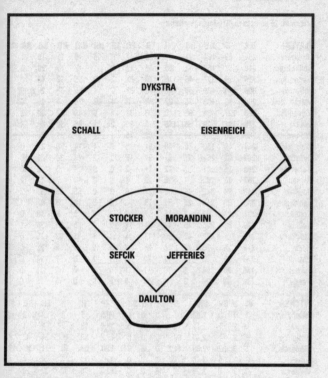

Capacity: 62,136
Turf: Artificial

LF Line: 330
RF Line: 330
Center: 408
Left CF: 371
Right CF: 371

Tickets:
215-463-1000

The 1993 pennant winners were an exemplary model of the type of players who succeed at the Vet: lefthanded linedrive hitters with some power—John Kruk, Darren Daulton, Lenny Dykstra—who the hard-nosed, often abusive Philly fans can relate to. The turf here is hard and fast, so it helps to have mobile outfielders and cornermen with quick reflexes.

Statistics

Minimum 25 at-bats or 10.0 innings pitched

PLAYER	BA	G	AB	RS	H	TB	2B	3B	HR	RBI	BB	SO	SB	CS
Longmire	.356	59	104	21	37	53	7	0	3	19	11	19	1	1
Gallagher	.318	62	157	12	50	65	12	0	1	12	16	20	0	0
Eisenreich	.316	129	377	46	119	175	22	2	10	55	38	43	10	0
Jefferies	.306	114	480	69	147	215	31	2	11	56	35	26	9	5
Marsh	.294	43	109	13	32	46	3	1	3	15	4	25	0	1
Morandini	.283	127	494	65	140	206	34	7	6	49	42	80	9	6
Hayes	.276	141	529	58	146	215	30	3	11	85	50	88	5	1
Whiten	.269	60	212	38	57	102	10	1	11	37	31	64	7	0
Webster	.267	49	150	18	40	61	9	0	4	14	16	27	0	0
Dykstra	.264	62	254	37	67	91	16	1	2	18	33	28	10	5
Lieberthal	.255	16	47	1	12	14	2	0	0	4	5	5	0	0
Varsho	.252	72	103	7	26	29	1	1	0	11	7	17	2	0
Daulton	.249	98	342	44	85	137	19	3	9	55	55	52	3	0
Van Slyke	.243	63	214	26	52	75	10	2	3	16	28	41	7	0
Schall	.231	24	65	2	15	17	2	0	0	5	6	16	0	0
Hollins	.229	65	205	46	47	84	12	2	7	25	53	38	1	1
Stocker	.218	125	412	42	90	113	14	3	1	31	43	75	6	1
Flora	.213	24	75	12	16	25	3	0	2	7	4	22	1	0
Elster	.208	26	53	10	11	20	4	1	1	9	7	14	0	0
Jordan	.185	25	54	6	10	17	1	0	2	6	2	11	0	0
Ready	.138	23	29	3	4	4	0	0	0	0	3	6	0	1

PITCHER	W	L	SV	ERA	G	GS	CG	SH	IP	H	R	ER	BB	SO
Ricci	1	0	0	1.80	7	0	0	0	10.0	9	2	2	3	9
Frey	0	1	1	2.12	18	0	0	0	17.0	10	7	4	4	7
Bottalico	5	3	1	2.46	62	0	0	0	87.2	50	25	24	42	87
Slocumb	5	6	32	2.89	61	0	0	0	65.1	64	26	21	35	63
Grace	1	1	0	3.18	2	2	0	0	11.1	10	4	4	4	7
Williams	3	3	0	3.29	35	8	0	0	87.2	78	37	32	29	57
Fernandez	6	1	0	3.34	11	11	0	0	64.2	48	25	24	21	79
Schilling	7	5	0	3.57	17	17	1	0	116.0	96	52	46	26	114
R. Springer	0	0	0	3.71	14	0	0	0	26.2	22	11	11	10	32
Borland	1	3	6	3.77	50	0	0	0	74.0	80	37	31	37	59
West	3	2	0	3.79	8	8	0	0	38.0	34	17	16	19	25
Abbott	2	0	0	3.81	18	0	0	0	28.1	28	12	12	16	21
Juden	2	4	0	4.02	13	10	1	0	62.2	53	31	28	31	47
Mimbs	9	7	1	4.15	35	19	2	1	136.2	127	70	63	75	93
Harris	2	2	0	4.26	21	0	0	0	19.0	19	9	9	8	9
Quantrill	11	12	0	4.67	33	29	0	0	179.1	212	102	93	44	103
D. Springer	0	3	0	4.84	4	4	0	0	22.1	21	15	12	9	15
Ty. Green	8	9	0	5.31	26	25	4	2	140.2	157	86	83	66	85
Fletcher	1	0	0	5.40	10	0	0	0	13.1	15	8	8	9	10
Munoz	0	2	0	5.74	3	0	0	0	15.2	15	13	10	9	6
Olivares	1	4	0	6.91	17	6	0	0	41.2	55	34	32	23	22
To. Greene	0	5	0	8.29	11	6	0	0	33.2	45	32	31	20	24

Roster

MANAGER: Jim Fregosi
COACHES: Larry Bowa, Denis Menke, Johnny Podres,
Mel Roberts, John Vukovich

NO	PITCHERS	B	T	HT	WT	DOB
39	Kyle Abbott	L	L	6-4	215	2/18/68
—	Willie Banks	R	R	6-1	195	2/27/69
42	Toby Borland	R	R	6-6	186	5/29/69
52	Ricky Bottalico	L	R	6-1	200	8/26/69
50	Sid Fernandez	L	L	6-1	225	10/12/62
58	Paul Fletcher	R	R	6-1	193	1/14/67
44	Mike Grace	R	R	6-4	210	6/20/70
28	Tyler Green	R	R	6-5	192	2/18/70
49	Tommy Greene	R	R	6-5	222	4/6/67
53	Ryan Karp	L	L	6-4	205	4/5/70
45	Michael Mimbs	L	L	6-2	182	2/13/69
35	Bobby Munoz	R	R	6-7	237	3/3/68
48	Paul Quantrill	L	R	6-1	184	11/3/68
37	Chuck Ricci	R	R	6-2	180	11/20/68
38	Curt Schilling	R	R	6-4	225	11/14/66
51	Heathcliff Slocumb	R	R	6-3	220	6/7/65
47	Dennis Springer	R	R	5-10	185	4/12/65
33	Russ Springer	R	R	6-4	195	11/7/68
40	David West	L	L	6-6	255	9/1/64
41	Mike Williams	R	R	6-2	199	7/29/68
	CATCHERS					
10	Darren Daulton	L	R	6-2	202	1/3/62
24	Mike Lieberthal	R	R	6-0	170	1/18/72
27	Lenny Webster	R	R	5-9	195	2/10/65
	INFIELDERS					
7	Mariano Duncan	R	R	6-0	200	3/13/63
3	Kevin Elster	R	R	6-2	200	8/3/64
25	Gregg Jefferies	S	R	5-10	185	8/1/67
23	Kevin Jordan	R	R	6-1	185	10/9/69
12	Mickey Morandini	L	R	5-11	180	4/22/66
31	Kevin Sefcik	R	R	5-10	175	2/10/71
19	Kevin Stocker	S	R	6-1	175	2/13/70
	OUTFIELDERS					
4	Lenny Dykstra	L	L	5-10	195	2/10/63
30	Kevin Flora	R	R	6-0	185	6/10/69
16	Tony Longmire	L	R	6-1	199	8/12/68
21	Tom Marsh	R	R	6-2	180	12/27/65
6	Gene Schall	R	R	6-3	201	6/5/70
5	Gary Varsho	L	R	5-11	185	6/20/61
22	Mark Whiten	S	R	6-3	215	11/25/66

FREE AGENTS: Jim Eisenreich, Charlie Hayes, Andy Van Slyke

Darren Daulton   C

Age: 34   **Seasons:** 12
Height: 6' 2"   **Weight:** 202
Bats: Left   **Throws:** Right
1995 OBP: .359   **1995 SLG:** .401

Daulton's work behind home plate is highly regarded, but his powerful bat is even more valuable. He's missed the bulk of the past two seasons with injuries, last year undergoing his eighth knee surgery.

	G	AB	H	2B	3B	HR	RS	RBI	BB	SB	CS	BA
1995	98	342	85	19	3	9	44	55	55	3	0	.249
Career	1020	3223	785	176	17	123	440	525	546	44	9	.244
Projected	124	421	119	24	1	25	74	78	64	2	1	.283

Lenny Dykstra   OF

Age: 33   **Seasons:** 11
Height: 5' 10"   **Weight:** 195
Bats: Left   **Throws:** Left
1995 OBP: .353   **1995 SLG:** .354

Age and his all-out style of play have taken a heavy toll on Dykstra's game of late. He sat out much of 1995 because of knee and back injuries, and there's little chance that he'll return to his 1993 performance level (.420 OBP, 143 runs scored).

	G	AB	H	2B	3B	HR	RS	RBI	BB	SB	CS	BA
1995	62	254	67	15	1	2	37	18	33	10	5	.264
Career	1238	4425	1263	275	40	78	781	391	614	282	71	.285
Projected	124	511	138	19	4	8	83	56	74	21	7	.270

Jim Eisenreich — OF

Age: 37	**Seasons:** 12
Height: 5' 11"	**Weight:** 200
Bats: Left	**Throws:** Left
1995 OBP: .375	**1995 SLG:** .464

Though he was second on the team in games played last year, Eisenreich is very near the end of his tenure as an everyday player, by his own admission. He's coming off a super season in which he was perfect as a fielder and a basestealer.

	G	AB	H	2B	3B	HR	RS	RBI	BB	SB	CS	BA
1995	129	377	119	22	2	10	46	55	38	10	0	.316
Career	1084	3173	915	175	33	46	390	389	247	88	37	.288
Projected	132	351	107	17	1	8	40	48	31	8	2	.305

Sid Fernandez — P

Age: 33	**Seasons:** 13
Height: 6' 1"	**Weight:** 225
Bats: Left	**Throws:** Left
1995 OBA: N/A	**1995 WHIP:** 1.32

Fernandez was less effective than a beached whale in Baltimore (0–4, 7.39 in eight appearances), but the Phils took a chance and were rewarded with El Sid's 5–0, 2.86 August performance. Lefties hit (if you can call it hitting) .103 against him.

	G	GS	IP	ER	ERA	H	BB	SO	W	L	SV
1995	19	18	92.2	47	4.56	84	38	110	6	5	0
Career	295	288	1798.2	670	3.35	1367	687	1663	110	90	1
Projected	31	31	217.1	81	3.35	195	54	177	13	10	0

Tyler Green   P

Age: 26   **Seasons:** 2
Height: 6' 5"   **Weight:** 192
Bats: Right   **Throws:** Right
1995 OBA: .290   **1995 WHIP:** 1.59

Green's wicked knuckle-curve proved to be a first-half mystery (8–4, 2.81 prior to the All-Star break), but his final 12 appearances were a disaster (0–5, 10.68). In 1994 he led the triple-A International League in losses, hit batters, and earned runs.

	G	GS	IP	ER	ERA	H	BB	SO	W	L	SV
1995	26	25	140.2	83	5.31	157	66	85	8	9	0
Career	29	27	148.0	89	5.41	173	71	92	8	9	0
Projected	21	15	112.1	71	5.69	128	57	60	4	8	0

Charlie Hayes   3B

Age: 30   **Seasons:** 8
Height: 6' 0"   **Weight:** 224
Bats: Right   **Throws:** Right
1995 OBP: .340   **1995 SLG:** .406

Hayes brings a quality glove to the hot corner; he has excellent range and ranked third in NL fielding percentage among third basemen last season. He's a mediocre all-around hitter, despite having some power.

	G	AB	H	2B	3B	HR	RS	RBI	BB	SB	CS	BA
1995	141	529	146	30	3	11	58	85	50	5	1	.276
Career	941	3370	904	175	13	94	361	452	212	32	24	.268
Projected	155	546	144	23	1	13	62	71	51	4	2	.264

Gregg Jefferies 1B

Age: 28	**Seasons:** 9
Height: 5' 10"	**Weight:** 185
Bats: Switch	**Throws:** Right
1995 OBP: .349	**1995 SLG:** .448

One of the toughest outs in the majors, Jefferies crushes lefties, rarely strikes out, and has the bat speed to go deep. His inaugural-year numbers in Philly, though not exactly shabby, weren't an accurate indicator of his true offensive abilities.

	G	AB	H	2B	3B	HR	RS	RBI	BB	SB	CS	BA
1995	114	480	147	31	2	11	69	56	35	9	5	.306
Career	976	3738	1106	214	18	91	522	474	325	149	42	.296
Projected	133	520	169	34	4	15	81	86	52	11	4	.325

Mickey Morandini 2B

Age: 30	**Seasons:** 6
Height: 5' 11"	**Weight:** 180
Bats: Left	**Throws:** Right
1995 OBP: .350	**1995 SLG:** .417

Morandini has been in the Phillies' system since 1989, and their patience is finally paying dividends. He hit .346 with runners in scoring position and finished among the league leaders in both doubles and triples.

	G	AB	H	2B	3B	HR	RS	RBI	BB	SB	CS	BA
1995	127	494	140	34	7	6	65	49	42	9	6	.283
Career	584	2019	537	92	33	16	256	161	170	56	18	.266
Projected	149	544	150	26	6	3	71	41	41	11	3	.276

Paul Quantrill   P

Age: 27   **Seasons:** 4
Height: 6' 1"   **Weight:** 184
Bats: Left   **Throws:** Right
1995 OBA: .295   **1995 WHIP:** 1.43

There are several things to like about Quantrill, including his makeup, his control (2.2 walks per nine innings, seventh in the NL), and the way he fields his position. Unfortunately, he has below-average stuff on both his sinker and slider.

	G	GS	IP	ER	ERA	H	BB	SO	W	L	SV
1995	33	29	179.1	93	4.67	212	44	103	11	12	0
Career	144	44	419.2	194	4.16	482	118	221	22	30	3
Projected	26	26	141.0	90	5.74	162	42	86	7	13	0

Curt Schilling   P

Age: 29   **Seasons:** 8
Height: 6' 4"   **Weight:** 225
Bats: Right   **Throws:** Right
1995 OBA: .220   **1995 WHIP:** 1.05

Schilling looked like his old self early last season (4–0), but he succumbed to season-ending shoulder surgery in July. He's one of the top pitchers in baseball when healthy, sporting terrific command of a deluxe power repertoire.

	G	GS	IP	ER	ERA	H	BB	SO	W	L	SV
1995	17	17	116.0	46	3.57	96	26	114	7	5	0
Career	206	95	805.0	317	3.56	731	241	618	43	42	13
Projected	22	22	141.2	49	3.11	131	41	118	10	6	0

Heathcliff Slocumb P

Age: 29	**Seasons:** 5
Height: 6' 3"	**Weight:** 220
Bats: Right	**Throws:** Right
1995 OBA: .257	**1995 WHIP:** 1.52

The NL's Pitcher of the Month in May (1.76 ERA, 14 saves), Slocumb was untouchable in the first half of last season. But he was roughed up after the All-Star break, losing five straight games in August.

	G	GS	IP	ER	ERA	H	BB	SO	W	L	SV
1995	61	0	65.1	21	2.89	64	35	63	5	6	32
Career	225	0	274.1	111	3.64	279	134	204	16	12	34
Projected	55	0	61.2	23	3.36	60	38	60	3	3	18

Mark Whiten OF

Age: 29	**Seasons:** 6
Height: 6' 3"	**Weight:** 215
Bats: Switch	**Throws:** Right
1995 OBP: .365	**1995 SLG:** .481

Whiten has been injury prone and much maligned since hitting 25 home runs for St. Louis in 1993, but his jaw-dropping power stroke and intimidating throwing arm can't be discounted. He's a much better hitter righthanded than lefthanded.

	G	AB	H	2B	3B	HR	RS	RBI	BB	SB	CS	BA
1995	92	320	77	13	1	12	51	49	39	8	0	.241
Career	633	2219	569	82	19	71	320	296	243	55	28	.256
Projected	138	452	125	25	1	26	65	78	43	9	1	.277

Denny Neagle

Pittsburgh
PIRATES

Scouting Report

Outfielders: The Pirates have been looking for a reliable center fielder since Andy Van Slyke left town. The club's number-one outfield prospect, Midre Cummings, hasn't developed as a hitter and will need to establish himself before minor leaguers like Charles Peterson arrive. Jacob Brumfield may continue to see most of the action in center by default. Al Martin, who logs spot duty in center but is usually found in left field, batted .132 versus southpaws last season. It's a good thing that Dave Clark, who hit .348 versus lefties, is around to platoon in left. Right fielder Orlando Merced is arguably Pittsburgh's best hitter. He could shift to first base to make room for rookie slugger Micah Franklin. Calgary's (triple-A) Trey Beamon, who hit .334 last season after winning a double-A batting title in 1994, needs to refine his fielding technique but should be in the majors soon.

Infielders: The anchor of the Pirates' infield is Jay Bell, who makes all the plays at shortstop and chips in his share of extra-base knocks at the plate. Carlos Garcia, the Bucs' All-Star representative in 1994, turned in another solid performance last season, batting .294 and showing great range at second base. Nelson Liriano was equally steady in a part-time role. Rich Aude will have every chance to nail down the first-base assignment. He showed big-time power in a tough park for hitters at triple-A Buffalo. Pittsburgh has re-signed third baseman Jeff King, who led the club in home runs last year.

Catchers: Angelo Encarnacion gunned down a healthy 36 percent of opposition basestealers as a rookie last year, but he drove in just 10 runs in 159 at-bats. Don Slaught batted .393 on the road and .304 overall, but he was an easy mark for thieves. Top prospect Jason Kendall may win the job.

Starting Pitchers: Denny Neagle was the only Pittsburgh starter whose ERA was under 4.50 last season. Esteban Loaiza, the organization's top pitching prospect, allowed a .317 batting average to righthanders. Paul Wagner has tremendous pure stuff, but it didn't keep him from losing more games than any other pitcher in baseball in 1995. Rick White made several ineffective late-season starts. Rookie righthander John Ericks cut loose 11 wild pitches and led the staff in walks per nine innings (4.25), but his ERA was the second lowest on the staff and he allowed just over a hit per inning.

Relief Pitchers: Dan Miceli struggled somewhat in the closer's role, allowing a .359 batting average to lefties, but he does have a live arm. Jason Christiansen will figure prominently in middle relief.

Outlook

Like a beautiful old estate that has fallen into disrepair, the Pirates have been a depressing spectacle of late. The sale of the franchise is on the verge of being formalized, and a new stadium is on the horizon, but attendance has been poor and the on-field action limited to fireworks by opposition batters. The Bucs were by far the worst team in the league last season, and they don't figure to be much better in 1996 unless probable call-ups Jason Kendall, Trey Beamon, and Micah Franklin blossom ahead of schedule. Expect a lengthy refurbishing project in Pittsburgh.

Fungoes

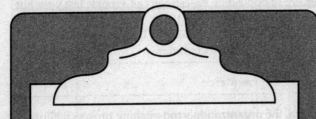

Quick Quiz: Which first baseman hit home runs in eight consecutive games in 1956?

Franchise Milestone: The Bucs have been in Pittsburgh since 1887 and have come out on top in five of their nine World Series appearances (1909, 1925, 1960, 1971, and 1979).

Top Pitcher: Vern Law, 1950–67

Top Player: Honus Wagner, 1900–1917

Top Manager: Fred Clarke, 1900–1915

Wacky Nickname: Big Poison and Little Poison (Paul Glee Waner and Lloyd James Waner)

Quick Quiz Answer: Dale Long

Lineup Card

NO	POS	PLAYER	OBP	SLG
30	CF	Midre Cummings	.303	.342
28	LF	Al Martin	.351	.442
6	RF	Orlando Merced	.365	.468
7	3B	Jeff King	.342	.456
48	1B	Rich Aude	.287	.376
3	SS	Jay Bell	.336	.404
13	2B	Carlos Garcia	.340	.420
2	C	Angelo Encarnacion	.285	.333

In a Nutshell: If the Pirates are going to make a move for a nonpitcher in the free-agent market after press time, it could be for a first-class center fielder, perhaps Otis Nixon, who can anchor the outfield defense and set the table from the leadoff spot. Top prospect Midre Cummings drew just 13 walks in 59 games last season, so he's not exactly cut from the same cloth as Florida's Quilvio Veras, and Jacob Brumfield isn't a fulltime solution. The Bucs get some punch from the middle of the order, but both King and Merced posted career highs in slugging last year and can't be counted on for much improvement, which leaves the heart of the lineup lacking a 30-homer bopper. Unless impressively built first-base prospect Rich Aude blossoms into a big-league longball threat, the Pirates aren't likely to improve on their eleventh-place rank in NL slugging, and things may get worse before they get better.

Three Rivers Stadium

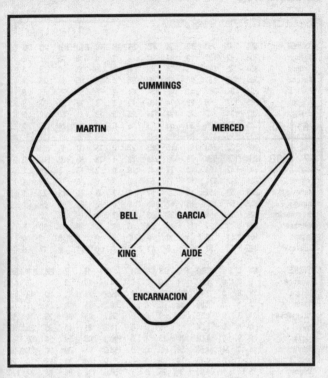

Capacity: 47,972
Turf: Artificial

LF Line: 335
RF Line: 335
Center: 400
Left CF: 375
Right CF: 375

Tickets:
412-323-5000

Three Rivers is one of the so-called "cookie cutter" stadiums, and it is essentially a neutral park (to the extent that any park is neutral). Home runs are reduced a little, but types of offense relating to linedrives are increased by about 5 percent. Perhaps the most notable aspect of the playing field is the extent to which the rough condition of the carpet increases errors.

Statistics

Minimum 25 at-bats or 10.0 innings pitched

PLAYER	BA	G	AB	RS	H	TB	2B	3B	HR	RBI	BB	SO	SB	CS
Wehner	.308	52	107	13	33	39	0	3	0	5	10	17	3	1
Slaught	.304	35	112	13	34	40	6	0	0	13	9	8	0	0
Merced	.300	132	487	75	146	228	29	4	15	83	52	75	7	2
C. Garcia	.294	104	367	41	108	154	24	2	6	50	25	55	8	4
Liriano	.286	107	259	29	74	103	12	1	5	38	24	34	2	2
Martin	.282	124	440	70	124	194	25	3	13	41	44	92	20	11
Clark	.281	77	196	30	55	73	6	0	4	24	24	38	2	3
Brumfield	.271	116	402	64	109	148	23	2	4	26	37	71	21	12
King	.265	122	445	61	118	203	27	2	18	87	55	63	7	4
Bell	.262	138	530	79	139	214	28	4	13	55	55	110	2	5
Aude	.248	42	109	10	27	41	8	0	2	19	6	20	1	2
Pegues	.246	82	171	17	42	68	8	0	6	16	4	36	1	2
Cummings	.243	59	152	13	37	52	7	1	2	15	13	27	1	0
Young	.232	56	181	13	42	69	9	0	6	22	8	53	1	3
Encarnacion	.226	58	159	18	36	53	7	2	2	10	13	28	1	1
Johnson	.208	79	221	32	46	93	6	1	13	28	37	66	5	2
Sasser	.154	14	26	1	4	5	1	0	0	0	0	0	0	0
F. Garcia	.140	42	57	5	8	11	1	1	0	1	8	17	0	0

PITCHER	W	L	SV	ERA	G	GS	CG	SH	IP	H	R	ER	BB	SO
Hancock	0	0	0	1.93	11	0	0	0	14.0	10	3	3	2	6
Neagle	13	8	0	3.43	32	31	5	1	209.2	221	91	80	45	150
Plesac	4	4	3	3.58	58	0	0	0	60.1	53	26	24	27	57
Christiansen	1	3	0	4.15	63	0	0	0	56.1	49	28	26	34	53
Dyer	4	5	0	4.34	55	0	0	0	74.2	81	40	36	30	53
Ericks	3	9	0	4.58	19	18	1	0	106.0	108	59	54	50	80
Miceli	4	4	21	4.66	58	0	0	0	58.0	61	30	30	28	56
White	2	3	0	4.75	16	9	0	0	55.0	66	33	29	18	29
Wagner	5	16	1	4.80	34	25	3	1	165.0	174	96	88	72	120
McCurry	1	4	1	5.02	55	0	0	0	61.0	82	38	34	30	27
Wilson	0	1	0	5.02	10	0	0	0	14.1	13	8	8	5	8
Loaiza	8	9	0	5.16	32	31	1	0	172.2	205	115	99	55	85
Parris	6	6	0	5.38	15	15	1	1	82.0	89	49	49	33	61
Gott	2	4	3	6.03	25	0	0	0	31.1	38	26	21	12	19
Lieber	4	7	0	6.32	21	12	0	0	72.2	103	56	51	14	45
Powell	0	2	0	6.98	27	3	0	0	29.2	36	26	23	21	20

Roster

MANAGER: Jim Leyland
COACHES: Rich Donnelly, Gene Lamont

NO	PITCHERS	B	T	HT	WT	DOB
41	Jason Christiansen	R	L	6-5	226	9/21/69
26	Steve Cooke	R	L	6-6	229	1/14/70
62	Mike Dyer	R	R	6-3	198	9/8/66
57	John Ericks	R	R	6-7	255	9/16/67
56	Jim Gott	R	R	6-4	220	8/3/59
42	Lee Hancock	L	L	6-4	215	6/27/67
47	Jon Lieber	L	R	6-3	220	4/2/70
34	Esteban Loaiza	R	R	6-4	190	12/31/71
53	Jeff McCurry	R	R	6-7	210	1/21/70
32	Dan Miceli	R	R	6-0	207	9/9/70
55	Ramon Morel	R	R	6-2	175	8/15/74
15	Denny Neagle	L	L	6-2	217	9/13/68
60	Steve Parris	R	R	6-0	190	12/17/67
52	Ross Powell	L	L	6-0	180	1/24/68
19	Dan Plesac	L	L	6-5	215	2/4/62
—	Kevin Rogers	S	L	6-2	198	8/20/68
43	Paul Wagner	R	R	6-1	202	11/14/67
44	Rick White	R	R	6-4	215	12/23/68
46	Gary Wilson	R	R	6-3	190	1/1/70
	CATCHERS					
2	Angelo Encarnacion	R	R	5-8	180	4/18/73
—	Jason Kendall	R	R	6-0	170	6/26/74
11	Don Slaught	R	R	6-1	185	9/11/58
	INFIELDERS					
48	Rich Aude	R	R	6-5	209	7/13/71
3	Jay Bell	R	R	6-0	185	12/11/65
13	Carlos Garcia	R	R	6-1	193	10/15/67
22	Freddy Garcia	R	R	6-2	190	8/1/72
7	Jeff King	R	R	6-1	183	12/26/64
16	Nelson Liriano	S	R	5-10	178	6/3/64
12	John Wehner	R	R	6-3	205	6/29/67
36	Kevin Young	R	R	6-2	219	6/16/69
	OUTFIELDERS					
—	Trey Beamon	L	R	6-3	195	2/11/74
5	Jacob Brumfield	R	R	6-0	185	5/27/65
35	Dave Clark	L	R	6-2	209	9/3/62
30	Midre Cummings	L	R	6-0	196	10/14/71
—	Micah Franklin	S	R	6-0	200	4/25/72
28	Al Martin	L	L	6-2	210	11/24/67
6	Orlando Merced	L	R	5-11	185	11/2/66
25	Steve Pegues	R	R	6-2	190	5/21/68

FREE AGENTS: Don Slaught

Jay Bell   SS

Age: 30   **Seasons:** 10
Height: 6' 0"   **Weight:** 185
Bats: Right   **Throws:** Right
1995 OBP: .336   **1995 SLG:** .404

Bell parlays soft hands and intelligent positioning into Gold Glove–quality shortstop play. The Pirates' most complete player, he is an excellent bunter and hit-and-run man. He's smacked at least 28 doubles in each of the past six seasons.

	G	AB	H	2B	3B	HR	RS	RBI	BB	SB	CS	BA
1995	138	530	139	28	4	13	79	55	55	2	5	.262
Career	1071	4002	1070	220	43	70	598	390	403	58	37	.267
Projected	156	610	169	33	5	11	88	50	61	9	6	.277

Carlos Garcia   2B

Age: 28   **Seasons:** 6
Height: 6' 1"   **Weight:** 193
Bats: Right   **Throws:** Right
1995 OBP: .340   **1995 SLG:** .420

Garcia had stolen 18 bases in each of the previous two seasons, though at a modest 64-percent success rate. Removed from the leadoff spot he ran less last year but continued to show some extra-base pop at the plate.

	G	AB	H	2B	3B	HR	RS	RBI	BB	SB	CS	BA
1995	104	367	108	24	2	6	41	50	25	8	4	.294
Career	381	1392	385	65	11	24	174	130	73	44	24	.277
Projected	120	395	111	20	3	5	44	45	26	10	4	.281

Jeff King   3B

Age: 31   **Seasons:** 7
Height: 6' 1"   **Weight:** 183
Bats: Right   **Throws:** Right
1995 OBP: .342   **1995 SLG:** .456

King isn't a bad player—he topped the Bucs in homers and RBIs in 1995 and chipped in decent defense at every infield position—but his status as a $5-million cleanup hitter says more about the Pirates than it does about King.

	G	AB	H	2B	3B	HR	RS	RBI	BB	SB	CS	BA
1995	122	445	118	27	2	18	61	87	55	7	4	.265
Career	739	2570	657	137	12	69	328	382	226	32	24	.256
Projected	144	466	119	25	1	15	68	85	51	5	3	.255

Al Martin   OF

Age: 28   **Seasons:** 4
Height: 6' 2"   **Weight:** 210
Bats: Left   **Throws:** Left
1995 OBP: .351   **1995 SLG:** .442

Martin has a quick bat and good foot speed—a 20/20 season wouldn't be at all surprising—but he's helpless against lefthanders, and his work in the outfield isn't polished. He'll need to step up soon or risk losing his job to younger prospects.

	G	AB	H	2B	3B	HR	RS	RBI	BB	SB	CS	BA
1995	124	439	124	25	3	13	70	41	44	20	11	.282
Career	361	1207	340	63	16	40	204	140	120	51	26	.282
Projected	140	445	136	26	5	14	75	54	40	17	10	.306

Orlando Merced   OF/1B

Age: 29   **Seasons:** 6
Height: 5' 11"   **Weight:** 185
Bats: Left   **Throws:** Right
1995 OBP: .365   **1995 SLG:** .468

Merced is a prototype Pirate. He's a mediocre (but versatile) fielder who contributes solid (but unspectacular) stats with the bat. He hit 99 points better against righties (.324) than lefties (.225) last season.

	G	AB	H	2B	3B	HR	RS	RBI	BB	SB	CS	BA
1995	132	487	146	29	4	15	75	83	52	7	2	.300
Career	656	2160	609	122	18	48	327	314	288	27	14	.282
Projected	149	522	154	23	3	12	70	74	60	5	2	.295

Denny Neagle   P

Age: 27   **Seasons:** 5
Height: 6' 2"   **Weight:** 217
Bats: Left   **Throws:** Left
1995 OBA: .273   **1995 WHIP:** 1.27

Neagle's fastball isn't much better than average, but his change-up can create excellent whiffs-to-walks ratios when his control is sharp, which it usually is. He did a fine job of cutting off the running game last season.

	G	GS	IP	ER	ERA	H	BB	SO	W	L	SV
1995	31	31	209.2	80	3.43	221	45	150	13	8	0
Career	167	71	534.1	258	4.35	547	181	436	29	30	3
Projected	34	34	226.1	83	3.30	232	47	166	11	9	0

St. Louis
CARDINALS

Scouting Report

Outfielders: Ray Lankford has been the Cardinals' best player over the past three seasons as a whole, combining exceptional range in center field with a rare mix of power and speed on offense. Ex–NFL standout Brian Jordan, whose skills are similar to Lankford's, signed a baseball-only deal that will make him the regular right fielder in St. Louis for at least the next three years. Left fielder Bernard Gilkey quietly compiled solid 1995 numbers, falling one RBI short of his career high despite logging the bulk of his at-bats in the leadoff spot. Two well-thought-of prospects, Allen Battle and Terry Bradshaw, will also see action in the St. Louis outfield.

Infielders: The Cardinals will probably delve into the free-agent market for a power-hitting first baseman. If they don't land one, the starting job will once again go to 1995 rookie surprise John Mabry. The organization would also like to locate a top-level second baseman via the open market, though it's unclear what would become of David Bell, the prospect acquired in exchange for Ken Hill. Bell could shift to his natural position at third base, but he's not likely to develop into the power threat that teams look for at the hot corner. Another young third sacker, Jose Oliva, has flashed eye-opening power but has yet to make consistent contact. Big-money free agent Scott Cooper washed out last season and may not return. Ozzie Smith is expected to return for a final campaign at shortstop, backed up by Tripp Cromer.

Catchers: It's not that Tom Pagnozzi isn't a valuable pro backstop, it's just that he can't stay healthy enough to use his vaunted arm and glove for a full season.

Starting Pitchers: The Cardinals could boast a terrific one-two southpaw punch if Donovan Osborne and Danny Jackson are of sound arm. Young lefty Allen Watson is wildly inconsistent but occasionally brilliant. The Redbirds have every reason to believe that rookie righthander Alan Benes, Andy's younger brother, can be a major league superstar. His fastball clocks out in the mid-90s, he has a veteran's grasp of pitching strategy, and his control is top notch. Mark Petkovsek, who was leading the American Association (triple-A) in ERA when he was called up in May, wound up leading the Cards in games started and innings pitched last season.

Relief Pitchers: Tom Henke was the NL's most consistent closer last season, but he may elect to retire on a high note. Rookie reliever Cory Bailey sliced and diced triple-A hitters last season and could be ready for the next level. Lefty batters cringe at the thought of facing veteran Tony Fossas.

Outlook

The Cardinals aren't nearly as lackluster as they appeared in 1995, but they clearly have problems to address: the lack of an intimidating slugger in the batting order or a frontline ace in the starting rotation; the inability of the established veterans to stay off the disabled list; and the failure of the rookies to pick up the slack. The Redbirds probably can't retool quickly enough to contend for the division title, but if they add a couple of big-name position players and let Tony La Russa work his magic on the pitching staff, anything is possible in the age of the wild card.

Fungoes

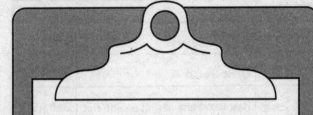

Quick Quiz: Which catcher threw out Babe Ruth attempting to steal second, ending the seventh game of the 1926 World Series?

Franchise Milestone: The tradition-rich Cardinals have been in St. Louis since 1892, winning nine World Series (1926, 1931, 1934, 1942, 1944, 1946, 1964, 1967, and 1987) in their storied history.

Top Pitcher: Bob Gibson, 1959–75

Top Player: Stan Musial, 1941–63

Top Manager: Whitey Herzog, 1980–90

Wacky Nickname: Slats (Martin Whitford Marion)

Quick Quiz Answer: Bob O'Farrell

Lineup Card

NO	POS	PLAYER	OBP	SLG
23	LF	Bernard Gilkey	.358	.490
1	SS	Ozzie Smith	.282	.244
16	CF	Ray Lankford	.360	.513
3	RF	Brian Jordan	.339	.488
47	1B	John Mabry	.347	.405
25	2B	David Bell	.278	.368
42	3B	Jose Oliva	.202	.284
19	C	Tom Pagnozzi	.254	.315

In a Nutshell: As we go to press, the Redbirds are on the lookout for a legitimate cleanup hitter–first baseman, which they desperately need, and a top-flight second baseman–leadoff hitter. The former would leave John Mabry, a natural outfielder who hit .307 with extra-base punch as a rookie last year while playing mostly at first base, in need of a spot in the team's oft-crowded outfield. The latter would allow young David Bell to shift back to the hot corner, his position in the minors. Last season the Cardinals ranked last in the majors in both slugging and on-base percentage, so there's nowhere to go but up. The club endured a 33-inning scoreless streak in late-July as the Cardinals plated just one run in a three-game set with the Marlins. The situation will be improved by filling in the above-mentioned gaps in the one- and four-holes, but the holdovers from 1995 must step up and contribute.

Busch Stadium

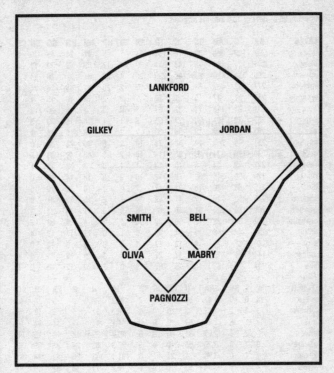

Capacity: 57, 078
Turf: Artificial

LF Line: 330
RF Line: 330
Center: 402
Left CF: 375
Right CF: 375

Tickets:
314-421-2400

Even in a dismal season, the Cards maintain a home-field advantage; nearly two-thirds of the Redbirds' 1995 wins came at home. The park isn't as unfriendly to sluggers as it once was—the fences have been moved in and shortened—but the plastic grass and expansive outfield dimensions still benefit the speedy linedrive hitters that have become a St. Louis trademark.

Statistics

Minimum 25 at-bats or 10.0 innings pitched

PLAYER	BA	G	AB	RS	H	TB	2B	3B	HR	RBI	BB	SO	SB	CS
Mabry	.307	129	388	35	119	157	21	1	5	41	24	45	0	3
Gilkey	.298	121	480	73	143	234	32	4	17	69	42	70	12	6
Jordan	.296	131	490	83	145	239	20	4	22	81	22	76	24	9
Lankford	.277	132	483	81	134	248	35	2	25	82	63	110	24	8
Sweeney	.273	37	77	5	21	29	2	0	2	13	10	15	1	1
Battle	.271	61	118	13	32	37	5	0	0	2	15	26	3	2
Pena	.267	32	101	20	27	38	6	1	1	8	16	30	3	2
Bell	.250	39	144	13	36	53	7	2	2	19	4	25	1	2
Sheaffer	.231	76	208	24	48	75	10	1	5	30	23	38	0	0
Cooper	.230	118	374	29	86	117	18	2	3	40	49	85	0	3
Bradshaw	.227	19	44	6	10	13	1	1	0	2	2	10	1	2
Cromer	.226	105	345	36	78	112	19	0	5	18	14	66	0	0
Coles	.225	63	138	13	31	47	7	0	3	16	16	20	0	0
Pagnozzi	.215	62	219	17	47	69	14	1	2	15	11	31	0	1
Oquendo	.209	88	220	31	46	66	8	3	2	17	35	21	2	1
Caraballo	.202	34	99	10	20	32	4	1	2	3	6	33	3	2
Smith	.199	44	156	16	31	38	5	1	0	11	17	12	4	3
Perry	.165	65	79	4	13	17	4	0	0	5	6	12	0	0
Hemond	.144	57	118	11	17	27	1	0	3	9	12	31	0	0
Oliva	.142	70	183	15	26	52	5	0	7	20	12	46	0	0

PITCHER	W	L	SV	ERA	G	GS	CG	SH	IP	H	R	ER	BB	SO
Fossas	3	0	0	1.47	58	0	0	0	36.2	28	6	6	10	40
Mathews	1	1	2	1.52	23	0	0	0	29.2	21	7	5	11	28
Henke	1	1	36	1.82	52	0	0	0	54.1	42	11	11	18	48
Habyan	3	2	0	2.88	31	0	0	0	40.2	32	18	13	15	35
DeLucia	8	7	0	3.39	56	0	0	0	82.3	63	38	31	36	76
Morgan	7	7	0	3.56	21	21	1	0	131.1	133	56	52	34	61
Parrett	4	7	0	3.64	59	0	0	0	76.2	71	33	31	28	71
Urbani	3	5	0	3.70	24	13	0	0	82.2	99	40	34	21	52
Osborne	4	6	0	3.81	19	19	0	0	113.1	112	58	48	34	82
Arocha	3	5	0	3.99	41	0	0	0	49.2	55	24	22	18	25
Petkovsek	6	6	0	4.00	26	21	1	1	137.1	136	71	61	35	71
Frascatore	1	1	0	4.41	14	4	0	0	32.2	39	19	16	16	21
Watson	7	9	0	4.96	21	19	0	0	114.1	126	68	63	41	49
Hill	6	7	0	5.06	18	18	0	0	110.1	125	71	62	45	50
Barber	2	1	0	5.22	9	4	0	0	29.1	31	17	17	16	27
Palacios	2	3	0	5.80	20	5	0	0	40.1	48	29	26	19	34
Jackson	2	12	0	5.90	19	19	2	1	100.2	120	82	66	48	52
Benes	1	2	0	8.44	3	3	0	0	16.0	24	15	15	4	20

Roster

MANAGER: Tony La Russa
COACHES: Mark DeJohn, Dave Duncan, Ron Hassey, George
Hendrick, Dave McKay, Tommie Reynolds

NO	PITCHERS	B	T	HT	WT	DOB
43	Rene Arocha	R	R	6-0	180	2/24/66
39	Cory Baily	R	R	6-1	202	1/24/71
—	Brian Barber	R	R	6-1	175	3/4/73
40	Alan Benes	R	R	6-5	215	1/21/72
41	Rich DeLucia	R	R	6-0	185	10/7/64
48	Tony Fossas	L	L	6-0	187	9/23/57
50	John Frascatore	R	R	6-1	200	2/4/70
29	Danny Jackson	R	L	6-0	220	1/5/62
—	T.J. Mathews	R	R	6-2	200	1/19/70
31	Donovan Osborne	L	L	6-2	195	6/21/69
58	Vicente Palacios	R	R	6-3	175	7/19/63
46	Mark Petkovsek	R	R	6-0	185	11/18/65
33	Rich Rodriguez	L	L	6-0	200	3/1/63
34	Tom Urbani	L	L	6-1	190	1/21/68
38	Allen Watson	L	L	6-3	190	11/18/70
	CATCHERS					
19	Tom Pagnozzi	R	R	6-1	190	7/30/62
5	Danny Sheaffer	R	R	6-0	202	8/2/61
26	Scott Hemond	R	R	6-0	215	11/18/65
	INFIELDERS					
25	David Bell	R	R	5-10	170	9/14/72
—	Ramon Caraballo	S	R	5-7	150	5/23/69
15	Darnell Coles	R	R	6-1	180	6/2/62
34	Scott Cooper	L	R	6-3	205	10/13/67
7	Tripp Cromer	R	R	6-2	165	11/21/67
47	John Mabry	L	R	6-4	195	10/17/70
42	Jose Oliva	R	R	6-3	215	3/3/71
21	Geronimo Pena	S	R	6-1	195	3/29/67
28	Gerald Perry	L	L	6-0	201	10/30/60
1	Ozzie Smith	S	R	5-10	168	12/26/54
	OUTFIELDERS					
35	Allen Battle	R	R	6-0	170	11/29/68
55	Terry Bradshaw	L	R	6-0	195	2/3/69
23	Bernard Gilkey	R	R	6-0	190	9/24/66
3	Brian Jordan	R	R	6-1	205	3/29/67
16	Ray Lankford	L	L	5-11	198	6/5/67

FREE AGENTS: Tom Henke, Mike Morgan, Jose Oquendo,
Jeff Parrett

David Bell   2B/3B

Age: 23   **Seasons:** 1
Height: 5' 10"   **Weight:** 170
Bats: Right   **Throws:** Right
1995 OBP: .278   **1995 SLG:** .368

Bell, a third-generation major leaguer who was acquired from Cleveland for Ken Hill, hit .355 with 18 homers in 481 triple-A at-bats in 1994. He took over permanent duties at second base for St. Louis in the final six weeks of last season.

	G	AB	H	2B	3B	HR	RS	RBI	BB	SB	CS	BA
1995	39	144	36	7	2	2	13	19	4	1	2	.250
Career	39	144	36	7	2	2	13	19	4	1	2	.250
Projected	126	421	101	15	4	9	62	68	16	2	4	.240

Alan Benes   P

Age: 24   **Seasons:** R
Height: 6' 5"   **Weight:** 215
Bats: Right   **Throws:** Right
1995 OBA: .343   **1995 WHIP:** 1.75

Benes got rocked by Pittsburgh in his big-league debut (he beat the Pirates two weeks later for his first win), so his ERA is inflated, but having shredded minor-league hitting at every level, he's arguably the most exciting prospect in baseball.

	G	GS	IP	ER	ERA	H	BB	SO	W	L	SV
1995	3	3	16.0	15	8.44	24	4	20	1	2	0
Career	3	3	16.0	15	8.44	24	4	20	1	2	0
Projected	26	26	168.1	69	3.69	155	41	147	9	7	0

Bernard Gilkey OF

Age: 29   **Seasons:** 6
Height: 6' 0"   **Weight:** 190
Bats: Right   **Throws:** Right
1995 OBP: .358   **1995 SLG:** .490

After slumping in 1993, Gilkey came back to post strong numbers last year. He hit .326 with runners in scoring position and tagged righthanded pitchers for 15 of his 17 dingers. A quality left fielder, he registered ten outfield assists.

	G	AB	H	2B	3B	HR	RS	RBI	BB	SB	CS	BA
1995	121	480	143	33	4	17	73	69	42	12	6	.298
Career	593	2133	602	126	18	52	319	250	223	80	42	.282
Projected	149	515	139	25	2	14	74	65	47	13	8	.270

Tom Henke P

Age: 38   **Seasons:** 14
Height: 6' 5"   **Weight:** 225
Bats: Right   **Throws:** Right
1995 OBA: .209   **1995 WHIP:** 1.10

Henke stormed through the National League last season, botching just two save chances in 38 tries and becoming the seventh man in baseball history to reach the 300-saves plateau. He has indicated that retirement is a possibility.

	G	GS	IP	ER	ERA	H	BB	SO	W	L	SV
1995	52	0	54.1	11	1.82	42	18	48	1	1	36
Career	642	0	799.2	234	2.63	607	255	861	41	42	311
Projected	61	0	60.2	15	2.23	48	24	51	1	3	35

Danny Jackson   P

Age: 34   **Seasons:** 13
Height: 6' 0"   **Weight:** 220
Bats: Right   **Throws:** Left
1995 OBA: .303   **1995 WHIP:** 1.67

Jackson staggered to an 0–7 start in his first year as a Cardinal, due in part to adverse effects caused by medication he was taking for a cancerous thyroid. A severe ankle sprain ended his season in August.

	G	GS	IP	ER	ERA	H	BB	SO	W	L	SV
1995	19	19	100.2	66	5.90	120	48	52	2	12	0
Career	323	307	1968.2	848	3.88	1979	772	1166	109	121	1
Projected	25	25	144.1	61	3.80	154	51	92	6	10	0

Brian Jordan   OF

Age: 29   **Seasons:** 4
Height: 6' 1"   **Weight:** 205
Bats: Right   **Throws:** Right
1995 OBP: .339   **1995 SLG:** .488

A former Atlanta Falcon, Jordan is blessed with serious athletic prowess. He's surehanded in right field (.996 fielding percentage, second among NL outfielders), though his arm is nothing special, and he's a power/speed threat on offense.

	G	AB	H	2B	3B	HR	RS	RBI	BB	SB	CS	BA
1995	131	490	145	20	4	22	83	81	22	24	9	.296
Career	306	1084	300	47	16	42	147	162	60	41	20	.277
Projected	144	521	149	21	6	18	79	84	31	21	11	.286

Ray Lankford   OF

Age: 28   **Seasons:** 6
Height: 5' 11"   **Weight:** 198
Bats: Left   **Throws:** Left
1995 OBP: .360   **1995 SLG:** .513

Lankford strikes out too often (110 in 1995), and he doesn't always make good decisions on the bases and in the field, yet he's still one of the league's most dynamic players. Ten of his 25 homers last season came in September.

	G	AB	H	2B	3B	HR	RS	RBI	BB	SB	CS	BA
1995	132	483	134	35	2	25	81	82	63	24	8	.277
Career	711	2596	695	150	32	83	416	351	328	143	78	.268
Projected	151	546	156	29	4	22	91	85	72	31	15	.286

Donovan Osborne   P

Age: 26   **Seasons:** 3
Height: 6' 2"   **Weight:** 195
Bats: Left   **Throws:** Left
1995 OBA: .260   **1995 WHIP:** 1.29

Shoulder surgery forced Osborne to sit out the entire 1994 season, and he struggled with elbow soreness the first half of 1995, but he was 4–0, 2.20 in his six September starts, lowering his ERA from 4.73 to 3.81.

	G	GS	IP	ER	ERA	H	BB	SO	W	L	SV
1995	19	19	113.1	48	3.81	112	34	82	4	6	0
Career	79	74	448.0	188	3.78	458	119	269	25	22	0
Projected	26	26	158.2	53	3.01	142	29	117	12	7	0

Tom Pagnozzi C

Age: 33
Height: 6' 1"
Bats: Right
1995 OBP: .254

Seasons: 9
Weight: 190
Throws: Right
1995 SLG: .315

One of the league's better defensive backstops, Pagnozzi's game-calling abilities, throwing arm, and glovework are all exceptional, but last season's wrist and leg injuries marked the third straight year he's spent a big chunk of time on the shelf.

	G	AB	H	2B	3B	HR	RS	RBI	BB	SB	CS	BA
1995	62	219	47	14	1	2	17	15	11	0	1	.215
Career	732	2279	577	118	11	29	188	247	150	14	20	.253
Projected	110	354	88	19	0	5	41	39	22	1	2	.249

Ozzie Smith SS

Age: 41
Height: 5' 10"
Bats: Switch
1995 OBP: .282

Seasons: 18
Weight: 168
Throws: Right
1995 SLG: .244

The Wizard was batting .250 in May, but proceeded to lose 77 games to a shoulder injury. A 12-time All-Star, Smith currently ranks second on the Cards' all-time list for walks and sixth in hits. This will be his swan-song season.

	G	AB	H	2B	3B	HR	RS	RBI	BB	SB	CS	BA
1995	44	156	31	5	1	0	16	11	17	4	3	.199
Career	2491	9169	2396	392	67	26	1221	775	1047	573	143	.261
Projected	114	285	64	13	2	1	33	14	28	9	4	.225

San Diego
PADRES

Scouting Report

Outfielders: Steve Finley notched personal bests in runs scored and batting average last season after coming to San Diego from Houston. A fine center fielder who is blessed with speed and instincts in equal measure, he won his first Gold Glove in 1995. The incomparable Tony Gwynn makes all the plays in right field and is the most prolific hitter in the league. Though his place in the Hall of Fame is already secured, he continues to compile credentials anyway. If the Padres are ready to give up on uppercut slugger Phil Plantier, left field will belong to either veteran Bip Roberts, all-or-nothing young bopper Melvin Nieves, or highly touted 23-year-old Marc Newfield, who was the key component of the Andy Benes deal.

Infielders: Ken Caminiti made 27 errors last season and won the Gold Glove for third basemen, further fueling speculation that the honor has as much to do with lumber as with leather. Speaking of sticks, Caminiti wielded a big one, reaching career highs in virtually every category. At press time the Padres have question marks around the horn. The first-base platoon of Scott Livingstone and Eddie Williams was reasonably productive, though no one in San Diego has forgotten Fred McGriff. Free agent Jody Reed was an anchor at second base last year but is a stopgap solution. Bip Roberts may become the second sacker by default unless Reed is re-signed or a prospect emerges. The situation at shortstop is equally muddled, as rookie Ray Holbert didn't pan out and Andujar Cedeno went bust.

Catchers: Brad Ausmus continues to push the envelope of his talents by approaching the .300 mark at the plate, stealing bases like a noncatcher, and eliminating almost half of opposition baserunners.

Starting Pitchers: Joey Hamilton—who is two years younger than last season's Rookie of the Year, Hideo Nomo—is one of the most promising young starters in the National League. Andy Ashby is also developing as planned, having ranked third in ERA among NL starters last season. Never hesitant to pitch inside, Ashby and Hamilton hit 22 batters between them. Scott Sanders pitched just 90 innings last year before landing on the DL with an elbow sprain, but he fanned just under one batter an inning and clearly has the stuff to emerge as a dominant pitcher. Young southpaw Glenn Dishman has torn up minor-league pitching and was tough on lefthanders in the Show last season.

Relief Pitchers: Trevor Hoffman wasn't always sharp in 1995, but he's one of the league's more intimidating closers. Bryce Florie handles primary setup duties.

Outlook

The Padres practically invented the concept of dumping salaries, but they've retooled in recent seasons and are now on solid ground located somewhere between title contention and mere respectability. The club's top two starters, Andy Ashby and Joey Hamilton, both finished among the NL's top six in ERA last season. If the able arms of Glenn Dishman and Scott Sanders develop, the San Diego rotation will be a match for the Dodgers' and a notch above the Giants' and Rockies'. Now, if the Padres only had a McGriff or a Sheffield to anchor the offense...

Fungoes

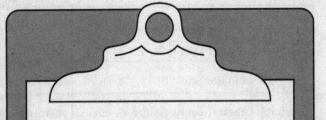

Quick Quiz: Which outfielder was drafted by the NFL's Minnesota Vikings and the NBA's Atlanta Hawks?

Franchise Milestone: The Padres have been to one World Series, losing to the Tigers in five games in 1984 despite the unexpected fireworks of the immortal Kurt Bevacqua, who smashed two home runs and batted .412 as the Padres' DH.

Top Pitcher: Andy Benes, 1989–95

Top Player: Tony Gwynn, 1982–

Top Manager: Dick Williams, 1982–85

Wacky Nickname: Downtown (Ollie Lee Brown)

Quick Quiz Answer: Dave Winfield

Lineup Card

NO	POS	PLAYER	OBP	SLG
12	CF	Steve Finley	.366	.420
3	2B	Bip Roberts	.346	.372
19	RF	Tony Gwynn	.404	.484
21	3B	Ken Caminiti	.380	.513
24	1B	Roberto Petagine	.367	.371
10	LF	Melvin Nieves	.276	.419
11	C	Brad Ausmus	.353	.412
10	SS	Andujar Cedeno	.271	.308

In a Nutshell: The Padres did a decent job of getting on base last season, ranking fifth in the league in OBP and third in batting average, and they were fairly efficient in bringing those runners home, considering that the club ranked tenth in slugging but sixth in runs scored. San Diego's table will be set often again this year, but the Padres need to get some power from the five- and six-holes, which is why prospects Petagine (a lefty slugger who was MVP of the double-A Texas League in 1993) and Nieves (the main element of the Fred McGriff trade) could be crucial to San Diego's run-producing ability this year. Steve Finley and Ken Caminiti can't be counted on to put up career-year numbers in back-to-back seasons. The first five spots in the batting order are all occupied by veterans who aren't likely to improve on their 1995 performances, so the kids will have to step up if the offense is to improve.

Jack Murphy Stadium

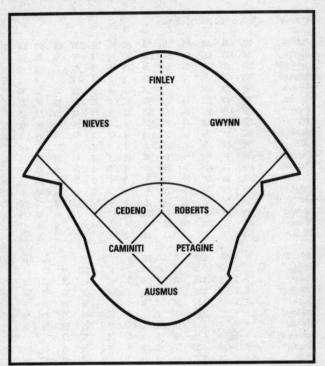

Capacity: 46,510
Turf: Natural

LF Line: 327
RF Line: 327
Center: 405
Left CF: 370
Right CF: 370

Tickets:
619-283-4494

The Murph has seen Roseanne's rendition of the national anthem, dearly departed president Chub Feeney's one-finger salute to the fans who booed him, and annual visits from a skunk living inside the seldom-used rain-delay tarp. The park isn't situated at a high altitude, but you'd never know that from the way home runs have been flying out the past few years.

Statistics

Minimum 25 at-bats or 10.0 innings pitched

PLAYER	BA	G	AB	RS	H	TB	2B	3B	HR	RBI	BB	SO	SB	CS
Gwynn	.368	135	535	82	197	259	33	1	9	90	35	15	17	5
Livingstone	.337	99	196	26	66	96	15	0	5	32	15	22	2	1
Newfield	.309	21	55	6	17	27	5	1	1	7	2	8	0	0
Roberts	.304	73	296	40	90	114	16	0	2	25	17	36	20	2
Caminiti	.302	143	526	74	159	270	33	0	26	94	69	94	12	4
Finley	.297	139	562	104	167	236	23	8	10	44	59	61	35	12
Ausmus	.293	103	328	44	96	135	16	4	5	34	31	56	16	5
Cianfrocco	.263	51	118	22	31	53	7	0	5	31	11	28	0	2
Williams	.260	97	296	35	77	126	11	1	12	47	22	47	0	0
Reed	.256	131	445	58	114	146	18	1	4	40	59	38	6	4
Plantier	.255	76	216	34	55	88	6	0	9	34	28	48	1	1
Johnson	.251	68	207	20	52	70	9	0	3	29	11	39	0	0
Petagine	.234	89	124	15	29	46	8	0	3	17	26	41	0	0
Clark	.216	74	97	12	21	30	3	0	2	7	8	18	0	2
Cedeno	.210	120	390	42	82	120	16	2	6	31	28	92	5	3
Nieves	.205	98	234	32	48	98	6	1	14	38	19	88	2	3
Holbert	.178	63	73	11	13	23	2	1	2	5	8	20	3	0

PITCHING	W	L	SV	ERA	G	GS	CG	SH	IP	H	R	ER	BB	SO
Ashby	12	10	0	2.94	31	31	2	2	192.2	180	79	63	62	150
Florie	2	2	1	3.01	47	0	0	0	68.2	49	30	23	38	68
Hamilton	6	9	0	3.08	31	30	2	2	204.1	189	89	70	56	123
Bochtler	4	4	1	3.57	34	0	0	0	45.1	38	18	18	19	45
Hoffman	7	4	31	3.88	55	0	0	0	53.1	48	25	23	14	52
Benes	4	7	0	4.17	19	19	1	1	118.2	121	65	55	45	126
Villone	2	1	0	4.21	19	0	0	0	25.2	24	12	12	11	37
Sanders	5	5	0	4.30	17	15	1	0	90.0	79	46	43	31	88
Blair	7	5	0	4.34	40	12	0	0	114	112	60	55	45	83
Worrell	1	0	0	4.73	9	0	0	0	13.1	16	7	7	6	13
Valenzuela	8	3	0	4.98	29	15	0	0	90.1	101	53	50	34	57
Dishman	4	8	0	5.01	19	16	0	0	97.0	104	60	54	34	43
Berumen	2	3	1	5.68	37	0	0	0	44.1	37	29	28	36	42
Williams	3	10	0	6.00	44	6	0	0	72.0	79	54	48	38	75
Hermanson	3	1	0	6.82	26	0	0	0	31.2	35	26	24	22	19

Roster

MANAGER: Bruce Bochy
COACHES: Davey Lopes, Rob Picciolo, Merv Rettenmund

NO	PITCHERS	B	T	HT	WT	DOB
43	Andy Ashby	R	R	6-5	190	7/11/67
55	Andres Berumen	R	R	6-2	205	4/5/71
49	Willie Blair	R	R	6-1	182	12/18/65
45	Doug Bochtler	R	R	6-3	200	7/5/70
44	Glenn Dishman	R	L	6-1	195	11/5/70
38	Donnie Elliott	R	R	6-5	225	9/20/68
39	Bryce Florie	R	R	5-11	190	5/21/70
50	Joey Hamilton	R	R	6-4	230	9/9/70
48	Dustin Hermanson	R	R	6-3	195	12/21/72
51	Trevor Hoffman	R	R	6-0	205	10/13/67
54	Marc Kroon	S	R	6-2	195	4/2/73
—	Pedro A. Martinez	R	L	6-2	185	11/29/68
27	Scott Sanders	R	R	6-4	215	3/25/69
49	Ron Villone	L	L	6-3	230	1/16/70
36	Tim Worrell	R	R	6-4	220	7/5/67
26	Brian Williams	R	R	6-2	195	2/15/69
	CATCHERS					
11	Brad Ausmus	R	R	5-11	190	4/14/69
25	Brian Johnson	R	R	6-2	210	1/8/68
	INFIELDERS					
21	Ken Caminiti	S	R	6-0	200	4/21/63
10	Andujar Cedeno	R	R	6-1	168	8/21/69
29	Archi Cianfrocco	R	R	6-5	215	10/6/66
8	Scott Livingstone	L	R	6-0	190	7/15/65
24	Roberto Petagine	L	L	6-1	170	6/7/71
3	Bip Roberts	S	R	5-7	165	10/27/63
23	Eddie Williams	R	R	6-0	210	11/1/64
	OUTFIELDERS					
12	Steve Finley	L	L	6-2	180	3/12/65
19	Tony Gwynn	L	L	5-11	215	5/9/60
20	Ray McDavid	L	R	6-2	200	7/20/71
28	Marc Newfield	R	R	6-4	205	10/19/71
10	Melvin Nieves	S	R	6-2	210	12/28/71
7	Phil Plantier	L	R	5-11	195	1/27/69

FREE AGENTS: Jody Reed, Fernando Valenzuela

Andy Ashby **P**

Age: 28   **Seasons:** 5
Height: 6' 5"   **Weight:** 190
Bats: Right   **Throws:** Right
1995 OBA: .253   **1995 WHIP:** 1.26

Ashby has had a history of injury and stamina problems, but he's developed nicely since former Padres GM Randy Smith brought him to San Diego, having allowed fewer hits than innings pitched over each of the past two seasons.

	G	GS	IP	ER	ERA	H	BB	SO	W	L	SV
1995	31	31	192.2	63	2.94	180	62	150	12	10	0
Career	105	92	559.0	277	4.46	576	201	398	23	39	1
Projected	34	34	217.1	75	3.11	213	65	179	14	9	0

Brad Ausmus **C**

Age: 27   **Seasons:** 3
Height: 5' 11"   **Weight:** 190
Bats: Right   **Throws:** Right
1995 OBP: .353   **1995 SLG:** .412

With skills that are reminiscent of those belonging to pre–second base Craig Biggio, Ausmus has good speed (not compared just to other catchers) and is an excellent contact hitter. He nailed 42 percent of would-be thieves last season.

	G	AB	H	2B	3B	HR	RS	RBI	BB	SB	CS	BA
1995	103	328	96	16	4	5	44	34	31	16	5	.293
Career	253	815	219	36	6	17	107	70	67	23	6	.269
Projected	127	364	103	17	3	6	48	40	33	13	2	.283

Ken Caminiti 3B

Age: 33   **Seasons:** 9
Height: 6' 0"   **Weight:** 200
Bats: Switch   **Throws:** Right
1995 OBP: .380   **1995 SLG:** .513

In a stunning four-day hot streak last year, Caminiti became the only player ever to belt homers from both sides of the plate three times in a single season. He made 20 errors before the All-Star break but only seven in the second half.

	G	AB	H	2B	3B	HR	RS	RBI	BB	SB	CS	BA
1995	143	526	159	33	0	26	74	94	69	12	5	.302
Career	1091	3967	1055	213	13	101	483	539	367	51	27	.266
Projected	155	580	161	29	1	22	71	83	54	9	4	.278

Andujar Cedeno SS

Age: 26   **Seasons:** 6
Height: 6' 1"   **Weight:** 168
Bats: Right   **Throws:** Right
1995 OBP: .271   **1995 SLG:** .308

Cedeno's stock has dropped like a rock in the time it takes to say "strike-zone," a word whose meaning this free swinger has yet to decipher. Since his defense lacks polish, too, it isn't unthinkable that he could be out of the majors soon.

	G	AB	H	2B	3B	HR	RS	RBI	BB	SB	CS	BA
1995	120	390	82	16	2	6	42	31	28	5	3	.210
Career	512	1716	414	92	10	37	191	185	128	21	14	.241
Projected	137	436	106	17	1	9	44	39	33	3	2	.243

Steve Finley   OF

Age: 31   **Seasons:** 7
Height: 6' 2"   **Weight:** 180
Bats: Left   **Throws:** Left
1995 OBP: .366   **1995 SLG:** .420

Finley crossed the plate 100 times for the first time in his career last year and was rewarded with a two-year contract worth $5.9 million. It's too bad that he had to have a career year at the plate for the Gold Glove voters to finally notice him.

	G	AB	H	2B	3B	HR	RS	RBI	BB	SB	CS	BA
1995	139	562	167	23	8	10	104	44	59	36	12	.297
Career	919	3364	935	132	55	47	486	292	262	185	64	.278
Projected	157	614	164	24	10	8	97	48	43	26	9	.267

Tony Gwynn   OF

Age: 35   **Seasons:** 14
Height: 5' 11"   **Weight:** 215
Bats: Left   **Throws:** Left
1995 OBP: .404   **1995 SLG:** .484

The first player since Ducky Medwick to hit .350 or better in three straight seasons, Gwynn won the sixth batting title of his career last season. His approach to hitting is analytical, but his execution is pure artistry.

	G	AB	H	2B	3B	HR	RS	RBI	BB	SB	CS	BA
1995	135	535	197	33	1	9	82	90	35	17	5	.368
Career	1830	7144	2401	384	80	87	1073	840	625	285	112	.336
Projected	142	570	203	30	2	10	86	81	42	12	3	.356

Joey Hamilton P

Age: 25 **Seasons:** 2
Height: 6' 4" **Weight:** 230
Bats: Right **Throws:** Right
1995 OBA: .246 **1995 WHIP:** 1.20

Hamilton already ranks with the best pitchers in baseball, though his whiff rates are barely average, and his future appears bright. He keeps the running game under control, isn't afraid to pitch inside, and stays composed under pressure.

	G	GS	IP	ER	ERA	H	BB	SO	W	L	SV
1995	31	30	204.1	70	3.08	189	56	123	6	9	0
Career	47	46	313.0	106	3.05	287	85	184	15	15	0
Projected	35	35	237.1	79	3.00	214	55	144	10	9	0

Trevor Hoffman P

Age: 28 **Seasons:** 3
Height: 6' 0" **Weight:** 205
Bats: Right **Throws:** Right
1995 OBA: .235 **1995 WHIP:** 1.16

Hoffman has the stuff and makeup to be the league's premier closer, but he took a small step backward last season. Righthanders hit 94 points higher off him than in 1994, and he relinquished an unacceptable ten home runs.

	G	GS	IP	ER	ERA	H	BB	SO	W	L	SV
1995	55	0	53.1	23	3.88	48	14	52	7	4	31
Career	169	0	199.1	78	3.52	167	73	199	15	14	56
Projected	63	0	60.2	20	2.97	42	16	63	3	4	34

Jody Reed   2B

Age: 33   **Seasons:** 9
Height: 5' 9"   **Weight:** 160
Bats: Right   **Throws:** Right
1995 OBP: .348   **1995 SLG:** .328

Reed is the second-base solution for desperate teams, and he's always on the bubble that separates marginal major leaguers from ex-ballplayers. As a hitter his value is intangible (in fact it barely exists at all), but he's a keystone middle infielder.

	G	AB	H	2B	3B	HR	RS	RBI	BB	SB	CS	BA
1995	131	445	114	18	1	4	58	40	59	6	4	.256
Career	1086	3947	1088	241	10	25	515	335	473	35	37	.276
Projected	141	426	108	13	0	2	44	32	41	4	3	.254

Bip Roberts   IF/OF

Age: 32   **Seasons:** 9
Height: 5' 7"   **Weight:** 165
Bats: Switch   **Throws:** Right
1995 OBP: .346   **1995 SLG:** .372

A versatile fielder, though not known as a standout at any position, Roberts is a handy player to have around. He keeps his average around .300 and contributes on the basepaths, though he's been prone to health problems in past seasons.

	G	AB	H	2B	3B	HR	RS	RBI	BB	SB	CS	BA
1995	73	296	90	14	0	2	40	25	17	20	2	.304
Career	897	3082	915	145	27	25	516	232	312	218	79	.297
Projected	144	522	166	27	4	3	82	34	41	25	5	.318

Scott Sanders **P**

Age: 27 **Seasons:** 3
Height: 6' 4" **Weight:** 215
Bats: Right **Throws:** Right
1995 OBA: .228 **1995 WHIP:** 1.22

Though he was shut down prematurely by an elbow sprain, the hard-throwing Sanders overpowered righties to the tune of a .198 OBA and struck out 8.8 batters per nine innings in half a season of work.

	G	GS	IP	ER	ERA	H	BB	SO	W	L	SV
1995	17	15	90.0	43	4.30	79	31	88	5	5	0
Career	49	44	253.1	126	4.48	236	102	234	12	16	1
Projected	28	28	157.2	51	2.91	131	55	149	13	6	0

Fernando Valenzuela **P**

Age: 35 **Seasons:** 15
Height: 5' 11" **Weight:** 200
Bats: Left **Throws:** Left
1995 OBA: .289 **1995 WHIP:** 1.49

The man just oozes professionalism, and his presence is always beneficial for fans and teammates. He won his final six decisions last season, which was quite a surprise considering that he was out of baseball entirely in 1992.

	G	GS	IP	ER	ERA	H	BB	SO	W	L	SV
1995	29	15	90.1	50	4.98	101	34	57	8	3	0
Career	402	375	2669.1	1036	3.49	2435	1038	1918	158	133	2
Projected	24	18	113.2	59	4.67	122	40	62	5	7	0

William VanLandingham

Scouting Report

Outfielders: Barry Bonds remains the best all-around player in the National League. Bank on 30 homers, 100 walks, 30 steals, and sparkling defense in left field. Deion Sanders, a charter member in the cult of personality, is a serviceable leadoff hitter/center fielder, but he comes with a prime-time price tag and a Cowboys logo. Instead of making a contribution to Dollars for Deion, the Giants might be better off giving a fulltime job to Marvin Benard, a young speedster who hit .382 in his first cup of coffee. Money matters may determine the status of Glenallen Hill, too. He's coming off a career year at the age of 30 and is eligible for arbitration. Free agent Mark Carreon will see some action in right field if he's re-signed, and so might grade-C prospect David McCarty.

Infielders: Matt Williams is an outrageously productive slugger and a Gold Glove third baseman. The two-plus months he spent on the disabled list last year took the Giants out of playoff contention, but it also cleared the way for Mark Carreon to emerge as the everyday first baseman. San Francisco was grateful for Carreon's performance, but it was predicated on the early-season struggles of blue-chip rookie J.R. Phillips. Popular second baseman Robby Thompson can't stay healthy, and the Giants miss his extra-base punch when he's on the DL. Royce Clayton set career highs in steals, doubles, and runs scored in 1995 while maintaining his usual great range at shortstop, but the Giants may look to forgo arbitration with Clayton and hand the job to Rich Aurilia, an impressive prospect acquired from Texas in the John Burkett deal.

Catchers: Kirt Manwaring is a blue-collar backstop—he played most of the second half of last season with five broken ribs—but his lunchpail talents are more admirable than productive.

Starting Pitchers: Jamie Brewington jumped from double-A to the Show last year and pitched well enough to secure a spot in the 1996 rotation. William VanLandingham was hampered by non-arm-related injuries, but he also has a potentially bright future. Mark Leiter, the only San Francisco starter who didn't miss a turn in the rotation last year, proved to be the unexpected ace of the staff. Expect to see Steve Bourgeois, 1995 Texas League Pitcher of the Year, starting at Candlestick this season.

Relief Pitchers: Rod Beck's .767 percentage of converted saves was the NL's second lowest, a major disappointment considering his previous dominance. Scott Service took over primary setup duties after his arrival from Cincinnati.

Outlook

San Francisco got hammered by the poststrike attendance drop, and most of their cash is tied up in a handful of guaranteed contracts. If the Giants are forced to dump the salaries of talented players such as Glenallen Hill and Rod Beck, the remaining core of stars—in particular Bonds and Williams—must stay injury free and fully productive. The pitching staff lacks an established ace, but if Mark Leiter doesn't regress and young guns VanLandingham and Brewington step up, the Giants will have a break-even shot at being in contention down the stretch in the West.

Fungoes

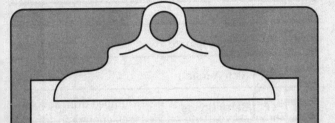

Quick Quiz: Most baseball fans know that the Giants were originally from New York, but which city was home to the franchise in its initial incarnation?

Franchise Milestone: San Francisco has yet to win a World Series title, but the Giants won four in New York (1905, 1921, 1922, and 1954). Since moving to the Bay Area, the club has won two league titles, in 1962 and 1989.

Top Pitcher: Christy Mathewson, 1900–16

Top Player: Willie Mays, 1951–72

Top Manager: John McGraw, 1902–32

Wacky Nickname: Moonlight (Archibald Wright Graham)

Quick Quiz Answer: Troy

Lineup Card

NO	POS	PLAYER	OBP	SLG
56	CF	Marvin Benard	.400	.529
57	SS	Rich Aurilia	.476	.947
25	LF	Barry Bonds	.431	.577
9	3B	Matt Williams	.399	.647
46	RF	Mark Carreon	.343	.490
31	1B	J.R. Phillips	.256	.351
6	2B	Robby Thompson	.317	.339
8	C	Kirt Manwaring	.314	.332

In a Nutshell: J.R. Phillips, who belted 27 taters in 360 triple-A at-bats in 1994, failed to keep his batting average above the dreaded Mendoza line for the Giants last year, but his "potential" (speaking of dread) may warrant one more shot at the first-base assignment. In no way should Mark Carreon, who probably has no long-term future in San Francisco, block Phillips if he can do the job, especially since Carreon can play right field. If J.R. bombs again or doesn't get another chance, Carreon will be at first base, and right field will be a question, assuming that arbitration-eligible Glenallen Hill isn't offered a contract after press time. The Giants probably can't afford to keep Royce Clayton and Deion Sanders, but the youngsters— Benard and Aurilia—could reenergize the top of the order. Bonds and Williams can carry an offense, but it helps if the table is already set when the big boys dig in at the plate.

Candlestick Park

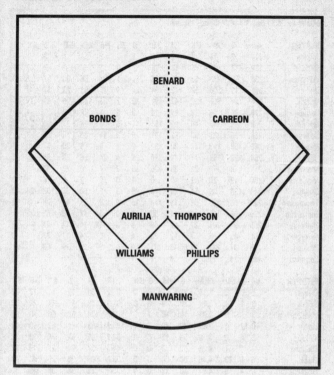

Capacity: 63,000
Turf: Natural

LF Line: 335
RF Line: 328
Center: 400
Left CF: 365
Right CF: 365

Tickets:
415-467-8000

If places have feelings, this place can't be feeling very loved. Sure it gets cold and windy and foggy—that's its charm! Is that the Hound of the Baskervilles baying in left field? The 'Stick has a great name, too, a name that can't be bought or sold, except perhaps in the sad realm of corporations and politics. The park is generally unfriendly to lefthanded hitters.

Statistics

Minimum 25 at-bats or 10.0 innings pitched

PLAYER	BA	G	AB	RS	H	TB	2B	3B	HR	RBI	BB	SO	SB	CS
Aurilia	.474	9	19	4	9	18	3	0	2	4	1	2	1	0
Benard	.382	13	34	5	13	18	2	0	1	4	1	7	1	0
Williams	.336	76	283	53	95	183	17	1	23	65	30	57	2	0
Carreon	.301	117	396	53	119	194	24	0	17	65	23	37	0	1
Bonds	.294	144	506	109	147	292	30	7	33	104	120	83	31	10
Lampkin	.276	65	76	8	21	26	2	0	1	9	9	8	2	0
Sanders	.268	85	343	48	92	137	11	8	6	28	27	60	24	9
Scarsone	.266	80	233	33	62	111	10	3	11	29	18	82	3	2
Reed	.265	66	113	12	30	32	2	0	0	9	20	17	0	0
Hill	.264	132	497	71	131	240	29	4	24	86	39	98	25	5
Manwaring	.251	118	379	21	95	126	15	2	4	36	27	72	1	0
McCarty	.250	12	20	1	5	6	1	0	0	2	2	4	1	0
Clayton	.244	138	509	56	124	174	29	3	5	58	38	109	24	9
Thompson	.223	95	336	51	75	114	15	0	8	23	42	76	1	2
Benjamin	.220	68	186	19	41	56	6	0	3	12	8	51	11	1
Patterson	.205	95	205	27	42	56	5	3	1	14	14	41	4	2
Faneyte	.198	45	86	7	17	23	4	1	0	4	11	27	1	0
Phillips	.195	91	231	27	45	81	9	0	9	28	19	69	1	1
Leonard	.190	14	21	4	4	8	1	0	1	4	5	2	0	0

PITCHER	W	L	SV	ERA	G	GS	CG	SH	IP	H	R	ER	BB	SO
Dewey	1	0	0	3.13	27	0	0	0	31.2	30	12	11	17	32
Service	3	1	0	3.19	28	0	0	0	31.0	31	11	11	20	30
VanLandingham	6	3	0	3.67	18	18	1	0	122.2	124	58	50	40	95
Leiter	10	12	0	3.82	30	29	7	1	195.2	185	91	83	55	129
Wilson	3	4	0	3.92	19	17	0	0	82.2	82	42	36	38	38
Barton	4	1	1	4.26	52	0	0	0	44.1	37	22	21	19	22
Beck	5	6	33	4.45	60	0	0	0	58.2	60	31	29	21	42
Brewington	6	4	0	4.54	13	13	0	0	75.1	68	38	38	45	45
S. Valdez	4	5	0	4.75	13	11	1	0	66.1	78	43	35	17	29
Aquino	0	3	2	5.10	34	0	0	0	42.1	57	34	24	13	26
Gomez	0	0	0	5.14	18	0	0	0	14.0	16	8	8	12	15
Greer	0	2	0	5.25	8	0	0	0	12.0	15	12	7	5	7
Hook	5	1	0	5.50	45	0	0	0	52.1	55	33	32	29	40
Mulholland	5	13	0	5.80	30	24	2	0	149.0	190	112	96	38	65
C. Valdez	0	1	0	6.14	11	0	0	0	14.2	19	10	10	8	7
Bautista	3	8	0	6.44	52	6	0	0	100.2	120	77	72	26	45
Estes	0	3	0	6.75	3	3	0	0	17.1	16	14	13	5	14
Mintz	1	2	0	7.45	14	0	0	0	19.1	26	16	16	5	14
Rosselli	2	1	0	8.70	9	5	0	0	30.0	39	29	29	20	7

Roster

MANAGER: Dusty Baker
COACHES: Bobby Bonds, Bob Brenly, Wendell Kim, Bob Lillis, Dick Pole

NO	PITCHERS	B	T	HT	WT	DOB
64	Shawn Barton	R	L	6-3	195	5/14/63
33	Jose Bautista	R	R	6-2	205	7/26/64
47	Rod Beck	R	R	6-1	236	8/3/68
30	Jamie Brewington	R	R	6-4	180	9/28/71
51	Enrique Burgos	L	L	6-5	230	10/7/65
40	Mark Dewey	R	R	6-0	216	1/3/65
36	Shawn Estes	L	R	6-2	185	2/18/73
61	Chris Hook	R	R	6-5	230	8/4/68
—	Jeff Juden	S	R	6-8	265	1/19/71
31	Mark Leiter	R	R	6-3	210	4/13/63
28	Kevin Rogers	S	L	6-1	198	8/20/68
42	John Roper	R	R	6-0	175	11/21/71
53	Joe Rosselli	R	L	6-1	170	5/28/72
34	Scott Service	R	R	6-6	226	2/26/67
35	Carlos Valzez	R	R	5-11	175	12/26/71
41	Sergio Valdez	R	R	6-1	190	9/7/65
50	William VanLandingham	R	R	6-2	210	7/16/70
	CATCHERS					
54	Marcus Jensen	S	R	6-4	195	12/14/72
49	Tom Lampkin	L	R	5-11	185	3/4/64
8	Kirt Manwaring	R	R	5-11	203	7/15/65
	INFIELDERS					
57	Rich Aurilia	R	R	6-1	170	9/2/71
10	Royce Clayton	R	R	6-0	183	1/2/70
22	David McCarty	R	L	6-5	213	11/23/69
31	J.R. Phillips	L	L	6-1	185	4/29/70
23	Steve Scarsone	R	R	6-2	195	4/11/66
6	Robby Thompson	R	R	5-11	173	5/10/62
9	Matt Williams	R	R	6-2	216	11/28/65
	OUTFIELDERS					
56	Marvin Benard	L	L	5-9	180	1/20/70
25	Barry Bonds	L	L	6-1	185	7/24/64
46	Mark Carreon	R	L	6-0	195	7/9/63
1	Glenallen Hill	R	R	6-2	220	3/22/65
—	Dax Jones	R	R	6-0	180	8/4/70
2	Mark Leonard	L	R	6-1	195	8/14/64
21	Deion Sanders	L	L	6-1	195	8/9/67

FREE AGENTS: Terry Mulholland, Jeff Reed, Trevor Wilson

Rod Beck **P**

Age: 27   **Seasons:** 5
Height: 6' 1"   **Weight:** 236
Bats: Right   **Throws:** Right
1995 OBA: .267   **1995 WHIP:** 1.38

Last year Beck ranked third in the NL in saves but also first in blown saves (10), marking his second consecutive subpar (by his standards) season. An intense individual, he challenges hitters with a good heater and a nasty forkball.

	G	GS	IP	ER	ERA	H	BB	SO	W	L	SV
1995	60	0	58.2	29	4.45	60	21	42	5	6	33
Career	280	0	331.0	103	2.80	281	75	292	14	15	127
Projected	68	0	70.2	21	2.67	59	14	74	3	4	36

Barry Bonds **OF**

Age: 31   **Seasons:** 10
Height: 6' 1"   **Weight:** 185
Bats: Left   **Throws:** Left
1995 OBP: .431   **1995 SLG:** .577

In 1995, Bonds hit .325 with runners in scoring position, joined the 30/30 club for the third time, and led the league in intentional walks for the fourth straight year. His instincts and sense of positioning in left field are impeccable.

	G	AB	H	2B	3B	HR	RS	RBI	BB	SB	CS	BA
1995	144	506	147	30	7	33	109	104	120	31	10	.294
Career	1425	5020	1436	306	48	292	999	864	931	340	103	.286
Projected	160	529	184	33	5	38	127	122	126	34	9	.348

Jamie Brewington P

Age: 24   **Seasons:** 1
Height: 6' 4"   **Weight:** 180
Bats: Right   **Throws:** Right
1995 OBA: .245   **1995 WHIP:** 1.50

San Francisco has a reputation for promoting young pitchers straight from double-A, and Brewington is part of that pattern. He overpowered minor-league hitters with his fastball and slider, then flashed equally stellar stuff with the big club.

	G	GS	IP	ER	ERA	H	BB	SO	W	L	SV
1995	13	13	75.1	38	4.54	68	45	45	6	4	0
Career	13	13	75.1	38	4.54	68	45	45	6	4	0
Projected	26	26	145.2	76	4.70	139	78	86	7	10	0

Mark Carreon 1B/OF

Age: 32   **Seasons:** 9
Height: 6' 0"   **Weight:** 195
Bats: Right   **Throws:** Left
1995 OBP: .343   **1995 SLG:** .490

Carreon stepped into the cleanup spot and just missed registering the first 400-at-bat season of his career. He makes contact, generates some power, and performs in the clutch. He's sure-handed in the field but has a so-so arm.

	G	AB	H	2B	3B	HR	RS	RBI	BB	SB	CS	BA
1995	117	396	119	24	0	17	53	65	23	0	1	.301
Career	619	1578	435	74	2	58	190	223	107	9	7	.276
Projected	134	421	118	21	0	16	56	58	26	1	1	.280

Royce Clayton   SS

Age: 26   **Seasons:** 5
Height: 6' 0"   **Weight:** 183
Bats: Right   **Throws:** Right
1995 OBP: .298   **1995 SLG:** .342

Clayton's range in the field is super and he turns the DP brilliantly, but he tends to pile up errors in streaks, making 20 last season despite a string of 30 games without a miscue. His skills with the bat are still developing.

	G	AB	H	2B	3B	HR	RS	RBI	BB	SB	CS	BA
1995	138	509	124	29	3	5	56	58	38	24	9	.244
Career	506	1790	445	72	18	18	179	184	133	66	26	.249
Projected	150	531	131	24	5	4	62	51	41	21	10	.247

Glenallen Hill   OF

Age: 31   **Seasons:** 7
Height: 6' 2"   **Weight:** 220
Bats: Right   **Throws:** Right
1995 OBP: .317   **1995 SLG:** .483

Posting career bests in nearly every major category—he even rang up a surprising ten outfield assists—Hill put together a season worthy of his talents. He would have picked up more steals had it not been for a late-season hamstring problem.

	G	AB	H	2B	3B	HR	RS	RBI	BB	SB	CS	BA
1995	132	497	131	29	4	24	71	86	39	25	5	.264
Career	595	1929	501	90	13	88	270	284	149	77	28	.260
Projected	146	531	143	23	2	18	68	75	41	32	7	.269

Mark Leiter   P

Age: 33	**Seasons:** 6
Height: 6' 3"	**Weight:** 210
Bats: Right	**Throws:** Right
1995 OBA: .254	**1995 WHIP:** 1.23

Leiter was cuffed around pretty good by lefties in 1994, but last season he held portsiders to a .241 batting average. He's known for making repeated throws to first (with marginal results) and for plunking batters (17 in 1995 to lead the league).

	G	GS	IP	ER	ERA	H	BB	SO	W	L	SV
1995	30	29	195.2	83	3.82	185	55	129	10	12	0
Career	178	81	670.2	324	4.35	669	236	469	38	38	3
Projected	32	32	218.0	95	3.92	214	61	138	11	12	0

Kirt Manwaring   C

Age: 30	**Seasons:** 9
Height: 5' 11"	**Weight:** 203
Bats: Right	**Throws:** Right
1995 OBP: .314	**1995 SLG:** .332

Strictly a contact hitter—and he was ultrastreaky in 1995—Manwaring is paid for his mobility and his glove behing home plate. Playing most of the year with busted ribs, he threw out just 23 percent of enemy thieves.

	G	AB	H	2B	3B	HR	RS	RBI	BB	SB	CS	BA
1995	118	379	95	15	2	4	21	36	27	1	0	.251
Career	660	1990	492	77	12	15	165	193	144	8	8	.247
Projected	126	414	107	16	1	3	30	41	35	1	2	.258

Deion Sanders   OF

Age: 28   **Seasons:** 7
Height: 6' 1"   **Weight:** 195
Bats: Left   **Throws:** Left
1995 OBP: .327   **1995 SLG:** .399

A poor man's Mickey Rivers, Sanders has excellent range in center field and tremendous speed on the basepaths. He doesn't get on base enough to make maximum use of his wheels, and his bat speed is below average.

	G	AB	H	2B	3B	HR	RS	RBI	BB	SB	CS	BA
1995	85	343	92	11	8	6	48	28	27	24	9	.268
Career	494	1583	418	57	36	33	249	141	121	127	46	.264
Projected	131	529	137	17	11	9	72	41	39	41	15	.259

Robby Thompson   2B

Age: 33   **Seasons:** 10
Height: 5' 11"   **Weight:** 173
Bats: Right   **Throws:** Right
1995 OBP: .317   **1995 SLG:** .339

His hitting skills may be deteriorating and his body is definitely falling apart, but when all is right with him, few second sackers can match Thompson's blend of great glovework in the field and extra-base pop at the plate.

	G	AB	H	2B	3B	HR	RS	RBI	BB	SB	CS	BA
1995	95	336	75	15	0	8	51	23	42	1	2	.223
Career	1241	4385	1147	227	38	114	319	437	415	101	60	.265
Projected	124	432	111	16	1	13	60	42	51	1	1	.257

William VanLandingham P

Age: 25 **Seasons:** 2
Height: 6' 2" **Weight:** 210
Bats: Right **Throws:** Right
1995 OBA: .264 **1995 WHIP:** 1.34

Despite being slowed by two separate muscle strains last season, his stamina and performance level both increased over his final 14 starts. Incredibly, VanLandingham is 9–0 lifetime at home, 12–0 in the daytime.

	G	GS	IP	ER	ERA	H	BB	SO	W	L	SV
1995	18	18	122.2	50	3.67	124	40	95	6	3	0
Career	32	30	206.2	83	3.61	194	81	149	14	5	0
Projected	28	28	177.1	68	3.45	169	52	139	13	8	0

Matt Williams 3B

Age: 30 **Seasons:** 9
Height: 6' 2" **Weight:** 216
Bats: Right **Throws:** Right
1995 OBP: .399 **1995 SLG:** .647

A fractured foot derailed his season, but Williams still posted better stats than all but a couple of the club's everyday players last year. Soft hands and snappy reflexes make him a Gold Glover at the hot corner.

	G	AB	H	2B	3B	HR	RS	RBI	BB	SB	CS	BA
1995	76	283	95	17	1	23	53	65	30	2	0	.336
Career	1015	3735	970	163	24	225	525	647	233	28	25	.260
Projected	151	542	144	25	2	47	94	111	38	1	2	.266

Kenny Rogers

American League

1995 Review

When the strike-stunted season finally got under way on April 26, AL fans willing to at least partially forgive their national pastime were rewarded with a classic campaign, albeit with a wild-card twist.

In the East the story was a nonstory—the collapse that never came. History-savvy fans in Boston and New York were ready for the Red Sox to fold (and if the season had lasted another 18 games, who knows?), but a 14-game cushion at the start of September protected the Bosox from a late Bombers rush as Boston took the division title and New York settled for a wild-card playoff berth.

In the Central the Indians wound up racing themselves (and winning!), setting their sights on a 100-victory year when it became apparent that their division competition would be providing little competition after all. The second-place Royals seemed to have command of the wild-card fight in early September, but a three-game sweep by the Mariners effectively put K.C. to bed.

The wild West offered the AL's only close division race. Seattle faced a 13-game, early-August deficit to the Angels, but Jay Buhner blasted 13 homers in September and the Mariners took the title by winning a one-game playoff.

Playoff highlights included a brilliantly contested five-game series between Seattle and New York, with the Mariners prevailing. Cleveland was denied home-field advantage despite owning baseball's best regular-season record, but neither Boston in the first round nor the M's in the ALCS could stop the Indians from making their first World Series appearance since 1954.

1995 Final Standings

EASTERN DIVISION

Team	Won	Lost	Pct	GB
Boston	86	58	.597	—
New York	79	65	.549	7.0
Baltimore	71	73	.493	15.0
Detroit	60	84	.417	26.0
Toronto	56	88	.389	30.0

CENTRAL DIVISION

Team	Won	Lost	Pct	GB
Cleveland	100	44	.694	—
Kansas City	70	74	.486	30.0
Chicago	68	76	.472	32.0
Milwaukee	65	79	.451	35.0
Minnesota	56	88	.389	44.0

WESTERN DIVISION

Team	Won	Lost	Pct	GB
Seattle	79	66	.545	—
California	78	67	.538	1.0
Texas	74	70	.514	4.5
Oakland	67	77	.465	11.5

First-Round Playoffs: Seattle 3, New York 2; Cleveland 3, Boston 0

League Championship: Cleveland 4, Seattle 2

World Series: Atlanta 4, Cleveland 2

Team Statistics

BATTING

TEAM	BA	G	RS	H	2B	3B	HR	RBI	BB	SB	SLG
Cleveland	.291	144	840	1461	279	23	207	803	542	132	.479
Boston	.280	144	791	1399	286	31	175	754	560	99	.455
Chicago	.280	145	755	1417	252	37	146	712	576	110	.431
Minnesota	.279	144	703	1398	270	34	120	662	471	105	.419
California	.277	145	801	1390	252	25	186	761	564	57	.448
New York	.276	145	749	1365	280	34	122	709	625	50	.420
Seattle	.276	145	796	1377	276	20	182	767	549	110	.448
Milwaukee	.266	144	740	1329	249	42	128	700	502	105	.409
Texas	.265	144	691	1304	247	24	138	651	526	90	.410
Oakland	.264	144	730	1296	228	18	169	694	565	112	.421
Baltimore	.262	144	704	1267	229	27	173	668	574	92	.428
Kansas City	.260	144	629	1275	240	35	119	578	475	120	.396
Toronto	.260	144	642	1309	275	27	140	613	492	75	.409
Detroit	.247	144	654	1204	228	29	159	619	551	73	.404

PITCHING

TEAM	W	L	ERA	G	SV	H	ER	HR	BB	SO	OBA
Cleveland	100	44	3.83	144	50	1261	554	135	445	926	.255
Baltimore	71	73	4.31	144	29	1165	607	149	523	930	.245
Boston	86	58	4.39	144	39	1338	631	127	476	888	.268
Kansas City	70	74	4.49	144	37	1323	642	142	503	763	.268
Seattle	79	66	4.50	145	39	1343	644	149	591	1068	.268
California	78	67	4.52	145	42	1310	645	163	486	901	.265
New York	79	65	4.56	145	35	1286	651	159	535	908	.261
Texas	74	70	4.66	144	34	1385	665	152	514	838	.278
Milwaukee	65	79	4.82	144	31	1391	689	146	603	699	.280
Chicago	68	76	4.85	145	36	1374	693	164	617	892	.275
Toronto	56	88	4.88	144	22	1336	701	145	654	894	.268
Oakland	67	77	4.93	144	34	1320	698	153	556	890	.269
Detroit	60	84	5.49	144	38	1509	778	170	536	729	.296
Minnesota	56	88	5.76	144	27	1450	815	210	533	790	.287

Edgar Martinez

Departmental Leaders

BATTING

Batting Average

Edgar Martinez, SEA	.356
Chuck Knoblauch, MIN	.333
Tim Salmon, CAL	.330
Wade Boggs, NY	.324
Eddie Murray, CLE	.323
B.J. Surhoff, MIL	.320
Chili Davis, CAL	.318
Albert Belle, CLE	.317
Carlos Baerga, CLE	.314
Kirby Puckett, MIN	.314
Jim Thome, CLE	.314

Hits

Lance Johnson, CHI	186
Edgar Martinez, SEA	182
Chuck Knoblauch, MIN	179
Tim Salmon, CAL	177
Carlos Baerga, CLE	175
Otis Nixon, TEX	174
Albert Belle, CLE	173
Bernie Williams, NY	173
Rafael Palmeiro, BAL	172
Kirby Puckett, MIN	169

Runs Scored

Albert Belle, CLE	121
Edgar Martinez, SEA	121
Jim Edmonds, CAL	120
Tony Phillips, CAL	119
Tim Salmon, CAL	111
Brady Anderson, BAL	108
John Valentin, BOS	108
Chuck Knoblauch, MIN	107
Frank Thomas, CHI	102
Lance Johnson, CHI	98
Mo Vaughn, BOS	98

Runs Batted In

Albert Belle, CLE	126
Mo Vaughn, BOS	126
Jay Buhner, SEA	121
Edgar Martinez, SEA	113
Tino Martinez, SEA	111
Frank Thomas, CHI	111
Jim Edmonds, CAL	107
Manny Ramirez, CLE	107
Tim Salmon, CAL	105
Rafael Palmeiro, BAL	104

At-Bats Per RBI

Jay Buhner, SEA	3.9
Albert Belle, CLE	4.3
Mo Vaughn, BOS	4.4
Frank Thomas, CHI	4.4
Edgar Martinez, SEA	4.5
Manny Ramirez, CLE	4.5
Mike Blowers, SEA	4.6
Tino Martinez, SEA	4.7
Paul O'Neill, NY	4.8
Mike Stanley, NY	4.8

Doubles

Albert Belle, CLE	52
Edgar Martinez, SEA	52
Kirby Puckett, MIN	39
John Valentin, BOS	37
Tino Martinez, SEA	35
Chuck Knoblauch, MIN	34
Tim Salmon, CAL	34
Brady Anderson, BAL	33
Cal Ripken, BAL	33
Kevin Seitzer, MIL	33

Triples

Kenny Lofton, CLE	13
Lance Johnson, CHI	12
Brady Anderson, BAL	10
Bernie Williams, NY	9
Chuck Knoblauch, MIN	8
Roberto Alomar, TOR	7
Fernando Vina, MIL	7
Vince Coleman, SEA	6
Gary DiSarcina, CAL	6
Ray Durham, CHI	6
Darryl Hamilton, MIL	6

Triples (continued)

David Hulse, MIL	6
Jon Nunnally, KC	6
Troy O'Leary, BOS	6

Home Runs

Albert Belle, CLE	50
Jay Buhner, SEA	40
Frank Thomas, CHI	40
Mark McGwire, OAK	39
Rafael Palmeiro, BAL	39
Mo Vaughn, BOS	39
Gary Gaetti, KC	35
Tim Salmon, CAL	34
Jim Edmonds, CAL	33
Mickey Tettleton, TEX	32

At-Bats Per Home Run

Albert Belle, CLE	10.9
Jay Buhner, SEA	11.8
Frank Thomas, CHI	12.3
Mickey Tettleton, TEX	13.4
Mo Vaughn, BOS	14.1
Rafael Palmeiro, BAL	14.2
Gary Gaetti, KC	14.7
Manny Ramirez, CLE	15.6
Tim Salmon, CAL	15.8
Cecil Fielder, DET	15.9

On-Base Percentage

Edgar Martinez, SEA	.479
Frank Thomas, CHI	.454
Jim Thome, CLE	.438
Chili Davis, CAL	.429
Tim Salmon, CAL	.429
Chuck Knoblauch, MIN	.424
Tim Naehring, BOS	.415
Wade Boggs, NY	.412
Rickey Henderson, OAK	.407
Harold Baines, BAL	.403

Slugging Percentage

Albert Belle, CLE	.690
Edgar Martinez, SEA	.628
Frank Thomas, CHI	.606
Tim Salmon, CAL	.594
Rafael Palmeiro, BAL	.583
Mo Vaughn, BOS	.575

Jay Buhner, SEA	.566
Manny Ramirez, CLE	.558
Jim Thome, CLE	.558
Jose Canseco, BOS	.556

Total Bases

Albert Belle, CLE	377
Rafael Palmeiro, BAL	323
Edgar Martinez, SEA	321
Tim Salmon, CAL	319
Mo Vaughn, BOS	316
Jim Edmonds, CAL	299
Frank Thomas, CHI	299
Tino Martinez, SEA	286
Kirby Puckett, MIN	277
John Valentin, BOS	277

Walks

Frank Thomas, CHI	136
Edgar Martinez, SEA	116
Tony Phillips, CAL	113
Mickey Tettleton, TEX	107
Jim Thome, CLE	97
Tim Salmon, CAL	91
Chili Davis, CAL	89
Mark McGwire, OAK	88
Brady Anderson, BAL	87
John Olerud, TOR	84

Strikeouts

Mo Vaughn, BOS	150
Benji Gil, TEX	147
Tony Phillips, CAL	135
Jim Edmonds, CAL	130
Mike Blowers, SEA	128
Jay Buhner, SEA	120
Cecil Fielder, DET	116
Alex Gonzalez, TOR	114
Jim Thome, CLE	113
Manny Ramirez, CLE	112

Stolen Bases

Kenny Lofton, CLE	54
Tom Goodwin, KC	50
Otis Nixon, TEX	50
Chuck Knoblauch, MIN	46
Vince Coleman, SEA	42
Lance Johnson, CHI	40

Stan Javier, OAK	36
Rickey Henderson, OAK	32
Roberto Alomar, TOR	30
Omar Vizquel, CLE	29

Caught Stealing

Otis Nixon, TEX	21
Tom Goodwin, KC	18
Chuck Knoblauch, MIN	18
Vince Coleman, SEA	16
Chad Curtis, DET	15
Kenny Lofton, CLE	15
Omar Vizquel, CLE	11
Mark McLemore, TEX	11
Tony Phillips, CAL	10
Luis Alicea, BOS	10
Rickey Henderson, OAK	10

PITCHING

Earned Run Average

Randy Johnson, SEA	2.48
Tim Wakefield, BOS	2.95
Dennis Martinez, CLE	3.08
Mike Mussina, BAL	3.29
Kenny Rogers, TEX	3.38
David Cone, NY	3.57
Kevin Brown, BAL	3.60
Al Leiter, TOR	3.64
Jim Abbott, CAL	3.70
Mark Gubicza, KC	3.75

Innings Pitched

David Cone, NY	229.1
Mike Mussina, BAL	221.2
Jack McDowell, NY	217.2
Randy Johnson, SEA	214.1
Mark Gubicza, KC	213.1
Todd Stottlemyre, OAK	209.2
Kenny Rogers, TEX	208.0
Alex Fernandez, CHI	203.2
Chuck Finley, CAL	203.0
Steve Sparks, MIL	202.0

Complete Games

Jack McDowell, NY	8
Scott Erickson, BAL	7

Mike Mussina, BAL	7
David Cone, NY	6
Randy Johnson, SEA	6
Tim Wakefield, BOS	6
Alex Fernandez, CHI	5
Jim Abbott, CAL	4
Kevin Appier, KC	4
Kevin Gross, TEX	4
Sterling Hitchcock, NY	4
Bob Tewksbury, TEX	4

Wins

Mike Mussina, BAL	19
David Cone, NY	18
Randy Johnson, SEA	18
Kenny Rogers, TEX	17
Orel Hershiser, CLE	16
Charles Nagy, CLE	16
Tim Wakefield, BOS	16
Kevin Appier, KC	15
Chuck Finley, CAL	15
Erik Hanson, BOS	15
Mark Langston, CAL	15
Jack McDowell, NY	15

Winning Percentage

Randy Johnson, SEA	.900
David Wells, DET	.769
Erik Hanson, BOS	.750
Orel Hershiser, CLE	.727
Charles Nagy, CLE	.727
Kenny Rogers, TEX	.708
Dennis Martinez, CLE	.706
David Cone, NY	.692
Mark Langston, CAL	.682
Mike Mussina, BAL	.679

Losses

Jason Bere, CHI	15
Kevin Gross, TEX	15
Mike Moore, DET	15
Mark Gubicza, KC	14
Juan Guzman, TOR	14
Pat Hentgen, TOR	14
Brad Radke, MIN	14
Felipe Lira, DET	13
Tim Belcher, SEA	12
Ricky Bones, MIL	12

Losses (continued)

Chuck Finley, CAL	12
Tom Gordon, KC	12

Saves

Jose Mesa, CLE	46
Lee Smith, CAL	37
Rick Aguilera, BOS	32
Roberto Hernandez, CHI	32
Jeff Montgomery, KC	31
John Wetteland, NY	31
Dennis Eckersley, OAK	29
Mike Fetters, MIL	22
Doug Jones, BAL	22
Jeff Russell, TEX	20

Strikeouts

Randy Johnson, SEA	294
Todd Stottlemyre, OAK	205
Chuck Finley, CAL	195
David Cone, NY	191
Kevin Appier, KC	185
Alex Fernandez, CHI	159
Mike Mussina, BAL	158
Jack McDowell, NY	157
Al Leiter, TOR	153
Roger Pavlik, TEX	149

Strikeouts Per Nine Innings

Randy Johnson, SEA	12.3
Todd Stottlemyre, OAK	8.8
Chuck Finley, CAL	8.6
Kevin Appier, KC	8.3
David Cone, NY	7.5
Al Leiter, TOR	7.5
Alex Fernandez, CHI	7.0
Charles Nagy, CLE	7.0
Roger Pavlik, TEX	7.0
Erik Hanson, BOS	6.7

Walks

Al Leiter, TOR	108
Jason Bere, CHI	106
Wilson Alvarez, CHI	93
Chuck Finley, CAL	93
Pat Hentgen, TOR	90
Roger Pavlik, TEX	90
Tom Gordon, KC	89

Kevin Gross, TEX	89
Tim Belcher, SEA	88
David Cone, NY	88

Walks Per Nine Innings

Mike Mussina, BAL	2.0
Dennis Martinez, CLE	2.2
Brad Radke, MIN	2.3
Kevin Brown, BAL	2.5
Mark Gubicza, KC	2.6
Orel Hershiser, CLE	2.7
Randy Johnson, SEA	2.7
Erik Hanson, BOS	2.8
Alex Fernandez, CHI	2.9
Mark Langston, CAL	2.9

Hits

Pat Hentgen, TOR	236
Todd Stottlemyre, OAK	228
Mark Gubicza, KC	222
Ricky Bones, MIL	218
Scott Erickson, BAL	213
Mark Langston, CAL	212
Chris Bosio, SEA	211
Jack McDowell, NY	211
Steve Sparks, MIL	210
Jim Abbott, CAL	209

Hits Per Nine Innings

Randy Johnson, SEA	6.68
Kevin Appier, KC	7.29
Tim Wakefield, BOS	7.51
Mike Mussina, BAL	7.59
David Cone, NY	7.65
Al Leiter, TOR	7.97
Kevin Brown, BAL	8.09
Orel Hershiser, CLE	8.12
Roger Pavlik, TEX	8.17
Sterling Hitchcock, NY	8.29

Opponents Batting Average

Randy Johnson, SEA	.201
Kevin Appier, KC	.221
Mike Mussina, BAL	.226
Tim Wakefield, BOS	.227
David Cone, NY	.228
Al Leiter, TOR	.238
Kevin Brown, BAL	.241

Roger Pavlik, TEX	.243
Kenny Rogers, TEX	.243
Orel Hershiser, CLE	.244

Home Runs

Brad Radke, MIN	32
Kevin Gross, TEX	27
Ricky Bones, MIL	26
Kenny Rogers, TEX	26
Todd Stottlemyre, OAK	26
Danny Darwin, TEX	25
Jack McDowell, NY	25
Brian Anderson, CAL	24
David Cone, NY	24
Mike Harkey, CAL	24
Pat Hentgen, TOR	24
Mike Moore, DET	24
Mike Mussina, BAL	24

Wild Pitches

Al Leiter, TOR	14
Sean Bergman, DET	13
Chuck Finley, CAL	13
David Cone, NY	11
Edwin Hurtado, TOR	11
Todd Stottlemyre, OAK	11
Tim Wakefield, BOS	11
Chris Bosio, SEA	10
Kirk McCaskill, CHI	10
Roger Pavlik, TEX	10

1996 Preview

There should be a three-way scramble in the East, and though free agency is likely to play a major role, young pitching could be the deciding factor. The Yankees will once again look to Sterling Hitchcock and Andy Pettitte to solidify their starting staff, while the Orioles have high expectations for Jimmy Haynes. The Red Sox will hope to re-create last year's patchwork-rotation magic, but injury-free seasons from Rocket Clemens and Aaron Sele would make things much simpler in Boston. Detroit will have a new manager but the same distinct lack of pitching, while the Blue Jays will also need six runs per game to make up for the absence of a deep starting staff.

The Indians are the class of the Central, and if injuries and age don't undercut Cleveland's veteran pitching staff, the small-market rivals in Minnesota, Milwaukee, and Kansas City will offer little challenge. Expect the White Sox to rebound somewhat from last year's collapse, but it will qualify as a big surprise if the Pale Hose can run with the Tribe.

The AL West is baseball's most unpredictable division, and any one of its four teams are capable of capturing the division crown. Seattle has to be an early favorite to repeat last year's first-place finish, but the M's have questionable pitching at press time. If the California hitters generate an encore of their 1995 fireworks, the Angels will be tough to beat. It won't be a shock if the Rangers make their first postseason appearance, but you wouldn't want to bet the ranch on it, either. Oakland appears to have completely relinquished its hold on the division, and only an infusion of fresh bats will keep the A's from occupying the cellar for the second straight year.

1996 Projected Standings

EASTERN DIVISION

Team	Won	Lost	Pct	GB
New York	92	70	.568	—
Baltimore	90	72	.556	2
Boston	84	78	.519	8
Detroit	72	90	.444	20
Toronto	69	93	.426	23

CENTRAL DIVISION

Team	Won	Lost	Pct	GB
Cleveland	101	61	.623	—
Chicago	84	78	.519	17
Kansas City	79	83	.488	22
Minnesota	70	92	.432	31
Milwaukee	69	93	.463	32

WESTERN DIVISION

Team	Won	Lost	Pct	GB
Seattle	88	74	.543	—
California	81	81	.500	7
Oakland	79	83	.488	9
Texas	76	86	.469	12

First-Round Playoffs: Cleveland 3, Baltimore 2; New York 3, Seattle 2

League Championship: New York 4, Cleveland 2

World Series: Atlanta 4, New York 3

Projected Statistical Leaders

BATTING

Batting Average
Kenny Lofton	.368
Edgar Martinez	.354
Wade Boggs	.336

Home Runs
Albert Belle	56
Ken Griffey	49
Frank Thomas	44

Runs Batted In
Albert Belle	137
Ken Griffey	135
Bobby Bonilla	131

PITCHING

Wins
Randy Johnson	24
Mike Mussina	22
Kevin Appier	20

Earned Run Average
Randy Johnson	2.60
Kevin Appier	2.62
Alex Fernandez	2.80

Strikeouts
Randy Johnson	304
Kevin Appier	213
David Cone	202

Projected All-Stars

First Team
First Base: Rafael Palmeiro
Second Base: Roberto Alomar
Shortstop: Cal Ripken
Third Base: Travis Fryman
Catcher: Ivan Rodriguez
Outfield: Albert Belle
Outfield: Tim Salmon
Outfield: Ken Griffey
Designated Hitter: Frank Thomas
Starting Pitcher: Randy Johnson
Relief Pitcher: Jose Mesa

Second Team
First Base: Mo Vaughn
Second Base: Chuck Knoblauch
Shortstop: John Valentin
Third Base: Jim Thome
Catcher: Sandy Alomar
Outfield: Bernie Williams
Outfield: Kenny Lofton
Outfield: Manny Ramirez
Designated Hitter: Edgar Martinez
Starting Pitcher: Mike Mussina
Relief Pitcher: John Wetteland

Mike Mussina

Baltimore
ORIOLES

Scouting Report

Outfielders: Brady Anderson, who is entering the final year of his contract, has great range and can be penciled in for 15 dingers and 25 steals per year. The O's young center fielder, Curtis Goodwin, possesses every trait of a super leadoff hitter except the most crucial—a knack for getting on base. As a switch-hitting slugger, Bobby Bonilla preys on mistakes, but as an erratic right fielder he's prone to mistakes. Neither of 1995's triple-A call-ups, Mark Smith and Sherman Obando, appear ready to play fulltime.

Infielders: The Birds used a platoon of Jeff Manto and Leo Gomez at third base last season. Manto offers big-time power and the offensive diversity of a sledgehammer. Bobby Bonilla could be inserted at the hot corner this year. The O's hope Roberto Alomar signs on to play second base, but at press time the position is open. Rookie Brad Tyler, coming off a stellar triple-A season, projects as the in-house frontrunner. Bret Barberie or Manny Alexander could provide depth. Cal Ripken is a legend at shortstop, while first baseman Rafael Palmeiro is Baltimore's best hitter.

Catchers: Underrated veteran Chris Hoiles displays plus power and top-level backstop skills. Greg Zaun came up from Rochester last season and played steady defense. He's not considered a top prospect, but he made good contact and flashed some longball pop.

Designated Hitters: Free agent bopper Harold Baines is the definition of a professional hitter, but the Orioles are reportedly trying to coax Eddie Murray back to Baltimore.

Starting Pitchers: The Orioles have an ace, Mike Mussina, who can match up with any starter in the league, but the rotation starts to wobble in spots two through five. Ben McDonald's stuff has gradually deteriorated due to arm injuries, but he's young enough to bounce back. Kevin Brown closed the 1995 season with a rush, then filed for free agency. Rick Krivda's breaking stuff keeps hitters in the dark, but he needs pinpoint control to keep from being lit up. Scott Erickson, who has been awful for the past three years, finished strongly enough to stay on the staff. The organization's top pitching prospect, Jimmy Haynes, flashed ace-quality stuff in his three late-season starts.

Relief Pitchers: Hard-throwing Armando Benitez has long been considered the Orioles' closer of the future, but he blew three of five save chances in his first extended trial. Jesse Orosco provides lefthanded setup, but the bullpen is thin at press time.

Outlook

The Orioles enter 1996 with several concerns, not the least of which is age. Baltimore's top players—Ripken, Bonilla, Palmeiro, Hoiles, and Anderson—are all past 30, so their window of opportunity to win as a group could soon be shut. The pitching staff is anchored brilliantly by Mike Mussina, but he'll need help from at least one of the kids, with Jimmy Haynes being the most likely young hurler to provide assistance. There are looming questions in the bullpen, too, but this much is certain—life with Cal is always a pleasure at Camden Yards.

Fungoes

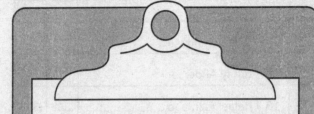

Quick Quiz: Which relief pitcher made ten starts in his first 400 appearances, then hurled three complete games (including a no-hitter) in his first season as an Oriole (1958)?

Franchise Milestone: Since moving to Baltimore in 1954, the organization has won three World Series titles (1966, 1970, and 1983).

Top Pitcher: Jim Palmer, 1965–84

Top Player: Cal Ripken, 1981–

Top Manager: Earl Weaver, 1968–86

Wacky Nickname: Hoover (Brooks Calbert Robinson)

Quick Quiz Answer: Hoyt Wilhelm

Lineup Card

NO	POS	PLAYER	OBP	SLG
28	CF	Curtis Goodwin	.301	.332
9	LF	Brady Anderson	.371	.444
25	1B	Rafael Palmeiro	.380	.583
26	RF	Bobby Bonilla	.392	.544
8	SS	Cal Ripken	.324	.422
00	DH	TBD	.000	.000
23	C	Chris Hoiles	.373	.460
12	3B	Jeff Manto	.325	.492
00	2B	TBD	.000	.000

In a Nutshell: Goodwin may eventually bat .300 and steal 60 or 70 bases, but his lack of an acquaintance with the base on balls is uncharacteristic of a leadoff hitter. If the O's win the Roberto Alomar sweepstakes, Alomar will probably bat second, with Brady Anderson taking the leadoff spot. The Orioles have home-run clout in slots three through seven, but the overall lineup is somewhat one-dimensional. The addition of Bobby Bo provides a pure slugger in the cleanup spot, and Ripken, though clearly in his twilight years, appears to have at least one or two productive seasons left in his bat. The DH slot remains unfilled at press time. Barring major injuries, the Orioles figure to have no trouble scoring runs.

Oriole Park at Camden Yards

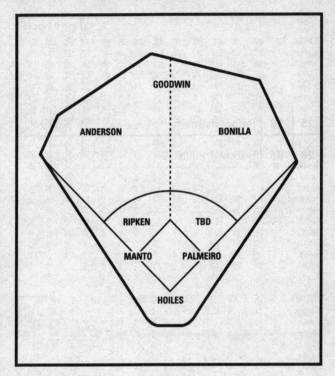

Capacity: 48,262
Turf: Natural

LF Line: 333
RF Line: 318
Center: 400
Left CF: 410
Right CF: 373

Tickets:
410-685-9800

Elegant and electrifying, this is a shrine for players and fans alike. The outfield fences are just the right height for the likes of Brady Anderson to take away potential home runs. And there are plenty of opportunities because the park is friendly to hitters, especially Rafael Palmeiro, who last year hit 49 points higher at Camden Yards (.336) than on the road (.287).

Statistics

Minimum 25 at-bats or 10.0 innings pitched

PLAYER	BA	G	AB	RS	H	TB	2B	3B	HR	RBI	BB	SO	SB	CS
Bonilla	.333	61	237	47	79	129	12	4	10	47	23	31	0	2
Palmeiro	.310	143	554	89	172	323	30	2	39	104	62	65	3	1
Baines	.299	127	385	60	115	208	19	1	24	63	70	45	0	2
Goodwin	.263	87	289	40	76	96	11	3	1	24	15	53	22	4
Obando	.263	16	38	0	10	11	1	0	0	3	2	12	1	0
Anderson	.262	143	554	108	145	246	33	10	16	64	87	111	26	7
Ripken	.262	144	550	71	144	232	33	2	17	88	52	59	0	1
Zaun	.260	40	104	18	27	41	5	0	3	14	16	14	1	1
Manto	.256	90	254	31	65	125	9	0	17	38	24	69	0	3
Hoiles	.250	114	352	53	88	162	15	1	19	58	67	80	1	0
Huson	.248	66	161	24	40	51	4	2	1	19	15	20	5	4
Bass	.244	111	295	32	72	99	12	0	5	32	24	47	8	8
Hammonds	.242	57	178	18	43	66	9	1	4	23	9	30	4	2
Barberie	.241	90	237	32	57	77	14	0	2	25	36	50	3	3
Alexander	.236	94	242	35	57	77	9	1	3	23	20	30	10	4
Gomez	.236	53	127	16	30	47	5	0	4	12	18	23	0	1
Smith	.231	37	104	11	24	38	5	0	3	15	12	22	3	0
Van Slyke	.159	17	63	6	10	20	1	0	3	8	5	15	0	0
Brown	.148	18	27	2	4	5	1	0	0	1	7	9	1	1
Nokes	.122	26	49	4	6	13	1	0	2	6	4	11	0	0
Buford	.063	24	32	6	2	2	0	0	0	2	6	7	3	1

PITCHER	W	L	SV	ERA	G	GS	CG	SH	IP	H	R	ER	BB	SO
Haynes	2	1	0	2.25	4	3	0	0	24.0	11	6	6	12	22
Orosco	2	4	3	3.26	65	0	0	0	49.2	28	19	18	27	58
Mussina	19	9	0	3.29	32	32	7	4	221.2	187	86	81	50	158
Clark	2	5	1	3.46	40	0	0	0	39.0	40	15	15	15	18
Brown	10	9	0	3.60	26	26	3	1	172.1	155	73	69	48	117
McDonald	3	6	0	4.16	14	13	1	0	80.0	67	40	37	38	62
Oquist	2	1	0	4.17	27	0	0	0	54.0	51	27	25	41	27
Krivda	2	7	0	4.54	13	13	1	0	75.1	76	40	38	25	53
Erickson	13	10	0	4.81	32	31	7	2	196.1	213	108	105	67	106
Lee	2	0	1	4.86	39	0	0	0	33.1	31	18	18	18	27
Jones	0	4	22	5.01	52	0	0	0	46.2	55	29	26	16	42
Hartley	1	0	0	5.14	8	0	0	0	14.0	13	8	8	3	6
Moyer	8	6	0	5.21	27	18	0	0	115.2	117	70	67	30	65
Benitez	1	5	2	5.66	44	0	0	0	47.2	37	33	30	37	56
Rhodes	2	5	0	6.21	19	9	0	0	75.1	68	53	52	48	77
Fernandez	0	4	0	7.39	8	7	0	0	28.0	36	26	23	17	31
Mills	3	0	0	7.43	21	0	0	0	23.0	30	20	19	18	16

Roster

MANAGER: Davey Johnson
COACHES: TBD

NO	PITCHERS	B	T	HT	WT	DOB
49	Armando Benitez	R	R	6-4	220	11/3/72
77	Joe Borowski	R	R	6-2	225	5/4/71
36	Terry Clark	R	R	6-2	196	10/10/60
21	Scott Erickson	R	R	6-4	222	2/2/68
29	Gene Harris	R	R	5-11	195	12/5/64
60	Jimmy Haynes	R	R	6-4	185	9/5/72
37	Rick Krivda	R	L	6-1	180	1/19/70
52	Mark Lee	L	L	6-3	215	7/20/64
19	Ben McDonald	R	R	6-7	214	11/24/67
35	Mike Mussina	R	R	6-2	185	12/8/68
56	Mike Oquist	R	R	6-2	170	5/30/68
47	Jesse Orosco	R	L	6-2	205	4/21/57
53	Arthur Rhodes	L	L	6-2	206	10/24/69
	CATCHERS					
59	Cesar Devarez	R	R	5-10	175	9/22/69
23	Chris Hoiles	R	R	6-0	213	3/20/65
24	Greg Zaun	S	R	5-10	170	4/14/71
	INFIELDERS					
1	Manny Alexander	R	R	5-10	165	3/20/71
2	Bret Barberie	S	R	5-11	180	8/16/67
10	Leo Gomez	R	R	6-0	208	3/2/67
30	Jeff Huson	L	R	6-3	180	8/15/64
12	Jeffrey Manto	R	R	6-3	210	8/23/64
25	Rafael Palmeiro	L	L	6-0	188	9/24/64
8	Cal Ripken	R	R	6-4	220	8/24/60
	OUTFIELDERS					
9	Brady Anderson	L	L	6-1	195	1/18/64
26	Bobby Bonilla	S	R	6-3	240	2/23/63
28	Curtis Goodwin	L	L	5-11	180	9/30/72
11	Jeffrey Hammonds	R	R	6-0	195	3/5/71
42	Sherman Obando	R	R	6-4	215	1/23/70
34	Mark Smith	R	R	6-3	205	5/7/70

FREE AGENTS: Harold Baines, Kevin Bass, Kevin Brown, Mark Eichhorn, Doug Jones, Jamie Moyer

Brady Anderson   *OF*

Age: 32   **Seasons:** 8
Height: 6' 1"   **Weight:** 195
Bats: Left   **Throws:** Left
1995 OBP: .371   **1995 SLG:** .444

Remember when Anderson was an underachieving prospect? It's enough to make you feel old, but he's entering the final year of his contract. A fine all-around player, he provides thrills in left field, speed on the basepaths, and pop at the plate.

	G	AB	H	2B	3B	HR	RS	RBI	BB	SB	CS	BA
1995	143	554	145	33	10	16	108	64	87	26	7	.262
Career	945	3271	817	164	44	72	512	346	459	187	53	.250
Projected	158	622	154	29	7	14	114	66	97	35	8	.248

Harold Baines   *DH*

Age: 37   **Seasons:** 16
Height: 6' 2"   **Weight:** 195
Bats: Left   **Throws:** Left
1995 OBP: .403   **1995 SLG:** .540

We hope he never retires. Watching him hit is pure church, and his ability to maintain a power stroke while walking more than he strikes out is truly rare. His career highlights include a league-topping .541 slugging percentage in 1984.

	G	AB	H	2B	3B	HR	RS	RBI	BB	SB	CS	BA
1995	127	385	115	19	1	24	60	63	70	0	2	.299
Career	2183	7871	2271	387	48	301	1033	1261	804	30	30	.289
Projected	139	419	129	22	0	23	58	71	77	0	1	.308

Armando Benitez P

Age: 23   **Seasons:** R
Height: 6' 4"   **Weight:** 220
Bats: Right   **Throws:** Right
1995 OBA: .213   **1995 WHIP:** 1.55

Thanks to his blazing heater, Benitez has been nearly untouchable at every minor-league level, but as most fans know, it takes more than velocity to succeed in the Show. If he ever develops command of a breaking ball, he'll be an imposing closer.

	G	GS	IP	ER	ERA	H	BB	SO	W	L	SV
1995	44	0	47.2	30	5.66	37	37	56	1	5	2
Career	47	0	57.2	31	4.84	45	41	70	1	5	2
Projected	49	0	55.1	29	4.72	42	44	71	2	5	21

Bobby Bonilla OF

Age: 33   **Seasons:** 10
Height: 6' 3"   **Weight:** 240
Bats: Switch   **Throws:** Right
1995 OBP: .388   **1995 SLG:** .575

Bobby Bo is a whale of a hitter from both sides of the plate, and contrary to his reputation, he usually plays hard. He isn't a natural fielder at either third base or in right field, though his ineptness has been vastly overstated.

	G	AB	H	2B	3B	HR	RS	RBI	BB	SB	CS	BA
1995	141	554	182	37	8	28	96	99	54	0	5	.329
Career	1434	5191	1472	306	49	217	809	849	644	36	44	.284
Projected	154	577	176	34	4	31	111	131	57	1	3	.305

Kevin Brown P

Age: 31   **Seasons:** 9
Height: 6' 4"   **Weight:** 195
Bats: Right   **Throws:** Right
1995 OBA: .241   **1995 WHIP:** 1.18

Once projected to be a future Rocket Clemens, the enigmatic Brown hasn't been able to build on his 21-victory performance in 1992, though he pitched well enough last season to finish with the league's seventh-best ERA.

	G	GS	IP	ER	ERA	H	BB	SO	W	L	SV
1995	26	26	172.1	69	3.60	155	48	117	10	9	0
Career	213	212	1451.0	610	3.78	1477	476	859	88	73	0
Projected	34	34	245.2	86	3.15	219	55	143	15	9	0

Scott Erickson P

Age: 28   **Seasons:** 6
Height: 6' 4"   **Weight:** 222
Bats: Right   **Throws:** Right
1995 OBA: .281   **1995 WHIP:** 1.43

Erickson's past successes (including 20 wins in 1991 and a no-hitter in early 1994) have earned him plenty of chances to prove his worth as a pitcher, but his plus-5.00 aggregate ERA over the past three seasons is unsightly.

	G	GS	IP	ER	ERA	H	BB	SO	W	L	SV
1995	32	31	196.1	105	4.81	213	67	106	13	10	0
Career	172	169	1088.0	506	4.19	1146	402	588	70	64	0
Projected	34	34	207.0	102	4.43	221	65	112	11	13	0

Curtis Goodwin OF

Age: 23   **Seasons:** 1
Height: 5' 11"   **Weight:** 180
Bats: Left   **Throws:** Left
1995 OBP: .301   **1995 SLG:** .332

A terrific percentage basestealer who plays an exhilarating center field, his value as a leadoff hitter is minimal because he doesn't get on base. He's young enough to develop, but at this stage Goodwin is a notch below a poor man's Vince Coleman.

	G	AB	H	2B	3B	HR	RS	RBI	BB	SB	CS	BA
1995	87	289	76	11	3	1	40	24	15	22	4	.263
Career	87	289	76	11	3	1	40	24	15	22	4	.263
Projected	147	586	168	17	8	2	74	36	32	46	7	.287

Jimmy Haynes P

Age: 23   **Seasons:** R
Height: 6' 4"   **Weight:** 185
Bats: Right   **Throws:** Right
1995 OBA: .136   **1995 WHIP:** 0.96

Haynes was one of the International League's top five starters last season, and he was very impressive in a late-season cup of coffee with the big club. His fastball runs 90-plus mph, and his curveball and command are both excellent.

	G	GS	IP	ER	ERA	H	BB	SO	W	L	SV
1995	4	3	24.0	6	2.25	11	12	22	2	1	0
Career	8	3	27.2	6	1.95	14	15	23	2	1	0
Projected	24	24	169.1	58	3.08	146	67	143	13	6	0

Chris Hoiles   C

Age: 31   **Seasons:** 7
Height: 6' 0"   **Weight:** 213
Bats: Right   **Throws:** Right
1995 OBP: .373   **1995 SLG:** .460

Hoiles rates as an acceptable-to-good defensive backstop, but he earns his pay with the bat. Though he's susceptible to sluggish starts, his power numbers are impressive and he draws a lion's share of walks per at-bat. He hit .310 back in 1993.

	G	AB	H	2B	3B	HR	RS	RBI	BB	SB	CS	BA
1995	114	352	88	15	1	19	53	58	67	1	0	.250
Career	571	1826	481	82	2	99	270	271	289	4	5	.263
Projected	121	404	121	21	0	24	75	86	73	1	1	.300

Rick Krivda   P

Age: 26   **Seasons:** 1
Height: 6' 1"   **Weight:** 180
Bats: Right   **Throws:** Left
1995 OBA: .266   **1995 WHIP:** 1.34

A finesse-type southpaw with a nifty curveball, Krivda racks up his share of strikeouts and can be very tough on lefty batters. His stats in triple-A were solid if not overwhelming, and he topped the entire minor leagues in strikeouts in 1992.

	G	GS	IP	ER	ERA	H	BB	SO	W	L	SV
1995	13	13	75.1	38	4.54	76	25	53	2	7	0
Career	13	13	75.1	38	4.54	76	25	53	2	7	0
Projected	19	19	129.2	55	3.82	136	42	104	8	7	0

Ben McDonald P

Age: 28   **Seasons:** 7
Height: 6' 7"   **Weight:** 214
Bats: Right   **Throws:** Right
1995 OBA: .224   **1995 WHIP:** 1.31

It's been two small steps forward and a giant stride backward for Big Ben. He spent time on the DL last season with tendinitis in his shoulder, which is clearly not the path to the consistency he's lacked throughout his career.

	G	GS	IP	ER	ERA	H	BB	SO	W	L	SV
1995	14	13	80.0	37	4.16	67	38	62	3	6	0
Career	155	142	937.0	404	3.88	838	334	638	58	53	0
Projected	29	29	204.1	74	3.26	192	77	181	16	9	0

Mike Mussina P

Age: 27   **Seasons:** 5
Height: 6' 2"   **Weight:** 185
Bats: Right   **Throws:** Right
1995 OBA: .226   **1995 WHIP:** 1.07

Mussina has won at least two-thirds of his decisions in each season since 1992, and he is clearly one of the top five starters in the majors. He pitches economically, varies his offerings, and makes perfect pitches in pressure situations.

	G	GS	IP	ER	ERA	H	BB	SO	W	L	SV
1995	32	32	221.2	81	3.29	187	50	158	19	9	0
Career	125	125	894.1	320	3.22	802	205	556	71	30	0
Projected	35	35	244.1	81	2.98	203	47	176	22	9	0

Rafael Palmeiro — 1B

Age: 31   **Seasons:** 10
Height: 6' 0" **Weight:** 188
Bats: Left   **Throws:** Left
1995 OBP: .380 **1995 SLG:** .583

Palmeiro is the most underrated star in the majors. A well-rounded hitter who has evolved into a consistent slugger, his power stats rate with those of Thomas and Vaughn, yet he's rarely mentioned in the same breath with the AL's top boppers.

	G	AB	H	2B	3B	HR	RS	RBI	BB	SB	CS	BA
1995	143	554	172	30	2	39	89	104	62	3	1	.310
Career	1300	4857	1455	296	27	194	758	706	494	60	24	.300
Projected	160	601	181	38	3	34	101	112	71	9	1	.301

Cal Ripken — SS

Age: 35   **Seasons:** 15
Height: 6' 4" **Weight:** 220
Bats: Right   **Throws:** Right
1995 OBP: .324 **1995 SLG:** .422

Cal loves baseball, and baseball loves Cal. It's a beautiful thing. Credit his first manager in the major leagues, Earl Weaver, with shifting him from third base to shortstop in the summer of 1982, a move that few people believed would work.

	G	AB	H	2B	3B	HR	RS	RBI	BB	SB	CS	BA
1995	144	550	144	33	2	17	71	88	52	0	1	.262
Career	2218	8577	2371	447	42	327	1272	1267	901	34	32	.276
Projected	162	641	162	31	2	21	80	91	67	1	2	.253

Scouting Report

Outfielders: The Red Sox have been graced with some of history's great outfield trios, and though the 1995 crew didn't rank with Rice, Lynn, and Evans, expect upgrades this season. Mike "Gator" Greenwell has been the man in the Monster's shadow for most of the past decade, but his hitting stats are nothing special for a lefty in Fenway Park. Promising prospects Jose Malave and Dwayne Hosey will challenge for playing time. Glenn Murray, a rookie with an NFL physique, has put up significant power numbers in triple-A, but he'll have to beat out Troy O'Leary, last year's club leader in batting average, in right field.

Infielders: MVP first baseman Mo Vaughn has immense power and is the cornerstone of Boston's offense. John Valentin isn't a slick fielder, but his lively bat is tops among AL shortstops. His partner on the pivot could be Craig Biggio or Delino DeShields, depending on what shakes down during the offseason. Tim Naehring can play any infield position, but he does his best work at third base.

Catchers: Injuries have impeded Eric Wedge's progress through the minor leagues, but he was the organization's brightest performer at Pawtucket last year. He'll compete with Bill Haselman and Scott Hatteberg.

Designated Hitters: Dramatic slugger Jose Canseco is a free agent at press time, and the Bosox will re-sign him only if the price isn't prohibitive.

Starting Pitchers: If the Red Sox are going to elevate to the next level, a healthy Rocket Clemens is essential. Aaron Sele was expected to solidify the staff in 1995, but a shoulder injury ended his season and put his future in doubt. The unlikely hero who redeemed the Bosox staff was, of course, knuckleballer Tim Wakefield, whose ugly windup and dopey pitch were beautiful brilliance for Red Sox fans. Unsigned free agent Erik Hanson has a great curveball, but he needs to prove that he can be a winner in back-to-back years. Vaughn Eshelman and Rheal Cormier, who both rely on control and breaking stuff, will be in the running for the fifth spot.

Relief Pitchers: Rick Aguilera is an experienced, consistent closer, but he has exercised his option to become a free agent. Setup work was in the hands of Stan Belinda and Mike Stanton last season, both of whom have been closers in the past. Ken Ryan converted 13 saves in 1994, but last year he was undermined by control problems. Another young reliever who could figure in the bullpen equation is hard-throwing Joe Hudson. He'll be joined in the spring by rookie righthander Matt Murray.

Outlook

The Boston faithful struck it rich in 1995 as their beloved Red Sox played great baseball for the entire season. The Bosox appear primed to contend for the AL pennant in 1996 as well. The core of the batting order is elite, and the already potent lineup may get a splash of fresh juice via free agency or from outfield prospects Glenn Murray and Jose Malave. The Bosox don't figure to execute flawless defense, but if Clemens and Sele have sound arms and Wakefield doesn't knuckle under, Boston will be basking in a summer pennant race.

Fungoes

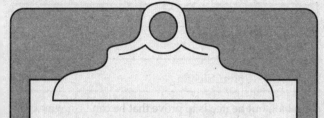

Quick Quiz: Which lefty hurler threw a league-record nine shoutouts in a single season?

Franchise Milestone: It's been too long between drinks. The Red Sox haven't won a World Series since 1918, though they've come within one victory in each of their last four appearances—1946, 1967, 1975, and 1986.

Top Pitcher: Cy Young, 1901–1908

Top Player: Ted Williams, 1939–60

Top Manager: Joe Cronin, 1935–47

Wacky Nickname: The Little Professor (Dominic Paul DiMaggio)

Quick Quiz Answer: Babe Ruth

Lineup Card

NO	POS	PLAYER	OBP	SLG
00	2B	TBD	.000	.000
13	SS	John Valentin	.399	.533
42	1B	Mo Vaughn	.388	.575
00	DH	TBD	.000	.000
39	LF	Mike Greenwell	.349	.459
25	RF	Troy O'Leary	.355	.491
46	CF	Dwayne Hosey	.408	.618
30	C	Scott Hatteberg	.500	.500
11	3B	Tim Naehring	.415	.448

In a Nutshell: The Red Sox will have some decisions to make regarding the replacement of any departed free agents. There will undoubtedly be new arrivals after press time—perhaps Craig Biggio or Delino DeShields at second base—so the regular batting order may not be set until after the season starts. Naehring gets on base more often than any other player in last year's lineup, and he can be used in any of several lineup slots. The Red Sox have a couple of rookie outfielders who posted big power stats at triple-A Pawtucket last season, Glenn Murray and Jose Malave, and it's possible that either Eric Wedge or a true rookie will be at catcher. There's talk of re-signing Jose Canseco and putting him in right field on a platoon basis.

Fenway Park

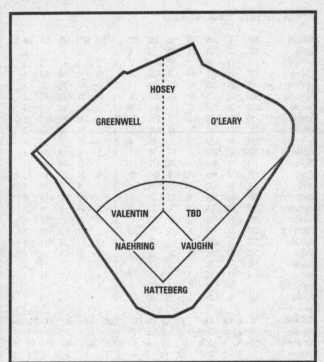

Capacity: 33,871
Turf: Natural

LF Line: 315
RF Line: 302
Center: 390
Left CF: 379
Right CF: 380

Tickets:
617-267-8661

Fenway's architectural oddities—the jutting angles in center field, the waist-high wall in right field, and, of course, the 37-foot Green Monster—can cause problems for even the most instinctive and agile outfielders. All types of offense are increased here, as are infield errors. The park is like heaven for fans and lefty batters, but it's something farther south for most pitchers.

Statistics

Minimum 25 at-bats or 10.0 innings pitched

PLAYER	BA	G	AB	RS	H	TB	2B	3B	HR	RBI	BB	SO	SB	CS
Hosey	.338	24	68	20	23	42	8	1	3	7	8	16	6	0
Rodriguez	.333	13	30	5	10	12	2	0	0	5	2	1	0	0
O'Leary	.308	112	399	60	123	196	31	6	10	49	29	64	5	3
Naehring	.307	126	433	61	133	194	27	2	10	57	77	66	0	2
Canseco	.306	102	396	64	121	220	25	1	24	81	42	93	4	0
Vaughn	.300	140	550	98	165	316	28	3	39	126	68	150	11	4
Valentin	.298	135	520	108	155	277	37	2	27	102	81	67	20	5
Greenwell	.297	120	481	67	143	221	25	4	15	76	38	35	9	5
Jefferson	.289	46	121	21	35	58	8	0	5	26	9	24	0	0
McGee	.285	67	200	32	57	80	11	3	2	15	9	41	5	2
Tinsley	.284	100	341	61	97	137	17	1	7	41	39	74	18	7
Alicea	.270	132	419	64	113	157	20	3	6	44	62	61	13	9
James	.268	42	82	8	22	32	4	0	2	8	7	14	1	0
Stairs	.261	39	88	8	23	35	7	1	1	17	4	14	0	1
Donnels	.253	40	91	13	23	35	2	2	2	11	9	18	0	0
Haselman	.243	64	152	22	37	60	6	1	5	23	17	30	0	2
Shumpert	.234	21	47	6	11	14	3	0	0	3	4	13	3	1
Macfarlane	.225	115	364	45	82	147	18	1	15	51	38	78	2	1
Whiten	.185	32	108	13	20	26	3	0	1	10	8	23	1	0
Rowland	.172	14	29	1	5	6	1	0	0	1	0	11	0	0
Bell	.154	17	26	7	4	9	2	0	1	2	2	10	0	0
Chamberlain	.119	19	42	4	5	9	1	0	1	1	3	11	1	0
Rhodes	.080	10	25	2	2	3	1	0	0	1	3	4	0	0

PITCHER	W	L	SV	ERA	G	GS	CG	SH	IP	H	R	ER	BB	SO
Aguilera	3	3	32	2.60	52	0	0	0	55.1	46	16	16	13	52
Wakefield	16	8	0	2.95	27	27	6	1	195.1	163	76	64	68	119
Stanton	1	0	0	3.00	22	0	0	0	21.0	17	9	7	8	10
Sele	3	1	0	3.06	6	6	0	0	32.1	32	14	11	14	21
Belinda	8	1	10	3.10	63	0	0	0	69.2	51	25	24	28	57
Maddux	4	1	1	3.61	36	4	0	0	89.2	86	40	36	15	65
Cormier	7	5	0	4.07	48	12	0	0	115.0	132	59	52	31	69
Hudson	0	1	1	4.11	39	0	0	0	46.0	53	21	21	23	29
Clemens	10	5	0	4.18	23	23	0	0	140.0	141	70	65	60	132
Hanson	15	5	0	4.24	29	29	1	1	186.2	187	94	88	59	139
Eshelman	6	3	0	4.85	23	14	0	0	81.2	86	47	44	36	41
Ryan	0	4	7	4.96	28	0	0	0	32.2	34	20	18	24	34
Gunderson	2	1	0	5.11	19	0	0	0	12.1	13	7	7	9	9
Smith	8	8	0	5.61	24	21	0	0	110.2	144	78	69	23	47
Suppan	1	2	0	5.96	8	3	0	0	22.2	29	15	15	5	19
Lilliquist	2	1	0	6.26	28	0	0	0	23.0	27	17	16	9	9
Pierce	0	3	0	6.60	12	0	0	0	15.0	16	12	11	14	12
Pena	1	1	0	7.40	17	0	0	0	24.1	33	23	20	12	25

Roster

MANAGER: Kevin Kennedy
COACHES: Tim Johnson, Al Nipper, Dave Oliver, Jim Rice, Herman Starrette, Frank White

NO	PITCHERS	B	T	HT	WT	DOB
43	Stan Belinda	R	R	6-3	187	8/6/66
57	Brian Bark	L	L	5-9	170	8/26/68
21	Roger Clemens	R	R	6-4	220	8/4/62
34	Rheal Cormier	L	L	5-10	185	4/23/67
52	Vaughn Eshelman	L	L	6-3	205	5/22/69
28	Eric Gunderson	R	L	6-0	195	3/29/66
45	Joe Hudson	R	R	6-1	180	9/29/70
45	Matt Murray	L	R	6-6	235	9/26/70
—	Brad Pennington	L	L	6-6	215	4/14/69
50	Ken Ryan	R	R	6-3	200	10/24/68
36	Aaron Sele	R	R	6-5	218	6/25/70
30	Mike Stanton	L	L	6-1	190	6/2/67
55	Jeff Suppan	R	R	6-2	210	1/2/75
49	Tim Wakefield	R	R	6-2	204	8/2/66
	CATCHERS					
37	Bill Haselman	R	R	6-3	215	5/25/66
30	Scott Hatteberg	L	R	6-1	185	12/14/69
—	Eric Wedge	R	R	6-3	215	1/27/68
	INFIELDERS					
6	Chris Donnels	L	R	6-0	185	4/21/66
27	Dave Hollins	S	R	6-1	215	5/25/66
10	Reggie Jefferson	L	L	6-4	215	9/25/68
11	Tim Naehring	R	R	6-2	200	2/1/67
3	Carlos Rodriguez	S	R	5-9	160	11/1/67
—	Jim Tatum	R	R	6-2	200	10/9/67
13	John Valentin	R	R	6-0	185	2/18/67
42	Mo Vaughn	L	R	6-1	230	12/15/67
	OUTFIELDERS					
39	Mike Greenwell	L	R	6-0	200	7/18/63
46	Dwayne Hosey	S	R	5-10	175	3/11/67
—	Jose Malave	R	R	6-2	195	5/31/71
—	Glenn Murray	R	R	6-2	200	11/23/70
25	Troy O'Leary	L	L	6-0	175	8/4/69
26	Lee Tinsley	S	R	5-10	185	3/4/69
35	Matt Stairs	L	R	5-9	175	2/27/69

FREE AGENTS: Rick Aguilera, Jose Canseco, Erik Hanson, Mike Macfarlane, Mike Maddux, Willie McGee, Zane Smith

Roger Clemens

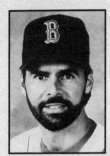

Rick Aguilera P

Age: 34　　　　　**Seasons:** 11
Height: 6' 5"　　　**Weight:** 203
Bats: Right　　　　**Throws:** Right
1995 OBA: .225　　　**1995 WHIP:** 1.07

Aggie has good control and a more varied selection of offerings—fastball, slider, splitter—than most closers, but he's still essentially a power pitcher, if not an overpowering one. He's saved at least 30 games in every nonstrike season since 1990.

	G	GS	IP	ER	ERA	H	BB	SO	W	L	SV
1995	52	0	55.1	16	2.60	46	13	52	3	3	32
Career	469	70	922.0	333	3.25	868	257	739	59	56	211
Projected	57	0	65.1	20	2.76	51	19	59	2	4	35

Stan Belinda P

Age: 29　　　　　**Seasons:** 7
Height: 6' 3"　　　**Weight:** 187
Bats: Right　　　　**Throws:** Right
1995 OBA: .205　　　**1995 WHIP:** 1.13

Belinda was on the verge of pitching himself out of the league until he came to Boston last year. He's prone to arm fatigue and bouts of wildness, but if he's used in brief setup stints, his sidearm slider can be very tough on righties.

	G	GS	IP	ER	ERA	H	BB	SO	W	L	SV
1995	63	0	69.2	24	3.10	51	28	57	8	1	10
Career	345	0	406.2	167	3.70	332	164	342	30	19	72
Projected	60	0	65.1	27	3.72	59	37	54	7	4	7

Jose Canseco   DH

Age: 31   **Seasons:** 11
Height: 6' 4"   **Weight:** 240
Bats: Right   **Throws:** Right
1995 OBP: .378   **1995 SLG:** .556

Last season provided the battle that fans had been hoping for years to see: Canseco vs. the Green Monster. His prime has passed and his average was inflated at home (.337 at Fenway, .274 on the road), but he remains a compelling slugger.

	G	AB	H	2B	3B	HR	RS	RBI	BB	SB	CS	BA
1995	102	396	121	25	1	24	64	81	42	4	0	.306
Career	1245	4711	1275	229	12	300	796	951	560	153	67	.271
Projected	122	458	131	30	0	26	71	84	54	6	1	.286

Roger Clemens   P

Age: 33   **Seasons:** 12
Height: 6' 4"   **Weight:** 220
Bats: Right   **Throws:** Right
1995 OBA: .259   **1995 WHIP:** 1.44

Rocket remains an imposing presence on the mound, particularly at Fenway, where he has always been almost untouchable, but his recent injury problems are not minor. Factor in his age and there has to be some uncertainty about his future.

	G	GS	IP	ER	ERA	H	BB	SO	W	L	SV
1995	23	23	140.0	65	4.18	141	60	132	10	5	0
Career	349	348	2533.1	844	3.00	2143	750	2333	182	98	0
Projected	32	32	233.2	81	3.12	224	51	209	16	7	0

Mike Greenwell   *OF*

Age: 32	**Seasons:** 11
Height: 6' 0"	**Weight:** 200
Bats: Left	**Throws:** Right
1995 OBP: .349	**1995 SLG:** .459

Gator isn't the type of hitter who can carry an offense, but he consistently makes contact and strokes enough extra-base hits to be a viable part of Boston's lineup. He plays caroms off the Monster expertly, but his overall fielding is mediocre.

	G	AB	H	2B	3B	HR	RS	RBI	BB	SB	CS	BA
1995	120	481	143	25	4	15	67	76	38	9	5	.297
Career	1192	4328	1313	255	37	123	622	682	442	76	43	.303
Projected	133	510	145	22	1	14	65	69	41	6	5	.284

Erik Hanson   *P*

Age: 30	**Seasons:** 8
Height: 6' 6"	**Weight:** 215
Bats: Right	**Throws:** Right
1995 OBA: .258	**1995 WHIP:** 1.32

Owner of a state-of-the-art curveball, Hanson has been an 18-game winner (1990) and a 17-game loser (1992) in his career. He was a key member of the Boston rotation last year but could be pitching elsewhere this season.

	G	GS	IP	ER	ERA	H	BB	SO	W	L	SV
1995	29	29	186.2	88	4.24	187	59	139	15	5	0
Career	196	195	1276.2	541	3.81	1273	367	980	76	64	0
Projected	30	30	202.1	99	4.40	211	60	151	14	9	0

Mike Macfarlane   C

Age: 32   **Seasons:** 9
Height: 6' 1"   **Weight:** 205
Bats: Right   **Throws:** Right
1995 OBP: .319   **1995 SLG:** .404

His knees are bad and he hit just .201 versus righthanders, but Macfarlane does have two outstanding characteristics: longball pop and a knack for being hit by pitches. He cut down a solid 35 percent of would-be basestealers last season.

	G	AB	H	2B	3B	HR	RS	RBI	BB	SB	CS	BA
1995	115	364	82	18	1	15	45	51	38	2	1	.225
Career	808	2522	633	154	13	91	313	360	215	8	11	.251
Projected	120	356	90	17	0	14	42	49	42	1	1	.253

Tim Naehring   3B

Age: 29   **Seasons:** 6
Height: 6' 2"   **Weight:** 200
Bats: Right   **Throws:** Right
1995 OBP: .415   **1995 SLG:** .448

Prior to last year Naehring had never stayed healthy long enough to have a 300-at-bat season. He's a versatile infielder and Boston's most patient hitter, but he lacks the extra-base knock of a top-flight cornerman.

	G	AB	H	2B	3B	HR	RS	RBI	BB	SB	CS	BA
1995	126	433	133	27	2	10	61	57	77	0	2	.307
Career	361	1183	329	70	3	23	139	145	149	2	5	.278
Projected	137	429	125	33	0	11	65	61	84	0	1	.291

Troy O'Leary OF

Age: 26	**Seasons:** 3
Height: 6' 0"	**Weight:** 175
Bats: Left	**Throws:** Left
1995 OBP: .355	**1995 SLG:** .491

Eight seasons in the minors (including a .334, 28-steal showing at double-A El Paso in 1992) and two cups of coffee weren't enough to convince the Brewers that O'Leary can hit, but he was a revelation at the plate for the Red Sox last season.

	G	AB	H	2B	3B	HR	RS	RBI	BB	SB	CS	BA
1995	112	399	123	31	6	10	60	49	29	5	3	.308
Career	158	506	153	35	7	12	72	59	39	6	4	.302
Projected	129	456	149	35	5	8	69	50	36	12	5	.327

Aaron Sele P

Age: 25	**Seasons:** 3
Height: 6' 5"	**Weight:** 218
Bats: Right	**Throws:** Right
1995 OBA: .252	**1995 WHIP:** 1.42

Sele's curveball is amazing, but his projected progression from neophyte prospect to rotation anchor was derailed by a season-ending arm injury. The Red Sox are hoping he can be an elemental ingredient of their 1996 rotation.

	G	GS	IP	ER	ERA	H	BB	SO	W	L	SV
1995	6	6	32.1	11	3.06	32	14	21	3	1	0
Career	46	46	287.1	106	3.32	272	122	219	18	10	0
Projected	24	24	156.1	74	4.26	151	67	124	10	7	0

Mike Stanton   P

Age: 29   **Seasons:** 7
Height: 6' 1"   **Weight:** 190
Bats: Left   **Throws:** Left
1995 OBA: N/A   **1995 WHIP:** 1.54

Stanton didn't live up to expectations in Atlanta, but he could still become a closer (depending on his command of the strikezone), and he'll at least be a factor as a one-batter specialist. Lefthanders hit just .160 off him after his arrival in Boston.

	G	GS	IP	ER	ERA	H	BB	SO	W	L	SV
1995	48	0	40.1	19	4.24	48	14	23	2	1	1
Career	326	0	310.2	136	3.94	294	122	233	19	21	55
Projected	61	0	72.2	27	3.34	68	18	47	5	3	12

John Valentin   SS

Age: 29   **Seasons:** 4
Height: 6' 0"   **Weight:** 185
Bats: Right   **Throws:** Right
1995 OBP: .399   **1995 SLG:** .533

Valentin's fielding technique doesn't rank with the league's best, but he has more discipline and power at the plate than any other AL shortstop. He had stolen seven bases in 954 career at-bats but swiped almost three times that amount in 1995.

	G	AB	H	2B	3B	HR	RS	RBI	BB	SB	CS	BA
1995	135	520	155	37	2	27	108	102	81	20	5	.298
Career	421	1474	431	116	7	52	232	242	192	27	10	.292
Projected	159	604	177	40	1	25	113	100	92	14	6	.293

Mo Vaughn 1B

Age: 28   **Seasons:** 5
Height: 6' 1"   **Weight:** 230
Bats: Left   **Throws:** Right
1995 OBP: .388   **1995 SLG:** .575

One factor to consider when mulling over the suspect MVP vote: Hit Dog was absent from the top five in slugging and the top ten in on-base percentage, whereas Edgar Martinez ranked second and first, respectively, in those crucial categories.

	G	AB	H	2B	3B	HR	RS	RBI	BB	SB	CS	BA
1995	140	550	165	28	3	39	98	126	68	11	4	.300
Career	590	2057	587	115	7	111	312	398	277	24	15	.285
Projected	155	602	183	32	1	35	100	130	81	6	5	.304

Tim Wakefield P

Age: 29   **Seasons:** 3
Height: 6' 2"   **Weight:** 204
Bats: Right   **Throws:** Right
1995 OBA: .227   **1995 WHIP:** 1.18

Watching Wakefield wing that wobbly knuckler (with a motion that would be well suited to tossing a paper airplane) is a fascinating experience. If his deliveries stay low in the strikezone, 62 mph might as well be 100.

	G	GS	IP	ER	ERA	H	BB	SO	W	L	SV
1995	27	27	195.1	64	2.95	163	68	119	16	8	0
Career	64	60	415.2	166	3.59	384	178	229	30	20	0
Projected	34	34	241.2	91	3.39	225	77	178	14	9	0

Tim Salmon

California
ANGELS

Scouting Report

Outfielders: Tim Salmon is an aggressive right fielder who hits for power and average. Center fielder Jim Edmonds chases down flies with little regard for his own personal safety, and his production at the plate last season was a revelation. The junior member of this young trio is Garret Anderson, who covers a lot of real estate in left field and can hit just about any pitch—inside the strikezone or out.

Infielders: The Angels get brilliant glovework from J.T. Snow at first base, and he's made great strides as a hitter. Second base is a question mark. Damion Easley has yet to establish himself in three seasons, so the Angels have signed free-agent utility infielder Randy Velarde. Free agent Tim Wallach is slated to play third base, and the club may not give 26-year-old Eduardo Perez another try if prospect George Arias develops on schedule. Scrappy shortstop Gary DiSarcina improved as a hitter last season before going on the injured list.

Catchers: Slugging minor leaguer Todd Greene, who has a strong arm but unpolished overall defensive skills, may be ready for the Show. If Greene needs more seasoning, backstop duties will go to light-hitting Jorge Fabregas.

Designated Hitters: Veteran slugger Chili Davis, who probably would have exited the league by now if not for the DH rule, has been consistently spectacular over the past three seasons.

Starting Pitchers: The Angels love lefties. Chuck Finley and Mark Langston are durable, experienced workhorses who throw hard and keep games close. Jim Abbott, who has had to adjust to the loss of his best stuff, returned to Anaheim after two tumultuous years in New York. At press time only Langston is signed for 1996. The other spots in California's rotation are open. Young lefty Brian Anderson, a finesse pitcher, has yet to blossom but should be more effective as he gains experience. The Angels' top prospects from the minors are Shad Williams, who's on a bullet train to the major leagues after a strong showing at Vancouver last year, and Andrew Lorraine, a 23-year-old southpaw with good stamina and control.

Relief Pitchers: It's not clear that Lee Smith can still serve as a fulltime closer, though he still intimidates hitters when he's on. Troy Percival, a potential late-inning ace, throws white light with movement, and another hard thrower, Mike James, gave up less than one hit per inning as a rookie last year. Julian Heredia, Erik Bennett, and Ken Edenfield could move up from triple-A.

Outlook

No team in the league, not even the Red Sox, took a more impressive step forward than the Angels last year. Hitting coach Rod Carew got much of the credit for assisting the development of struggling youngsters J.T. Snow, Gary DiSarcina, and Jim Edmonds, while a tip o' the halo also goes to the front office for its blending of underachievers and past-prime veterans. There is always the possibility of a setback after instant success, especially now that Tony Phillips is gone, but California should at least be a player in the Western Division shuffle.

Fungoes

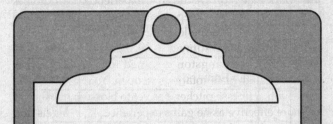

Quick Quiz: Which pitcher became the Angels' first 20-game winner in 1964, two years before they moved from L.A. to Anaheim?

Franchise Milestone: The Angels have never been to a World Series, but they came within one pitch in 1986. They also suffered a heartbreaker in 1982, becoming the first team ever to lose an LCS after winning the first two games.

Top Pitcher: Nolan Ryan, 1972–79

Top Hitter: Bobby Grich, 1977–86

Top Manager: Gene Mauch, 1981–87

Wacky Nickname: Chili (Charles Theodore Davis)

Quick Quiz Answer: Dean Chance

Lineup Card

NO	POS	PLAYER	OBP	SLG
33	SS	Gary DiSarcina	.344	.459
25	CF	Jim Edmonds	.352	.536
15	RF	Tim Salmon	.429	.594
44	DH	Chili Davis	.429	.514
6	1B	J.T. Snow	.353	.465
16	LF	Garret Anderson	.352	.505
00	3B	Tim Wallach	.326	.428
8	C	Todd Greene	.000	.000
00	2B	Randy Velarde	.375	.392

In a Nutshell: Having entered spring training with only one proven, in-prime hitter (Salmon), the Angels conjured up one of the league's most balanced batting orders last season. Their unexpected offensive explosion was fascinating, and it creates some equally interesting questions for 1996. Snow and Edmonds had generated just 29 home runs in a combined five seasons before they unloaded 57 together in 1995. DiSarcina doubled his previous season's doubles output. And while Chili Davis seems to defy time, when your cleanup hitter is on the wrong side of 35 years old there has to be some concern. The trick for the Angels hitters will be to produce a group encore and to finish what they start.

Anaheim Stadium

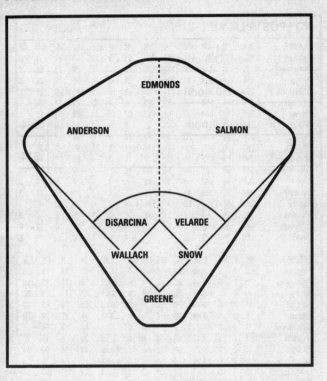

Capacity: 64,593
Turf: Natural

LF Line: 333
RF Line: 333
Center: 404
Left CF: 370
Right CF: 370

Tickets:
714-634-2000

Forget past reports—the Big A no longer favors pitchers and is, in fact, a fine park for power hitters from both sides of the plate. The outfield fences in both corners are comparatively low, giving fans and fielders an equal chance to snare borderline longballs. By the way, the infield won't do double duty as an NFL red zone now that the Rams have split town.

Statistics

Minimum 25 at-bats or 10.0 innings pitched

PLAYER	BA	G	AB	RS	H	TB	2B	3B	HR	RBI	BB	SO	SB	CS
Salmon	.330	143	537	111	177	319	34	3	34	105	91	111	5	5
Anderson	.321	106	374	50	120	189	19	1	16	69	19	66	6	2
Davis	.318	119	424	81	135	218	23	0	20	86	89	79	3	3
DiSarcina	.307	99	362	61	111	166	28	6	5	41	20	25	7	4
Edmonds	.290	141	558	120	162	299	30	4	33	107	51	130	1	4
Snow	.289	143	544	80	157	253	22	1	24	102	52	91	2	1
Aldrete	.268	78	149	19	40	60	8	0	4	24	19	31	0	0
Hudler	.265	84	223	30	59	93	16	0	6	27	10	48	12	0
Phillips	.261	139	525	120	137	241	21	1	27	61	113	135	13	10
Myers	.260	85	273	35	71	114	12	2	9	38	17	49	0	1
Fabregas	.247	73	227	24	56	69	10	0	1	22	17	28	0	2
Lind	.236	44	140	9	33	38	5	0	0	7	6	12	0	1
Owen	.229	82	218	17	50	68	9	3	1	28	18	22	3	2
Easley	.216	114	357	35	77	107	14	2	4	35	32	47	5	3
Martinez	.180	26	61	7	11	15	1	0	1	9	6	7	0	0
Allanson	.171	35	82	5	14	26	3	0	3	10	7	12	0	1
Perez	.169	29	71	9	12	21	4	1	1	7	12	9	0	2

PITCHER	W	L	SV	ERA	G	GS	CG	SH	IP	H	R	ER	BB	SO
Percival	3	2	3	1.95	62	0	0	0	74.0	37	19	16	26	94
Patterson	5	2	0	3.04	62	0	0	0	53.1	48	18	18	13	41
Smith	0	5	37	3.47	52	0	0	0	49.1	42	19	19	25	43
Abbott	11	8	0	3.70	30	30	4	1	197.0	209	93	81	64	86
James	3	0	1	3.88	46	0	0	0	55.2	49	27	24	26	36
Sanderson	1	3	0	4.12	7	7	0	0	39.1	48	23	18	4	23
Habyan	1	2	0	4.13	28	0	0	0	32.2	36	16	15	12	25
Finley	15	12	0	4.21	32	32	2	1	203.0	192	106	95	93	195
Edenfield	0	0	0	4.26	7	0	0	0	12.2	15	7	6	5	6
Langston	15	7	0	4.63	31	31	2	1	200.1	212	109	103	64	142
Butcher	6	1	0	4.73	40	0	0	0	51.1	49	28	27	31	29
Harkey	8	9	0	5.44	26	20	1	0	127.1	155	78	77	47	56
Boskie	7	7	0	5.64	20	20	1	0	111.2	127	73	70	25	51
Anderson	6	8	0	5.87	18	17	1	0	99.2	110	66	65	30	45
Bielecki	4	6	0	5.97	22	11	0	0	75.1	80	56	50	31	45
Springer	1	2	0	6.10	19	6	0	0	51.2	60	37	35	25	38
Williams	1	2	0	6.75	20	0	0	0	10.2	13	10	8	21	9

Roster

MANAGER: Marcel Lachemann
COACHES: Rick Burleson, Rod Carew, Chuck Hernandez, Bobby Knopp, Bill Lachemann, Joe Maddon

NO	PITCHERS	B	T	HT	WT	DOB
52	Jim Abbott	L	L	6-3	210	9/19/67
56	Brian Anderson	S	L	6-1	190	4/26/72
66	Shawn Boskie	R	R	6-3	200	3/28/67
48	Ken Edenfield	R	R	6-1	165	3/18/67
31	Chuck Finley	L	L	6-6	214	11/26/62
34	Mike Harkey	R	R	6-5	235	10/25/66
—	David Holdridge	R	R	6-3	195	2/5/69
42	Mark Holzemer	L	L	6-0	165	8/20/69
46	Mike James	R	R	6-4	216	8/15/67
12	Mark Langston	R	L	6-2	184	8/20/60
45	Phil Leftwich	R	R	6-5	205	5/19/69
37	Bob Patterson	R	L	6-2	192	5/16/59
40	Troy Percival	R	R	6-3	200	8/9/69
47	Lee Smith	R	R	6-6	269	12/4/57
59	Shad Williams	R	R	6-0	185	3/10/71
	CATCHERS					
14	Jorge Fabregas	L	R	6-3	205	3/13/70
8	Todd Greene	R	R	5-9	195	5/8/71
20	Chris Turner	R	R	6-1	190	3/23/69
	INFIELDERS					
5	Rod Correia	R	R	5-11	185	9/13/67
33	Gary DiSarcina	R	R	6-1	178	11/19/67
1	Damion Easley	R	R	5-11	185	11/11/69
10	Rex Hudler	R	R	6-0	195	9/2/60
24	Eduardo Perez	R	R	6-4	215	9/11/69
6	J.T. Snow	S	L	6-2	202	2/26/68
—	Randy Velarde	R	R	6-0	192	11/24/62
	Tim Wallach	R	R	6-3	202	9/14/57
	OUTFIELDERS					
16	Garret Anderson	L	L	6-3	190	6/30/72
44	Chili Davis	S	R	6-3	217	1/17/60
25	Jim Edmonds	L	L	6-1	190	6/27/70
3	Orlando Palmeiro	L	R	5-11	155	1/19/69
—	Marquis Riley	R	R	5-11	170	12/27/70
15	Tim Salmon	R	R	6-3	220	8/24/68

FREE AGENTS: Jim Abbott, Mike Aldrete, Mike Bielecki, Chuck Finley, Dave Gallagher, Rene Gonzalez, John Habyan, Greg Myers, Spike Owen, Bob Patterson, Tony Phillips, Scott Sanderson, Dick Schofield

Brian Anderson

Jim Abbott P

Age: 28	**Seasons:** 7
Height: 6' 3"	**Weight:** 210
Bats: Left	**Throws:** Left
1995 OBA: .274	**1995 WHIP:** 1.39

Lacking both overpowering stuff and phenomenal control, Abbott relies on tenacity and brains to keep games close. His peripheral numbers are mediocre, but he's experienced, lefthanded, and comparatively young—three valuable qualities.

	G	GS	IP	ER	ERA	H	BB	SO	W	L	SV
1995	30	30	197.0	81	3.70	209	64	86	11	8	0
Career	211	211	1418.1	594	3.77	1463	488	779	78	82	0
Projected	32	32	212.1	99	4.20	223	66	95	12	13	0

Brian Anderson P

Age: 24	**Seasons:** 3
Height: 6' 1"	**Weight:** 190
Bats: Switch	**Throws:** Left
1995 OBA: .282	**1995 WHIP:** 1.40

Anderson is a John Tudor type. His mechanics, makeup, and move to first are each above average, but his repertoire is strictly finesse and his future success will depend on location (of his pitches) and information (about batters).

	G	GS	IP	ER	ERA	H	BB	SO	W	L	SV
1995	18	17	99.2	65	5.87	110	30	45	6	8	0
Career	40	36	212.2	121	5.12	241	59	96	13	13	0
Projected	18	18	121.1	61	4.52	135	34	58	7	6	0

Garret Anderson   OF

Age: 23   **Seasons:** 2
Height: 6' 3"   **Weight:** 190
Bats: Left   **Throws:** Left
1995 OBP: .352   **1995 SLG:** .505

Anderson's natural lefty stroke cranks out linedrives in streaks. A pure hitter who has produced at every level since high school, he doesn't have an excess of discipline or speed, but his power should increase as he matures.

	G	AB	H	2B	3B	HR	RS	RBI	BB	SB	CS	BA
1995	106	374	120	19	1	16	50	69	19	6	2	.321
Career	111	387	125	19	1	16	50	70	19	6	2	.323
Projected	152	599	174	24	4	17	76	82	34	9	3	.290

Chili Davis   DH

Age: 36   **Seasons:** 15
Height: 6' 3"   **Weight:** 217
Bats: Switch   **Throws:** Right
1995 OBP: .429   **1995 SLG:** .514

A patient, professional hitter who can really drive the low fastball, Davis is just your typical 15-year vet who registers the highest batting average of his career at the age of 35. Amazing. His bat has to slow down someday, just not today.

	G	AB	H	2B	3B	HR	RS	RBI	BB	SB	CS	BA
1995	119	424	135	23	0	20	81	86	89	3	3	.318
Career	1969	7087	1934	348	29	270	1026	1100	936	127	91	.273
Projected	146	520	147	22	0	21	79	91	77	3	2	.283

Gary DiSarcina SS

Age: 28   **Seasons:** 7
Height: 6' 1"   **Weight:** 178
Bats: Right   **Throws:** Right
1995 OBP: .344   **1995 SLG:** .459

Formerly a contact hitter with almost no extra-base pop, DiSarcina actually led all Angels batters in doubles through mid-August, but his breakthrough season was cut short by a torn ligament in his thumb. He's a super shortstop with soft hands.

	G	AB	H	2B	3B	HR	RS	RBI	BB	SB	CS	BA
1995	99	362	111	28	6	5	61	41	20	7	4	.307
Career	532	1799	459	84	10	14	219	164	79	25	25	.255
Projected	150	510	132	22	3	7	55	49	27	8	6	.259

Jim Edmonds OF

Age: 25   **Seasons:** 3
Height: 6' 1"   **Weight:** 190
Bats: Left   **Throws:** Left
1995 OBP: .352   **1995 SLG:** .536

Last season a respected publication wrote of Edmonds, "...does not have much power." Another suggested he "would be better suited (to) playing left field." He pried some eyes wide open with his glove in center and his pop at the plate.

	G	AB	H	2B	3B	HR	RS	RBI	BB	SB	CS	BA
1995	141	558	162	30	4	33	120	107	51	1	4	.290
Career	253	908	256	47	6	38	160	148	83	5	8	.282
Projected	160	624	177	24	5	22	103	94	64	2	3	.284

Jorge Fabregas C

Age: 26   **Seasons:** 1
Height: 6' 3"   **Weight:** 205
Bats: Left   **Throws:** Right
1995 OBP: .298   **1995 SLG:** .304

His bat isn't potent and he has an odd penchant for dropping the ball, but he threw out almost 40 percent of would-be basestealers, so Fabregas should see at least 250 at-bats this season if he doesn't win the starting job outright.

	G	AB	H	2B	3B	HR	RS	RBI	BB	SB	CS	BA
1995	73	227	56	10	0	1	24	22	17	0	2	.247
Career	116	354	92	13	0	1	36	38	24	2	3	.260
Projected	88	269	64	12	0	3	29	30	24	0	1	.238

Chuck Finley P

Age: 33   **Seasons:** 10
Height: 6' 6"   **Weight:** 214
Bats: Left   **Throws:** Left
1995 OBA: .249   **1995 WHIP:** 1.40

Finley is a skilled and durable veteran, and, except for an occasional bout with wildness, there are few blanks in his arsenal. When he's on a roll the strikeouts come in bunches, thanks to one of the league's nastier splitters.

	G	GS	IP	ER	ERA	H	BB	SO	W	L	SV
1995	32	32	203.0	95	4.21	192	93	195	15	12	0
Career	309	252	1836.1	731	3.58	1744	756	1369	114	98	0
Projected	34	34	252.2	94	3.35	224	85	234	17	11	0

Mark Langston P

Age: 35   **Seasons:** 12
Height: 6' 2"   **Weight:** 184
Bats: Right   **Throws:** Left
1995 OBA: .272   **1995 WHIP:** 1.38

One of the majors' top lefties for more than a decade, Langston still has a good curve and an above-average slider. He helps himself with slick fielding and an elusive move to first, and the Angels helped him last season with positive run support.

	G	GS	IP	ER	ERA	H	BB	SO	W	L	SV
1995	31	31	200.1	103	4.63	212	64	142	15	7	0
Career	383	380	2648.2	1120	3.81	2370	1145	2252	166	141	0
Projected	33	33	216.1	97	4.04	219	63	163	16	10	0

Troy Percival P

Age: 26   **Seasons:** 1
Height: 6' 3"   **Weight:** 200
Bats: Right   **Throws:** Right
1995 OBA: .147   **1995 WHIP:** 0.85

A converted catcher with a history of arm trouble, Percival wields a clock-busting fastball that looks like a garbanzo bean shot from a howitzer. He's also got a closer's makeup, so look for him to step into that role in the near future.

	G	GS	IP	ER	ERA	H	BB	SO	W	L	SV
1995	62	0	74.0	16	1.95	37	26	94	3	2	3
Career	62	0	74.0	16	1.95	37	26	94	3	2	3
Projected	70	0	84.1	17	1.81	40	30	103	5	1	13

Tony Phillips   IF/OF

Age: 37   **Seasons:** 14
Height: 5' 10"   **Weight:** 175
Bats: Switch   **Throws:** Right
1995 OBP: .394   **1995 SLG:** .459

Timeless and intense, Tony will be a contributor wherever he plays. He can handle a variety of positions and is ultra productive at the plate. On the downside, he's never been an effective basestealer and occasionally gets nasty with umpires.

	G	AB	H	2B	3B	HR	RS	RBI	BB	SB	CS	BA
1995	139	525	137	21	1	27	119	61	113	13	10	.261
Career	1696	5860	1557	257	41	121	975	629	974	139	92	.266
Projected	154	575	152	29	2	22	124	55	118	10	6	.264

Tim Salmon   OF

Age: 27   **Seasons:** 4
Height: 6' 3"   **Weight:** 220
Bats: Right   **Throws:** Right
1995 OBP: .429   **1995 SLG:** .594

Salmon is the most formidable hitter in the California lineup, with a quick, powerful stroke, an excellent eye, and the ability to make adjustments at the plate. He's entering the heart of his prime and his numbers are already eye-popping.

	G	AB	H	2B	3B	HR	RS	RBI	BB	SB	CS	BA
1995	143	537	177	34	3	34	111	105	91	5	5	.330
Career	408	1504	444	88	6	90	279	276	238	12	15	.295
Projected	162	617	201	39	2	35	108	112	101	6	4	.326

Lee Smith   P

Age: 38   **Seasons:** 16
Height: 6' 6"   **Weight:** 269
Bats: Right   **Throws:** Right
1995 OBA: .237   **1995 WHIP:** 1.36

For what it's worth, he is starting to slip a little, but the operative words are *a* and *little*. He's been giving up more walks and can be used only for short stints, but the league's all-time saves leader continues to be an intimidating closer.

	G	GS	IP	ER	ERA	H	BB	SO	W	L	SV
1995	52	0	49.1	19	3.47	42	25	43	0	5	37
Career	943	6	1213.0	397	2.95	1048	452	1195	68	87	471
Projected	44	0	46.1	21	4.08	45	31	40	1	5	31

J.T. Snow   1B

Age: 28   **Seasons:** 4
Height: 6' 2"   **Weight:** 202
Bats: Switch   **Throws:** Left
1995 OBP: .353   **1995 SLG:** .465

After batting an uninspiring .232 in his first 656 career at-bats, last season Snow belatedly began to justify his status as a perennial prospect. He doesn't figure to move up another level as a hitter, but he is one smooth-fielding first baseman.

	G	AB	H	2B	3B	HR	RS	RBI	BB	SB	CS	BA
1995	143	544	157	22	1	24	80	102	52	2	1	.289
Career	340	1200	309	45	3	48	163	191	131	5	2	.257
Projected	161	596	166	23	0	19	81	84	55	1	0	.278

Frank Thomas

Chicago
WHITE SOX

Scouting Report

Outfielders: The White Sox neglected to pick up the option on Lance Johnson's contract, reducing their payroll but leaving a question in center field that is unanswered at press time. Look for a free-agent signing or a battle of rookies to emerge in the spring. Classy veteran Tim Raines is only adequate in left field, but he's a high-percentage basestealer who does some good things with the bat. Lyle Mouton hit .354 at home and made just one error while splitting time between right and left fields as a rookie.

Infielders: Ozzie Guillen's production level has slipped, and the Chisox need to make room in their infield for a couple of strong prospects. Chris Snopek could be the new shortstop if Olmedo Saenz bumps him off his natural position, third base. Robin Ventura, who's won three Gold Gloves at the hot corner, will probably be installed at first base, with Frank Thomas becoming a fulltime DH. Second base belongs to Ray Durham, a solid fielder with a lively stick and plus speed.

Catchers: Ron Karkovice cuts off the running game and has a reputation for being a savvy handler of pitchers. As a hitter he's a feast-or-famine type who often goes unfed. As great as Karko is on defense, backup backstop Spanky LaValliere may be even better. He made just one error in 268 innings and nailed an impressive 53 percent of would-be thieves.

Designated Hitters: It appears that two-time AL MVP Frank "The Big Hurt" Thomas will be penciled in as the club's rent-a-stick on a daily basis.

Starting Pitchers: Fireballing young righthander Jason Bere walked more than 100 batters and registered a plus-7.00 ERA. Hefty lefty Wilson Alvarez passed out 90-plus walks and also had a disappointing year. After a poor (5–7, 5.62) beginning, ace Alex Fernandez turned his season around and didn't lose in any of his final ten starts (seven wins). The Chisox need to sign another starter or get help from the farm system. The top prospects are Mike Bertotti, who has unbelievable raw stuff, and Luis Andujar, who recovered from 1993 shoulder problems to flash great potential with the big club last season. James Baldwin has been dominant in the minors.

Relief Pitchers: Top stopper Roberto Hernandez blew ten save chances in 1995. Matt Karchner, Bill Simas, and Larry Thomas are all up-and-coming young hurlers who were impressive in their big-league debuts.

Outlook

On paper the White Sox have enough talent to make the playoffs. The top three members of the starting rotation—Fernandez, Alvarez, and Bere—are expected to bounce back from a collectively sub-par 1995, and the club has at least four rookies who could round out the staff. Look for significant reshuffling in the infield to reinvigorate the offense but possibly put a strain on the defense. At press time the White Sox are in need of a replacement for free agent Lance Johnson in center field. If things fall into place, Chicago will be in the thick of the wild-card hunt.

Fungoes

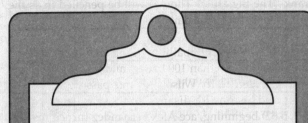

Quick Quiz: Which infamous pitcher went 0–3, 6.61 in the tainted 1919 World Series after going 23–11, 2.64 during the regular season?

Franchise Milestone: Since 1901 the Chisox have won just one more World Series than they've thrown, the first coming in 1906 and the second in 1917. The 1917 pitching staff included the names Slim Sallee, Pol Perritt, Rube Benton, and Ferdie Schupp.

Top Pitcher: Ed Walsh, 1904–16

Top Player: Luke Appling, 1930–50

Top Manager: Al Lopez, 1957–69

Wacky Nickname: Cracker (Raymond William Schalk)

Quick Quiz Answer: Lefty Williams

Lineup Card

NO	POS	PLAYER	OBP	SLG
30	LF	Tim Raines	.374	.422
27	3B	Chris Snopek	.403	.426
23	1B	Robin Ventura	.384	.498
35	DH	Frank Thomas	.454	.606
28	RF	Lyle Mouton	.373	.475
00	CF	TBD	.000	.000
52	2B	Ray Durham	.309	.384
20	C	Ron Karkovice	.306	.387
13	SS	Ozzie Guillen	.270	.318

In a Nutshell: The White Sox didn't struggle to generate offense last season, finishing fifth in the league in runs scored and in the top five in both slugging and on-base percentage. Lance Johnson's $3.1-million option was not picked up during the offseason, but the Chisox have a ready-made leadoff hitter in Tim Raines, or they can delve into free agency to find a replacement for Johnson's speed at the top of the order. Another priority is the acquisition or development of a four- or five-hole slugger who can protect Frank Thomas, though Robin Ventura has done an effective job in that capacity. The bottom of the order sports some rock-bottom on-base percentages, but the club will lose some defense if Ozzie or Karko sit.

Comiskey Park

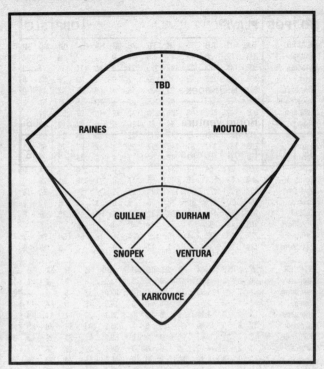

Capacity: 44,321
Turf: Natural

LF Line: 347
RF Line: 347
Center: 400
Left CF: 375
Right CF: 375

Tickets:
312-924-1000

The playing surface is lush and smooth at Comiskey, so infield and outfield errors are reduced by about 15 percent. Righthanders generally hit better here than at other parks, but lefties are affected in a negative way. For example, Lyle Mouton had a 96-point BA differential at home, while Lance Johnson's batting average was 35 points lower at Comiskey.

Statistics

Minimum 25 at-bats or 10.0 innings pitched

PLAYER	BA	G	AB	RS	H	TB	2B	3B	HR	RBI	BB	SO	SB	CS
Snopek	.324	22	68	12	22	29	4	0	1	7	9	12	1	0
Thomas	.308	145	493	102	152	299	27	0	40	111	136	74	3	2
Kruk	.308	45	159	13	49	62	7	0	2	23	26	33	0	1
Martinez	.307	119	303	48	93	132	16	4	5	37	32	41	8	2
Devereaux	.306	92	333	48	102	155	21	1	10	55	25	51	6	6
Johnson	.306	142	607	98	186	258	18	12	10	57	32	31	40	6
Mouton	.302	58	179	23	54	85	16	0	5	27	19	46	1	0
Ventura	.295	135	492	79	145	245	22	0	26	93	75	98	4	3
Raines	.285	133	502	81	143	212	25	4	12	67	70	52	13	2
Martin	.269	71	160	17	43	64	7	4	2	17	3	25	5	0
Lyons	.266	27	64	8	17	34	5	0	5	16	4	14	0	0
Grebeck	.260	53	154	19	40	55	12	0	1	18	21	23	0	0
Durham	.257	125	471	68	121	181	27	6	7	51	31	83	18	5
Sabo	.254	20	71	10	18	26	5	0	1	8	3	12	2	0
Guillen	.248	122	415	50	103	132	20	3	1	41	13	25	6	7
LaValliere	.245	46	98	7	24	33	6	0	1	19	9	15	0	0
Karkovice	.217	113	323	44	70	125	14	1	13	51	39	84	2	3
Cameron	.184	27	38	4	7	12	2	0	1	2	3	15	0	0

PITCHER	W	L	SV	ERA	G	GS	CG	SH	IP	H	R	ER	BB	SO
Thomas	0	0	0	1.32	17	0	0	0	13.2	8	2	2	6	12
Karchner	4	2	0	1.69	31	0	0	0	32.0	33	8	6	12	24
Simas	1	1	0	2.57	14	0	0	0	14.0	15	5	4	10	16
Andujar	2	1	0	3.26	5	5	0	0	30.1	26	12	11	14	9
Fernandez	12	8	0	3.80	30	30	5	2	203.2	200	98	86	65	159
Hernandez	3	7	32	3.92	60	0	0	0	59.2	63	30	26	28	84
Sirotka	1	2	0	4.19	6	6	0	0	34.1	39	16	16	17	19
Righetti	3	2	0	4.20	10	9	0	0	49.1	65	24	23	18	29
Alvarez	8	11	0	4.32	29	29	3	0	175.0	171	96	84	93	118
McCaskill	6	4	2	4.89	55	1	0	0	81.0	97	50	44	33	50
Keyser	5	6	0	4.97	23	10	0	0	92.1	114	53	51	27	48
Deleon	5	3	0	5.19	38	0	0	0	67.2	60	41	39	28	53
Radinsky	2	2	1	5.45	46	0	0	0	38.0	46	23	23	17	14
Fortugno	1	3	0	5.59	37	0	0	0	38.2	30	24	24	19	24
Bere	8	15	0	7.19	27	27	1	0	137.2	151	120	110	106	110
Bolton	0	2	0	8.18	8	3	0	0	22.0	33	23	20	14	10
Bertotti	1	1	0	12.56	4	3	0	0	14.1	23	20	20	11	15
Baldwin	0	1	0	12.89	6	4	0	0	14.2	32	22	21	9	10

Roster

MANAGER: Terry Bevington
COACHES: Roly de Armas, Ron Jackson, Doug Mansolino,
Joe Nossek, Mike Pazlik

NO	PITCHERS	B	T	HT	WT	DOB
40	Wilson Alvarez	L	L	6-1	235	3/24/70
49	Luis Andujar	R	R	6-2	175	11/22/72
37	James Baldwin	R	R	6-3	210	7/15/71
46	Jason Bere	R	R	6-3	185	5/26/71
52	Mike Bertotti	L	L	6-1	185	1/18/70
42	Rod Bolton	R	R	6-2	190	9/23/68
—	Jeff Darwin	R	R	6-3	180	7/6/69
44	Robert Ellis	R	R	6-5	220	12/15/70
32	Alex Fernandez	R	R	6-1	215	8/13/69
39	Roberto Hernandez	R	R	6-4	235	11/11/64
51	Matt Karchner	R	R	6-4	245	6/28/67
26	Brian Keyser	R	R	6-1	180	10/31/66
34	Andrew Lorraine	L	L	6-3	195	8/11/72
15	Kirk McCaskill	R	R	6-1	205	4/9/61
31	Scott Radinsky	L	L	6-3	204	3/3/68
36	Scott Ruffcorn	R	R	6-4	210	12/29/69
43	Steve Schrenk	R	R	6-3	185	11/20/68
48	Jeff Shaw	R	R	6-2	200	7/7/66
41	Bill Simas	L	R	6-3	220	11/28/71
38	Mike Sirotka	L	L	6-1	200	5/13/71
50	Larry Thomas	R	L	6-1	195	10/25/69
	CATCHERS					
20	Ron Karkovice	R	R	6-1	219	8/8/63
53	Chris Tremie	R	R	6-0	200	10/17/69
	INFIELDERS					
33	Doug Brady	S	R	5-11	165	11/23/69
52	Ray Durham	S	R	5-8	170	11/30/71
12	Craig Grebeck	R	R	5-7	148	12/29/64
13	Ozzie Guillen	L	R	5-11	164	1/20/64
7	Norberto Martin	R	R	5-10	164	12/10/66
—	Olmedo Saenz	R	R	6-0	185	10/8/70
27	Chris Snopek	R	R	6-1	185	9/20/70
35	Frank Thomas	R	R	6-5	257	5/27/68
23	Robin Ventura	L	R	6-1	198	7/14/67
	OUTFIELDERS					
24	Mike Cameron	R	R	6-2	190	1/8/73
—	Jimmy Hurst	R	R	6-6	225	3/1/72
14	Dave Martinez	L	L	5-10	175	9/26/64
28	Lyle Mouton	R	R	6-4	240	5/13/69
30	Tim Raines	S	R	5-8	186	9/16/59

FREE AGENTS: Lance Johnson, Dave Righetti

Wilson Alvarez   P

Age: 26   **Seasons:** 6
Height: 6' 1"   **Weight:** 235
Bats: Left   **Throws:** Left
1995 OBA: .258   **1995 WHIP:** 1.51

He's lefthanded, he throws a mid-90s heater, and his best pitch is a hard-breaking curve—all elements of a star in the making—yet except for a 7–0 second half in 1993, Alvarez has failed to consistently locate either his pitches or success.

	G	GS	IP	ER	ERA	H	BB	SO	W	L	SV
1995	29	29	175.0	84	4.32	171	93	118	8	11	0
Career	129	103	701.0	296	3.80	639	373	479	43	33	1
Projected	31	31	215.2	77	3.21	210	71	143	15	10	0

Jason Bere   P

Age: 24   **Seasons:** 3
Height: 6' 3"   **Weight:** 185
Bats: Right   **Throws:** Right
1995 OBA: .277   **1995 WHIP:** 1.87

What happened? Bere (mentioned in the same sentence with, gulp, Rocket Clemens prior to last season) was a monumental bust in 1995, getting bombed quickly and often in most of his starts, due to chart-topping control problems.

	G	GS	IP	ER	ERA	H	BB	SO	W	L	SV
1995	27	27	137.2	110	7.19	151	106	110	8	15	0
Career	75	75	422.0	225	4.80	379	267	366	32	22	0
Projected	29	29	165.1	85	4.63	158	83	144	10	9	0

Ray Durham 2B

Age: 24	**Seasons:** 1
Height: 5' 8"	**Weight:** 170
Bats: Switch	**Throws:** Right
1995 OBP: .309	**1995 SLG:** .384

Despite his smallish stature, Durham smacked 16 taters at triple-A Nashville in 1994 and exhibited extra-base pop at the big-league level last season. He could blossom into a 20/20 threat, making him a rare commodity among second sackers.

	G	AB	H	2B	3B	HR	RS	RBI	BB	SB	CS	BA
1995	125	471	121	27	6	7	68	51	31	18	5	.257
Career	125	471	121	27	6	7	68	51	31	18	5	.257
Projected	154	580	146	28	8	12	76	56	42	15	6	.252

Alex Fernandez P

Age: 26	**Seasons:** 6
Height: 6' 1"	**Weight:** 215
Bats: Right	**Throws:** Right
1995 OBA: .255	**1995 WHIP:** 1.30

Fernandez, the best pitcher in Chicago even before the departure of Black Jack McDowell, has yet to find the consistency teams look for in an ace, but he did win 18 games in 1993 and should be one of the league's top starters this season.

	G	GS	IP	ER	ERA	H	BB	SO	W	L	SV
1995	30	30	203.2	86	3.80	200	65	159	12	8	0
Career	164	162	1088.1	467	3.86	1058	354	751	63	53	0
Projected	35	35	251.0	78	2.80	220	64	188	17	7	0

Ozzie Guillen   SS

Age: 32   **Seasons:** 11
Height: 5' 11"   **Weight:** 164
Bats: Left   **Throws:** Right
1995 OBP: .270   **1995 SLG:** .318

Was there a less effective hitter per at-bat in the majors last season? He doesn't draw walks, he doesn't steal bases, and he has no power. Age and a 1992 knee injury have stripped his skills, but a fat longterm contract may keep him in the lineup.

	G	AB	H	2B	3B	HR	RS	RBI	BB	SB	CS	BA
1995	122	415	103	20	3	1	50	41	13	6	7	.248
Career	1451	5078	1357	195	54	16	572	468	161	152	93	.267
Projected	131	455	114	18	2	1	45	38	15	5	5	.251

Roberto Hernandez   P

Age: 31   **Seasons:** 5
Height: 6' 4"   **Weight:** 235
Bats: Right   **Throws:** Right
1995 OBA: .266   **1995 WHIP:** 1.52

A late bloomer who saved 38 games in 1993, Hernandez has been stung by the wildness bug and bitten by the gopher ball in each of the past two seasons. He has the tools to dominate, but who knows if he will.

	G	GS	IP	ER	ERA	H	BB	SO	W	L	SV
1995	60	0	59.2	26	3.92	63	28	84	3	7	32
Career	227	3	272.0	98	3.24	236	94	279	18	18	96
Projected	65	0	65.1	24	3.31	66	25	88	3	4	35

Lance Johnson OF

Age: 32 | **Seasons:** 9
Height: 5' 11" | **Weight:** 160
Bats: Left | **Throws:** Left
1995 OBP: .341 | **1995 SLG:** .425

Johnson had knocked seven homers in his first 3,000-plus at-bats, so last season's double-figure dingers total was something of a surprise. He fell one triple short of leading the league for the fifth straight season.

	G	AB	H	2B	3B	HR	RS	RBI	BB	SB	CS	BA
1995	142	607	186	18	12	10	98	57	32	40	6	.306
Career	979	3618	1031	108	78	17	487	334	214	232	72	.285
Projected	161	685	199	22	15	5	107	49	41	37	5	.291

Ron Karkovice C

Age: 32 | **Seasons:** 10
Height: 6' 1" | **Weight:** 219
Bats: Right | **Throws:** Right
1995 OBP: .306 | **1995 SLG:** .387

Karko has few peers behind the plate, and his throwing arm ranks with the most feared in the majors. Though he's stroked double-figure dingers for four straight years, his batting average has set up house in the low-rent district.

	G	AB	H	2B	3B	HR	RS	RBI	BB	SB	CS	BA
1995	113	323	70	14	1	13	44	51	39	2	3	.217
Career	777	2104	471	95	6	80	282	279	198	24	14	.224
Projected	124	366	85	16	0	13	45	55	44	1	2	.232

Lyle Mouton   OF

Age: 26   **Seasons:** 1
Height: 6' 4"   **Weight:** 240
Bats: Right   **Throws:** Right
1995 OBP: .373   **1995 SLG:** .475

Snatched from the Yankees in the Jack McDowell trade, Mouton seems to have straightened out the kinks in his swing and is on the verge of becoming a solid everyday player. He lacks a right fielder's arm but has 20-homer potential.

	G	AB	H	2B	3B	HR	RS	RBI	BB	SB	CS	BA
1995	58	179	54	16	0	5	23	27	19	1	0	.302
Career	58	179	54	16	0	5	23	27	19	1	0	.302
Projected	142	420	122	26	2	14	73	52	50	5	2	.290

Tim Raines   OF

Age: 36   **Seasons:** 17
Height: 5' 8"   **Weight:** 186
Bats: Switch   **Throws:** Right
1995 OBP: .374   **1995 SLG:** .422

Rock compiled six consecutive years of 70-plus steals in his prime—if he'd played in a nonsluggers era there'd be no questioning his Hall of Fame credentials. His wheels aren't what they were, but he draws walks and has added a dash of power.

	G	AB	H	2B	3B	HR	RS	RBI	BB	SB	CS	BA
1995	133	502	143	25	4	12	81	67	70	13	2	.285
Career	2053	7766	2295	371	109	146	1374	829	1134	777	136	.296
Projected	148	551	156	26	3	10	79	62	77	10	1	.283

Frank Thomas   1B/DH

Age: 27   **Seasons:** 6
Height: 6' 5"   **Weight:** 257
Bats: Right   **Throws:** Right
1995 OBP: .454   **1995 SLG:** .606

Thomas has been baseball's top hitter over the past three years and, barring unforeseen disaster, he'll be marking milestones on the road to Cooperstown for the next decade. He slumped slightly versus righties in 1995, hitting .281 against them.

	G	AB	H	2B	3B	HR	RS	RBI	BB	SB	CS	BA
1995	145	493	152	27	0	40	102	111	136	3	2	.308
Career	789	2764	893	185	8	182	565	595	661	16	13	.323
Projected	159	564	184	33	1	44	112	117	131	3	4	.326

Robin Ventura   3B/1B

Age: 28   **Seasons:** 7
Height: 6' 1"   **Weight:** 198
Bats: Left   **Throws:** Right
1995 OBP: .384   **1995 SLG:** .498

Ventura is a superb all-around player who posts higher batting averages on the road than at home (20-point differential in 1995). A three-time Gold Glover at third, he may be permanently shifted to first base to make room for Chris Snopek.

	G	AB	H	2B	3B	HR	RS	RBI	BB	SB	CS	BA
1995	135	492	145	22	0	26	79	93	75	4	3	.295
Career	881	3183	873	147	5	110	451	519	477	13	22	.274
Projected	157	588	171	31	1	21	87	95	90	3	6	.291

Carlos Baerga

Cleveland
INDIANS

Scouting Report

Outfielders: Kenny Lofton is a run-scoring catalyst at the top of the lineup and a fleetfooted flycatcher in center field. Cleveland's corner outfielders, Albert Belle in left and Manny Ramirez in right, are a devastating duo with lumber but a paltry pair with leather. With an All-Star at each outfield spot there are few opportunities for prospects like Brian Giles and Jeromy Burnitz to crack the starting lineup.

Infielders: Jim Thome is the AL's brightest young hitting star at third base, though his fielding still needs some refinement. First baseman Paul Sorrento had a break-through season at the plate, but the Tribe declined on his option in order to make room for young Herbert Perry. Second sacker Carlos Baerga is arguably the club's most complete player. His defensive skills are solid and his hitting prowess is unsurpassed among middle infielders. At shortstop the silky glovework of Omar Vizquel keeps the Cleveland pitchers smiling.

Catchers: Sandy Alomar has never stayed healthy long enough to become a star, but he's a fine nine-hole hitter and his work behind the dish is top-notch. Fiery veteran Tony Pena, a fine backup, is a free agent at press time.

Designated Hitters: An over-the-hill Eddie Murray is a better hitter than most hot prospects, but an expensive free-agent price tag might prohibit his return.

Starting Pitchers: Dennis Martinez has so-so stuff at age 40, but he knows how to set up hitters and keep games close. Orel Hershiser's rejuvenated arm was practically untouchable in the second half of last season. Charles Nagy has shown flashes of a return to the level he'd reached prior to undergoing shoulder surgery in 1993, but his status in Cleveland will depend on offseason contract talks. If both Nagy and Ken Hill prove too pricey, the Indians can start any of three promising righthanders who pitched beautifully in relief last season. Lanky youngster Julian Tavarez has the potential to be an ace starter, Chad Ogea made 14 starts and was 8–3 overall, and Albie Lopez is also on the verge of excellence.

Relief Pitchers: Jose Mesa, who was utterly dominant in his first season as the Tribe's closer, blew just two saves in 48 tries. Eric Plunk, perhaps the most underrated setup man in the league, allowed opponents a scant .211 batting average against him last season. Look for prospect Paul Shuey to step up as a major leaguer. Paul Assenmacher and Jim Poole are both unsigned at press time, leaving the status of Cleveland's lefthanded relief uncertain.

Outlook

With their core group of young stars—Baerga, Thome, and Lofton—signed to longterm deals, the Indians figure to run roughshod over the AL Central competition for at least the next two seasons. (Weren't people saying similar things about the Blue Jays not long ago?) The Cleveland lineup assaults opponents with speed and power, and though the starting rotation has some veteran anchors, the farm system is also overflowing with live arms. It's hard to imagine the Tribe failing to run away and hide with its second consecutive division crown.

Fungoes

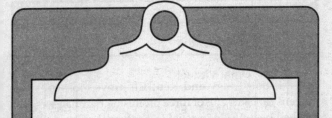

Quick Quiz: Name the now-infamous outfielder who hit .408 for Cleveland in 1911 yet didn't win a batting title.

Franchise Milestone: The Indians have won two World Series titles, beating the Brooklyn Robins in 1920 and the Boston Braves in 1948.

Top Pitcher: Bob Feller, 1936–56

Top Player: Earl Averill, 1929–39

Top Manager: Al Lopez, 1951–56

Wacky Nickname: The Human Rain Delay (Michael Dudley Hargrove)

Quick Quiz Answer: Joe Jackson

Lineup Card

NO	POS	PLAYER	OBP	SLG
7	CF	Kenny Lofton	.362	.453
13	SS	Omar Vizquel	.333	.351
9	2B	Carlos Baerga	.355	.452
8	LF	Albert Belle	.401	.690
25	3B	Jim Thome	.438	.558
24	RF	Manny Ramirez	.402	.558
34	1B	Herbert Perry	.376	.463
00	DH	TBD	.000	.000
15	C	Sandy Alomar	.332	.478

In a Nutshell: Baseball's scariest batting order has Lofton at the top and eye-popping pop from three through eight. The Tribe hitters keep whiffs to a minimum despite their fence-busting abilities, partially compensating for their free-swinging lack of patience at the plate. Most teams are searching for one .500-slugging-percentage hitter who can fill the cleanup slot, but the Indians are blessed with three such players, including the best four-hole bopper in the business. If there are any weaknesses in the lineup, they were exposed by the Braves for all the baseball-watching world to see. Attribute it to cockiness or lack of discipline if you like, but whatever the reason, the Indians don't always "bat smart"—they usually don't have to.

Jacobs Field

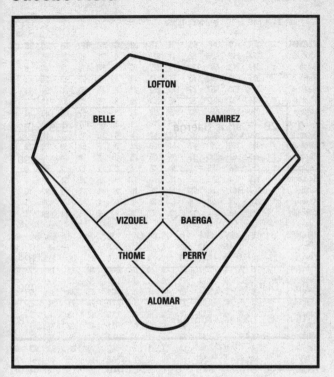

Capacity: 42,400
Turf: Natural

LF Line: 325
RF Line: 325
Center: 405
Left CF: 370
Right CF: 375

Tickets:
216-241-8888

The grass is plush so ground balls hop true, a helpful circumstance for some of the Indians' less sure-handed fielders. The visibility is good, so power pitchers are not at a premium. The park is slightly favorable to power hitters, but Tribe batting averages tend to be much higher at home. Cleveland fans are some of baseball's most dedicated.

Statistics

Minimum 25 at-bats or 10.0 innings pitched

PLAYER	BA	G	AB	RS	H	TB	2B	3B	HR	RBI	BB	SO	SB	CS
Murray	.323	113	436	68	141	225	21	0	21	82	39	65	5	1
Belle	.317	143	546	121	173	377	52	1	50	126	73	80	5	2
Perry	.315	52	162	23	51	75	13	1	3	23	13	28	1	3
Baerga	.314	135	557	87	175	252	28	2	15	90	35	31	11	2
Thome	.314	137	452	92	142	252	29	3	25	73	97	113	4	3
Lofton	.310	118	481	93	149	218	22	13	7	53	40	49	54	15
Ramirez	.308	137	484	85	149	270	26	1	31	107	75	112	6	6
Alomar	.300	66	203	32	61	97	6	0	10	35	7	26	3	1
Vizquel	.266	136	542	87	144	190	28	0	6	56	59	59	29	11
Pena	.262	91	263	25	69	99	15	0	5	28	14	44	1	0
Espinoza	.252	66	143	15	36	46	4	0	2	17	2	16	0	2
Sorrento	.235	104	323	50	76	165	14	0	25	79	51	71	1	1
Kirby	.207	101	188	29	39	56	10	2	1	14	13	32	10	3
Amaro	.200	28	60	5	12	18	3	0	1	7	4	6	1	3
Winfield	.191	46	115	11	22	33	5	0	2	4	14	26	1	0

PITCHER	W	L	SV	ERA	G	GS	CG	SH	IP	H	R	ER	BB	SO
Mesa	3	0	46	1.13	62	0	0	0	64.0	49	9	8	17	58
Tavarez	10	2	0	2.44	57	0	0	0	85.0	76	36	23	21	68
Plunk	6	2	2	2.67	56	0	0	0	64.0	48	19	19	27	71
Assenmacher	6	2	0	2.82	47	0	0	0	38.1	32	13	12	12	41
Ogea	8	3	0	3.05	20	14	1	0	106.1	95	38	36	29	57
Martinez	12	5	0	3.08	28	28	3	2	187.0	174	71	64	46	99
Lopez	0	0	0	3.13	6	2	0	0	23.0	17	8	8	7	22
Poole	3	3	0	3.75	42	0	0	0	50.1	40	22	21	7	22
Hershiser	16	6	0	3.87	26	26	1	1	167.1	151	76	72	51	111
Hill	4	1	0	3.98	12	11	1	0	74.2	77	36	33	32	48
Nagy	16	6	0	4.55	29	29	2	1	178.0	194	95	90	61	139
Embree	3	2	1	5.11	23	0	0	0	24.2	23	16	14	16	23
Clark	9	7	0	5.27	22	21	2	0	124.2	143	77	73	42	68
Grimsley	0	0	1	6.09	15	2	0	0	34.0	37	24	23	32	25
Black	4	2	0	6.85	11	10	0	0	47.1	63	42	36	16	34

Roster

MANAGER: Mike Hargrove
COACHES: Luis Isaac, Charlie Manuel, Dave Nelson,
Jeffrey Newman, Mark Wiley

NO	PITCHERS	B	T	HT	WT	DOB
45	Paul Assenmacher	L	L	6-3	210	12/10/60
—	John Carter	R	R	6-1	195	2/16/72
54	Mark Clark	R	R	6-5	225	5/12/68
—	Carlos Crawford	R	R	6-1	185	10/4/71
56	Alan Embree	L	L	6-2	185	1/23/70
55	Orel Hershiser	R	R	6-3	195	9/16/58
59	Albie Lopez	R	R	6-2	205	8/18/71
32	Dennis Martinez	R	R	6-1	180	5/14/55
49	Jose Mesa	R	R	6-3	225	5/22/66
41	Charles Nagy	L	R	6-3	200	5/5/67
37	Chad Ogea	R	R	6-0	200	11/9/70
38	Eric Plunk	R	R	6-6	220	9/3/63
62	Jim Poole	L	L	6-2	203	4/28/66
53	Paul Shuey	R	R	6-3	215	9/16/70
50	Julian Tavarez	R	R	6-2	165	5/22/73
	CATCHERS					
15	Sandy Alomar	R	R	6-5	215	6/18/66
—	Einar Diaz	R	R	5-10	160	12/28/72
	INFIELDERS					
9	Carlos Baerga	S	R	5-11	200	11/4/68
34	Herbert Perry	R	R	6-2	210	9/15/69
25	Jim Thome	L	R	6-4	220	8/27/70
13	Omar Vizquel	S	R	5-9	165	4/24/67
	OUTFIELDERS					
30	Ruben Amaro	S	R	5-10	175	2/12/65
8	Albert Belle	R	R	6-2	210	8/25/66
23	Jeromy Burnitz	L	R	6-0	190	4/15/69
58	Brian Giles	L	L	5-11	195	1/20/71
35	Wayne Kirby	L	R	5-10	185	1/22/64
7	Kenny Lofton	L	L	6-0	180	5/31/67
24	Manny Ramirez	R	R	6-0	190	5/30/72

FREE AGENTS: Alvaro Espinoza, John Farrell, Ken Hill, Eddie
Murray, Tony Pena, Billy Ripken, Dave Winfield

Sandy Alomar   C

Age: 29   **Seasons:** 8
Height: 6' 5"   **Weight:** 215
Bats: Right   **Throws:** Right
1995 OBP: .332   **1995 SLG:** .478

Alomar is an excellent receiver with an accurate arm, but a continuous string of injuries has plagued his career. He compiled strong numbers versus lefties last season after batting a puny .189 against portsiders in 1994.

	G	AB	H	2B	3B	HR	RS	RBI	BB	SB	CS	BA
1995	66	203	61	6	0	10	32	35	7	3	1	.300
Career	490	1658	451	80	4	42	193	215	92	21	14	.272
Projected	107	349	107	14	1	16	52	58	15	4	2	.306

Carlos Baerga   2B

Age: 27   **Seasons:** 6
Height: 5' 11"   **Weight:** 200
Bats: Switch   **Throws:** Right
1995 OBP: .355   **1995 SLG:** .452

Baerga is a free swinger and his glove-work is erratic, yet he's one of the two most valuable players in the league at his position. As a switch-hitting middle infielder with extra-base pop, his mix of skills is extremely rare.

	G	AB	H	2B	3B	HR	RS	RBI	BB	SB	CS	BA
1995	135	557	175	28	2	15	87	90	35	11	2	.314
Career	819	3185	971	165	15	93	491	505	178	47	14	.305
Projected	160	651	201	32	4	24	100	115	41	14	3	.308

Albert Belle OF

Age: 29
Height: 6' 2"
Bats: Right
1995 OBP: .401

Seasons: 7
Weight: 210
Throws: Right
1995 SLG: .690

With a quick, compact stroke Belle will crush any low fastball that's not kept outside his reach, and he's patient enough to wait for a good pitch to hit. He's the only player in baseball annals to smack 50 doubles and 50 homers in a single season.

	G	AB	H	2B	3B	HR	RS	RBI	BB	SB	CS	BA
1995	142	546	173	52	1	50	121	126	73	5	2	.317
Career	755	2839	827	185	13	194	468	603	297	50	25	.291
Projected	157	590	196	57	1	56	130	137	85	6	3	.332

Orel Hershiser P

Age: 37
Height: 6' 3"
Bats: Right
1995 OBA: .244

Seasons: 13
Weight: 195
Throws: Right
1995 WHIP: 1.21

Smart as they come and hard-nosed to boot, Hershiser's arm strength seems to have returned. His whiffs-to-walks ratio was above two-to-one for the first time since 1991, and he won 12 of his last 14 decisions and was the ALCS MVP.

	G	GS	IP	ER	ERA	H	BB	SO	W	L	SV
1995	26	26	167.1	72	3.87	151	51	111	16	6	0
Career	369	329	2323.1	791	3.06	2085	704	1554	150	108	5
Projected	32	32	212.1	77	3.26	191	44	138	18	6	0

Ken Hill P

Age: 30   **Seasons:** 8
Height: 6' 2"   **Weight:** 200
Bats: Right   **Throws:** Right
1995 OBA: N/A   **1995 WHIP:** 1.51

A quality starter, Hill has put together five consecutive winning seasons. There's reason to believe that last year's struggles (prior to his arrival in Cleveland) were just a sore arm–related glitch and that he can reestablish himself as an ace.

	G	GS	IP	ER	ERA	H	BB	SO	W	L	SV
1995	30	29	185.0	95	4.62	202	77	98	10	8	0
Career	198	191	1212.0	494	3.67	1125	475	720	74	61	0
Projected	35	35	226.1	83	3.30	211	74	145	16	8	0

Kenny Lofton OF

Age: 28   **Seasons:** 5
Height: 6' 0"   **Weight:** 180
Bats: Left   **Throws:** Left
1995 OBP: .362   **1995 SLG:** .453

Despite noticeable declines in most categories last season, Lofton remains the key that starts the Indians' engine. His range and arm strength in center field are exceptional, and he's arguably the league's most dynamic leadoff hitter.

	G	AB	H	2B	3B	HR	RS	RBI	BB	SB	CS	BA
1995	118	481	149	22	13	7	93	53	40	54	15	.310
Career	546	2159	673	98	38	25	419	194	246	252	54	.312
Projected	161	608	224	31	10	13	119	66	71	77	15	.368

Dennis Martinez P

Age: 40   **Seasons:** 20
Height: 6' 1"   **Weight:** 180
Bats: Right   **Throws:** Right
1995 OBA: .247   **1995 WHIP:** 1.18

El Presidente is, in certain respects, pitching the most masterful ball of his inspiring career. His record over the past five years is 68–42 (.618). He isn't showing signs of an imminent decline, but his arm did seem to tire in the postseason.

	G	GS	IP	ER	ERA	H	BB	SO	W	L	SV
1995	28	28	187.0	64	3.08	174	46	99	12	5	0
Career	610	528	3748.1	1500	3.60	3601	1080	2022	231	176	6
Projected	32	32	228.2	86	3.38	235	59	116	16	7	0

Jose Mesa P

Age: 29   **Seasons:** 7
Height: 6' 3"   **Weight:** 225
Bats: Right   **Throws:** Right
1995 OBA: .216   **1995 WHIP:** 1.03

Mesa's fastballs (a sinker and a riser) have more action than a Bruce Lee movie, but in five seasons as a starter he'd logged an ERA of about 5.00. His mild success as a setup man in 1994 was a subtle prelude to last year's dominance.

	G	GS	IP	ER	ERA	H	BB	SO	W	L	SV
1995	62	0	64.0	8	1.13	49	17	58	3	0	46
Career	211	95	708.0	350	4.45	747	279	406	37	45	48
Projected	74	0	75.2	15	1.78	58	23	65	2	1	54

Eddie Murray   DH

Age: 40   **Seasons:** 19
Height: 6' 2"   **Weight:** 220
Bats: Switch   **Throws:** Right
1995 OBP: .375   **1995 SLG:** .516

Murray has driven in at least 75 runs for 19 consecutive seasons, a mark equaled only by Hank Aaron. He's a lock for Cooperstown when his time comes due, but he clearly doesn't appear ready to accept statue status just yet.

	G	AB	H	2B	3B	HR	RS	RBI	BB	SB	CS	BA
1995	113	436	141	21	0	21	68	82	39	5	1	.323
Career	2819	10603	3071	532	34	479	1545	1820	1257	105	43	.290
Projected	120	441	118	18	0	15	57	75	28	4	2	.268

Charles Nagy   P

Age: 28   **Seasons:** 6
Height: 6' 3"   **Weight:** 200
Bats: Left   **Throws:** Right
1995 OBA: .278   **1995 WHIP:** 1.43

Nagy's control wasn't always sharp last season, but when his hard curve is on target it induces plenty of whiffs and grounders. He had a 17-win, 2.96 season in 1992 before undergoing shoulder surgery.

	G	GS	IP	ER	ERA	H	BB	SO	W	L	SV
1995	29	29	178.0	90	4.55	194	61	139	16	6	0
Career	136	135	905.0	399	3.97	966	266	581	57	49	0
Projected	31	31	194.2	88	4.07	203	65	154	18	8	0

Chad Ogea   P

Age: 25   **Seasons:** 2
Height: 6' 0"   **Weight:** 200
Bats: Right   **Throws:** Right
1995 OBA: .234   **1995 WHIP:** 1.17

Ogea (pronounced like "Ojay") was making steady progress to the big leagues before a knee injury knocked him off track in late 1994. A control pitcher who adjusts smoothly from setup work to the rotation, he'll see plenty of work this year.

	G	GS	IP	ER	ERA	H	BB	SO	W	L	SV
1995	20	14	106.1	36	3.05	95	29	57	8	3	0
Career	24	15	122.2	47	3.45	116	39	68	8	4	0
Projected	26	22	142.2	53	3.34	144	34	82	14	5	0

Herbert Perry   1B

Age: 26   **Seasons:** 2
Height: 6' 2"   **Weight:** 210
Bats: Right   **Throws:** Right
1995 OBP: .376   **1995 SLG:** .463

Wrist and shoulder injuries prevent Perry's tearing up the minor leagues and establishing himself as Cleveland's first baseman of the near future. A former University of Florida quarterback, he's mobile around the bag.

	G	AB	H	2B	3B	HR	RS	RBI	BB	SB	CS	BA
1995	52	162	51	13	1	3	23	23	13	1	3	.315
Career	56	171	52	13	1	3	24	24	16	1	3	.304
Projected	149	495	151	21	3	16	59	61	43	3	4	.305

Eric Plunk   P

Age: 32   **Seasons:** 10
Height: 6' 6"   **Weight:** 220
Bats: Right   **Throws:** Right
1995 OBA: .211   **1995 WHIP:** 1.17

Plunk is a vastly underrated and, at times, utterly overpowering pitcher. He blew three of five save chances last season, but when his heater is moving and his control is sound, there may not be a more reliable setup man in the league.

	G	GS	IP	ER	ERA	H	BB	SO	W	L	SV
1995	56	0	64.0	19	2.67	48	27	71	6	2	2
Career	472	41	859.2	356	3.75	743	504	793	57	44	32
Projected	61	0	72.0	17	2.12	51	25	80	5	1	4

Manny Ramirez   OF

Age: 23   **Seasons:** 3
Height: 6' 0"   **Weight:** 190
Bats: Right   **Throws:** Right
1995 OBP: .402   **1995 SLG:** .558

With ultra-quick wrists à la Henry Aaron, Ramirez is perhaps the most exciting young slugger in the league, though his all-around skills lack polish. His fielding is spotty and his baserunning is occasionally comical.

	G	AB	H	2B	3B	HR	RS	RBI	BB	SB	CS	BA
1995	137	484	149	26	1	31	85	107	75	6	6	.308
Career	250	827	236	49	1	50	141	172	119	10	8	.285
Projected	155	521	169	30	0	36	99	118	83	5	4	.324

Paul Sorrento   1B

Age: 30   **Seasons:** 7
Height: 6' 2"   **Weight:** 220
Bats: Left   **Throws:** Right
1995 OBP: .336   **1995 SLG:** .511

Sorrento isn't one of the AL's elite first basemen, but his bat has home-run pop and his glove is no worse than average. The Indians have prospects with more star potential than Sorrento, but he'll be a starter somewhere, if not in Cleveland.

	G	AB	H	2B	3B	HR	RS	RBI	BB	SB	CS	BA
1995	104	323	76	14	0	25	50	79	51	1	1	.235
Career	568	1755	450	84	3	84	239	293	215	5	7	.256
Projected	144	455	124	22	0	24	55	81	59	0	1	.273

Julian Tavarez   P

Age: 22   **Seasons:** 3
Height: 6' 2"   **Weight:** 165
Bats: Right   **Throws:** Right
1995 OBA: .235   **1995 WHIP:** 1.14

Getting his first extended big-league trial last year, Tavarez pitched well in a setup role. His ERA was deceptively spiffy thanks to an unusually high percentage of unearned runs allowed (36 of 59), but he has the talent to be an outstanding starter.

	G	GS	IP	ER	ERA	H	BB	SO	W	L	SV
1995	57	0	85.0	23	2.44	76	21	68	10	2	0
Career	66	8	123.2	54	3.93	135	35	87	12	5	0
Projected	32	20	161.1	53	2.96	153	38	126	14	5	0

Jim Thome   3B

Age: 25   **Seasons:** 5
Height: 6' 4"   **Weight:** 220
Bats: Left   **Throws:** Right
1995 OBP: .438   **1995 SLG:** .558

Thome is entering his prime with a bang, and though he wasn't batting in an RBI slot in the lineup last season, he could move up this year. His glovework is nothing special at this point, but he has the tools to be above average.

	G	AB	H	2B	3B	HR	RS	RBI	BB	SB	CS	BA
1995	137	452	142	29	3	25	92	73	97	4	3	.314
Career	349	1142	318	67	7	55	193	168	187	12	8	.278
Projected	160	531	165	37	1	29	102	88	102	3	2	.311

Omar Vizquel   SS

Age: 29   **Seasons:** 7
Height: 5' 9"   **Weight:** 165
Bats: Switch   **Throws:** Right
1995 OBP: .333   **1995 SLG:** .351

Vizquel's flashy style, excellent range, and soft hands make him an electric presence in the middle of Cleveland's infield. Though he has shown vast improvement as a basestealer, Omar's on-base percentages have never been good.

	G	AB	H	2B	3B	HR	RS	RBI	BB	SB	CS	BA
1995	136	542	144	28	0	6	87	56	59	29	11	.266
Career	865	2939	753	98	16	13	349	220	255	81	49	.231
Projected	155	622	171	24	2	4	91	62	52	22	12	.275

Detroit
TIGERS

Scouting Report

Outfielders: Chad Curtis is coming off his best year so far and is expected to improve further this season. He's a go-getter in center field and is developing an impressive power/speed repertoire on offense. Bobby Higginson has been a pleasant surprise, showing unanticipated pop at the plate and gunning down runners from both right and left fields. The Tigers had high hopes for Danny Bautista, but he has failed to hit in two extended trials. He's young and talented, so expect him to get at least one more chance to secure a job in right field. Rudy Pemberton hit .344 in 67 games at Toledo last year and looked good with the big club in a May cup of coffee, so look for him to see time in left field, with rookies Todd Steverson and Phil Nevin also battling for at-bats.

Infielders: After 19 years Detroit's dynamic double-play duo, Alan Trammell and Lou Whitaker, could be ready to hang up their spikes, though no official announcement had been made at press time. If they do retire, Chris Gomez will be an adequate fulltime shortstop with some extra-base pop in his bat, while prospect Shannon Penn could blossom into a solid second baseman and stolen-base threat. The Tigers have an all-star at the hot corner, veteran Travis Fryman, who is due for a career year. Taking over at first base will be yet another youngster, Tony Clark, an unpolished fielder with an unproven bat.

Catchers: At age 28, John Flaherty can't be considered a prospect. His reputation for defense notwithstanding, he proved an easy mark for basestealers last season, but he made a solid contribution with the bat.

Designated Hitters: Cecil Fielder is set to become Detroit's fulltime DH, a role for which he is perfectly suited.

Starting Pitchers: Detroit starters posted the second-worst ERA in the majors last year, so management will throw some prospects on the wall and hope one sticks. Clint Sodowsky kept his ERA under 3.00 at two minor-league levels last season. Felipe Lira registered the lowest ERA and most wins among Detroit's returning starters. Sean Bergman led the club in games started and pitched well at times. Jose Lima showed marked improvement in his last five starts. Look for lefthanders C.J. Nitkowski or Justin Thompson to compete for the fifth spot in the rotation.

Relief Pitchers: The Tigers are locked in to a fat contract with Joe Boever, but Greg Gohr might surprise if he gets a shot at being the closer.

Outlook

Detroit has pared down its payroll and jettisoned most of its past-prime veterans—a drastic step predicated as much on financial considerations as on baseball ones—but a step in the right direction nevertheless. It remains to be seen whether the infusion of Tigers prospects will produce any big-league caliber ballplayers, but the sheer numbers are in the franchise's favor. Fans in Detroit are going to witness either the birth of a fine young ballclub or the Toledo Mud Hens dressed up like Jack Morris and Chet Lemon.

Fungoes

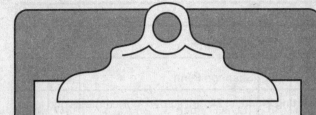

Quick Quiz: Which second baseman led the American League in both errors (a four-way tie) and fielding percentage among players at his position in 1936?

Franchise Milestone: Detroit has won four World Series titles (1935, 1945, 1968, and 1984), but the Tigers came up short in five other Series, including three straight from 1907 through 1909.

Top Pitcher: Jack Morris, 1977–90

Top Player: Ty Cobb, 1905–26

Top Manager: Sparky Anderson, 1979–95

Wacky Nickname: The Georgia Peach (Tyrus Raymond Cobb)

Quick Quiz Answer: Charlie Gehringer

Lineup Card

NO	POS	PLAYER	OBP	SLG
9	CF	Chad Curtis	.349	.435
7	2B	Shannon Penn	.400	.333
24	3B	Travis Fryman	.347	.409
45	DH	Cecil Fielder	.346	.472
17	1B	Tony Clark	.294	.396
18	LF	Rudy Pemberton	.344	.467
4	RF	Bobby Higginson	.329	.393
12	C	John Flaherty	.284	.404
35	SS	Chris Gomez	.292	.355

In a Nutshell: Detroit tied St. Louis for the worst batting average in the majors last season at .247, yet the Tigers still found a way to ground into 121 double plays (fifth most in the league). It's an equation that explains how a club that plays half its games in a bandbox ballpark, and ranks seventh in the league in both homers and walks, can still manage to rank twelfth in the league in runs scored and runs driven in. Fryman, Fielder, and Higginson each piled up at least 100 whiffs, while Curtis and Gomez (who hit leadoff and second, respectively, for much of the year) both cracked the 90-mark in fanning futility. In the words of Chevy Chase: See the ball, be the ball...

Tiger Stadium

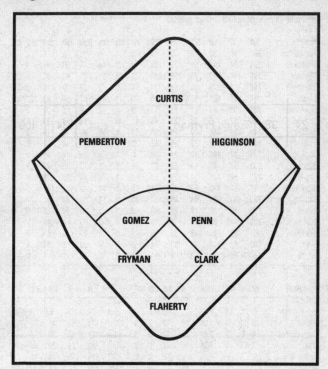

Capacity: 52,416
Turf: Natural

LF Line: 340
RF Line: 325
Center: 440
Left CF: 365
Right CF: 375

Tickets:
313-962-4000

A hallowed sanctuary for baseball lovers, Tiger Stadium is the first place we'd send a virgin baseball fan to see a ballgame. It's also a heaven on Earth for lefty sluggers, with its excellent visibility, small foul territory, and short porch in right field. Somewhat countering the advantages for hitters is the deepest center-field area in the big leagues, where fly balls go to die.

Statistics

Minimum 25 at-bats or 10.0 innings pitched

PLAYER	BA	G	AB	RS	H	TB	2B	3B	HR	RBI	BB	SO	SB	CS
Pemberton	.300	12	30	3	9	14	3	1	0	3	1	5	0	0
Whitaker	.293	84	249	36	73	129	14	0	14	44	31	41	4	0
Fryman	.275	144	567	79	156	232	21	5	15	81	63	100	4	2
Trammell	.269	74	223	28	60	78	12	0	2	23	27	19	3	1
Curtis	.268	144	586	96	157	255	29	3	21	67	70	93	27	15
Steverson	.262	30	42	11	11	17	0	0	2	6	6	10	2	0
Stubbs	.250	62	116	13	29	46	11	0	2	19	19	27	0	1
Fielder	.243	136	494	70	120	233	18	1	31	82	75	116	0	1
Flaherty	.243	112	354	39	86	143	22	1	11	40	18	47	0	0
Clark	.238	27	101	10	24	39	4	1	3	11	6	28	0	0
Fletcher	.231	67	182	19	42	57	10	1	1	17	19	27	1	0
Tingley	.226	54	124	14	28	50	8	1	4	18	15	38	0	1
Higginson	.224	131	410	61	92	161	17	5	14	43	62	107	6	4
Gomez	.223	123	431	49	96	153	20	2	11	50	41	96	4	1
Nevin	.219	29	96	9	21	32	3	1	2	12	11	27	0	0
Cuyler	.205	41	88	15	18	27	1	4	0	5	8	16	2	1
Bautista	.203	89	271	28	55	85	9	0	7	27	12	68	4	1
Hiatt	.202	52	114	11	23	41	6	0	4	12	9	38	1	0
White	.188	39	48	3	9	11	2	0	0	2	0	7	0	0
Rodriguez	.179	18	39	5	7	8	1	0	0	0	6	10	2	2

PITCHER	W	L	SV	ERA	G	GS	CG	SH	IP	H	R	ER	BB	SO
Gohr	1	0	0	0.87	10	0	0	0	10.1	9	1	1	3	12
Henneman	0	1	18	1.53	29	0	0	0	29.1	24	5	5	9	24
Wells	10	3	0	3.04	18	18	3	0	130.1	120	54	44	37	83
Christopher	4	0	1	3.82	36	0	0	0	61.1	71	28	26	14	34
Lira	9	13	1	4.31	37	22	0	0	146.1	151	74	70	56	89
Sodowsky	2	2	0	5.01	6	6	0	0	23.1	24	15	13	18	14
Doherty	5	9	6	5.10	48	2	0	0	113.0	130	66	64	37	46
Bergman	7	10	0	5.12	28	28	1	1	135.1	169	95	77	67	86
Bohanon	1	1	1	5.54	52	10	0	0	105.2	121	68	65	41	63
Lima	3	9	0	6.11	15	15	0	0	73.2	85	52	50	18	37
Boever	5	7	3	6.39	60	0	0	0	98.2	128	74	70	44	71
Maxcy	4	5	0	6.88	41	0	0	0	52.1	61	48	40	31	20
Nitkowski	1	4	0	7.09	11	11	0	0	39.1	53	32	31	20	12
Groom	1	3	0	7.52	23	4	0	0	40.2	55	35	34	26	33
Moore	5	15	0	7.53	25	25	1	0	132.2	179	118	111	68	64
Blomdahl	0	0	1	7.77	14	0	0	0	24.1	36	21	21	13	15
Ahearne	0	2	0	11.70	4	3	0	0	10.0	20	13	13	5	4
Gardiner	0	0	0	14.59	9	0	0	0	12.1	27	20	20	2	7

Roster

MANAGER: Buddy Bell
COACHES: Glenn Ezell, Terry Francona, Larry Herndon, Fred Kendall, Jon Matlack, Ron Oester

NO	PITCHERS	B	T	HT	WT	BORN
43	Sean Bergman	R	R	6-4	205	4/11/70
26	Ben Blomdahl	R	R	6-2	185	12/30/70
37	Joe Boever	R	R	6-1	200	10/4/60
49	Brian Bohanon	L	L	6-3	220	8/1/68
33	Mike Christopher	R	R	6-5	205	11/3/63
44	John Doherty	R	R	6-4	210	6/11/67
46	Mike Gardiner	S	R	6-0	200	10/19/65
34	Greg Gohr	R	R	6-3	205	10/29/67
32	Jose Lima	R	R	6-2	170	9/30/72
40	Felipe Lira	R	R	6-0	170	4/26/72
15	Brian Maxcy	R	R	6-1	170	5/4/71
27	Mike Myers	L	L	6-3	197	6/26/69
36	C.J. Nitkowski	L	L	6-3	190	3/3/73
—	Justin Thompson	L	L	6-3	175	3/8/73
	CATCHERS					
12	John Flaherty	R	R	6-1	202	10/21/67
25	Ron Tingley	R	R	6-2	195	5/27/59
	INFIELDERS					
17	Tony Clark	S	R	6-8	240	6/15/72
45	Cecil Fielder	R	R	6-3	250	9/21/63
36	Scott Fletcher	R	R	5-11	170	7/30/58
24	Travis Fryman	R	R	6-1	194	3/25/69
35	Chris Gomez	R	R	6-1	183	6/16/71
—	Mark Lewis	R	R	6-1	190	11/30/69
7	Shannon Penn	S	R	5-10	163	9/11/69
3	Alan Trammell	R	R	6-0	185	2/21/58
1	Lou Whitaker	L	R	5-11	180	5/12/57
	OUTFIELDERS					
29	Danny Bautista	R	R	5-11	170	5/24/72
9	Chad Curtis	R	R	5-10	175	11/6/68
22	Milt Cuyler	S	R	5-10	185	10/7/68
4	Bobby Higginson	L	R	5-11	180	8/18/70
42	Phil Nevin	R	R	6-2	185	1/19/71
18	Rudy Pemberton	R	R	6-1	185	12/17/69
13	Todd Steverson	R	R	6-2	194	11/15/71

FREE AGENTS: Scott Fletcher, Franklin Stubbs, Lou Whitaker

Sean Bergman   P

Age: 25   **Seasons:** 3
Height: 6' 4"   **Weight:** 205
Bats: Right   **Throws:** Right
1995 OBA: .307   **1995 WHIP:** 1.74

Bergman doesn't throw hard but has an effective changeup and is capable of improving on his mediocre strikeout rate. (He whiffed 145 batters in 154.2 innings at Toledo in 1994.) He tends to be either an utter mystery or an easy target for hitters.

	G	GS	IP	ER	ERA	H	BB	SO	W	L	SV
1995	28	28	135.1	77	5.12	169	67	86	7	10	0
Career	40	37	192.2	113	5.28	238	97	117	10	15	0
Projected	34	34	226.1	132	5.25	241	71	95	9	15	0

Tony Clark   1B

Age: 23   **Seasons:** R
Height: 6' 8"   **Weight:** 240
Bats: Switch   **Throws:** Right
1995 OBP: .294   **1995 SLG:** .396

An intriguing (and tall) prospect whose development has been slow, Tony the Tiger will take over at first base this season but may be an even poorer fielder than Fielder. Clark figures to hit homers in bunches, but it's too early to bet on his future.

	G	AB	H	2B	3B	HR	RS	RBI	BB	SB	CS	BA
1995	27	101	24	5	1	3	10	11	8	0	0	.238
Career	27	101	24	5	1	3	10	11	8	0	0	.238
Projected	148	555	136	15	1	14	56	68	32	0	1	.245

Chad Curtis OF

Age: 27 **Seasons:** 4
Height: 5' 10" **Weight:** 175
Bats: Right **Throws:** Right
1995 OBP: .349 **1995 SLG:** .435

A tough, talented center fielder who works hard to maximize his skills, Curtis became the Tigers' first 20/20 man since 1987 and set career highs in runs scored and runs batted in. He's in his prime and is getting better every year.

	G	AB	H	2B	3B	HR	RS	RBI	BB	SB	CS	BA
1995	144	586	157	29	3	21	96	67	70	27	15	.268
Career	549	2063	553	93	12	48	316	222	228	143	68	.268
Projected	161	644	185	31	4	17	95	66	68	33	16	.287

Cecil Fielder DH

Age: 32 **Seasons:** 10
Height: 6' 3" **Weight:** 250
Bats: Right **Throws:** Right
1995 OBP: .346 **1995 SLG:** .472

Cecil is a low-ball slugger, and it'll be interesting to see how well he adjusts to enforcement of the high strike. Not playing the field should help his aching back, but he won't be winning any more RBI crowns without Tony Phillips leading off.

	G	AB	H	2B	3B	HR	RS	RBI	BB	SB	CS	BA
1995	136	494	120	18	1	31	70	82	75	0	1	.243
Career	1095	3789	973	148	6	250	570	762	502	0	5	.257
Projected	150	512	127	20	0	27	72	84	72	0	0	.248

John Flaherty   C

Age: 28   **Seasons:** 4
Height: 6' 1"   **Weight:** 202
Bats: Right   **Throws:** Right
1995 OBP: .284   **1995 SLG:** .404

Of his 11 dingers, six came during a nine-game streak, so it's not clear that he can deliver consistent pop (nor is it certain that he can't). Flaherty topped all AL backstops in errors and didn't exactly present a challenge to opposing basestealers.

	G	AB	H	2B	3B	HR	RS	RBI	BB	SB	CS	BA
1995	112	354	86	22	1	11	39	40	18	0	0	.243
Career	194	485	108	27	1	11	47	48	24	0	1	.223
Projected	125	390	96	19	0	9	41	43	22	0	0	.246

Travis Fryman   3B

Age: 27   **Seasons:** 6
Height: 6' 1"   **Weight:** 194
Bats: Right   **Throws:** Right
1995 OBP: .347   **1995 SLG:** .409

Fryman started slowly in 1995, so his final numbers don't reflect his talent level. He struck out just 28 times after mid-July, he had a four-hit game in every month from May to September, and his play at third base was the steadiest of his career.

	G	AB	H	2B	3B	HR	RS	RBI	BB	SB	CS	BA
1995	144	567	156	21	5	15	79	81	63	4	2	.275
Career	785	3086	848	170	23	105	427	477	287	38	20	.275
Projected	162	651	179	34	3	24	89	94	72	6	4	.275

Greg Gohr P

Age: 28   **Seasons:** 3
Height: 6' 3"   **Weight:** 205
Bats: Right   **Throws:** Right
1995 OBA: .243   **1995 WHIP:** 1.19

A former first-round pick (1989) and an annual disappointment, Gohr was on the injured list for most of last season but, as evidenced by his numbers, was overpowering in short relief after his September return.

	G	GS	IP	ER	ERA	H	BB	SO	W	L	SV
1995	10	0	10.1	1	0.87	9	3	12	1	0	0
Career	34	6	67.0	33	4.43	71	38	56	3	2	0
Projected	34	10	108.1	45	3.74	106	44	87	4	4	4

Chris Gomez 2B/SS

Age: 24   **Seasons:** 3
Height: 6' 1"   **Weight:** 183
Bats: Right   **Throws:** Right
1995 OBP: .292   **1995 SLG:** .355

Gomez alternated between second and short to substitute for the greatest DP combo in history and is expected to be the fulltime shortstop this season. His secondary hitting skills are developing nicely, but he needs to make more contact.

	G	AB	H	2B	3B	HR	RS	RBI	BB	SB	CS	BA
1995	123	431	96	20	2	11	49	50	41	4	1	.223
Career	253	855	204	46	3	19	92	114	83	11	6	.239
Projected	145	500	119	21	1	12	51	55	44	6	2	.238

Bobby Higginson   OF

Age: 25   **Seasons:** 1
Height: 5' 11"   **Weight:** 180
Bats: Left   **Throws:** Right
1995 OBP: .329   **1995 SLG:** .393

Higginson has already gone beyond the expectations of most scouts. He topped all AL outfielders in assists (13) and flashed good power, though 10 of his homers came in the first half and he often failed to make contact (107 whiffs).

	G	AB	H	2B	3B	HR	RS	RBI	BB	SB	CS	BA
1995	131	410	92	17	5	14	61	43	62	6	4	.224
Career	131	410	92	17	5	14	61	43	62	6	4	.224
Projected	152	484	115	21	3	18	64	51	60	9	5	.238

Jose Lima   P

Age: 23   **Seasons:** 2
Height: 6' 2"   **Weight:** 170
Bats: Right   **Throws:** Right
1995 OBA: .288   **1995 WHIP:** 1.40

Detroit's top pitching prospect saw half a season of action in the majors last year and finished on a high note, allowing just seven earned runs in his final 28 innings (2.25 ERA). He isn't overpowering but throws a nifty circle change.

	G	GS	IP	ER	ERA	H	BB	SO	W	L	SV
1995	15	15	73.2	50	6.11	85	18	37	3	9	0
Career	18	16	80.1	60	6.72	96	21	44	3	10	0
Projected	28	28	154.2	81	4.71	166	29	78	6	10	0

Felipe Lira P

Age: 23   **Seasons:** 1
Height: 6' 0"   **Weight:** 170
Bats: Right   **Throws:** Right
1995 OBA: .271   **1995 WHIP:** 1.41

Shuttled between the bullpen and the starting rotation in his first season, the superstitious Lira flashed decent control and an above-average split-finger pitch. A 1–0 outing versus the Rangers in late June provided evidence of his potential.

	G	GS	IP	ER	ERA	H	BB	SO	W	L	SV
1995	37	22	146.1	70	4.31	151	56	89	9	13	1
Career	37	22	146.1	70	4.31	151	56	89	9	13	1
Projected	27	27	147.0	67	4.10	150	45	97	10	14	0

C.J. Nitkowski P

Age: 23   **Seasons:** 1
Height: 6' 3"   **Weight:** 190
Bats: Left   **Throws:** Left
1995 OBA: N/A   **1995 WHIP:** 1.80

Acquired from Cincinnati (where his ERA was 6.12 in nine appearances) in exchange for David Wells, Nitkowski's struggles weren't alleviated in the Motor City. His knuckle-curve is a nasty pitch, but he needs to locate and mix it more effectively.

	G	GS	IP	ER	ERA	H	BB	SO	W	L	SV
1995	20	18	71.2	53	6.66	94	35	31	2	7	0
Career	20	18	71.2	53	6.66	94	35	31	2	7	0
Projected	25	25	118.0	74	5.64	133	43	49	4	11	0

Kevin Appier

Kansas City
ROYALS

Scouting Report

Outfielders: They aren't well known outside of Kansas City, but the Royals' outfielders all have talent. Johnny Damon has shown good range in center field and the raw tools to be a top-level leadoff hitter. Michael Tucker may be K.C.'s best hitting prospect, but he'll need to make more contact versus lefties if he's going to be a fulltime left fielder. Tom Goodwin, who escaped the bench and stole 50 bases, will see action in both left and center. Right fielder Jon Nunnally endured a late-season home-run drought, but he's capable of providing some of the power the Royals desperately need.

Infielders: Wally Joyner owns one of baseball's prettiest swings, and though his power stats won't knock your socks off, he's a quality hitter and fielder. As a 30-year-old rookie, Keith Lockhart sparked the Royals with a .321 average and scrappy play at second base. Greg Gagne took advantage of his free-agent status, which opens the shortstop job for utility man David Howard. Third sacker Gary Gaetti was K.C.'s MVP and only significant power source. It's doubtful that so-so prospect Joe Randa will hit enough to replace Gaetti at the hot corner.

Catchers: Brent Mayne can't hit lefties and is probably best equipped to be a backup, but his glovework is steady. The Royals are hoping that rookie Mike Sweeney and/or second-year backstop Henry Mercedes will challenge for playing time.

Designated Hitters: Bob Hamelin will try to regain the power stroke that made him 1994's AL Rookie of the Year. Jeff Grotewold and Joe Vitiello will also see at-bats at DH.

Starting Pitchers: If the Royals lose staff ace Kevin Appier to free agency, he will be difficult to replace. Another free agent, Tom Gordon, is still a mediocre pitcher with above-average stuff, but he could turn the corner any year now. Mark Gubicza has made a successful transition from power to finesse, and he led all Royals starters in ERA and innings pitched. The team will depend on rookie arms to bolster the rotation. Jim Pittsley, who has ace-type stuff, underwent simple elbow surgery in August. Dilson Torres pitched brilliantly in the minors but found major-league batters a more difficult puzzle. Jason Jacome (pronounced Hock-a-mee) has the makeup but may lack the stuff.

Relief Pitchers: Veteran closer Jeff Montgomery, who is tough as a week-old bagel on righthanders, is a free agent at press time. There are several inexperienced, live-armed options available in the bullpen, including Melvin Bunch, Mark Huisman, Billy Brewer, and Hipolito Pichardo.

Outlook

The Royals sliced about $10 million off their payroll in 1995, and it's likely that at least a few of their big-name holdovers—Montgomery, Gaetti, Gordon, Appier, and Gubicza—will have vacated via free agency prior to Opening Day 1996. That will clear the way for several hungry prospects to emerge as regulars, but the growth process is as likely to be slow and painful as accelerated and glorious. Kansas City should be very solid on defense and dangerous on the basepaths, but they'll need to get tremendous pitching to compensate for their lack of pop.

Fungoes

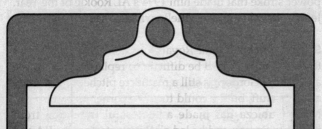

Quick Quiz: Which K.C. outfielder won the 1969 Rookie of the Year Award and can still be seen in the clubhouse of a major-league team?

Franchise Milestone: Down three games to one, the underdog Royals stormed back to beat St. Louis in the 1985 World Series. Bret Saberhagen allowed just one run in two complete-game victories.

Top Pitcher: Dan Quisenberry, 1979–88

Top Player: George Brett, 1973–92

Top Manager: Whitey Herzog, 1975–79

Wacky Nickname: Blue Moon (Johnny Lee Odom)

Quick Quiz Answer: Lou Piniella

Lineup Card

NO	POS	PLAYER	OBP	SLG
51	CF	Johnny Damon	.324	.441
47	LF	Tom Goodwin	.346	.358
12	1B	Wally Joyner	.394	.447
44	DH	Joe Vitiello	.317	.446
43	2B	Keith Lockhart	.355	.478
9	RF	Jon Nunnally	.357	.472
6	SS	David Howard	.310	.325
24	C	Brent Mayne	.313	.326
18	3B	Joe Randa	.237	.243

In a Nutshell: The Royals really struggled against left-handed pitching (14–27) last season. Keith Lockhart hit .188, Jon Nunnally .162, and Brent Mayne .178 versus southpaws. If free agency removes the bat of Gary Gaetti, the K.C. batting order will be hard pressed to produce a proven power source. No team in baseball will rely as heavily on its designated-hitter slot. If the Hammer splits his wood the way he did last year, Joe Vitiello (who was a notorious slow starter in the minors) could become the cleanup hitter. The Royals are fun to watch, topping the league in sacrifice bunts, finishing second in steals, and ranking third in triples last season. Unfortunately they were also last in home runs and next to last in walks.

Kauffman Stadium

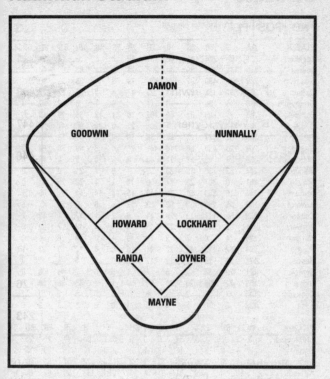

Capacity: 40,625
Turf: Natural

LF Line: 330
RF Line: 330
Center: 400
Left CF: 375
Right CF: 375

Tickets:
816-921-8000

The Royals were the only Central Division club that failed to win more games at home than on the road. With the artificial turf taken out and the alley fences moved in ten feet, speed isn't the factor that it once was in Kansas City. The organization may need to rethink its player-development strategy in order to mold a team that better suits its home park.

Statistics

Minimum 25 at-bats or 10.0 innings pitched

PLAYER	BA	G	AB	RS	H	TB	2B	3B	HR	RBI	BB	SO	SB	CS
Lockhart	.321	94	274	41	88	131	19	3	6	33	14	21	8	1
Joyner	.310	131	465	69	144	208	28	0	12	83	69	65	3	2
Goodwin	.288	133	480	72	138	172	16	3	4	28	38	72	50	18
Damon	.282	47	188	32	53	83	11	5	3	23	12	22	7	0
Grotewold	.278	15	36	4	10	14	1	0	1	6	9	7	0	0
Samuel	.263	91	205	31	54	102	10	1	12	39	29	49	6	4
Gaetti	.261	137	514	76	134	266	27	0	35	96	47	91	3	3
Tucker	.260	62	177	23	46	68	10	0	4	17	18	51	2	3
Gagne	.256	120	430	58	110	161	25	4	6	49	38	60	3	5
Mercedes	.256	23	43	7	11	13	2	0	0	9	8	13	0	0
Vitiello	.254	53	130	13	33	58	4	0	7	21	8	25	0	0
Mayne	.251	110	307	23	77	100	18	1	1	28	25	41	0	1
Nunnally	.244	119	303	51	74	143	15	6	14	42	51	86	6	4
Howard	.243	94	255	23	62	83	13	4	0	19	24	41	6	1
Caceres	.239	55	117	13	28	41	6	2	1	17	8	15	2	2
Borders	.231	52	143	14	33	55	8	1	4	13	7	22	0	0
Norman	.225	24	40	6	9	11	0	1	0	4	6	6	0	1
Hiatt	.204	52	113	11	23	41	6	0	4	12	9	37	1	0
Randa	.171	34	70	6	12	17	5	0	0	1	5	17	0	1
Stynes	.171	22	35	7	6	7	1	0	0	2	4	3	0	0
Hamelin	.168	72	208	20	35	65	7	1	7	25	26	56	0	1
Cookson	.143	22	35	2	5	6	1	0	0	5	2	7	1	0
Jose	.133	9	30	2	4	5	1	0	0	1	2	9	0	0

PITCHER	W	L	SV	ERA	G	GS	CG	SH	IP	H	R	ER	BB	SO
Montgomery	2	3	31	3.43	54	0	0	0	65.2	60	27	25	25	49
Haney	3	4	0	3.65	16	13	1	0	81.1	78	35	33	33	31
Gubicza	12	14	0	3.75	33	33	3	2	213.1	222	97	89	62	81
Appier	15	10	0	3.89	31	31	4	1	201.1	163	90	87	80	185
Olson	3	3	3	4.09	23	0	0	0	33.0	28	15	15	19	21
Magnante	1	1	0	4.23	28	0	0	0	44.2	45	23	21	16	28
Pichardo	8	4	1	4.36	44	0	0	0	64.0	66	34	31	30	43
Gordon	12	12	0	4.43	31	31	2	0	189.0	204	110	93	89	119
Meacham	4	3	2	4.98	49	0	0	0	59.2	72	36	33	19	30
Anderson	1	0	0	5.33	6	4	0	0	25.1	29	15	15	8	6
Jacome	4	6	0	5.36	15	14	1	0	84.0	101	52	50	21	39
Brewer	2	4	0	5.56	48	0	0	0	45.1	54	28	28	20	31
Bunch	1	3	0	5.63	13	5	0	0	40.0	42	25	25	14	19
Fleming	1	6	0	5.96	25	12	1	0	80.0	84	61	53	53	40
Torres	1	2	0	6.09	24	2	0	0	44.1	56	30	30	17	28
Converse	1	3	1	6.56	15	1	0	0	23.1	28	17	17	16	14
Linton	0	1	0	7.25	7	2	0	0	22.1	22	21	18	10	13
Browning	0	2	0	8.10	2	2	0	0	10.0	13	9	9	5	3
Rasmussen	0	1	0	9.00	5	1	0	0	10.0	13	10	10	8	6

Roster

MANAGER: Bob Boone
COACHES: Jeff Cox, Bruce Kison, Greg Luzinski, Mitchell Page, Jamie Quirk

NO	PITCHERS	B	T	HT	WT	DOB
55	Kevin Appier	R	R	6-2	195	12/6/67
58	Brian Bevil	R	R	6-3	190	9/5/71
59	Mike Bovee	R	R	5-10	200	8/21/73
41	Billy Brewer	L	L	6-1	185	4/15/68
50	Melvin Bunch	R	R	6-1	165	11/4/71
53	Jim Converse	L	R	5-9	180	8/17/71
62	Bart Evans	R	R	6-1	190	12/30/70
47	Dave Fleming	L	L	6-3	205	11/7/69
—	Jeff Granger	R	L	6-4	200	12/16/71
33	Chris Haney	L	L	6-3	195	11/16/68
37	Rick Huisman	R	R	6-3	210	5/17/69
45	Jason Jacome	L	L	6-0	180	11/24/70
57	Mike Magnante	L	L	6-1	190	6/17/65
28	Rusty Meacham	R	R	6-2	175	1/27/68
35	Hipolito Pichardo	R	R	6-1	185	8/22/69
—	Jim Pittsley	R	R	6-7	215	4/3/74
52	Dilson Torres	R	R	6-3	200	5/31/70
	CATCHERS					
24	Brent Mayne	L	R	6-1	190	4/19/68
15	Henry Mercedes	R	R	5-11	185	7/23/69
29	Mike Sweeney	R	R	6-1	195	7/22/73
	INFIELDERS					
46	Edgar Caceres	S	R	6-0	170	6/6/64
3	Bob Hamelin	L	L	6-0	235	11/29/67
6	David Howard	S	R	6-0	175	2/26/67
12	Wally Joyner	L	L	6-2	200	6/16/62
43	Keith Lockhart	L	R	5-10	170	11/10/64
18	Joe Randa	R	R	5-11	190	12/18/69
38	Chris Stynes	R	R	5-9	170	2/19/73
44	Joe Vitiello	R	R	6-2	215	4/11/70
	OUTFIELDERS					
48	Brent Cookson	R	R	6-0	195	9/7/69
51	Johnny Damon	L	L	6-0	175	11/5/73
47	Tom Goodwin	L	R	6-1	170	7/27/68
64	Les Norman	R	R	6-1	185	2/25/69
9	Jon Nunnally	L	R	5-10	190	11/9/71
31	Michael Tucker	L	R	6-2	185	6/25/71

FREE AGENTS: Tom Browning, Gary Gaetti, Greg Gagne, Tom Gordon, Mark Gubicza, Jeff Montgomery, Gregg Olson, Juan Samuel

Kevin Appier   P

Age: 28   **Seasons:** 7
Height: 6' 2"   **Weight:** 195
Bats: Right   **Throws:** Right
1995 OBA: .221   **1995 WHIP:** 1.21

Appier floundered in the second half of last season after going 11–2 with a 2.04 ERA in his first 14 starts, but he's one of the league's most effective hurlers when his mechanics are right. He's murder on righthanders—they hit just .179 against him.

	G	GS	IP	ER	ERA	H	BB	SO	W	L	SV
1995	31	31	201.1	87	3.89	163	80	185	15	10	0
Career	190	178	1218.1	436	3.22	1068	419	961	81	54	0
Projected	34	34	247.1	72	2.62	171	64	213	20	8	0

Johnny Damon   OF

Age: 22   **Seasons:** 1
Height: 6' 0"   **Weight:** 175
Bats: Left   **Throws:** Left
1995 OBP: .324   **1995 SLG:** .441

Damon has a poor throwing arm and only marginal power, but he makes good use of his other talents, in particular his speed. He was drafted in 1992 and is essentially learning his trade in the majors, so look for him to improve dramatically.

	G	AB	H	2B	3B	HR	RS	RBI	BB	SB	CS	BA
1995	47	188	53	11	5	3	32	23	12	7	0	.282
Career	47	188	53	11	5	3	32	23	12	7	0	.282
Projected	134	487	142	16	12	4	61	34	35	18	4	.292

Gary Gaetti 3B

Age: 37	**Seasons:** 15
Height: 6' 0"	**Weight:** 200
Bats: Right	**Throws:** Right
1995 OBP: .329	**1995 SLG:** .518

Though he batted just .212 versus lefthanders and his overall offensive numbers resemble those of Dave Kingman circa 1984, Gaetti was the Royals' only power source last season, racking up the highest home-run total of his fine career.

	G	AB	H	2B	3B	HR	RS	RBI	BB	SB	CS	BA
1995	137	514	134	27	0	35	76	96	47	3	3	.261
Career	1972	7203	1832	349	32	292	914	1075	499	86	58	.254
Projected	152	569	143	22	1	24	61	75	52	0	2	.251

Greg Gagne SS

Age: 34	**Seasons:** 13
Height: 5' 11"	**Weight:** 180
Bats: Right	**Throws:** Right
1995 OBP: .316	**1995 SLG:** .374

Respected around the league for his top-level fielding skills and willingness to sweat the details, Gagne is a valuable veteran who will certainly be an improvement over Jose Offerman, though that doesn't mean he'll be worth what L.A. is paying him.

	G	AB	H	2B	3B	HR	RS	RBI	BB	SB	CS	BA
1995	120	430	110	25	4	6	58	49	38	3	5	.256
Career	1526	4731	1202	263	45	92	615	492	286	102	89	.254
Projected	139	412	101	23	2	7	50	44	29	2	5	.245

Tom Goodwin   OF

Age: 27   **Seasons:** 5
Height: 6' 1"   **Weight:** 170
Bats: Left   **Throws:** Right
1995 OBP: .346   **1995 SLG:** .358

Another minor-league refugee who should thank the Royals for rescuing his career, Goodwin's output on offense was a pleasant surprise. He'll need to hit the ball on the ground more often this season to take full advantage of his speed.

	G	AB	H	2B	3B	HR	RS	RBI	BB	SB	CS	BA
1995	133	480	138	16	3	4	72	28	38	50	18	.288
Career	238	579	161	18	4	4	96	32	45	59	24	.278
Projected	149	544	165	17	7	2	89	33	47	55	22	.303

Tom Gordon   P

Age: 28   **Seasons:** 8
Height: 5' 9"   **Weight:** 180
Bats: Right   **Throws:** Right
1995 OBA: .279   **1995 WHIP:** 1.55

The smallish hurler with the A+ curve is still searching for consistency. He was far more hittable in 1995 than in previous years, with lefties clubbing him at a .314 pace, and he continues to struggle with his control.

	G	GS	IP	ER	ERA	H	BB	SO	W	L	SV
1995	31	31	189.0	93	4.43	204	89	119	12	12	0
Career	274	144	1149.2	513	4.01	1040	587	999	79	71	2
Projected	33	33	219.1	90	3.69	227	71	181	13	7	0

Mark Gubicza **P**

Age: 33	**Seasons:** 12
Height: 6' 5"	**Weight:** 230
Bats: Right	**Throws:** Right
1995 OBA: .272	**1995 WHIP:** 1.33

Another former power pitcher who has made the transition to finesse late in his career, Gubicza capped off a solid 1995 season by tossing a four-hit shutout. He works fast, keeps walks to a minimum, and limits the running game.

	G	GS	IP	ER	ERA	H	BB	SO	W	L	SV
1995	33	33	213.1	89	3.75	222	62	81	12	14	0
Career	363	308	2099.1	898	3.85	2094	749	1311	128	123	2
Projected	35	35	219.0	94	3.86	231	55	91	10	10	0

Bob Hamelin **DH**

Age: 28	**Seasons:** 3
Height: 6' 0"	**Weight:** 235
Bats: Left	**Throws:** Left
1995 OBP: .278	**1995 SLG:** .313

The Hammer took a hit of his own last season, going from a 1994 Rookie of the Year Award to a minor-league demotion. He whiffed in a quarter of his total at-bats and hit just .157 versus righthanders after having clobbered them the year before.

	G	AB	H	2B	3B	HR	RS	RBI	BB	SB	CS	BA
1995	72	208	35	7	1	7	20	25	26	0	1	.168
Career	189	569	134	35	2	33	86	95	88	4	4	.236
Projected	111	298	74	15	0	14	37	42	37	0	1	.248

Chris Haney   **P**

Age: 27   **Seasons:** 5
Height: 6' 3"   **Weight:** 195
Bats: Left   **Throws:** Left
1995 OBA: .262   **1995 WHIP:** 1.36

Haney posted two straight seasons (1993 and 1994) of plus-6.00 ERAs, but last year he seemed to be on track until a herniated disk landed him on the 60-day DL. His stuff is average at best, and his career could go either way at this point.

	G	GS	IP	ER	ERA	H	BB	SO	W	L	SV
1995	16	13	81.1	33	3.65	78	33	31	3	4	0
Career	77	71	398.1	218	4.93	424	166	219	21	28	0
Projected	19	18	107.0	51	4.29	121	48	42	4	7	0

Jason Jacome   **P**

Age: 25   **Seasons:** 2
Height: 6' 1"   **Weight:** 155
Bats: Left   **Throws:** Left
1995 OBA: N/A   **1995 WHIP:** 1.62

Jacome may not have the skills his 1994 ERA (2.67 in eight starts) would suggest, but he should be able to solve some of last year's problems. He's a smart, gritty lefthander who relies on mixing his pitches and keeping them low in the zone.

	G	GS	IP	ER	ERA	H	BB	SO	W	L	SV
1995	20	19	105.0	74	5.36	134	36	50	4	10	0
Career	28	27	159.0	90	5.09	188	53	80	8	13	0
Projected	21	21	123.1	67	4.89	142	29	64	5	8	0

Wally Joyner 1B

Age: 33 **Seasons:** 10
Height: 6' 2" **Weight:** 200
Bats: Left **Throws:** Left
1995 OBP: .394 **1995 SLG:** .447

The hitting gods blessed Joyner with a textbook swing—it's too bad they didn't infuse a bit more pop into his bat. He's arguably the smoothest first baseman in the league and his stats (121 DPs, three errors) are Gold Glove caliber.

	G	AB	H	2B	3B	HR	RS	RBI	BB	SB	CS	BA
1995	131	465	144	28	0	12	69	83	69	3	2	.310
Career	1364	5105	1481	290	19	158	725	789	560	50	27	.290
Projected	149	569	161	22	2	14	75	81	76	4	3	.283

Keith Lockhart 2B

Age: 31 **Seasons:** 2
Height: 5' 10" **Weight:** 170
Bats: Left **Throws:** Right
1995 OBP: .355 **1995 SLG:** .478

Lockhart spent a decade in the minors before solidifying the Royals' middle infield last season. He flashed good pop for his size, played it smart on the bases, and developed quickly as a second baseman after having played third base at Omaha.

	G	AB	H	2B	3B	HR	RS	RBI	BB	SB	CS	BA
1995	94	274	88	19	3	6	41	33	14	8	1	.321
Career	121	317	97	19	3	8	45	39	18	9	1	.306
Projected	135	405	126	20	6	5	55	42	21	16	3	.311

Jeff Montgomery   P

Age: 34   **Seasons:** 9
Height: 5' 11"   **Weight:** 180
Bats: Right   **Throws:** Right
1995 OBA: .252   **1995 WHIP:** 1.29

Montgomery is one of several aging closers—Aggie, Eck, Lee Smith—who are still racking up saves without having dominant years. He's always very tough on righthanders but was toasted by portsiders for the second straight season.

	G	GS	IP	ER	ERA	H	BB	SO	W	L	SV
1995	54	0	65.2	25	3.43	60	25	49	2	3	31
Career	492	1	638.2	193	2.72	543	216	559	38	33	218
Projected	65	0	76.1	24	2.83	69	22	62	2	2	36

Jon Nunnally   OF

Age: 24   **Seasons:** 1
Height: 5' 10"   **Weight:** 190
Bats: Left   **Throws:** Right
1995 OBP: .357   **1995 SLG:** .472

A young power/speed player who can play any outfield position, Nunnally made the move from single-A to the Show and walloped 14 taters by early August. He won't play every day if he doesn't improve on last year's .162 versus lefties.

	G	AB	H	2B	3B	HR	RS	RBI	BB	SB	CS	BA
1995	119	303	74	15	6	14	51	42	51	6	4	.244
Career	119	303	74	15	6	14	51	42	51	6	4	.244
Projected	134	351	86	17	9	12	54	44	49	12	5	.245

Milwaukee
BREWERS

Scouting Report

Outfielders: Not believing that prospect Duane Singleton would be able to handle fulltime duty in center field, the Brewers traded for speedy Chuck Carr. Switch hitter Turner Ward has some pop and can cover acreage in left field, but his value as an everyday player is limited. Dave Nilsson is one of the Brewers' best hitters, but he's another player without a position, having been flip-flopped between the outfield, catcher, first base, and DH. Matt Mieske is an adequate right fielder with a strong arm who hits lefties about 100 points better than he hits righties.

Infielders: First baseman John Jaha was the only man in the Milwaukee lineup who provided a power threat in 1995. Jeff Cirillo should be solid at the hot corner, but don't count on seeing 1992 Rookie of the Year Pat Listach at any position on a regular basis unless his game undergoes a miraculous transformation. Jose Valentin, who took the shortstop job that Listach lost but hit just .133 against lefties, may be replaced by prospect Mark Loretta. Valentin could wind up in a second-base platoon with valuable but limited Fernando Vina.

Catchers: Mike Matheny, a reliable young backstop, hits righties and lefties with equal mediocrity. He enjoys home cooking, having hit .306 in Milwaukee, .138 on the road.

Designated Hitters: The Brewers hope for a return to form from struggling slugger Greg Vaughn.

Starting Pitchers: Cal Eldred, the true ace of Milwaukee's rotation, underwent season-ending elbow surgery after just four starts. The Brewers will be in a pickle if he can't come back strong. Would-be ace Ricky Bones proved to be an unfortunate substitute. The American League's "other" knuckleballer, Steve Sparks, will try to match the unexpected success of his now-famous Boston counterpart. Scott Karl, who tries to keep hitters off balance with off-speed stuff, threw well enough to remain penciled in to the rotation for 1996. Mark Kiefer, who bounced between triple-A and the majors last year, has pitched serviceably well in middle relief for the Brewers and could earn a shot at the fifth starting spot. He went 8–2, 2.82 at New Orleans in 12 starts after being designated for assignment in June.

Relief Pitchers: Mike Fetters, who toiled in middle relief before becoming a closer by default, presents a tough task for batters when he's able to spot his pitches and utilize his sinker. Southpaw Kevin Wickander held righthanders to a .209 batting average last year, and righthander Al Reyes (1–1, 2.43, .167) was very impressive before elbow surgery washed out his season.

Outlook

The Brewers expect to see increased revenues when the city's new stadium opens in 1999, but until then the club will probably be treading water far from contention. The probable free-agent departures of familiar faces Surhoff, Seitzer, and Hamilton could open the door for either the emergence of productive newcomers or a 100-loss season. Milwaukee finished 1995 on a downward slide that will only get more precipitous if the youngsters don't step up or the veterans don't have career years, but even a best-case scenario could equal last place in the division.

Fungoes

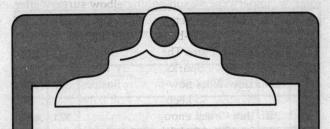

Quick Quiz: Which outfielder joined Reggie Jackson atop the home-run list in 1980, and which one accomplished the same feat in 1982?

Franchise Milestone: Since the Seattle Pilots flew into Milwaukee in 1970, the franchise has been to one World Series, a 4–3 loss to St. Louis in 1982.

Top Pitcher: Teddy Higuera, 1985–94

Top Player: Robin Yount, 1974–92

Top Manager: George Bamberger, 1978–80 and 1985–86

Wacky Nickname: The Ignitor (Paul Leo Molitor)

Quick Quiz Answer: Ben Oglivie and Gorman Thomas

Lineup Card

NO	POS	PLAYER	OBP	SLG
00	CF	Chuck Carr	.330	.312
11	LF	Dave Nilsson	.337	.468
56	3B	Jeff Cirillo	.371	.442
23	DH	Greg Vaughn	.317	.408
32	1B	John Jaha	.389	.579
2	2B	Jose Valentin	.293	.402
30	RF	Matt Mieske	.323	.442
22	C	Mike Matheny	.306	.313
8	SS	Mark Loretta	.327	.380

In a Nutshell: Milwaukee finished eleventh in the league in slugging and on-base percentage in 1995, which tells you quite a lot about the Brewers' blasé attack. This year's Brew Crew is in need of a quality leadoff hitter, and it's unclear whether Chuck Carr is qualified to fill that role. The heart of the order doesn't look too shabby in relation to itself, but compare Milwaukee's 3-4-5 to the Cleveland's 6-7-8 and a problem emerges. If Greg Vaughn vanishes again, the Brewers will face the prospect of having no one on base and no one to drive runners home. From the more optimistic angle, John Jaha, Jeff Cirillo, and Jose Valentin could each be on the verge of a breakthrough year. In any case, efficiency will be crucial for this lineup.

Milwaukee County Stadium

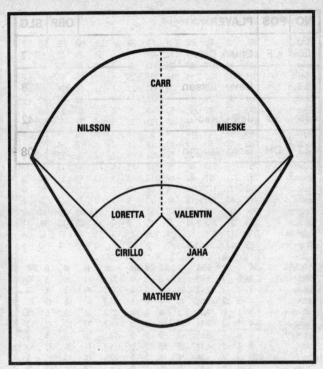

Capacity: 53,192
Turf: Natural

LF Line: 315
RF Line: 315
Center: 402
Left CF: 392
Right CF: 392

Tickets:
414-933-1818

The short dimensions down the lines and the history of prodigious sluggers may give the impression that this park favors hitters, but that isn't really true. The early- and late-summer cold can be tough on batters, while the alleys are forbiddingly deep. Most types of offense are cut by 5 percent over time, but several Brewers performed better at home than on the road in 1995.

Statistics

Minimum 25 at-bats or 10.0 innings pitched

PLAYER	BA	G	AB	RS	H	TB	2B	3B	HR	RBI	BB	SO	SB	CS
Surhoff	.320	117	415	72	133	204	26	3	13	73	37	43	7	3
Jaha	.313	88	316	59	99	183	20	2	20	65	36	66	2	1
Seitzer	.311	132	492	56	153	207	33	3	5	69	64	57	2	0
Nilsson	.278	81	263	41	73	123	12	1	12	53	24	41	2	0
Cirillo	.277	125	328	57	91	145	19	4	9	39	47	42	7	2
Oliver	.273	97	337	43	92	148	20	0	12	51	27	66	2	4
Hamilton	.271	112	398	54	108	155	20	6	5	44	47	35	11	1
Ward	.264	44	129	19	34	51	3	1	4	15	14	21	6	1
Loretta	.260	19	50	13	13	19	3	0	1	3	4	7	1	1
Vina	.257	113	288	46	74	104	7	7	3	29	22	28	6	1
Hulse	.251	119	339	46	85	117	11	6	3	47	18	60	15	3
Mieske	.251	117	267	42	67	118	13	1	12	48	27	45	2	4
May	.248	32	113	15	28	36	3	1	1	9	5	18	0	1
Matheny	.247	80	166	13	41	52	9	1	0	21	12	28	2	1
Vaughn	.224	108	392	67	88	160	19	1	17	59	55	89	10	4
Listach	.219	101	333	35	73	85	8	2	0	25	25	61	13	3
Valentin	.219	112	338	62	74	136	23	3	11	49	37	83	16	9
Singleton	.065	13	31	0	2	2	0	0	0	0	1	10	1	0

PITCHER	W	L	SV	ERA	G	GS	CG	SH	IP	H	R	ER	BB	SO
Wickander	0	0	1	1.93	29	0	0	0	23.1	19	6	5	12	11
Reyes	1	1	1	2.43	27	0	0	0	33.1	19	9	9	18	29
Fetters	0	3	22	3.38	40	0	0	0	34.2	40	16	13	20	33
Eldred	1	1	0	3.42	4	4	0	0	23.2	24	10	9	10	18
Kiefer	4	1	0	3.44	24	0	0	0	49.2	37	20	19	27	41
Bronkey	0	0	0	3.65	8	0	0	0	12.1	15	6	5	6	5
Karl	6	7	0	4.14	25	18	1	0	124.0	141	65	57	50	59
Lloyd	0	5	4	4.50	33	0	0	0	32.0	28	16	16	8	13
Bones	10	12	0	4.63	32	31	3	0	200.1	218	108	103	83	77
Sparks	9	11	0	4.63	33	27	3	0	202.0	210	111	104	86	96
McAndrew	2	3	0	4.71	10	4	0	0	36.1	37	21	19	12	19
Givens	5	7	0	4.95	19	19	0	0	107.1	116	71	59	54	73
Miranda	4	5	1	5.23	30	10	0	0	74.0	83	47	43	49	45
Wegman	5	7	2	5.35	38	4	0	0	70.2	89	45	42	21	50
Rightnowar	2	1	1	5.40	34	0	0	0	36.2	35	23	22	18	22
Slusarski	1	1	0	5.40	12	0	0	0	15.0	21	11	9	6	6
Roberson	6	4	0	5.76	26	13	0	0	84.1	102	55	54	37	40
Ignasiak	4	1	0	5.90	25	0	0	0	39.2	51	27	26	23	26
Scanlan	4	7	0	6.59	17	14	0	0	83.1	101	66	61	44	29
Dibble	1	1	1	7.18	31	0	0	0	26.1	16	21	21	46	26

Roster

MANAGER: Phil Garner
COACHES: Chris Bando, Bill Castro, Jim Gantner, LaMar Johnson, Don Rowe

NO	PITCHERS	B	T	HT	WT	DOB
25	Ricky Bones	R	R	6-0	190	4/7/69
29	Jeff Bronkey	R	R	6-3	215	9/18/65
21	Cal Eldred	R	R	6-4	235	11/24/67
36	Mike Fetters	R	R	6-4	215	12/19/64
13	Brian Givens	R	L	6-6	220	11/6/65
40	Michael Ignasiak	S	R	5-11	190	3/12/66
42	Scott Karl	L	L	6-2	195	8/9/71
37	Graeme Lloyd	L	L	6-7	230	4/9/67
49	Jamie McAndrew	R	R	6-2	190	9/2/67
41	Jose Mercedes	R	R	6-1	180	3/5/71
38	Angel Miranda	L	L	6-1	195	11/9/69
47	Al Reyes	R	R	6-1	193	4/10/71
39	Bob Scanlan	R	R	6-8	215	8/9/66
48	Joe Slusarski	R	R	6-4	195	12/19/66
50	Steve Sparks	R	R	6-0	187	7/2/65
52	Kevin Wickander	L	L	6-2	202	1/4/65
	CATCHERS					
22	Mike Matheny	R	R	6-3	205	9/22/70
11	Dave Nilsson	L	R	6-3	215	12/14/69
	INFIELDERS					
56	Jeff Cirillo	R	R	6-2	180	9/23/69
32	John Jaha	R	R	6-1	205	5/27/66
16	Pat Listach	S	R	5-9	170	9/12/67
8	Mark Loretta	R	R	6-0	175	8/14/71
8	Tim Unroe	R	R	6-3	200	10/7/70
2	Jose Valentin	S	R	5-10	175	10/12/69
1	Fernando Vina	L	R	5-9	170	4/16/69
	OUTFIELDERS					
—	Chuck Carr	S	R	5-10	165	8/10/68
15	David Hulse	L	L	5-11	170	2/25/68
30	Matt Mieske	R	R	6-0	185	2/13/68
18	Duane Singleton	L	L	6-1	171	8/6/72
23	Greg Vaughn	R	R	6-0	205	7/3/65
27	Turner Ward	S	R	6-2	182	4/11/65

FREE AGENTS: Rob Dibble, Darryl Hamilton, Joe Oliver, Kevin Seitzer, B.J. Surhoff, Bill Wegman

Cal Eldred

Ricky Bones   P

Age: 27   **Seasons:** 5
Height: 6' 0"   **Weight:** 190
Bats: Right   **Throws:** Right
1995 OBA: .281   **1995 WHIP:** 1.50

Any major-league finesse pitcher who throws 200-plus innings and walks more men than he whiffs is destined for obscurity. His stuff is barely average and he'll never win consistently without perfect location.

	G	GS	IP	ER	ERA	H	BB	SO	W	L	SV
1995	32	31	200.1	103	4.63	218	83	77	10	12	0
Career	130	125	792.0	390	4.43	832	257	293	44	48	0
Projected	33	33	186.1	102	4.93	223	78	74	7	14	0

Jeff Cirillo   3B

Age: 26   **Seasons:** 2
Height: 6' 2"   **Weight:** 180
Bats: Right   **Throws:** Right
1995 OBP: .371   **1995 SLG:** .442

Set to take over fulltime duties at third base, Cirillo is an overachiever who hit in the .300 range at every minor-league level. He flashed decent pop in the Show last year and walked more than he whiffed.

	G	AB	H	2B	3B	HR	RS	RBI	BB	SB	CS	BA
1995	125	328	91	19	4	9	57	39	47	7	2	.277
Career	164	454	121	28	4	12	74	51	58	7	3	.267
Projected	149	401	115	20	2	11	62	41	44	10	3	.287

Cal Eldred   P

Age: 28	**Seasons:** 5
Height: 6' 4"	**Weight:** 235
Bats: Right	**Throws:** Right
1995 OBA: .261	**1995 WHIP:** 1.44

In 1993, Eldred pitched to more than 1,000 batters in a chart-topping 258 innings pitched. The next season he strung together five straight complete games at one point. Now he's trying to return from elbow surgery and may never be the same.

	G	GS	IP	ER	ERA	H	BB	SO	W	L	SV
1995	4	4	23.2	9	3.42	24	10	18	1	1	0
Career	82	82	577.0	245	3.82	510	214	368	41	30	0
Projected	26	26	184.1	82	4.00	177	65	124	8	8	0

Mike Fetters   P

Age: 31	**Seasons:** 7
Height: 6' 4"	**Weight:** 215
Bats: Right	**Throws:** Right
1995 OBA: .286	**1995 WHIP:** 1.73

At his best, Fetters throws a leaden sinker that virtually eliminates the longball. His whiffs-to-walks ratio is not that of a first-class closer, but he'll do until someone more dominant comes along.

	G	GS	IP	ER	ERA	H	BB	SO	W	L	SV
1995	40	0	34.2	13	3.38	40	20	33	0	3	22
Career	223	6	318.1	119	3.36	313	142	193	12	17	42
Projected	45	0	41.0	13	2.93	42	18	42	1	4	24

John Jaha   1B

Age: 29   **Seasons:** 4
Height: 6' 1"   **Weight:** 205
Bats: Right   **Throws:** Right
1995 OBP: .389   **1995 SLG:** .579

Jaha spent time on the DL last year and still hasn't confirmed that he can offer big-time run production over a full season, but his 1995 slugging percentage would have ranked in the league's top ten if he'd had enough at-bats to qualify.

	G	AB	H	2B	3B	HR	RS	RBI	BB	SB	CS	BA
1995	88	316	99	20	2	20	59	65	36	2	1	.313
Career	372	1255	335	58	3	53	199	184	131	28	13	.267
Projected	154	510	147	23	0	26	81	83	43	3	2	.288

Scott Karl   P

Age: 24   **Seasons:** 1
Height: 6' 2"   **Weight:** 195
Bats: Left   **Throws:** Left
1995 OBA: .288   **1995 WHIP:** 1.54

He's not a hard thrower, but Karl was a winner in his minor-league career. His change-up is effective, and his offerings are usually near the plate. The extent to which he keeps righthanders in check may determine the length of his career.

	G	GS	IP	ER	ERA	H	BB	SO	W	L	SV
1995	25	18	124.0	57	4.14	141	50	59	6	7	0
Career	25	18	124.0	57	4.14	141	50	59	6	7	0
Projected	32	32	174.1	72	3.72	184	45	71	7	11	0

Dave Nilsson   OF

Age: 26   **Seasons:** 4
Height: 6' 3"   **Weight:** 215
Bats: Left   **Throws:** Right
1995 OBP: .337   **1995 SLG:** .468

Nilsson was slowed by injury in 1995, but he's upped his average each year of his career and added a little power along the way. He handles righties and lefties equally well, but there was an 83-point split in his home and road BAs, .317 to .234.

	G	AB	H	2B	3B	HR	RS	RBI	BB	SB	CS	BA
1995	81	263	73	12	1	12	41	53	24	2	0	.278
Career	341	1120	296	58	6	35	142	187	112	8	8	.264
Projected	118	403	113	15	2	10	47	55	30	1	2	.280

Kevin Seitzer   3B

Age: 34   **Seasons:** 10
Height: 5' 11"   **Weight:** 190
Bats: Right   **Throws:** Right
1995 OBP: .395   **1995 SLG:** .421

Seitzer has been a solid player, but the Brewers were wise to let him leave via free agency. He doesn't contribute much in the field and he has little power at the plate. He'll probably sign on somewhere as a stopgap or utility infielder.

	G	AB	H	2B	3B	HR	RS	RBI	BB	SB	CS	BA
1995	132	492	153	33	3	5	56	69	64	2	0	.311
Career	1221	4507	1317	236	32	59	627	511	564	74	48	.292
Projected	126	450	126	24	1	5	44	48	52	4	2	.280

Steve Sparks   P

Age: 30	**Seasons:** 1
Height: 6' 0"	**Weight:** 187
Bats: Right	**Throws:** Right
1995 OBA: .274	**1995 WHIP:** 1.47

Sparks, a standard-issue 30-year-old rookie knuckleballer, wasn't a profound mystery to minor-league hitters in 1993 and 1994, and the situation was essentially the same at the big-league level last season.

	G	GS	IP	ER	ERA	H	BB	SO	W	L	SV
1995	33	27	202.0	104	4.63	210	86	96	9	11	0
Career	33	27	202.0	104	4.63	210	86	96	9	11	0
Projected	30	30	212.1	98	4.15	219	72	101	7	10	0

B.J. Surhoff   OF/1B

Age: 31	**Seasons:** 9
Height: 6' 1"	**Weight:** 200
Bats: Left	**Throws:** Right
1995 OBP: .378	**1995 SLG:** .492

Surhoff used to be an underachiever, but he lowered expectations to the point where everything he does well is a nice surprise. His top-ten finish in 1995's AL batting race certainly qualifies—he hit 52 points over his previous career average.

	G	AB	H	2B	3B	HR	RS	RBI	BB	SB	CS	BA
1995	117	415	133	26	3	13	72	73	37	7	3	.320
Career	1102	3884	1064	194	24	57	472	524	294	102	64	.274
Projected	129	464	125	22	1	12	68	61	40	3	1	.269

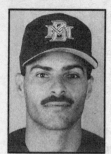

Jose Valentin   2B/SS

Age: 26   **Seasons:** 4
Height: 5' 10"   **Weight:** 175
Bats: Switch   **Throws:** Right
1995 OBP: .293   **1995 SLG:** .402

A broken finger and a susceptibility to strikeouts spoiled his 1995 season, and the play of rookie Mark Loretta could prompt a shift to second base for Valentin, but he has 20/20 tools and spectacular range at either middle-infield position.

	G	AB	H	2B	3B	HR	RS	RBI	BB	SB	CS	BA
1995	112	338	74	23	3	11	62	49	37	16	8	.219
Career	232	679	155	43	5	23	120	103	82	29	11	.228
Projected	120	346	84	20	2	14	54	50	41	17	7	.243

Greg Vaughn   DH

Age: 30   **Seasons:** 7
Height: 6' 0"   **Weight:** 205
Bats: Right   **Throws:** Right
1995 OBP: .317   **1995 SLG:** .408

Reported to be making about a third of the Brewers' total payroll, Vaughn didn't hold up his end of the bargain. He bopped 30 home runs in 1993 but hasn't been as productive since. Injuries are partially to blame for the dropoff.

	G	AB	H	2B	3B	HR	RS	RBI	BB	SB	CS	BA
1995	108	392	88	19	1	17	67	59	55	10	4	.224
Career	801	2869	694	142	13	138	450	471	363	57	38	.242
Projected	131	446	106	21	1	21	70	72	58	8	4	.238

Minnesota
TWINS

Scouting Report

Outfielders: Right fielder Kirby Puckett, who sat out the last of the 1995 season with a broken jaw, is an institution in Minnesota. Rich Becker was supposed to be the center fielder of the future, but he was basically a bust last year. Young speedster Matt Lawton will challenge for a fulltime job. Left fielder Marty Cordova was the AL's 1995 Rookie of the Year and has the talent to build on his excellent first-year numbers. Pedro Munoz sees action in right field on an occasional basis.

Infielders: Chuck Knoblauch has added a power dimension to his game, making him one of the most complete second basemen in the majors. The rest of the infield is unsettled. Jeff Reboulet is a valuable utility infielder and a consistent contributor with the bat, but he isn't an everyday third baseman. Tom Quinlan isn't being counted on to provide much help despite a strong season at triple-A. It could be up to Ron Coomer, who was picked up from the Dodgers for Kevin Tapani, to solidify the hot corner. Shortstop Pat Meares is just average defensively and at the plate, though he did muscle up to contribute double-figure homers last year. His competition is prospect Denny Hocking, whose triple-A numbers are solid but won't knock your socks off. The Twins have a plethora of prospects at first base, but Pedro Munoz may claim the everyday job.

Catchers: Matt Walbeck, picked up from the Cubs in 1994 in exchange for Willie Banks, raised his dismal lifetime batting average to a livable level last season, but he has little potential on offense.

Designated Hitters: Paul Molitor has returned to the area where he was born, to carry on his pursuit of 3,000 hits and anchor the Twins' batting order.

Starting Pitchers: Among Minnesota's young starters, the best bet to have an impact in the win column is probably Frankie Rodriguez, though he posted awful stats last year. Brad Radke, LaTroy Hawkins, and Rich Robertson have shown some promise, but overall the rotation was rickety in its inaugural run. Robertson finished 1995 on a roll and could be the ace of the staff this season. Radke actually pitched better than his mediocre stats indicate, and vast improvement from him wouldn't be surprising.

Relief Pitchers: The Twins' bullpen is divided between those with plus-5.00 ERAs—Eddie Guardado, Dave Stevens, Oscar Munoz—and others, such as Pat Mahomes and Scott Klingenbeck, who are even worse. Stevens is first in line for the role of late-inning stopper.

Outlook

Minnesota has the right idea—avoid paying megadollar salaries that will probably only result in expensive mediocrity—but the second element of the youth-movement equation is to cultivate quality prospects, a trick the Twins are struggling to turn. In 1982 the organization produced one of the most bountiful rookie crops in modern annals, a harvest that included names like Puckett, Gaetti, and Hrbek. Such results are hard to repeat, and the Twinkies didn't come close last season, but they'll keep promoting farmhands to the big club until something good happens.

Fungoes

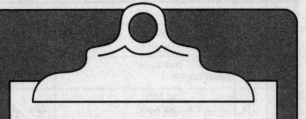

Quick Quiz: Which pitcher holds the Minnesota record for wins in a single season with 25?

Franchise Milestone: The Senators were champs in 1924 as Walter Johnson got the win in Game Seven. The Twins captured World Series titles in 1987 and 1991.

Top Pitcher: Walter Johnson, 1907–27

Top Player: Harmon Killebrew, 1954–74

Top Manager: Tom Kelly, 1986–

Wacky Nickname: Superjew (Michael Peter Epstein)

Quick Quiz Answer: Jim Kaat

Lineup Card

NO	POS	PLAYER	OBP	SLG
—	DH	Paul Molitor	.350	.423
50	CF	Matt Lawton	.414	.467
11	2B	Chuck Knoblauch	.424	.487
34	RF	Kirby Puckett	.379	.515
40	LF	Marty Cordova	.352	.486
5	1B	Pedro Munoz	.338	.489
2	SS	Pat Meares	.311	.431
17	3B	Jeff Reboulet	.373	.398
9	C	Matt Walbeck	.302	.316

In a Nutshell: The lower half of the Twinkies' lineup reads like a Who's Who of Who's That? The batting order is rife with wild swingers, some of whom connect frequently—such as Puckett and Munoz—but most of whom can be easily handled by any savvy hurler. The signing of Molitor will create some balance, but the Minnesota batters still draw fewer walks and homer less often than any other AL crew. Such characteristics make this a negative image of a successful offense, so the benefits of a respectable overall batting average are largely usurped. Nevertheless, if the youngsters make progress and the role players hold their own, the offense should be good enough to produce some thrills.

Hubert H. Humphrey Metrodome

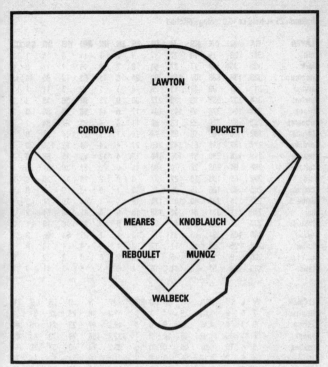

Capacity: 56,783
Turf: Artificial

LF Line: 343
RF Line: 327
Center: 408
Left CF: 385
Right CF: 367

Tickets:
612-375-7444

The Homerdome's bizarre design elements—tricky ceiling lights, hard turf, and plastic bags in the outfield—are less than conducive to classic baseball, but when the team is rolling and the fans are rocking, the closed environment can create deafening noise and a decided home-field advantage. Righty power hitters thrive here, and control pitchers are valuable.

Statistics

Minimum 25 at-bats or 10.0 innings pitched

PLAYER	BA	G	AB	RS	H	TB	2B	3B	HR	RBI	BB	SO	SB	CS
Cole	.342	28	79	10	27	37	3	2	1	14	8	15	1	3
Clark	.339	36	109	17	37	60	8	3	3	15	2	11	3	0
Knoblauch	.333	136	538	107	179	262	34	8	11	63	78	95	46	18
Lawton	.317	21	60	11	19	28	4	1	1	12	7	11	1	1
Puckett	.314	137	538	83	169	277	39	0	23	99	56	89	3	2
Munoz	.301	104	376	45	113	184	17	0	18	58	19	86	0	3
Reboulet	.292	87	216	39	63	86	11	0	4	23	27	34	1	2
Merullo	.282	76	195	19	55	74	14	1	1	27	14	27	0	1
Cordova	.277	137	512	81	142	249	27	4	24	84	52	111	20	7
Meares	.269	116	390	57	105	168	19	4	12	49	15	68	10	4
Stahoviak	.266	94	263	28	70	98	19	0	3	23	30	61	5	1
Hale	.262	69	103	10	27	37	4	0	2	18	11	20	0	0
Coomer	.260	36	100	15	26	46	3	1	5	19	9	10	0	1
Walbeck	.257	115	393	40	101	124	18	1	1	44	25	71	3	1
Leius	.248	117	371	51	92	130	16	5	4	45	49	54	2	1
Masteller	.237	71	198	21	47	68	12	0	3	21	18	19	1	2
Becker	.236	106	394	45	93	116	15	1	2	33	34	96	8	8
McCarty	.218	25	55	10	12	17	3	1	0	4	4	18	0	1
Hocking	.200	9	25	4	5	9	0	2	0	3	2	2	1	0
Maas	.193	22	57	5	11	18	4	0	1	5	7	11	0	0

PITCHER	W	L	SV	ERA	G	GS	CG	SH	IP	H	R	ER	BB	SO
Robertson	2	0	0	3.83	25	4	1	0	51.2	48	28	22	31	38
Guthrie	5	3	0	4.46	36	0	0	0	42.1	47	22	21	16	48
Tapani	6	11	0	4.92	20	20	3	1	133.2	155	79	73	34	88
Stevens	5	4	10	5.07	56	0	0	0	65.2	74	40	37	32	47
Guardado	4	9	2	5.12	51	5	0	0	91.1	99	54	52	45	71
Sanford	0	0	0	5.30	11	0	0	0	18.2	16	11	11	16	17
Radke	11	14	0	5.32	29	28	2	1	181.0	195	112	107	47	75
Watkins	0	0	0	5.40	27	0	0	0	21.2	22	14	13	11	12
Munoz	2	1	0	5.60	10	3	0	0	35.1	40	28	22	17	25
Trombley	4	8	0	5.62	20	18	0	0	97.2	107	68	61	42	68
Rodriguez	5	8	0	6.13	25	18	0	0	105.2	114	83	72	57	59
Mahomes	4	10	3	6.37	47	7	0	0	94.2	100	74	67	47	67
Schullstrom	0	0	0	6.89	37	0	0	0	47.0	66	36	36	22	21
Klingenbeck	2	4	0	7.12	24	9	0	0	79.2	101	65	63	42	42
Parra	1	5	0	7.59	12	12	0	0	61.2	83	59	52	22	29
Hawkins	2	3	0	8.67	6	6	1	0	27.0	39	29	26	12	9
Harris	0	5	0	8.82	7	6	0	0	32.2	50	35	32	16	21

Roster

MANAGER: Tom Kelly
COACHES: Terry Crowley, Ron Gardenhire, Rick Stelmaszek, Dick Such, Scott Ullger

NO	PITCHERS	B	T	HT	WT	DOB
—	Marc Barcelo	R	R	6-3	215	1/10/72
49	Gus Gandarillas	R	R	6-0	183	7/19/71
18	Eddie Guardado	R	L	6-0	193	10/2/70
—	Greg Hansell	R	R	6-5	215	3/12/71
32	LaTroy Hawkins	R	R	6-5	193	12/21/72
52	Scott Klingenbeck	R	R	6-2	205	2/3/71
20	Pat Mahomes	R	R	6-4	210	8/9/70
—	Mike Misuraca	R	R	6-0	188	8/21/68
—	Dan Naulty	R	R	6-6	211	1/6/70
56	Jose Parra	R	R	5-11	165	11/28/72
59	Brad Radke	R	R	6-2	186	10/27/72
30	Todd Ritchie	R	R	6-3	190	11/7/71
—	Brett Roberts	R	R	6-7	230	3/24/70
47	Rich Robertson	L	L	6-4	175	9/15/68
33	Frank Rodriguez	R	R	6-0	193	12/11/72
—	Dan Serafini	S	L	6-1	180	1/25/74
41	Dave Stevens	R	R	6-3	210	3/4/70
23	Hector Trinidad	R	R	6-2	190	9/8/73
21	Mike Trombley	R	R	6-2	208	4/14/67
51	Scott Watkins	L	L	6-3	180	5/15/70
	CATCHERS					
27	Mike Durant	R	R	6-2	200	9/14/69
23	Matt Walbeck	S	R	5-11	190	10/2/69
	INFIELDERS					
15	Ron Coomer	R	R	5-11	195	11/18/66
7	Denny Hocking	S	R	5-10	174	4/2/70
11	Chuck Knoblauch	R	R	5-9	181	7/7/68
2	Pat Meares	R	R	6-0	184	9/6/68
—	Paul Molitor	R	R	6-0	180	8/22/56
—	Tom Quinlan	R	R	6-3	214	3/27/68
17	Jeff Reboulet	R	R	6-0	169	4/30/64
37	Scott Stahoviak	L	R	6-5	208	3/6/70
	OUTFIELDERS					
25	Rich Becker	S	L	5-10	180	2/1/72
40	Marty Cordova	R	R	6-0	200	7/10/69
—	J.J. Johnson	R	R	6-0	195	8/31/73
—	Chris Latham	S	R	6-0	195	5/26/73
50	Matt Lawton	L	R	5-10	196	11/3/71
5	Pedro Munoz	R	R	5-10	203	9/19/68
—	Jamie Ogden	L	L	6-5	233	1/19/72
34	Kirby Puckett	R	R	5-9	215	3/14/61

FREE AGENTS: None

Rich Becker   OF

Age: 24   **Seasons:** 3
Height: 5' 10"   **Weight:** 180
Bats: Switch   **Throws:** Left
1995 OBP: .302   **1995 SLG:** .294

Whatever the Twins' scouts see (or saw) in Becker hasn't been manifested in his play. He trashed his knee in 1993, which may partly explain his poor success rate on steal attempts last year. He's prone to slumps with both the bat and glove.

	G	AB	H	2B	3B	HR	RS	RBI	BB	SB	CS	BA
1995	106	394	93	15	1	2	45	33	34	8	8	.236
Career	137	497	121	20	1	3	60	41	52	15	10	.243
Projected	115	412	99	18	2	3	49	34	37	10	6	.240

Marty Cordova   OF

Age: 26   **Seasons:** 1
Height: 6' 0"   **Weight:** 200
Bats: Right   **Throws:** Right
1995 OBP: .352   **1995 SLG:** .486

Cordova is a young, sweet-swinging hitter with substantial linedrive pop and good speed who could be the Twins' best hitter this season, especially if he cuts down on his strikeouts. His defense in left field needs some work.

	G	AB	H	2B	3B	HR	RS	RBI	BB	SB	CS	BA
1995	137	512	142	27	4	24	81	84	52	20	7	.277
Career	137	512	142	27	4	24	81	84	52	20	7	.277
Projected	158	592	174	29	6	26	91	94	64	24	6	.294

LaTroy Hawkins P

Age: 23   **Seasons:** 2
Height: 6' 5"   **Weight:** 193
Bats: Right   **Throws:** Right
1995 OBA: .339   **1995 WHIP:** 1.89

Young, athletic, and dominant in the minors, Hawkins entered 1995 as the Twins' top pitching prospect. His overall numbers don't reflect much initial success, but he did toss a five-hit complete game versus Chicago in late September.

	G	GS	IP	ER	ERA	H	BB	SO	W	L	SV
1995	6	6	27.0	26	8.67	39	12	9	2	3	0
Career	6	6	27.0	26	8.67	39	12	9	2	3	0
Projected	24	24	125.0	74	5.33	141	32	51	6	11	0

Chuck Knoblauch 2B

Age: 27   **Seasons:** 5
Height: 5' 9"   **Weight:** 181
Bats: Right   **Throws:** Right
1995 OBP: .424   **1995 SLG:** .487

Knoblauch jacked more taters in 1995 than in his previous four seasons combined. He's a prolific basestealer (though last year's success rate was the lowest of his career), a superior fielder—and he's still improving.

	G	AB	H	2B	3B	HR	RS	RBI	BB	SB	CS	BA
1995	136	538	179	34	8	11	107	63	78	46	18	.333
Career	704	2750	822	149	27	21	456	261	331	169	53	.299
Projected	154	601	191	30	5	13	109	66	83	35	12	.318

Pat Meares   SS

Age: 27   **Seasons:** 3
Height: 6' 0"   **Weight:** 184
Bats: Right   **Throws:** Right
1995 OBP: .311   **1995 SLG:** .431

Meares is a marginal starter who must maximize his talents to keep his job. An offseason weightlifting regimen led to a quantum leap in his power stats, but he doesn't get on base much and isn't considered a wizard with the glove.

	G	AB	H	2B	3B	HR	RS	RBI	BB	SB	CS	BA
1995	116	390	105	19	4	12	57	49	15	10	4	.269
Career	307	965	253	45	8	14	119	106	36	19	10	.262
Projected	124	423	110	21	2	9	52	53	18	13	5	.260

Pedro Munoz   DH

Age: 27   **Seasons:** 6
Height: 5' 10"   **Weight:** 203
Bats: Right   **Throws:** Right
1995 OBP: .338   **1995 SLG:** .489

Despite being one of the least disciplined hitters in the league, Munoz is talented enough to contribute solid offensive numbers, but he probably won't continue to develop unless he forces pitchers to throw him strikes.

	G	AB	H	2B	3B	HR	RS	RBI	BB	SB	CS	BA
1995	104	376	113	17	0	18	45	58	19	0	3	.301
Career	483	1587	436	70	8	61	186	234	91	11	10	.275
Projected	124	417	119	19	1	20	49	61	23	0	2	.285

Kirby Puckett OF

Age: 35   **Seasons:** 12
Height: 5' 9"   **Weight:** 215
Bats: Right   **Throws:** Right
1995 OBP: .379   **1995 SLG:** .515

Baseball's lovable fireplug just keeps on spraying linedrives with authority. He's even showing more patience at the plate these days, registering more walks and fewer whiffs. His strong and accurate arm still makes meat of those who test it.

	G	AB	H	2B	3B	HR	RS	RBI	BB	SB	CS	BA
1995	137	538	169	39	0	23	83	99	56	3	2	.314
Career	1783	7244	2304	414	57	207	1071	1085	450	134	76	.318
Projected	152	611	189	32	2	21	94	96	48	5	3	.309

Brad Radke P

Age: 23   **Seasons:** 1
Height: 6' 2"   **Weight:** 186
Bats: Right   **Throws:** Right
1995 OBA: .275   **1995 WHIP:** 1.34

Radke got rocked by Cleveland in his final start of 1995, but he was a fixture in the rotation for the entire season, leading the Twins in starts and strikeouts while fashioning the team's only complete-game shutout of the year.

	G	GS	IP	ER	ERA	H	BB	SO	W	L	SV
1995	29	28	181.0	107	5.32	195	47	75	11	14	0
Career	29	28	181.0	107	5.32	195	47	75	11	14	0
Projected	33	33	223.0	121	4.88	231	53	123	10	14	0

Rich Robertson   P

Age: 27   **Seasons:** 3
Height: 6' 4"   **Weight:** 175
Bats: Left   **Throws:** Left
1995 OBA: .253   **1995 WHIP:** 1.53

Robertson was a washout in previous big-league trials with Pittsburgh, but he seems to be making progress, as evidenced by his final two starts last season (18 innings, 1.50 ERA) after a late-season call-up.

	G	GS	IP	ER	ERA	H	BB	SO	W	L	SV
1995	25	4	51.2	22	3.83	48	31	38	2	0	0
Career	42	4	76.1	40	4.72	83	45	51	2	1	0
Projected	28	21	143.1	61	3.83	137	54	101	9	8	0

Frank Rodriguez   P

Age: 23   **Seasons:** 1
Height: 6' 0"   **Weight:** 193
Bats: Right   **Throws:** Right
1995 OBA: .277   **1995 WHIP:** 1.62

The top prospect in Boston's system, Rodriguez was acquired by the Twins in midseason for Rick Aguilera. His wicked stuff, relative youth, and overall athleticism are reasons for excitement, but his lack of control is cause for concern.

	G	GS	IP	ER	ERA	H	BB	SO	W	L	SV
1995	25	18	105.2	72	6.13	114	57	59	5	8	0
Career	25	18	105.2	72	6.13	114	57	59	5	8	0
Projected	34	34	216.2	113	4.69	210	82	131	8	13	0

Dave Stevens P

Age: 26   **Seasons:** 2
Height: 6' 3"   **Weight:** 210
Bats: Right   **Throws:** Right
1995 OBA: .285   **1995 WHIP:** 1.61

A component of the Willie Banks deal in 1994, Stevens is considered the top in-house candidate to fill the void left by Rick Aguilera's departure. He has a pretty good heater but inconsistent command of the strikezone.

	G	GS	IP	ER	ERA	H	BB	SO	W	L	SV
1995	56	0	65.2	37	5.07	74	32	47	5	4	10
Career	80	0	110.2	71	5.77	129	55	71	10	6	10
Projected	62	0	71.1	27	3.41	61	28	56	3	4	22

Matt Walbeck C

Age: 26   **Seasons:** 3
Height: 5' 11"   **Weight:** 190
Bats: Switch   **Throws:** Right
1995 OBP: .302   **1995 SLG:** .316

Walbeck showed slight progress at the plate last season, lifting his lifetime batting average to a respectable level, but he rarely walks and has no power, so his days in the majors are probably numbered. He does have an excellent throwing arm.

	G	AB	H	2B	3B	HR	RS	RBI	BB	SB	CS	BA
1995	115	393	101	18	1	1	40	44	25	3	1	.257
Career	223	761	176	32	1	7	73	85	43	4	2	.231
Projected	142	475	127	17	0	4	42	48	33	2	0	.267

Paul O'Neill

New York
YANKEES

Scouting Report

Outfielders: Paul O'Neill is the Yankees' most balanced hitter and a natural right fielder. Bernie Williams ranks among the AL's top glovemen in center while offering a power/speed blend that's otherwise lacking in the New York lineup. Gerald Williams can cover any of the three outfield spots and chip in some extra-base punch at the plate, but he's not an everyday player. The best bet to cover left is Ruben Rivera, who may need more seasoning in the minors but who has big-league power at age 22.

Infielders: Don Mattingly's retirement leaves an opening at first base. If the Bombers can't deal for a big bopper, look for Wade Boggs to move across the diamond from third. If a deal is made involving blue-chip prospect Russ Davis, look for Boggs to remain at the hot corner. Second baseman Pat Kelly is a stellar fielder and no slouch with the stick, but the Yanks appear bent on signing a big-name free agent to replace him. Highly touted Derek Jeter has little left to prove as a minor-league hitter, but his skills at shortstop have been questioned. Young third sacker Andy Fox batted .348 and slugged .530 at triple-A Columbus last year, but it isn't likely that he'll be handed the everyday job in the Bronx.

Catchers: Joe Girardi is a quality receiver but not much of a hitter. The backup should be prospect Jorge Posada, who lashed 32 doubles and struck out 101 times in 108 games at triple-A Columbus.

Designated Hitters: Ruben Sierra offers explosive power and production

Starting Pitchers: Jack McDowell—a free agent at press time—is a quality starter with a nasty streak. Free agent David Cone is ready to take his pitching-mercenary show back on the road, but the Yanks would love to pencil him in as their staff ace. Jimmy Key has had four shoulder surgeries in his career and may not return to his prior form. There may be room in the rotation for righthanded prospects Brian Boehringer and Mariano Rivera. Sterling Hitchcock, the subject of trade rumors, has ace potential, and Andy Pettitte looked like a future star during the 1995 stretch run. Scott Kamieniecki could see action as a spot starter. The wild card is Doc Gooden, who missed all of 1995 because of a drug suspension.

Relief Pitchers: John Wetteland is one of the league's toughest closers, but he's unsigned at press time. Setup men Steve Howe and Bob Wickman underachieved last season. Mariano Rivera will bolster the bullpen if he isn't in the starting rotation.

Outlook

If a World Series ring could be acquired with cash, the Yankees wouldn't be enduring a 17-year drought. New York has a poor track record in regard to the development of fresh talent—when they haven't given it away they've blocked it with past-prime veterans. It's a lack of wisdom and courage that fuels the compulsion to acquire "proven" players from outside the organization, but the Bombers may find themselves being infiltrated by youngsters who are too talented to ignore, and the franchise may wind up winning in spite of itself.

Fungoes

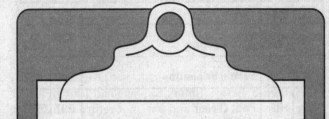

Quick Quiz: Which Yankees hurler threw two no-hitters in his career?

Franchise Milestone: Since 1921 the Bronx Bombers have won 24 World Series titles, including five consecutive starting in 1949. The most recent came in 1978 as New York roared back from a two-game deficit to defeat the Dodgers in six.

Top Pitcher: Whitey Ford, 1950–67

Top Player: Babe Ruth, 1920–34

Top Manager: Casey Stengel, 1949–60

Wacky Nickname: Poosh 'Em Up Tony (Anthony Michael Lazzeri)

Quick Quiz Answer: Allie Reynolds

Lineup Card

NO	POS	PLAYER	OBP	SLG
12	1B	Wade Boggs	.412	.422
51	CF	Bernie Williams	.392	.487
21	RF	Paul O'Neill	.387	.526
25	DH	Ruben Sierra	.323	.449
24	3B	Russ Davis	.349	.429
17	LF	Ruben Rivera	.000	.000
2	SS	Derek Jeter	.294	.375
14	2B	Pat Kelly	.307	.333
00	C	Joe Girardi	.308	.359

In a Nutshell: Free agency will, as always, be a prevailing force in shaping the Yankees' batting order, giving fans plenty to talk about. What fresh faces will grace the back pages of New York's tabloid newspapers, and which young prospects will go on to star for other teams? Bernie Williams, New York's most versatile offensive weapon, is certain to score 100 runs in a full season near the top of the order. If Davis and Rivera are allowed to develop, there should be substantial pop in spots two through five, though there won't be an ideal amount of lefthanded power unless a trade is made. Expect the rookies to be the key to success in the Bronx, if Boss Steinbrenner gives them a snowball's chance....

Yankee Stadium

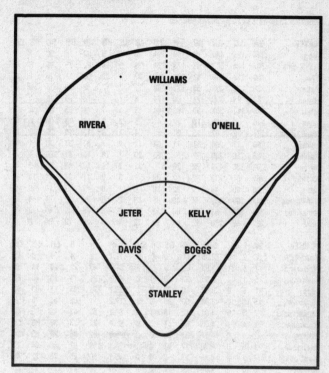

Capacity: 57,545
Turf: Natural

LF Line: 312
RF Line: 310
Center: 410
Left CF: 411
Right CF: 385

Tickets:
718-293-6000

Due to the caverous depths of the outfield in center and left center, righthanded hitters such as Russ Davis are at a disadvantage in the House that Ruth Built. Though the choking-off effect is less severe for lefties, only extreme pull hitters are equipped to take advantage of the short porch in left. Lou Gehrig, for example, put up better career numbers away from the Bronx.

Statistics

Minimum 25 at-bats or 10.0 innings pitched

PLAYER	BA	G	AB	RS	H	TB	2B	3B	HR	RBI	BB	SO	SB	CS
Boggs	.324	126	460	76	149	194	22	4	5	63	74	50	1	1
B. Williams	.307	144	563	93	173	274	29	9	18	82	75	98	8	6
O'Neill	.300	127	460	82	138	242	30	4	22	96	71	76	1	2
Mattingly	.288	128	458	59	132	189	32	2	7	49	40	35	0	2
James	.287	85	209	22	60	74	6	1	2	26	20	16	4	1
Velarde	.278	111	367	60	102	144	19	1	7	46	55	64	5	1
Davis	.276	39	98	14	27	42	5	2	2	12	10	26	0	0
Strawberry	.276	32	87	15	24	39	4	1	3	13	10	22	0	0
Leyritz	.269	77	264	37	71	104	12	0	7	37	37	73	1	1
Stanley	.268	118	399	63	107	192	29	1	18	83	57	106	1	1
Sierra	.263	126	479	73	126	215	32	0	19	86	46	76	5	4
Polonia	.261	67	238	37	62	83	9	3	2	15	25	29	10	4
Jeter	.250	15	48	5	12	18	4	1	0	7	3	11	0	0
G. Williams	.247	100	182	33	45	85	18	2	6	28	22	34	4	2
Fernandez	.245	108	384	57	94	133	20	2	5	45	42	40	6	6
Kelly	.237	89	270	32	64	90	12	1	4	29	23	65	8	3

PITCHER	W	L	SV	ERA	G	GS	CG	SH	IP	H	R	ER	BB	SO
Manzanillo	0	0	0	2.08	11	0	0	0	17.1	19	4	4	9	11
Wetteland	1	5	31	2.93	60	0	0	0	61.1	40	22	20	14	66
Honeycutt	5	1	2	2.96	52	0	0	0	45.2	39	16	15	10	21
Cone	18	8	0	3.57	30	30	6	2	229.1	195	95	91	88	191
McDowell	15	10	0	3.93	30	30	8	2	217.2	211	106	95	78	157
Kamieniecki	7	6	0	4.01	17	16	1	0	89.2	83	43	40	49	43
Wickman	2	4	1	4.05	63	1	0	0	80.0	77	38	36	33	51
Pettitte	12	9	0	4.17	31	26	3	0	175.0	182	86	81	63	114
Hitchcock	11	10	0	4.70	27	27	4	1	168.1	155	91	88	68	121
MacDonald	1	1	0	4.86	33	0	0	0	46.1	50	25	25	22	41
Howe	6	3	2	4.96	56	0	0	0	49.0	66	29	27	17	28
Rivera	5	3	0	5.51	19	10	0	0	67.0	71	43	41	30	51
Perez	5	5	0	5.58	13	12	1	0	69.1	70	46	43	31	44
Key	1	2	0	5.64	5	5	0	0	30.1	40	20	19	6	14
Ausanio	2	0	1	5.73	28	0	0	0	37.2	42	24	24	23	36
Bankhead	1	1	0	6.00	20	1	0	0	39.0	44	26	26	16	20
Eiland	1	1	0	6.30	4	1	0	0	10.0	16	10	7	3	6
Boehringer	0	3	0	13.75	7	3	0	0	17.2	24	27	27	22	10

Roster

MANAGER: Joe Torre
COACHES: Jose Cardenal, Chris Chambliss, Tony Cloninger, Willie Randolph, Mel Stottlemyre, Don Zimmer

NO	PITCHERS	B	T	HT	WT	DOB
54	Joe Ausanio	R	R	6-1	205	2/9/65
—	Brian Boehringer	S	R	6-2	190	1/8/70
—	Dwight Gooden	R	R	6-3	210	11/16/64
41	Sterling Hitchcock	L	L	6-1	192	4/29/71
28	Scott Kamieniecki	R	R	6-0	195	4/19/64
22	Jimmy Key	R	L	6-1	185	4/22/61
34	Bob MacDonald	L	L	6-3	208	4/27/65
33	Melido Perez	R	R	6-4	210	2/15/66
46	Andy Pettitte	L	L	6-5	220	6/15/72
42	Mariano Rivera	R	R	6-2	168	11/29/69
35	John Wetteland	R	R	6-2	215	8/21/66
27	Bob Wickman	R	R	6-1	212	2/6/69
	CATCHERS					
—	Joe Girardi	R	R	5-11	195	10/14/64
13	Jim Leyritz	R	R	6-0	195	12/27/63
62	Jorge Posada	S	R	6-2	205	8/17/71
	INFIELDERS					
12	Wade Boggs	L	R	6-2	197	6/15/58
24	Russ Davis	R	R	6-0	195	9/13/69
—	Robert Eenhoorn	R	R	6-3	185	2/9/68
6	Tony Fernandez	S	R	6-2	175	6/30/62
45	Andy Fox	L	R	6-4	205	1/12/71
2	Derek Jeter	R	R	6-3	185	6/26/74
14	Pat Kelly	R	R	6-0	180	10/14/67
	OUTFIELDERS					
—	Matt Luke	L	L	6-5	220	2/26/71
21	Paul O'Neill	L	L	6-4	215	2/25/63
17	Ruben Rivera	R	R	6-3	200	11/14/73
25	Ruben Sierra	S	R	6-1	200	10/6/65
26	Darryl Strawberry	L	L	6-6	215	3/12/62
51	Bernie Williams	S	R	6-2	205	9/13/68
29	Gerald Williams	R	R	6-2	190	8/10/66

FREE AGENTS: David Cone, Rick Honeycutt, Steve Howe, Dion James

Wade Boggs   3B/1B

Age: 37   **Seasons:** 14
Height: 6' 2"   **Weight:** 197
Bats: Left   **Throws:** Right
1995 OBP: .412   **1995 SLG:** .422

A lock to make the Hall of Fame, Boggs remains a tough out and a steady glove. He has failed to hit .300 in only one season of his career, and his 11 straight All-Star appearances are topped at his position only by Brooks Robinson's 15.

	G	AB	H	2B	3B	HR	RS	RBI	BB	SB	CS	BA
1995	126	460	149	22	4	5	76	63	74	1	1	.324
Career	1991	7599	2541	489	53	103	1287	864	1213	19	30	.334
Projected	143	562	189	27	2	4	89	47	78	1	2	.311

David Cone   P

Age: 33   **Seasons:** 10
Height: 6' 1"   **Weight:** 190
Bats: Left   **Throws:** Right
1995 OBA: .228   **1995 WHIP:** 1.23

Cone the carpetbagger (Mets, Blue Jays, Royals, back to the Blue Jays, Yankees—all since 1992) is less reliant on strikeouts than he once was, though his nasty repertoire still generates plenty of whiffs. He led the AL in innings pitched in 1995.

	G	GS	IP	ER	ERA	H	BB	SO	W	L	SV
1995	30	30	229.1	91	3.57	195	88	191	18	8	0
Career	288	259	1922.0	678	3.17	1589	716	1841	129	78	1
Projected	33	33	249.2	89	3.21	213	111	202	18	11	0

Russ Davis 3B

Age: 26	**Seasons:** R
Height: 6' 0"	**Weight:** 195
Bats: Right	**Throws:** Right
1995 OBP: .349	**1995 SLG:** .429

Davis has shown substantial pop in the minors—he was the 1992 Eastern League (double-A) MVP—but his progress to the Show has been impeded by Boggs. He sports a lively bat, but Yankee Stadium will constrict his power numbers.

	G	AB	H	2B	3B	HR	RS	RBI	BB	SB	CS	BA
1995	39	98	27	5	2	2	14	12	10	0	0	.276
Career	44	112	29	5	2	2	14	13	10	0	0	.259
Projected	137	445	105	22	4	17	55	62	38	3	1	.236

Sterling Hitchcock P

Age: 25	**Seasons:** 4
Height: 6' 1"	**Weight:** 192
Bats: Left	**Throws:** Left
1995 OBA: .245	**1995 WHIP:** 1.32

Hitchcock boasts a nifty assortment of breaking balls, and his southpaw status points to the probability of a long career. If the Yankees resist the urge to mess with his head or trade him, they'll have a great third starter.

	G	GS	IP	ER	ERA	H	BB	SO	W	L	SV
1995	27	27	168.1	88	4.70	155	68	121	11	10	0
Career	59	41	261.2	139	4.79	258	117	190	16	15	2
Projected	30	30	184.2	93	4.53	167	75	135	17	12	0

Pat Kelly 2B

Age: 28   **Seasons:** 5
Height: 6' 0"   **Weight:** 180
Bats: Right   **Throws:** Right
1995 OBP: .307   **1995 SLG:** .333

Kelly has a knack for the sprawling catch and he's fearless on the DP, but his kamikaze work in the field often results in nagging injuries. He figures to bounce back with a solid year if he doesn't permanently lose his job to a free agent.

	G	AB	H	2B	3B	HR	RS	RBI	BB	SB	CS	BA
1995	89	270	64	12	1	4	32	29	23	8	3	.237
Career	511	1578	399	91	10	24	189	171	106	48	25	.253
Projected	124	390	104	20	1	5	50	42	27	11	4	.267

Jimmy Key P

Age: 35   **Seasons:** 12
Height: 6' 1"   **Weight:** 185
Bats: Right   **Throws:** Left
1995 OBA: .323   **1995 WHIP:** 1.52

It's probably unreasonable to expect a 35-year-old finesse pitcher with an oft-damaged rotator cuff to anchor a staff, but if he hasn't lost his ability to set up batters, Key will have a shot at Comeback Player of the Year.

	G	GS	IP	ER	ERA	H	BB	SO	W	L	SV
1995	5	5	30.1	19	5.64	40	6	14	1	2	0
Career	381	314	2130.2	804	3.39	2060	505	1228	152	93	10
Projected	26	26	147.1	65	3.97	156	21	104	13	6	0

Don Mattingly 1B

Age: 35	**Seasons:** 14
Height: 6' 0"	**Weight:** 200
Bats: Left	**Throws:** Left
1995 OBP: .341	**1995 SLG:** .413

Mattingly's numbers are pretty puny, and his body is falling apart, but there is more to life (and baseball) than objective analysis, and it'll be a shame if he doesn't come back for one more postseason in blue pinstripes.

	G	AB	H	2B	3B	HR	RS	RBI	BB	SB	CS	BA
1995	128	458	132	32	2	7	59	49	40	0	2	.288
Career	1785	7003	2153	442	20	222	1007	1099	588	13	9	.307
Projected	135	440	122	23	0	8	46	43	41	1	1	.277

Jack McDowell P

Age: 30	**Seasons:** 8
Height: 6' 5"	**Weight:** 188
Bats: Right	**Throws:** Right
1995 OBA: .254	**1995 WHIP:** 1.33

Black Jack—baseball's answer to petulant rock diva Courtney Love—has seen his ERA rise and his winning percentage sag in the two seasons since he won the Cy Young Award, but he's still a gritty competitor and a quality starter.

	G	GS	IP	ER	ERA	H	BB	SO	W	L	SV
1995	30	30	217.2	95	3.93	211	78	157	15	10	0
Career	221	221	1561.1	617	3.56	1469	497	1075	106	68	0
Projected	33	33	247.1	91	3.31	229	77	180	16	9	0

Paul O'Neill   OF

Age: 33   **Seasons:** 11
Height: 6' 4"   **Weight:** 215
Bats: Left   **Throws:** Left
1995 OBP: .387   **1995 SLG:** .526

Despite his second-half struggles last season, the intense and intelligent O'Neill has been New York's most productive hitter since his 1993 arrival. Don't expect him to win another batting title, but bank on his consistent, all-around excellence.

	G	AB	H	2B	3B	HR	RS	RBI	BB	SB	CS	BA
1995	127	460	138	30	4	22	82	96	71	1	2	.300
Career	1170	3944	1104	236	13	159	542	665	493	69	43	.280
Projected	149	501	148	30	2	25	94	105	79	2	2	.295

Andy Pettitte   P

Age: 23   **Seasons:** 1
Height: 6' 5"   **Weight:** 220
Bats: Left   **Throws:** Left
1995 OBA: .272   **1995 WHIP:** 1.41

Pettitte has good control of a sweeping curveball, plus the requisite 90-mph fastball. He's physically imposing (though his strikeout rates aren't overwhelming), and his brilliance during the Yankees' pennant drive indicates a bright future.

	G	GS	IP	ER	ERA	H	BB	SO	W	L	SV
1995	31	26	175.0	81	4.17	183	63	114	12	9	0
Career	31	26	175.0	81	4.17	183	63	114	12	9	0
Projected	30	30	205.0	84	3.69	201	60	141	14	9	0

Mariano Rivera   **P**

Age: 26   **Seasons:** 1
Height: 6' 2"   **Weight:** 168
Bats: Right   **Throws:** Right
1995 OBA: .266   **1995 WHIP:** 1.51

Rivera is built slender and his arm is still developing, but he's shown brief flashes of great command, composure, and stuff. He has nothing left to prove in the minors, but another season of middle-relief seasoning could be in store for 1996.

	G	GS	IP	ER	ERA	H	BB	SO	W	L	SV
1995	19	10	67.0	41	5.51	71	30	51	5	3	0
Career	19	10	67.0	41	5.51	71	30	51	5	3	0
Projected	32	13	126.1	61	4.35	131	48	74	9	5	0

Ruben Rivera   **OF**

Age: 22   **Seasons:** R
Height: 6' 3"   **Weight:** 200
Bats: Right   **Throws:** Right
1995 OBP: .000   **1995 SLG:** .000

We've all watched a thousand minor-league all-stars flame-out in the Show, but to see this youngster's languorous fly balls just carry and carry is to get excited about baseball again. If he doesn't make it, the breaking ball will be his undoing.

	G	AB	H	2B	3B	HR	RS	RBI	BB	SB	CS	BA
1995	5	1	0	0	0	0	0	0	0	0	0	.000
Career	5	1	0	0	0	0	0	0	0	0	0	.000
Projected	117	312	83	14	2	9	38	42	9	2	1	.266

Ruben Sierra **OF**

Age: 30   **Seasons:** 10
Height: 6' 1"   **Weight:** 200
Bats: Switch   **Throws:** Right
1995 OBP: .323   **1995 SLG:** .449

Though his overall skills seem to have deteriorated—his speed is gone and he's a liability in right field—Sierra can still contribute as a switch-hitting RBI man. After his arrival in New York he hit a team-high .353 with runners in scoring position.

	G	AB	H	2B	3B	HR	RS	RBI	BB	SB	CS	BA
1995	126	479	126	32	0	19	73	86	46	5	4	.263
Career	1454	5679	1547	306	50	220	809	952	419	126	47	.273
Projected	153	554	131	24	1	23	70	88	49	6	3	.236

Mike Stanley **C**

Age: 32   **Seasons:** 10
Height: 6' 0"   **Weight:** 190
Bats: Right   **Throws:** Right
1995 OBP: .360   **1995 SLG:** .481

Since bashing more homers in 1993 (26) than he'd hit in his previous seven seasons combined, Stanley has consistently produced above-average power numbers. The Yankees elected not to re-sign him in the offseason.

	G	AB	H	2B	3B	HR	RS	RBI	BB	SB	CS	BA
1995	118	399	107	29	1	18	63	83	57	1	1	.268
Career	850	2272	614	116	6	85	325	371	333	8	2	.271
Projected	125	409	112	22	0	22	66	79	62	0	0	.274

Darryl Strawberry *OF/DH*

Age: 34   **Seasons:** 13
Height: 6' 6"   **Weight:** 215
Bats: Left   **Throws:** Left
1995 OBP: .364   **1995 SLG:** .448

Given a full season, there's a better-than-even chance that he'd play his way out of baseball permanently, but these 100–at-bat seasons keep everyone just curious enough to wonder. This much is clear: he still *looks* like a ballplayer.

	G	AB	H	2B	3B	HR	RS	RBI	BB	SB	CS	BA
1995	32	87	24	4	1	3	15	13	10	0	0	.276
Career	1384	4843	1256	226	36	297	808	899	722	205	87	.259
Projected	75	185	49	10	0	9	21	24	24	2	2	.265

Randy Velarde *SS/2B*

Age: 33   **Seasons:** 9
Height: 6' 0"   **Weight:** 192
Bats: Right   **Throws:** Right
1995 OBP: .375   **1995 SLG:** .392

Though somewhat overrated by the fans in New York, the new Angel can do some damage with the bat, and he's not a liability at either middle-infield position. Versatility and consistency are his trademarks.

	G	AB	H	2B	3B	HR	RS	RBI	BB	SB	CS	BA
1995	111	367	102	19	1	7	60	46	55	5	1	.278
Career	659	1935	511	99	10	43	263	204	186	23	15	.264
Projected	122	377	99	14	2	8	48	40	49	4	2	.263

John Wetteland   **P**

Age: 29   **Seasons:** 7
Height: 6' 2"   **Weight:** 215
Bats: Right   **Throws:** Right
1995 OBA: .185   **1995 WHIP:** 0.88

A wicked fastball-curveball combo and good control make Wetteland one of the league's dominant late-inning stoppers, though he's been susceptible to brief streaks of ineffectiveness and nagging injuries in each of the past three years.

	G	GS	IP	ER	ERA	H	BB	SO	W	L	SV
1995	60	0	61.1	20	2.93	40	14	66	1	5	31
Career	308	17	448.1	146	2.93	338	143	487	26	30	137
Projected	72	0	75.1	16	1.91	49	17	82	2	3	41

Bernie Williams   **OF**

Age: 27   **Seasons:** 5
Height: 6' 2"   **Weight:** 205
Bats: Switch   **Throws:** Right
1995 OBP: .392   **1995 SLG:** .487

Tantalizingly close to stardom, Bernie is coming off his best season. He gets on base, hits well in the clutch, and makes sparkling catches in center field. Bad baserunning is perhaps his only flaw as a player.

	G	AB	H	2B	3B	HR	RS	RBI	BB	SB	CS	BA
1995	144	563	173	29	9	18	93	82	75	8	6	.307
Career	538	2119	592	122	20	50	322	267	266	50	35	.279
Projected	160	601	193	35	7	21	114	94	89	13	9	.321

Oakland
ATHLETICS

Scouting Report

Outfielders: Last season's outfield trio consisted of Stan Javier (CF), Geronimo Berroa (RF), and Rickey Henderson (LF), but there'll be a full-scale youth movement in 1996. Jose Herrera, a raw but talented prospect who came to Oakland (with Steve Karsay) in 1993's Henderson deal, will have every chance to lock up a fulltime job in center field if Javier goes the free-agent route. Ernie Young has logged some inspiring numbers in triple-A, but he hasn't hit a lick with the big club. He'll be vying for a starting slot, probably in right field.

Infielders: In theory, first base is anchored by the steady glove of Mark McGwire, the league's most injury-prone star. Oakland's only remaining Bash Brother, the mammoth redhead is outrageously productive when healthy. Across the diamond at third, Jason Giambi will try to build on his modestly successful rookie campaign. The A's expect to see more consistency from talented second baseman Brent Gates. Mike Bordick was a keystone at shortstop and a steady contributor at the plate in 1995. His understudy is young glove wizard Fausto Cruz. Mike Gallego will only be re-signed at a bargain-basement price.

Catchers: Terry Steinbach has been an important part of the A's winning legacy, but the club might dump his salary if switch-hitting prospect George Williams shows that he can handle the fulltime job this season.

Designated Hitters: Oft-injured Danny Tartabull will be back, but Geronimo Berroa, who many considered to be the A's MVP in 1995, is eligible for arbitration.

Starting Pitchers: Fans in Oakland will see a procession of new faces on the mound this season. It's a cockeyed baseball universe when annually average Todd Stottlemyre is the ace of any starting staff. The key to this rotation may be perennial prospect Todd Van Poppel, with his newfound control and improved curveball. Another large question mark with great potential is Steve Karsay, whose career has been undercut by elbow injuries. Oft-injured Steve Ontiveros, the 1994 ERA champ, will try to come back in top form. Youngsters Doug Johns, Steve Wojciechowski, and Ariel Prieto will all contend for spots in the starting five.

Relief Pitchers: Dennis Eckersley struggled during the 1995 stretch run and is reportedly thinking of retirement. The A's get solid setup work from their deep bullpen, led by righthanders Jim Corsi and Don Wengert and southpaws Mike Mohler and Dave Leiper. No fewer than five other prospects will battle for positions.

Outlook

The A's are a reeling franchise, and patience will be needed if fans in Oakland want to see a quality rebuilding effort. The other Western Division clubs aren't loaded with top-level pitching, so there's no reason to believe that Oakland can't get an edge in that area by developing their young guns and trying to duplicate their legendary reclamation successes (Dave Stewart, Dennis Eckersley). The A's may get a full season from Mark McGwire eventually, and 50 homers could be the result. Even in transition, this is the type of organization that shouldn't be counted out.

Fungoes

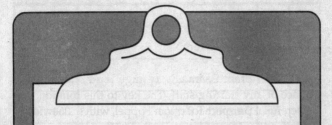

Quick Quiz: Which Athletics player saw action at all nine positions in a single game (1965)?

Franchise Milestone: The Athletics have won nine championships—five in Philly, none in KC, and four in Oakland. The most recent came in 1989 as the A's beat cross-Bay rival San Francisco (4–0) in an earthquake-marred Series.

Top Pitcher: Lefty Grove, 1925–33

Top Player: Mickey Cochrane, 1925–33

Top Manager: Connie Mack, 1901–50

Wacky Nickname: Catfish (James Augustus Hunter)

Quick Quiz Answer: Bert Campaneris

Lineup Card

NO	POS	PLAYER	OBP	SLG
44	CF	Jose Herrera	.219	.314
13	2B	Brent Gates	.308	.344
29	RF	Geronimo Berroa	.351	.451
25	1B	Mark McGwire	.441	.685
45	DH	Danny Tartabull	.335	.379
36	C	Terry Steinbach	.322	.458
16	3B	Jason Giambi	.364	.398
14	SS	Mike Bordick	.325	350
9	LF	Ernie Young	.310	.380

In a Nutshell: If both Stan Javier and Rickey Henderson leave Oakland, the A's could be minus a legitimate leadoff hitter. Brent Gates actually hit in the cleanup spot for an extended period when Mark McGwire was hurt, a sign of the degree to which the A's struggled to drive in runs in 1995. For all the heat that Rickey takes for the things he won't do (hustle, play with pain, etc.), he's an exceedingly valuable catalyst at the top of the order and a primary reason that Oakland ranked fourth in the league in walks last season. He will be missed in terms of the offense he can generate. At its worst—McGwire gets hurt, Steinbach has a down year at age 34, none of the rookies produce—the Oakland lineup will struggle to score three runs per game.

Oakland Coliseum

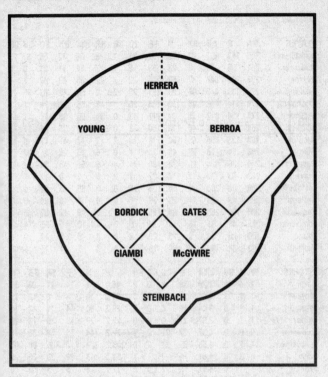

Capacity: 46,942
Turf: Natural

LF Line: 330
RF Line: 330
Center: 400
Left CF: 372
Right CF: 372

Tickets:
510-638-0500

The Coliseum offers Bay Area fans a perfect baseball atmosphere, but it's not so easy on hitters. Batting averages are suppressed drastically, especially for lefties, a factor partly attributable to the immense foul territory. The park affects power stats as well, though to a lesser extent. The Coliseum has housed six AL home-run kings but never a batting champion.

Statistics

Minimum 25 at-bats or 10.0 innings pitched

PLAYER	BA	G	AB	RS	H	TB	2B	3B	HR	RBI	BB	SO	SB	CS
Henderson	.300	112	407	67	122	182	31	1	9	54	72	66	32	10
Williams	.291	29	79	13	23	39	5	1	3	14	11	21	0	0
Berroa	.278	141	546	87	152	246	22	3	22	88	63	98	7	4
Javier	.278	130	442	81	123	171	20	2	8	56	49	63	36	5
Steinbach	.278	114	406	43	113	186	26	1	15	65	25	74	1	3
McGwire	.274	104	317	75	87	217	13	0	39	90	88	77	1	1
Bordick	.264	126	428	46	113	150	13	0	8	44	35	48	11	3
Brosius	.263	123	388	69	102	176	19	2	17	47	41	67	4	2
Giambi	.256	54	176	27	45	70	7	0	6	25	28	31	2	1
Gates	.254	136	524	60	133	180	24	4	5	56	46	84	3	3
Herrera	.243	33	70	9	17	24	1	2	0	2	6	11	1	3
Tartabull	.236	83	280	34	66	106	16	0	8	35	43	82	0	2
Gallego	.233	43	120	11	28	28	0	0	0	8	9	24	0	1
Paquette	.226	105	283	42	64	118	13	1	13	49	12	88	5	2
Tomberlin	.212	46	85	15	18	30	0	0	4	10	5	22	4	1
Young	.200	26	50	9	10	19	3	0	2	5	8	12	0	0
Helfand	.163	38	86	9	14	18	2	1	0	7	11	25	0	0

PITCHER	W	L	SV	ERA	G	GS	CG	SH	IP	H	R	ER	BB	SO
Corsi	2	4	2	2.20	38	0	0	0	45.0	31	14	11	26	26
Mohler	1	1	1	3.04	28	0	0	0	23.2	16	8	8	18	15
Wengert	1	1	0	3.34	19	0	0	0	29.2	30	14	11	12	16
Leiper	1	1	0	3.57	21	0	0	0	22.2	23	10	9	13	10
Ontiveros	9	6	0	4.37	22	22	2	1	129.2	144	75	63	38	77
Stottlemyre	14	7	0	4.55	31	31	2	0	209.2	228	117	106	80	205
Johns	5	3	0	4.61	11	9	1	1	54.2	44	32	28	26	25
Wasdin	1	1	0	4.67	5	2	0	0	17.1	14	9	9	3	6
Eckersley	4	6	29	4.83	52	0	0	0	50.1	53	29	27	11	40
Van Poppel	4	8	0	4.88	36	14	1	0	138.1	125	77	75	56	122
Prieto	2	6	0	4.97	14	9	1	0	58.0	57	35	32	32	37
Reyes	4	6	0	5.09	40	1	0	0	69.0	71	43	39	28	48
Wojciechowski	2	3	0	5.18	14	7	0	0	48.2	51	28	28	28	13
Acre	1	2	0	5.71	43	0	0	0	52.0	52	35	33	28	47
Darling	4	7	0	6.23	21	21	1	0	104.0	124	79	72	46	69
Stewart	3	7	0	6.89	16	16	0	0	81.0	101	65	62	39	58
Briscoe	0	1	0	8.35	16	0	0	0	18.1	25	17	17	21	19

Roster

MANAGER: Art Howe
COACHES: TBD

NO	PITCHERS	B	T	HT	WT	DOB
55	Mark Acre	R	R	6-8	240	9/16/68
53	John Briscoe	R	R	6-3	190	9/22/67
41	Jim Corsi	R	R	6-1	220	9/9/61
43	Dennis Eckersley	R	R	6-2	195	10/3/54
40	Rick Honeycutt	L	L	6-1	191	6/29/54
51	Doug Johns	R	L	6-2	185	12/19/67
20	Steve Karsay	R	R	6-3	205	3/24/72
58	Mike Mohler	R	L	6-2	195	7/26/68
48	Ariel Prieto	R	R	6-3	225	10/22/69
40	Carlos Reyes	S	R	6-1	190	4/4/69
32	Todd Stottlemyre	L	R	6-3	200	5/20/65
22	Bill Taylor	R	R	6-8	200	10/16/61
59	Todd Van Poppel	R	R	6-5	210	12/9/71
31	John Wasdin	R	R	6-2	190	8/5/72
56	Don Wengert	R	R	6-2	205	11/6/69
39	Steve Wojciechowski	L	L	6-2	185	7/29/70
	CATCHERS					
6	Eric Helfand	L	R	6-0	195	3/25/69
36	Terry Steinbach	R	R	6-1	195	3/2/62
56	George Williams	S	R	5-10	190	4/22/69
	INFIELDERS					
23	Mike Aldrete	L	L	5-11	185	1/29/61
14	Mike Bordick	R	R	5-11	175	7/21/65
7	Scott Brosius	R	R	6-1	185	8/15/66
13	Brent Gates	S	R	6-1	180	3/14/70
16	Jason Giambi	L	R	6-2	200	1/8/71
25	Mark McGwire	R	R	6-5	250	10/1/63
3	Craig Paquette	R	R	6-0	190	3/28/69
	OUTFIELDERS					
29	Geronimo Berroa	R	R	6-0	195	9/18/65
44	Jose Herrera	L	L	6-0	165	8/30/72
45	Danny Tartabull	R	R	6-1	204	10/30/62
9	Ernie Young	R	R	6-1	190	7/8/69

FREE AGENTS: Mike Gallego, Brian Harper, Rickey Henderson, Stan Javier, Steve Ontiveros

Geronimo Berroa   OF

Age: 31   **Seasons:** 6
Height: 6' 0"   **Weight:** 195
Bats: Right   **Throws:** Right
1995 OBP: .351   **1995 SLG:** .451

An unlikely success story, Berroa has become an everyday player for the A's, the seventh organization of his career. He draws a healthy share of walks for a free swinger, flashes good linedrive power, and fields his position adequately.

	G	AB	H	2B	3B	HR	RS	RBI	BB	SB	CS	BA
1995	141	546	152	22	3	22	87	88	63	7	4	.278
Career	252	1075	300	46	5	37	154	162	116	14	8	.279
Projected	153	579	161	25	1	24	92	93	65	7	3	.278

Mike Bordick   SS

Age: 30   **Seasons:** 6
Height: 5' 11"   **Weight:** 175
Bats: Right   **Throws:** Right
1995 OBP: .325   **1995 SLG:** .350

A fan favorite and a manager's dream, Bordick makes up for his lukewarm talents at the plate by being a details man, executing bunts and hit-and-run plays to perfection. He sparkles in the field, especially when turning two.

	G	AB	H	2B	3B	HR	RS	RBI	BB	SB	CS	BA
1995	126	428	113	13	0	8	46	44	35	11	3	.264
Career	668	2118	556	76	11	16	227	198	188	43	25	.263
Projected	135	441	116	17	2	5	49	48	37	12	5	.263

Dennis Eckersley   P

Age: 41	**Seasons:** 21
Height: 6' 2"	**Weight:** 195
Bats: Right	**Throws:** Right
1995 OBA: .269	**1995 WHIP:** 1.27

He has struggled to shut down lefties in recent seasons and his ERA has suffered, but Eck still exhibits pinpoint location and, of course, a closer's makeup. He could either retire or, given a full spring training, regain his dominant form.

	G	GS	IP	ER	ERA	H	BB	SO	W	L	SV
1995	52	0	50.1	27	4.83	53	11	40	4	6	29
Career	901	361	3133.0	1212	3.48	2916	716	2285	192	159	323
Projected	58	0	56.0	22	3.54	51	11	44	3	5	34

Brent Gates   2B

Age: 26	**Seasons:** 3
Height: 6' 1"	**Weight:** 180
Bats: Switch	**Throws:** Right
1995 OBP: .308	**1995 SLG:** .344

Gates is an average fielder with good range, but the A's were hoping he'd be more than average with the bat. A linedrive hitter who strikes out too often, he's yet to improve on a promising 1993 rookie season (.290, 29 doubles).

	G	AB	H	2B	3B	HR	RS	RBI	BB	SB	CS	BA
1995	136	524	133	24	4	5	60	56	46	3	3	.254
Career	339	1292	354	64	7	14	157	149	123	13	6	.274
Projected	157	603	157	32	3	6	81	78	53	4	1	.260

Rickey Henderson   OF

Age: 37   **Seasons:** 17
Height: 5' 10"   **Weight:** 190
Bats: Right   **Throws:** Left
1995 OBP: .407   **1995 SLG:** .447

Arguably the greatest leadoff man of all time in his prime, Henderson still does his job better than most, though his value as a basestealer has declined. No one will ever refer to him as Rickey Baseball, except perhaps sarcastically.

	G	AB	H	2B	3B	HR	RS	RBI	BB	SB	CS	BA
1995	112	407	122	31	1	9	67	54	72	32	10	.300
Career	2192	8063	2338	395	57	235	1719	858	1550	1149	265	.290
Projected	138	501	142	25	2	11	75	51	75	46	14	.283

Stan Javier   OF

Age: 32   **Seasons:** 11
Height: 6' 0"   **Weight:** 185
Bats: Switch   **Throws:** Right
1995 OBP: .353   **1995 SLG:** .387

A slick defensive outfielder and a quality leadoff-type hitter, Javier is yet another successful reclamation project in Oakland. He has no star potential but should continue to be a solid regular for at least one more year.

	G	AB	H	2B	3B	HR	RS	RBI	BB	SB	CS	BA
1995	130	442	123	20	2	8	81	56	49	36	5	.278
Career	1089	2896	748	120	23	31	439	275	316	155	30	.258
Projected	145	526	133	22	3	9	84	61	53	31	4	.253

Mark McGwire   **1B**

Age: 32   **Seasons:** 10
Height: 6' 5"   **Weight:** 250
Bats: Right   **Throws:** Right
1995 OBP: .441   **1995 SLG:** .685

McGwire is one powerful individual, and he presents a compact strikezone by utilizing a crouched, open stance. He's become a chronic feature on the injury list, but he's a devastating slugger when healthy.

	G	AB	H	2B	3B	HR	RS	RBI	BB	SB	CS	BA
1995	104	317	87	13	0	39	75	90	88	1	1	.274
Career	1094	3659	921	150	5	277	621	747	673	7	8	.252
Projected	133	448	117	21	0	31	88	97	95	0	1	.261

Steve Ontiveros   **P**

Age: 35   **Seasons:** 9
Height: 6' 0"   **Weight:** 190
Bats: Right   **Throws:** Right
1995 OBA: .283   **1995 WHIP:** 1.40

Ontiveros returned to Earth last year after being 1994's unlikely AL leader in ERA. A control pitcher who does a nice job of changing speeds, he's struggled with elbow problems throughout his career.

	G	GS	IP	ER	ERA	H	BB	SO	W	L	SV
1995	22	22	129.2	63	4.37	144	38	77	9	6	0
Career	204	72	656.1	263	3.61	613	203	381	33	30	19
Projected	18	18	109.2	52	4.27	121	29	68	10	6	0

Terry Steinbach   C

Age: 34   **Seasons:** 10
Height: 6' 1"   **Weight:** 195
Bats: Right   **Throws:** Right
1995 OBP: .322   **1995 SLG:** .458

Steinbach is a steady contributor with the stick, and last season was perhaps the most productive of his career. He's even more valuable as a receiver, throwing well and earning kudos for his work with the team's steady influx of new pitchers.

	G	AB	H	2B	3B	HR	RS	RBI	BB	SB	CS	BA
1995	114	406	113	26	1	15	43	65	25	1	3	.278
Career	1054	3648	1004	180	13	97	419	495	258	15	17	.275
Projected	115	404	111	21	0	12	40	58	30	0	2	.275

Todd Stottlemyre   P

Age: 30   **Seasons:** 8
Height: 6' 3"   **Weight:** 200
Bats: Left   **Throws:** Right
1995 OBA: .276   **1995 WHIP:** 1.47

Stottlemyre's career has been an odd mix of promise and failure, and his 1995 numbers are a distilled measure of that fact. He an electric arm and his whiff totals are super, but his ERA is mediocre and his WHIP ratio is poor.

	G	GS	IP	ER	ERA	H	BB	SO	W	L	SV
1995	31	31	209.2	106	4.55	228	80	205	14	7	0
Career	237	206	1348.2	661	4.41	1410	494	867	83	77	1
Projected	36	36	233.1	123	4.74	246	81	226	16	9	0

Danny Tartabull DH

Age: 33
Height: 6' 1"
Bats: Right
1995 OBP: .335

Seasons: 12
Weight: 204
Throws: Right
1995 SLG: .379

Oakland acquired the Baby Bull in midseason and received an upclose gander at his susceptibility to injuries and deteriorating skills as a slugger. He's played most of his career in parks that have hurt his power numbers.

	G	AB	H	2B	3B	HR	RS	RBI	BB	SB	CS	BA
1995	83	280	66	16	0	8	34	35	43	0	2	.236
Career	1271	4532	1246	266	19	235	696	824	700	36	28	.275
Projected	128	413	107	17	0	21	51	62	55	1	3	.259

Todd Van Poppel P

Age: 24
Height: 6' 5"
Bats: Right
1995 OBA: .244

Seasons: 4
Weight: 210
Throws: Right
1995 WHIP: 1.31

Van Poppel was rushed to the majors and, as a result, has posted numbers in direct contrast to his formidable stuff. He's still young and talented, and his 1995 stats were a vast improvement over those of his previous three seasons.

	G	GS	IP	ER	ERA	H	BB	SO	W	L	SV
1995	36	14	138.1	75	4.88	125	56	122	4	8	0
Career	76	54	343.2	206	5.39	316	209	258	17	24	0
Projected	34	34	215.2	84	3.51	194	64	199	12	7	0

Randy Johnson

Scouting Report

Outfielders: Center fielder Ken Griffey is the center of the Seattle universe. Already recognized as perhaps the best all-around player in the majors, he's just entering his prime years. Jay Buhner is a power hitter's power hitter, and the throws he uncorks from right field are champagne laced with strychnine for opposition baserunners. The Mariners have a pair of potentially great young hitters to patrol left field. Marc Newfield is a middle-of-the-order type and a poor fielder, while Darren Bragg is cut from the same cloth as Rickey Henderson.

Infielders: First baseman Tino Martinez finally output a season's worth of production in line with his enormous abilities. He's a slick gloveman and a dangerous power hitter. Second sacker Joey Cora is small in stature but big on the details that win ballgames. Cora's new partner in the pivot has rare size and talent. Young shortstop Alex Rodriguez is being touted as a future star, and he figures to displace Luis Sojo. Third baseman Mike Blowers is now a Dodger, so the M's may deal for a third baseman. Room also needs to be made for prospect Arquimedez Pozo.

Catchers: Dan Wilson is agile behind the plate, but his prowess in the batter's box is a surprise. He elevated his slugging percentage more than 100 points from 1994. His backup is Chris Widger, who developed a reputation in the minors for his handling of pitchers but appeared to be overmatched at the plate in his first big-league trial.

Designated Hitters: Edgar Martinez, one of the league's most perfect hitters, not only stayed healthy but also raised his production to an MVP level in 1995.

Starting Pitchers: Randy Johnson is baseball's dominant southpaw, intimidating batters with his wicked slider and aggressive demeanor. Andy Benes continues to compile yearly stats that don't quite jibe with his star-quality stuff. He'll test the waters of free agency and won't be back in Seattle this season. Chris Bosio still puts on a pitching clinic everytime he toes the rubber, while Tim Belcher is experienced and intense, but the Seattle rotation is going to need help from youngsters like Bob Wolcott, who made a big splash by shutting down the Indians in his first post-season start.

Relief Pitchers: Bobby Ayala washed out as the closer, but Norm Charlton came back from obscurity to save the day. Bill Risley and Jeff Nelson are a super setup combo. Ayala, Charlton, and Nelson could all be too expensive for the M's to retain. Long-injured lefty Greg Hibbard, a drain on the Seattle budget, could return to contribute long relief.

Outlook

Seattle fans can take for granted the pleasure of watching the AL's best all-around player in Ken Griffey and its top pitcher in Randy Johnson, not to mention second-tier stars Edgar Martinez and Jay Buhner. Unfortunately, those big names cost the small-market Mariners big money, so it will be a challenge for the club to retain an Andy Benes, a Norm Charlton, and a Tino Martinez—players who could be essential in the quest for a second straight division title. Several M's will be in the running for postseason awards, but the M's must solve their pitching puzzle to contend.

Fungoes

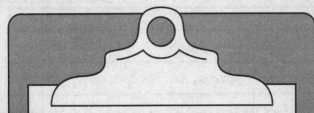

Quick Quiz: Who posted five straight years of at least 40 steals for Seattle, plus a career success rate of over 80 percent?

Franchise Milestone: After almost two decades of losing, the franchise hit its high-water mark in 1995, rising from what appeared to be an insurmountable deficit to catch California and bring home the Mariners' first division title.

Top Pitcher: Randy Johnson, 1989–

Top Player: Ken Griffey, 1989–

Top Manager: Lou Piniella, 1993–

Wacky Nickname: The Big Unit (Randall David Johnson)

Quick Quiz Answer: Julio Cruz

Lineup Card

NO	POS	PLAYER	OBP	SLG
34	LF	Darren Bragg	.331	.345
28	2B	Joey Cora	.359	.372
24	CF	Ken Griffey	.379	.481
11	DH	Edgar Martinez	.479	.628
19	RF	Jay Buhner	.343	.566
00	3B	TBD	.000	.000
23	1B	Tino Martinez	.369	.551
6	C	Dan Wilson	.336	.416
3	SS	Alex Rodriguez	.264	.408

In a Nutshell: Seattle's batting order has an extreme bell shape—light hitters on top and bottom, heavy hitters through the middle. The wild card for this season is Alex Rodriguez, who may or may not be ready to hit in the majors on an everyday basis. Several of the Mariners had career years in 1995. With the notable exception of broken-wristed Griffey, the entire M's lineup was gliding at full sail, and though there's no guarantee that Blowers, for example, can approach the 100-RBI plateau for a second straight year, a healthy Junior is sure to pick up any slack in the offense. One caveat: power doesn't always translate into runs, as these same Mariners proved in 1993, and much this year will depend on what the table setters do.

The Kingdome

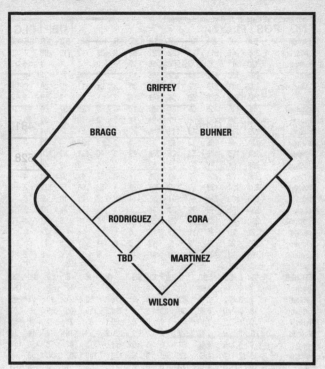

GRIFFEY

BRAGG   BUHNER

RODRIGUEZ   CORA

TBD   MARTINEZ

WILSON

Capacity: 59,166
Turf: Artificial

LF Line: 331
RF Line: 312
Center: 405
Left CF: 389
Right CF: 380

Tickets:
206-296-3663

The turf in Seattle is arguably the fastest in the league, making this a fine park in which to steal bases. Of course, this is also a friendly venue for power hitters. It may be sacrilege to mention this in Seattle, but there'd be less talk of Griffey being the game's best player if Barry Bonds were playing half his games in the Kingdome. It's the ideal place for his offensive skills.

Statistics

Minimum 25 at-bats or 10.0 innings pitched

PLAYER	BA	G	AB	RS	H	TB	2B	3B	HR	RBI	BB	SO	SB	CS
E. Martinez	.356	145	511	121	182	321	52	0	29	113	116	89	4	3
Thurman	.320	13	25	3	8	10	2	0	0	3	1	3	4	2
Cora	.297	120	427	64	127	159	19	3	3	39	37	31	18	7
T. Martinez	.293	141	519	92	152	286	35	3	31	111	62	89	0	0
Sojo	.289	102	339	50	98	141	18	2	7	39	23	19	4	2
Coleman	.288	115	455	66	131	181	23	6	5	29	37	80	42	16
Amaral	.282	88	238	45	67	91	14	2	2	19	21	33	20	2
Wilson	.278	119	399	40	111	166	22	3	9	51	33	64	2	1
Strange	.271	74	155	19	42	61	9	2	2	21	10	25	0	3
Buhner	.262	126	470	86	123	266	23	0	40	121	60	120	0	1
Newson	.261	84	157	34	41	62	2	2	5	15	39	45	2	1
Griffey	.258	72	260	52	67	125	7	0	17	42	52	53	4	2
Blowers	.257	134	439	59	113	208	24	1	23	96	53	128	2	1
Diaz	.248	103	270	44	67	90	14	0	3	27	13	27	18	8
Bragg	.234	52	145	20	34	50	5	1	3	12	18	37	9	0
Rodriguez	.232	48	142	15	33	58	6	2	5	19	6	42	4	2
Kreuter	.227	25	75	12	17	25	5	0	1	8	5	22	0	0
Widger	.200	23	45	2	9	12	0	0	1	2	3	11	0	0
Fermin	.195	73	200	21	39	45	6	0	0	15	6	6	2	0

PITCHER	W	L	SV	ERA	G	GS	CG	SH	IP	H	R	ER	BB	SO
Charlton	2	1	14	1.51	30	0	0	0	47.2	23	12	8	16	58
Nelson	7	3	2	2.17	62	0	0	0	78.2	58	21	19	27	96
Johnson	18	2	0	2.48	30	30	6	3	214.1	159	65	59	65	294
Risley	2	1	1	3.13	45	0	0	0	60.1	55	21	21	18	65
Wolcott	3	2	0	4.42	7	6	0	0	36.2	43	18	18	14	19
Ayala	6	5	19	4.44	63	0	0	0	71.0	73	42	35	30	77
Belcher	10	12	0	4.52	28	28	2	0	179.1	188	101	90	88	96
Frey	0	3	0	4.76	13	0	0	0	11.1	16	7	6	6	7
Bosio	10	8	0	4.92	31	31	0	0	170.0	211	98	93	69	85
Carmona	2	4	1	5.66	15	3	0	0	47.2	55	31	30	34	28
Wells	4	3	0	5.75	30	4	0	0	76.2	88	51	49	39	38
Krueger	2	1	0	5.85	6	5	0	0	20.0	37	17	13	4	10
Benes	7	2	0	5.86	12	12	0	0	63.0	72	42	41	33	45
Torres	3	8	0	6.00	16	13	1	0	72.0	87	53	48	42	45
Davis	2	1	0	6.38	5	5	0	0	24.0	30	21	17	18	19
Guetterman	0	0	1	6.88	23	0	0	0	17.0	21	13	13	11	11
Villone	0	2	0	7.91	19	0	0	0	19.1	20	19	17	23	26

Roster

MANAGER: Lou Piniella
COACHES: Bobby Cuellar, Lee Elia, John McLaren, Sam Mejias,
Sam Perlozzo, Matt Sinatro

NO	PITCHERS	B	T	HT	WT	DOB
13	Bobby Ayala	R	R	6-3	200	7/8/69
29	Chris Bosio	R	R	6-3	225	4/3/63
32	Rafael Carmona	L	R	6-2	185	10/2/72
37	Norm Charlton	S	L	6-3	205	1/6/63
35	Scott Davison	R	R	6-0	175	10/16/70
36	Greg Hibbard	L	L	6-0	185	9/13/64
51	Randy Johnson	R	L	6-10	225	9/10/63
42	Jim Mecir	S	R	6-1	195	5/16/70
43	Jeff Nelson	R	R	6-8	235	11/17/66
55	Bill Risley	R	R	6-2	215	5/29/67
38	Salomon Torres	R	R	5-11	165	3/11/72
45	Bob Wells	R	R	6-0	180	11/1/66
33	Bob Wolcott	R	R	6-0	190	9/8/73
	CATCHERS					
31	Chris Widger	R	R	6-3	195	5/21/71
6	Dan Wilson	R	R	6-3	190	3/25/69
	INFIELDERS					
8	Rich Amaral	R	R	6-0	175	4/1/62
28	Joey Cora	S	R	5-8	155	5/14/65
10	Felix Fermin	R	R	5-11	170	10/9/63
11	Edgar Martinez	R	R	5-11	190	1/2/63
23	Tino Martinez	L	R	6-2	210	12/7/67
20	Greg Pirkl	R	R	6-5	240	8/7/70
41	Arquimedez Pozo	R	R	5-10	180	8/24/73
3	Alex Rodriguez	R	R	6-3	190	7/27/75
9	Luis Sojo	R	R	5-11	174	1/3/66
12	Doug Strange	S	R	6-1	185	4/13/64
	OUTFIELDERS					
34	Darren Bragg	L	R	5-9	180	9/7/69
19	Jay Buhner	R	R	6-3	210	8/13/64
27	Alex Diaz	S	R	5-11	180	10/5/68
24	Ken Griffey	L	L	6-3	205	11/21/69
29	Warren Newson	L	L	5-7	202	7/3/64

FREE AGENTS: Tim Belcher, Andy Benes, Vince Coleman,
Lee Guetterman

Jay Buhner

Andy Benes P

Age: 28   **Seasons:** 7
Height: 6' 4"   **Weight:** 240
Bats: Right   **Throws:** Right
1995 OBA: N/A   **1995 WHIP:** 1.49

After years in San Diego of pitching much better than his won-lost records indicated, Benes reversed that pattern in Seattle. He's a workhorse and a fine pitcher when his fastball isn't flat, but it's difficult not to think of him as an underachiever.

	G	GS	IP	ER	ERA	H	BB	SO	W	L	SV
1995	31	31	181.2	96	4.75	193	78	171	11	9	0
Career	199	198	1298.0	531	3.68	1200	435	1081	76	77	0
Projected	34	34	229.1	78	3.06	232	61	216	16	9	0

Mike Blowers 3B

Age: 31   **Seasons:** 7
Height: 6' 2"   **Weight:** 210
Bats: Right   **Throws:** Right
1995 OBP: .335   **1995 SLG:** .474

Blowers, who was acquired for the immortal Jim Blueberg in 1991, blew away lefties at a .341 clip and took full advantage of his RBI opportunities last year, generating the best numbers of his career. A trip to L.A. via free agency is his reward.

	G	AB	H	2B	3B	HR	RS	RBI	BB	SB	CS	BA
1995	134	439	113	24	1	23	59	96	53	2	1	.257
Career	453	1378	355	67	4	64	179	229	147	6	8	.258
Projected	150	518	129	31	0	25	68	88	59	0	2	.249

Chris Bosio   P

Age: 33   **Seasons:** 10
Height: 6' 3"   **Weight:** 225
Bats: Right   **Throws:** Right
1995 OBA: .313   **1995 WHIP:** 1.65

Bosio has always been something of an underdog, having been bitten by poor run support and injuries. He works quickly and is a master at changing speeds and mixing pitches, but his stamina is poor and he seems to be losing his stuff.

	G	GS	IP	ER	ERA	H	BB	SO	W	L	SV
1995	31	31	170.0	93	4.92	211	69	85	10	8	0
Career	291	237	1649.1	713	3.89	1670	457	1020	90	89	9
Projected	27	27	151.1	86	5.11	194	65	79	9	12	0

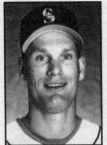

Jay Buhner   OF

Age: 31   **Seasons:** 9
Height: 6' 3"   **Weight:** 210
Bats: Right   **Throws:** Right
1995 OBP: .343   **1995 SLG:** .566

Buhner is one of the game's most dramatic players, unleashing fantastic power from a unique batting stance. His throwing arm, one of baseball's best, is rarely tested by baserunners, and he keeps the routine plays routine in right field.

	G	AB	H	2B	3B	HR	RS	RBI	BB	SB	CS	BA
1995	126	470	123	23	0	40	86	121	60	0	1	.262
Career	875	2990	769	146	16	169	463	548	415	6	21	.257
Projected	155	559	151	31	1	33	91	108	74	1	2	.270

Norm Charlton P

Age: 33	**Seasons:** 7
Height: 6' 3"	**Weight:** 205
Bats: Switch	**Throws:** Left
1995 OBA: N/A	**1995 WHIP:** 1.11

Just when it looked like Charlton was on his way out of baseball and the M's would have no closer down the stretch, the former Nasty Boy reemerged in devastating fashion. Righties hit just .129 off him after his arrival in Seattle.

	G	GS	IP	ER	ERA	H	BB	SO	W	L	SV
1995	55	0	69.2	26	3.35	46	31	70	4	6	14
Career	327	37	605.0	202	3.00	497	238	539	36	33	61
Projected	42	0	43.2	11	2.27	32	17	55	2	3	34

Joey Cora 2B

Age: 30	**Seasons:** 8
Height: 5' 8"	**Weight:** 155
Bats: Switch	**Throws:** Right
1995 OBP: .359	**1995 SLG:** .372

The diminutive Cora walks more than he whiffs, is a terrific bunter, and has improved as a basestealer. He flashes some spectacular diving grabs in the field, but he also makes too many errors and is merely average on the double play.

	G	AB	H	2B	3B	HR	RS	RBI	BB	SB	CS	BA
1995	120	427	127	19	3	3	64	39	37	18	7	.297
Career	671	2028	543	67	25	7	318	163	319	91	42	.268
Projected	125	434	116	17	5	2	61	37	51	12	8	.267

Ken Griffey   OF

Age: 26   **Seasons:** 7
Height: 6' 3"   **Weight:** 205
Bats: Left   **Throws:** Left
1995 OBP: .379   **1995 SLG:** .481

Barring another injury and/or the M's moving to a park less conducive to the longball, Junior has a reasonable shot at hitting 60. He's entering his prime, he'll have universal fan support (unlike Maris), and, of course, he's got that perfect stroke.

	G	AB	H	2B	3B	HR	RS	RBI	BB	SB	CS	BA
1995	72	260	67	7	0	17	52	42	52	4	2	.258
Career	917	3440	1039	201	19	189	570	585	426	92	43	.302
Projected	158	597	181	32	3	49	109	135	72	14	5	.303

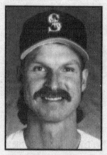

Randy Johnson   P

Age: 32   **Seasons:** 8
Height: 6' 10"   **Weight:** 225
Bats: Right   **Throws:** Left
1995 OBA: .201   **1995 WHIP:** 1.05

His reputation for wildness is nothing but hype these days. At 2.73 walks per nine innings, Johnson has harnessed his killer stuff to become one of the most overpowering lefthanders in baseball history.

	G	GS	IP	ER	ERA	H	BB	SO	W	L	SV
1995	30	30	214.1	59	2.48	159	65	294	18	2	0
Career	218	216	1459.2	571	3.52	1125	755	1624	99	64	1
Projected	36	36	263.1	76	2.60	176	72	304	24	5	0

Edgar Martinez **DH**

Age: 33	**Seasons:** 9
Height: 5' 11"	**Weight:** 190
Bats: Right	**Throws:** Right
1995 OBP: .479	**1995 SLG:** .628

'Gar didn't go more than eight at-bats without a hit last season—perhaps the Stat of the Year—en route to his second batting title. Being a DH helps him stay off the DL and allows him to concentrate on what he does so brilliantly—hit.

	G	AB	H	2B	3B	HR	RS	RBI	BB	SB	CS	BA
1995	145	511	182	52	0	29	121	113	116	4	3	.356
Career	797	2777	868	204	9	91	483	381	432	27	17	.313
Projected	157	560	198	45	1	23	120	102	121	2	3	.354

Tino Martinez **1B**

Age: 28	**Seasons:** 6
Height: 6' 2"	**Weight:** 210
Bats: Left	**Throws:** Right
1995 OBP: .369	**1995 SLG:** .551

Everyone was waiting for Tino to put together an entire season (even a strike-shortened one) of offensive fireworks. It may turn out to have been a career year for him, and he's been the subject of trade talks.

	G	AB	H	2B	3B	HR	RS	RBI	BB	SB	CS	BA
1995	141	519	152	35	3	31	92	111	62	0	0	.293
Career	543	1896	502	106	6	88	250	312	198	3	6	.265
Projected	154	547	154	31	2	29	96	115	66	0	1	.282

Jeff Nelson   P

Age: 29   **Seasons:** 4
Height: 6' 8"   **Weight:** 235
Bats: Right   **Throws:** Right
1995 OBA: .209   **1995 WHIP:** 1.08

A sidearmer who formerly suffered from a huge platoon split (lefties had hit him nearly 200 points better than righties), Nelson was able to clamp down on his portside nemeses in 1995, holding them to a .233 BA.

	G	GS	IP	ER	ERA	H	BB	SO	W	L	SV
1995	62	0	78.2	19	2.17	58	27	96	7	3	2
Career	227	0	262.0	92	3.16	221	125	247	13	13	9
Projected	70	0	87.2	26	2.67	65	38	103	8	4	4

Alex Rodriguez   SS

Age: 20   **Seasons:** R
Height: 6' 3"   **Weight:** 190
Bats: Right   **Throws:** Right
1995 OBP: .264   **1995 SLG:** .408

He may not fit the physical mold of a typical shortstop, but neither does that fellow in Baltimore. Rodriguez has rare athletic gifts and, though he's still extremely raw, he could be the best nonpitching prospect since Junior Griffey.

	G	AB	H	2B	3B	HR	RS	RBI	BB	SB	CS	BA
1995	48	142	33	6	2	5	15	19	6	4	2	.232
Career	65	196	44	6	2	5	19	21	9	7	2	.224
Projected	137	404	111	17	5	14	66	68	21	6	1	.275

Dan Wilson   C

Age: 27   **Seasons:** 4
Height: 6' 3"   **Weight:** 190
Bats: Right   **Throws:** Right
1995 OBP: .336   **1995 SLG:** .416

Wilson was a marginal hitter prior to last year, but if he can maintain his 1995 regular-season level, he'll be a valuable player. He's ultramobile behind the plate and cuts off the running game with a quick release.

	G	AB	H	2B	3B	HR	RS	RBI	BB	SB	CS	BA
1995	119	399	111	22	3	9	40	51	33	2	1	.278
Career	258	782	198	40	5	12	72	89	55	3	3	.253
Projected	135	420	112	19	1	13	45	49	42	1	1	.267

Bob Wolcott   P

Age: 22   **Seasons:** R
Height: 6' 0"   **Weight:** 190
Bats: Right   **Throws:** Right
1995 OBA: .297   **1995 WHIP:** 1.55

An overnight sensation in Seattle after he shut down the Indians in Game One of the ALCS, young Mr. Wolcott will contend for a spot in the starting rotation. Lacking an overpowering fastball, he needs pinpoint location to be successful.

	G	GS	IP	ER	ERA	H	BB	SO	W	L	SV
1995	7	6	36.2	18	4.42	43	14	19	3	2	0
Career	7	6	36.2	18	4.42	43	14	19	3	2	0
Projected	18	17	121.2	56	4.14	114	36	55	9	6	0

Will Clark

Texas
RANGERS

Scouting Report

Outfielders: The Rangers can't afford to lose Otis Nixon's range and experience in center field, but they may not have enough money available to re-sign him. Rusty Greer is reasonably productive on offense and versatile enough to cover any outfield spot, though he did make six errors last season. Texas wants to retain the services of slugging outfielder/DH Mickey Tettleton—who closed the 1995 season on a tear, blasting five homers and batting .556 in his final 18 at-bats—but financial concerns will affect that decision, too. Juan Gonzalez will try to stay healthy and regain his status as a premier power hitter and perhaps his position in left field, as well. Mark McLemore worked 69 games in left field last season when Gonzalez was hurt.

Infielders: Will Clark is a cornerstone at first base, and his bat has come alive since his arrival in Texas two years ago. The Rangers need a healthy Dean Palmer at third base. His absence due to injury created a gaping vacancy in the batting order. Palmer's backup is prospect Luis Ortiz, who was a component of the Jose Caseco deal. Benji Gil can really pick 'em at shortstop, but he doesn't connect nearly as often at the plate. His 147 strikeouts were just three short of tops in the majors, but his nine longballs were very impressive for a neophyte middle infielder. Mark McLemore has quick feet and sure hands at second base, plus leadoff-type characteristics as a hitter. Jeff Frye played 83 games at second last season, making consistent contact at the plate and turning the double play beautifully.

Catchers: Ivan Rodriguez is the state of the art among AL catchers, eradicating baserunners with his cannon arm and keeping his batting average in the .300 range. Dave Valle is an overpaid backup backstop.

Designated Hitters: Juan Gonzalez has missed dozens of games and suffered diminished performance levels the past two years due to a variety of injuries. Fulltime DH duty might help keep his bat in the lineup.

Starting Pitchers: If they can't afford to keep free-agent Kenny Rogers, the team's only plus-.500 starter last season, the new ace might turn out to be hard-throwing Roger Pavlik. Veteran workhorse Kevin Gross will return, but Bobby Witt and Bob Tewksbury are free-agent veterans coming off poor 1995 performances.

Relief Pitchers: Jeff Russell saved 20 games in 24 chances last season, but Darren Oliver's shoulder injury spells trouble for a bullpen that lacks quality arms. The club held open tryouts for prospects in September, but none emerged as potential go-to middle relievers.

Outlook

With attendance down and salaries up, the Rangers are hurting financially. The farm system that produced such young stars as Gonzalez and Rodriguez (but, it should be noted, passed over Frank Thomas in the 1989 draft) has generally come up short in the pitching department, and the club may not have the resources to build a rotation via free agency. Perhaps most disturbing for a team built around sluggers, the Rangers ranked tenth in slugging and on-base percentage last season, outperforming only the league's most anemic offenses.

Fungoes

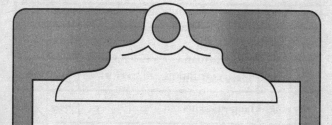

Quick Quiz: Kenny Rogers tossed a perfect game in 1994, but which two pitchers threw no-hitters for Texas in the 1970s?

Franchise Milestone: Since the Senators moved to Arlington in 1972 to become the Rangers, the organization has won only the incomplete 1994 AL West title. The Rangers have finished second in the division six times.

Top Pitcher: Charlie Hough, 1980–90

Top Player: Ruben Sierra, 1986–92

Top Manager: Billy Martin, 1973–75

Wacky Nickname: The Gambler (Kenneth Scott Rogers)

Quick Quiz Answer: Jim Bibby (1973) and Bert Blyleven (1977)

Lineup Card

NO	POS	PLAYER	OBP	SLG
2	CF	Otis Nixon	.357	.338
3	LF	Mark McLemore	.346	.358
22	1B	Will Clark	.389	.480
19	DH	Juan Gonzalez	.324	.594
16	3B	Dean Palmer	.448	.613
7	C	Ivan Rodriguez	.327	.449
29	RF	Rusty Greer	.355	.424
1	2B	Jeff Frye	.335	.377
23	SS	Benji Gil	.266	.347

In a Nutshell: Otis Nixon is unsigned at press time, and the lineup shown above is based on a presumption of his presence (or someone like Darryl Hamilton, who won't be back with the Brewers this year). Without him the Rangers might wind up using McLemore in the leadoff spot, Frye in the two-hole, and Greer in center field. Other unknowns include the future contract status of Mickey Tettleton and the ability of Juan Gonzalez to play left field. The heart of the order—one of baseball's most dangerous just a couple of years ago—has become somewhat soft, and the slack in Gonzalez's power stats is a prime culprit. If the lineup loses Tettleton to free agency, it will be even more crucial that Gonzalez and Palmer stay injury free.

The Ballpark in Arlington

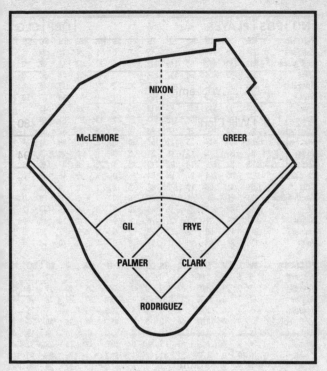

Capacity: 49,292
Turf: Natural

LF Line: 332
RF Line: 325
Center: 400
Left CF: 390
Right CF: 377

Tickets:
817-273-5100

Unless the batter is a pull-hitting lefty, the Ballpark is not friendly to sluggers. The outfield dimensions are deep, and the amount of home runs hit by righthanders can be cut by as much as 35 percent over the course of a season—just ask Juan Gonzalez, whose home-run stroke went missing shortly after the Rangers moved in to their new stadium.

Statistics

Minimum 25 at-bats or 10.0 innings pitched

PLAYER	BA	G	AB	RS	H	TB	2B	3B	HR	RBI	BB	SO	SB	CS
Palmer	.336	36	119	30	40	73	6	0	9	24	21	21	1	1
Rodriguez	.303	130	492	56	149	221	32	2	12	67	16	48	0	2
Clark	.302	123	454	85	137	218	27	3	16	92	68	50	0	1
Gonzalez	.295	90	352	57	104	209	20	2	27	82	17	66	0	0
Nixon	.295	139	589	87	174	199	21	2	0	45	58	85	50	21
Frye	.278	90	313	38	87	118	15	2	4	29	24	45	3	3
Greer	.271	131	417	58	113	177	21	2	13	61	55	66	3	1
Maldonado	.263	74	190	28	50	93	16	0	9	30	32	50	1	2
McLemore	.261	129	467	73	122	167	20	5	5	41	59	71	21	11
Valle	.240	36	75	7	18	21	3	0	0	5	6	18	1	0
Tettleton	.238	134	429	76	102	219	19	1	32	78	107	110	0	0
Pagliarulo	.232	86	241	27	56	84	16	0	4	27	15	49	0	0
Ortiz	.231	41	108	10	25	37	5	2	1	18	6	18	0	1
Worthington	.221	26	28	4	15	25	4	0	2	6	7	8	0	0
Gil	.219	130	415	36	91	144	20	3	9	46	26	147	2	4
Beltre	.217	54	92	7	20	28	8	0	0	7	4	15	0	0
Frazier	.212	49	99	19	21	23	2	0	0	8	7	20	9	1
Voigt	.175	36	63	9	11	20	3	0	2	8	10	14	0	0

PITCHER	W	L	SV	ERA	G	GS	CG	SH	IP	H	R	ER	BB	SO
Vosberg	5	5	4	3.00	44	0	0	0	36.0	32	15	12	16	36
Russell	1	0	20	3.03	37	0	0	0	32.2	36	12	11	9	21
Rogers	17	7	0	3.38	31	31	3	1	208.0	192	87	78	76	140
Heredia	0	1	0	3.75	6	0	0	0	12.0	9	5	5	15	6
McDowell	7	4	4	4.02	64	0	0	0	85.0	86	39	38	34	49
Whiteside	5	4	3	4.08	40	0	0	0	53.0	48	24	24	19	46
Oliver	4	2	0	4.22	17	7	0	0	49.0	47	25	23	32	39
Pavlik	10	10	0	4.37	31	31	2	1	191.2	174	96	93	90	149
Cook	0	2	2	4.53	46	1	0	0	57.2	63	32	29	26	53
Witt	3	4	0	4.55	10	10	1	0	61.1	81	35	31	21	46
Tewksbury	8	7	0	4.58	22	21	4	1	129.2	169	75	66	20	53
Gross	9	15	0	5.54	31	30	4	0	183.2	200	124	113	89	106
Brandenberg	0	1	0	5.93	11	0	0	0	27.1	36	18	18	7	21
Burrows	2	2	1	6.45	28	3	0	0	44.2	60	37	32	19	22
Helling	0	2	0	6.57	3	3	0	0	12.1	17	11	9	8	5
Nichting	0	0	0	7.03	13	0	0	0	24.1	36	19	19	13	6
Alberro	0	0	0	7.40	12	0	0	0	20.2	26	18	17	12	10
Darwin	3	10	0	7.45	20	15	1	0	99.0	131	87	82	31	58
Fajardo	0	0	0	7.80	5	0	0	0	15.0	19	13	13	5	9
Taylor	1	2	0	9.39	3	3	0	0	15.1	25	16	16	5	10

Roster

MANAGER: Johnny Oates
COACHES: Dick Bosman, Bucky Dent, Larry Hardy, Rudy Jaramillo,
Ed Napoleon, Jerry Narron

NO	PITCHERS	B	T	HT	WT	DOB
—	Jose Alberro	R	R	6-2	190	6/29/69
—	Mark Brandenburg	R	R	6-0	180	7/14/70
—	Terry Burrows	L	L	6-1	185	11/28/68
42	Dennis Cook	L	L	6-3	190	10/4/62
44	Danny Darwin	R	R	6-3	202	10/25/55
24	Steve Dreyer	R	R	6-3	188	11/19/69
—	Hector Fajardo	R	R	6-4	200	11/6/70
46	Kevin Gross	R	R	6-5	227	6/5/61
—	Rick Helling	R	R	6-3	215	12/15/70
—	Chris Nichting	R	R	6-1	205	5/13/66
28	Darren Oliver	R	L	6-2	200	10/6/70
59	Roger Pavlik	R	R	6-2	220	10/4/67
40	Jeff Russell	R	R	6-3	205	9/2/61
35	Dan Smith	L	L	6-5	195	4/20/69
52	Ed Vosberg	L	L	6-1	190	9/28/61
27	Matt Whiteside	R	R	6-0	205	8/8/67
	CATCHERS					
7	Ivan Rodriguez	R	R	5-9	205	11/30/71
10	Dave Valle	R	R	6-2	220	10/30/60
	INFIELDERS					
6	Esteban Beltre	R	R	5-10	172	12/26/67
22	Will Clark	L	L	6-1	196	3/13/64
1	Jeff Frye	R	R	5-9	165	8/31/66
23	Benji Gil	R	R	6-2	182	10/6/72
3	Mark McLemore	S	R	5-11	207	10/4/64
—	Luis Ortiz	R	R	6-0	195	2/25/70
16	Dean Palmer	R	R	6-2	195	12/27/68
24	Craig Worthington	R	R	6-0	200	4/17/65
	OUTFIELDERS					
4	Lou Frazier	S	R	6-2	180	1/26/65
19	Juan Gonzalez	R	R	6-3	215	10/16/69
29	Rusty Greer	L	L	6-0	190	1/21/69
—	Terrell Lowery	R	R	6-3	175	10/25/70

FREE AGENTS: Candy Maldonado, Roger McDowell, Otis Nixon,
Mike Pagliarulo, Kenny Rogers, Mickey Tettleton, Bob Tewksbury,
Bobby Witt

Will Clark   1B

Age: 32   **Seasons:** 10
Height: 6' 1"   **Weight:** 196
Bats: Left   **Throws:** Left
1995 OBP: .389   **1995 SLG:** .480

Clark doesn't ring up the eye-popping power stats of the AL's slugging elite, but he fields his position deftly, hits the ball hard in every situation, and plays the game with fire and brains. He's ultraconsistent when not nagged by injuries.

	G	AB	H	2B	3B	HR	RS	RBI	BB	SB	CS	BA
1995	123	454	137	27	3	16	85	92	68	0	1	.302
Career	1393	5112	1543	300	42	205	845	881	645	57	43	.302
Projected	136	462	133	31	2	14	82	89	72	3	1	.288

Juan Gonzalez   OF

Age: 26   **Seasons:** 7
Height: 6' 3"   **Weight:** 215
Bats: Right   **Throws:** Right
1995 OBP: .324   **1995 SLG:** .594

The American League's home-run king in 1992 and 1993, Gonzalez has been plagued by assorted injuries the past two seasons. His bat is still quick, but he probably hasn't seen the last of the DL and may be relegated to DH duties.

	G	AB	H	2B	3B	HR	RS	RBI	BB	SB	CS	BA
1995	90	352	104	20	2	27	57	82	17	0	0	.295
Career	683	2589	717	139	11	167	391	515	169	14	11	.277
Projected	124	475	135	22	2	31	66	91	23	1	1	.284

Rusty Greer   OF

Age: 27   **Seasons:** 2
Height: 6' 0"   **Weight:** 190
Bats: Left   **Throws:** Left
1995 OBP: .355   **1995 SLG:** .424

Greer is a fan favorite who does some nice things on offense—draws some walks, strokes some extra-base knocks—though nothing spectacular. He's a versatile fielder whose sole weakness is a below-average arm.

	G	AB	H	2B	3B	HR	RS	RBI	BB	SB	CS	BA
1995	131	417	113	21	2	13	58	61	55	3	1	.271
Career	211	694	200	37	3	23	94	107	101	3	1	.288
Projected	154	504	136	24	4	13	66	68	54	5	1	.270

Kevin Gross   P

Age: 34   **Seasons:** 13
Height: 6' 5"   **Weight:** 227
Bats: Right   **Throws:** Right
1995 OBA: .280   **1995 WHIP:** 1.57

Gross is a workhorse in decline. His career pattern has been 150 strikeouts per year and an ERA around 4.00, but last season he ranked among the league's top ten in losses, hit batsmen, walks, and home runs allowed.

	G	GS	IP	ER	ERA	H	BB	SO	W	L	SV
1995	31	30	183.2	113	5.54	200	89	106	9	15	0
Career	434	346	2333.0	1042	4.02	2338	916	1629	129	149	5
Projected	32	32	182.1	109	5.38	198	81	115	7	14	0

Mark McLemore 2B

Age: 31 **Seasons:** 10
Height: 5' 11" **Weight:** 207
Bats: Switch **Throws:** Right
1995 OBP: .346 **1995 SLG:** .358

McLemore provides plus range and steady hands at second base. He's also a reliable replacement outfielder in a pinch. He lacks bat speed but runs well, draws a healthy share of walks, and can be inserted into the leadoff spot if needed.

	G	AB	H	2B	3B	HR	RS	RBI	BB	SB	CS	BA
1995	129	467	122	20	5	5	73	41	59	21	11	.261
Career	783	2513	632	95	19	17	361	244	286	118	54	.251
Projected	139	455	112	14	2	1	77	36	62	20	13	.246

Otis Nixon OF

Age: 37 **Seasons:** 13
Height: 6' 2" **Weight:** 180
Bats: Switch **Throws:** Right
1995 OBP: .357 **1995 SLG:** .338

Nixon still provides wheels and skill in center field and the leadoff spot. His 21 caught stealings equaled his career worst, but his 50 steals tied for second most in the league. It's surprising that his speed hasn't translated into more career triples.

	G	AB	H	2B	3B	HR	RS	RBI	BB	SB	CS	BA
1995	139	589	174	21	2	0	87	45	58	50	21	.295
Career	1245	3444	920	101	16	7	605	217	382	444	147	.267
Projected	157	661	179	13	1	0	85	29	52	40	15	.271

Darren Oliver P

Age: 25		**Seasons:** 3	
Height: 6' 2"		**Weight:** 200	
Bats: Right		**Throws:** Left	
1995 OBA: .257		**1995 WHIP:** 1.61	

Oliver began his minor-league career as a starter, suffered shoulder injuries in 1990 and 1991, and was shifted to relief. He made his first big-league starts last season and promptly wound up on the disabled list with a torn rotator cuff.

	G	GS	IP	ER	ERA	H	BB	SO	W	L	SV
1995	17	7	49.0	23	4.22	47	32	39	4	2	0
Career	62	7	102.1	43	3.78	89	68	93	8	2	2
Projected	17	0	24.2	14	5.11	26	18	21	1	1	0

Dean Palmer 3B

Age: 27		**Seasons:** 6	
Height: 6' 2"		**Weight:** 195	
Bats: Right		**Throws:** Right	
1995 OBP: .448		**1995 SLG:** .613	

Palmer is a streaky slugger who can leave the yard in a heartbeat. He leaped out to a sizzling start last year before a ruptured biceps tendon in his left arm landed him on the disabled list until the season's final week.

	G	AB	H	2B	3B	HR	RS	RBI	BB	SB	CS	BA
1995	36	119	40	6	0	9	30	24	21	1	1	.336
Career	526	1808	427	87	6	102	280	289	194	25	21	.236
Projected	147	505	124	25	1	27	71	74	54	4	5	.246

Roger Pavlik   P

Age: 28   **Seasons:** 4
Height: 6' 2"   **Weight:** 220
Bats: Right   **Throws:** Right
1995 OBA: .243   **1995 WHIP:** 1.38

Pavlik uncorked ten wild pitches last year and walked 4.23 batters per nine innings, but if he ever harnesses his wild streak and stops working from behind in the count, he'll be a dominant starting pitcher.

	G	GS	IP	ER	ERA	H	BB	SO	W	L	SV
1995	31	31	191.2	93	4.37	174	90	149	10	10	0
Career	81	80	470.1	228	4.36	452	234	356	28	25	0
Projected	34	34	215.1	87	3.64	188	84	163	13	9	0

Ivan Rodriguez   C

Age: 24   **Seasons:** 5
Height: 5' 9"   **Weight:** 205
Bats: Right   **Throws:** Right
1995 OBP: .327   **1995 SLG:** .449

Pudge puts the running game on ice—he nailed 48 percent of would-be thieves last season, the best rate in the majors—and he's also become a consistent .300-range hitter with extra-base punch. He's clearly the American League's top backstop.

	G	AB	H	2B	3B	HR	RS	RBI	BB	SB	CS	BA
1995	130	492	149	32	2	12	56	67	16	0	2	.303
Career	577	2028	569	111	8	49	231	254	105	14	13	.281
Projected	134	500	141	28	3	13	52	65	24	1	3	.282

Kenny Rogers   **P**

Age: 31   **Seasons:** 7
Height: 6' 1"   **Weight:** 205
Bats: Left   **Throws:** Left
1995 OBA: .243   **1995 WHIP:** 1.29

Texas probably can't afford to keep Rogers, which is too bad because he's coming off a great season. His ERA was the league's fifth best, while his 17 victories were the most ever by a Rangers southpaw.

	G	GS	IP	ER	ERA	H	BB	SO	W	L	SV
1995	31	31	208.0	78	3.38	192	76	140	17	7	0
Career	376	100	943.1	407	3.88	925	370	680	70	51	28
Projected	33	33	224.1	84	3.37	210	79	201	15	8	0

Mickey Tettleton   **OF/DH**

Age: 35   **Seasons:** 12
Height: 6' 2"   **Weight:** 212
Bats: Switch   **Throws:** Right
1995 OBP: .396   **1995 SLG:** .510

Tettleton is one of baseball's most unique hitters, from his mannerisms at the plate to the amazing amount of noncontact at-bats he collects. He's jacked 30-plus taters four times but has topped 90 RBIs only once.

	G	AB	H	2B	3B	HR	RS	RBI	BB	SB	CS	BA
1995	134	429	102	19	1	32	76	78	107	0	0	.238
Career	1325	4163	1007	183	15	218	628	645	851	21	28	.242
Projected	152	520	126	17	0	27	75	76	111	0	2	.242

John Olerud

Toronto
BLUE JAYS

Scouting Report

Outfielders: Left fielder Joe Carter is the soul of the Blue Jays, but at age 36 he is in the decline phase of his career. Shawn Green put together a solid rookie season in right field and was the only Toronto hitter to register a plus-.500 slugging percentage. Center fielder Devon White took a free-agent ride to Florida, and many believe the Blue Jays will be in deep trouble now that his speed and glove have departed Toronto. Rookie outfielders Robert Perez and Shannon Stewart were unimpressive in their major-league debuts, batting .188 and .211, respectively.

Infielders: Whether he's trying too hard or struggling with his mechanics, John Olerud's unexpected troubles at the plate have become the subject of worried discussion in Toronto. If the Jays lose Roberto Alomar to free agency, second base will be a question mark. Utility infielder Domingo Cedeno would be a stopgap at best, and rookie Tomas Perez might not be ready for fulltime duties. If youngster Alex Gonzalez cuts down on his 114 strikeouts and fulfills his potential in the field, Toronto will have a top-flight shortstop. The Blue Jays have a top prospect in third baseman Howard Battle, but incumbent Ed Sprague is coming off his best season at the plate.

Catchers: Sandy Martinez has a powerful arm—he threw out almost 40 percent of would-be thieves—but his overall mechanics need polishing. He has no plate discipline and can't hit southpaws. Randy Knorr provides backup.

Designated Hitters: Paul Molitor has moved back home to Minnesota, and Joe Carter might be best suited to DH duty at this stage of his career. The organization is still hoping that Carlos Delgado will not be remembered as a ballyhooed bust; he's shown little indication that his big talent will ever develop into big production.

Starting Pitchers: Toronto will probably say goodbye to free agent Al Leiter, leaving them with a pitching staff full of plus-5.00 ERAs. Pat Hentgen will try to regroup and find the strikezone, as will number-two starter Juan Guzman. The Blue Jays have few blue-chip prospects, but Jeff Ware kept his ERA near 3.00 at triple-A Syracuse and flashed a lively arm but poor command in five starts for Toronto. Rookie righthander Edwin Hurtado walked more batters than he whiffed but won five of his seven decisions.

Relief Pitchers: The loss of closer Duane Ward to injury was another key element of Toronto's collapse. Darren Hall hurt his elbow, and Tony Castillo blew eight saves in 21 opportunities. Mike Timlin and rookie Tim Crabtree were solid in middle relief.

Outlook

The Blue Jays aren't the first championship team to fall apart in short order, but that's of little comfort to fans in Toronto. The reasons range from age-related declines (Molitor, Carter) to flat-out underachievement (Olerud, Hentgen) to injuries (Ward). The farm system has produced precious few reliable arms to bolster the unstable starting rotation, and the top-rated young position players—Delgado, Battle, Martinez, Green, Gonzalez, and Perez—have so far shown more promise than production. It will be a shock if the Jays are in contention in August.

Fungoes

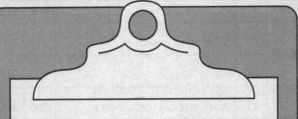

Quick Quiz: Which shortstop became the first player in Blue Jays history to surpass 200 hits in a season (1986)?

Franchise Milestone: Toronto won back-to-back World Series titles, defeating the Braves in 1992 and the Phillies in 1993, both in six games. The franchise also captured division titles in 1985, 1989, and 1991.

Top Pitcher: Dave Stieb, 1979–92

Top Player: Roberto Alomar, 1991–95

Top Manager: Cito Gaston, 1989–

Wacky Nickname: Crime Dog (Frederick Stanley McGriff)

Quick Quiz Answer: Tony Fernandez

Lineup Card

NO	POS	PLAYER	OBP	SLG
7	CF	Shannon Stewart	.318	.211
8	SS	Alex Gonzalez	.322	.398
29	LF	Joe Carter	.300	.428
9	1B	John Olerud	.398	.404
15	RF	Shawn Green	.326	.509
33	3B	Ed Sprague	.333	.407
6	DH	Carlos Delgado	.212	.297
20	2B	Domingo Cedeno	.289	.360
53	C	Sandy Martinez	.270	.335

In a Nutshell: The loss of Devon White to a broken foot in September brought home his importance to the team, and now that he's gone, the Jays may turn to rookie Shannon Stewart. He's not an ideal leadoff hitter, but the Blue Jays don't have anyone more qualified. In the past, Cito Gaston has inexplicably inserted run producer Joe Carter in front of the club's leader in on-base percentage, John Olerud, a decision that must be based on some factor other than a basic understanding of lineup selection. The Jays placed twelfth in the league in on-base percentage and slugging last year, and the free-agent defections of Paul Molitor and Roberto Alomar will deepen the holes in Toronto's lineup. Rookie slugger Howard Battle may start at the hot corner.

SkyDome

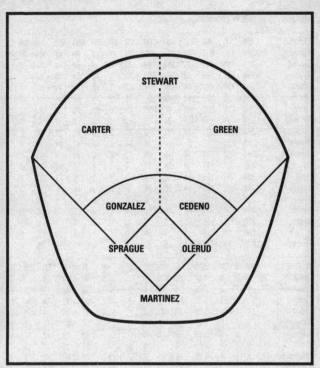

Capacity: 50,516
Turf: Artificial

LF Line: 328
RF Line: 328
Center: 400
Left CF: 375
Right CF: 375

Tickets:
416-341-1234

Of the three AL stadiums that use fake grass, SkyDome is perhaps the one that most resembles an NL home field in its dimensions and feel. Generally speaking, all types of offense are increased here, home runs in particular. Jose Canseco is a good example of a non–Blue Jay who unleashes an extra measure of power when visiting Toronto. The roof at SkyDome is retractable.

Statistics

Minimum 25 at-bats or 10.0 innings pitched

PLAYER	BA	G	AB	RS	H	TB	2B	3B	HR	RBI	BB	SO	SB	CS
Alomar	.300	130	517	71	155	232	24	7	13	66	47	45	30	3
Olerud	.291	135	492	72	143	199	32	0	8	54	84	54	0	0
Green	.288	121	379	52	109	193	31	4	15	54	20	68	1	2
White	.283	101	427	61	121	184	23	5	10	53	29	97	11	2
Molitor	.270	130	525	63	142	222	31	2	15	60	61	57	12	0
Carter	.253	139	558	70	141	239	23	0	25	76	37	87	12	1
T. Perez	.244	41	98	12	24	32	3	1	1	8	7	18	0	1
Sprague	.244	144	521	77	127	212	27	2	18	74	58	96	0	0
Gonzalez	.243	111	367	51	89	146	19	4	10	42	44	114	4	4
Martinez	.241	62	191	12	46	64	12	0	2	25	7	45	0	0
Cedeno	.236	51	161	18	38	58	6	1	4	14	10	35	0	1
Huff	.232	61	138	14	32	46	9	1	1	9	22	21	1	1
Knorr	.212	45	132	18	28	45	8	0	3	16	11	28	0	0
Stewart	.211	12	38	2	8	8	0	0	0	1	5	5	2	0
Parrish	.202	70	178	15	36	57	9	0	4	22	15	52	0	0
Battle	.200	9	15	3	3	3	0	0	0	0	4	8	1	0
R. Perez	.188	17	48	2	9	14	2	0	1	3	0	5	0	0
Delgado	.165	37	91	7	15	27	3	0	3	11	6	26	0	0

PITCHER	W	L	SV	ERA	G	GS	CG	SH	IP	H	R	ER	BB	SO
Timlin	4	3	5	2.14	31	0	0	0	42.0	38	13	10	17	36
Crabtree	0	2	0	3.09	31	0	0	0	32.0	30	16	11	13	21
Castillo	1	5	13	3.22	55	0	0	0	72.2	65	27	26	24	38
Leiter	11	11	0	3.64	28	28	2	1	183.0	162	80	74	108	153
Robinson	1	2	0	3.69	21	0	0	0	39.0	25	21	16	22	31
Williams	1	2	0	3.69	23	3	0	0	53.2	43	23	22	28	41
Hall	0	2	3	4.41	17	0	0	0	16.1	21	9	8	9	11
Menhart	1	4	0	4.92	21	9	1	0	78.2	72	49	43	47	50
Hentgen	10	14	0	5.11	30	30	2	0	200.2	236	129	114	90	135
Hurtado	5	2	0	5.45	14	10	1	0	77.2	81	50	47	40	33
Ware	2	1	0	5.47	5	5	0	0	26.1	28	18	16	21	18
Rogers	2	4	0	5.70	19	0	0	0	23.2	21	15	15	18	13
Guzman	4	14	0	6.32	24	24	3	0	135.1	151	101	95	73	94
Jordan	1	0	1	6.60	15	0	0	0	15.0	18	11	11	13	10
Carrara	2	4	0	7.21	12	7	1	0	48.2	64	46	39	25	27
Cox	1	3	0	7.40	24	0	0	0	45.0	57	40	37	33	38

Roster

MANAGER: Cito Gaston
COACHES: Alfredo Griffin, Nick Leyva, Mel Queen, Gene Tenace, Willie Upshaw

NO	PITCHERS	B	T	HT	WT	DOB
38	Giovanni Carrara	R	R	6-2	230	3/4/68
49	Tony Castillo	L	L	5-10	188	3/1/63
—	Brad Cornett	R	R	6-3	190	2/4/69
37	Tim Crabtree	R	R	6-4	205	10/13/69
44	Juan Guzman	R	R	5-11	195	10/28/66
36	Darren Hall	R	R	6-3	205	7/14/64
41	Pat Hentgen	R	R	6-2	200	11/13/68
—	Edwin Hurtado	R	R	6-3	215	2/1/70
48	Ricardo Jordan	L	L	6-0	175	6/27/70
55	Paul Menhart	R	R	6-2	190	3/25/69
40	Mike Timlin	R	R	6-4	210	3/10/66
—	Jeff Ware	R	R	6-3	190	11/11/70
54	Woody Williams	R	R	6-0	190	8/19/66
	CATCHERS					
27	Randy Knorr	R	R	6-2	215	11/12/68
53	Angel Martinez	L	R	6-4	200	10/3/72
	INFIELDERS					
14	Howard Battle	R	R	6-0	197	3/25/72
20	Domingo Cedeno	S	R	6-1	165	11/4/68
8	Alex Gonzalez	R	R	6-0	182	4/8/73
9	John Olerud	L	L	6-5	218	8/5/68
1	Tomas Perez	S	R	5-11	165	12/29/73
33	Ed Sprague	R	R	6-2	210	7/25/67
	OUTFIELDERS					
29	Joe Carter	R	R	6-3	225	3/7/60
6	Carlos Delgado	L	R	6-3	206	6/25/72
15	Shawn Green	L	L	6-4	190	11/10/72
26	Mike Huff	R	R	6-1	190	8/11/63
17	Robert Perez	R	R	6-3	205	6/4/69

FREE AGENTS: Roberto Alomar, Danny Cox, Al Leiter, Lance Parrish, Duane Ward

Roberto Alomar   2B

Age: 28   **Seasons:** 8
Height: 6' 0"   **Weight:** 185
Bats: Switch   **Throws:** Right
1995 OBP: .354   **1995 SLG:** .449

A perennial MVP candidate, Alomar combines speed, contact, and extra-base pop as a hitter with nonpareil fielding skills. He's a below-average hitter from the right side (.231), but that's his only weakness as a player.

	G	AB	H	2B	3B	HR	RS	RBI	BB	SB	CS	BA
1995	130	517	155	24	7	13	71	66	47	30	3	.300
Career	1151	4460	1329	230	48	77	697	499	470	296	76	.298
Projected	153	592	184	25	5	15	101	72	54	44	8	.311

Joe Carter   OF

Age: 36   **Seasons:** 13
Height: 6' 3"   **Weight:** 225
Bats: Right   **Throws:** Right
1995 OBP: .300   **1995 SLG:** .428

After six consecutive 100-RBI seasons, Carter posted his lowest RBI total in ten years, plus his typically abysmal on-base percentage. Combine those factors with his less-than-stellar fielding and you have an aging star whose value is negligible.

	G	AB	H	2B	3B	HR	RS	RBI	BB	SB	CS	BA
1995	139	558	141	23	0	25	70	76	37	12	1	.253
Career	1749	6797	1782	345	41	327	959	1173	419	212	57	.262
Projected	154	601	150	24	2	26	71	72	30	10	0	.250

Alex Gonzalez   SS

Age: 22   **Seasons:** 2
Height: 6' 0"   **Weight:** 182
Bats: Right   **Throws:** Right
1995 OBP: .322   **1995 SLG:** .398

Gonzalez weathered the trials of a top prospect, including 19 errors in 111 games, a .217 batting average on the road, and an eight-game stint on the bench. He's loaded with raw talent, but the operative word at this point is *raw*.

	G	AB	H	2B	3B	HR	RS	RBI	BB	SB	CS	BA
1995	111	367	89	19	4	10	51	42	44	4	4	.243
Career	126	420	97	22	5	10	58	43	48	7	4	.231
Projected	148	446	113	22	6	12	57	47	50	9	5	.253

Shawn Green   OF

Age: 23   **Seasons:** 3
Height: 6' 4"   **Weight:** 190
Bats: Left   **Throws:** Left
1995 OBP: .326   **1995 SLG:** .509

In his coming-out season Green set the franchise record for extra-base hits by a rookie (50). He also rang up a club-best nine outfield assists. He needs to improve against lefties (.222) and cut down on his fielding miscues.

	G	AB	H	2B	3B	HR	RS	RBI	BB	SB	CS	BA
1995	121	379	109	31	4	15	52	54	20	1	2	.288
Career	138	418	112	32	4	15	53	55	21	2	2	.268
Projected	154	480	131	26	2	22	65	69	25	3	2	.273

Juan Guzman   P

Age: 29   **Seasons:** 5
Height: 5' 11"   **Weight:** 195
Bats: Right   **Throws:** Right
1995 OBA: .281   **1995 WHIP:** 1.66

Guzman logged sub-3.00 ERAs in 1991 and 1992 but plus-5.00 ERAs the past two seasons. He's a slow worker who tries to blow hitters away, but his control is shaky and his velocity has been questioned, perhaps because of arm problems.

	G	GS	IP	ER	ERA	H	BB	SO	W	L	SV
1995	24	24	135.1	95	6.32	151	73	94	4	14	0
Career	133	133	823.0	385	4.21	760	397	700	56	36	0
Projected	29	29	152.1	100	5.91	163	81	100	5	13	0

Pat Hentgen   P

Age: 27   **Seasons:** 5
Height: 6' 2"   **Weight:** 200
Bats: Right   **Throws:** Right
1995 OBA: .290   **1995 WHIP:** 1.63

Hentgen had risen from mediocrity to become the ace of a championship club in 1993, but last season he fell apart. Poor control was his undoing, and his ability to bounce back could depend on how well he locates his curve.

	G	GS	IP	ER	ERA	H	BB	SO	W	L	SV
1995	30	30	200.2	114	5.11	236	90	135	10	14	0
Career	119	89	649.1	305	4.23	663	258	446	47	33	0
Projected	31	31	211.1	101	4.30	121	79	143	9	13	0

Al Leiter P

Age: 30	**Seasons:** 9
Height: 6' 3"	**Weight:** 215
Bats: Left	**Throws:** Left
1995 OBA: .238	**1995 WHIP:** 1.48

Leiter's career has long been stunted by injuries and wildness, but he was the only Toronto starter whose ERA was under 5.00 last season. His arm is a live wire—he topped the league in wild pitches and walks.

	G	GS	IP	ER	ERA	H	BB	SO	W	L	SV
1995	28	28	183.0	74	3.64	162	108	153	11	11	0
Career	113	83	522.0	253	4.19	490	309	439	33	32	2
Projected	33	33	219.0	84	3.45	174	95	177	15	10	0

Paul Molitor DH

Age: 39	**Seasons:** 18
Height: 6' 0"	**Weight:** 180
Bats: Right	**Throws:** Right
1995 OBP: .350	**1995 SLG:** .423

He began to show signs of decline last season, but Molitor might last long enough to reach 3,000 hits and gain well-deserved entrance into the Hall of Fame. A brilliant basestealer, Molitor is 85 for 95 in steal attempts the past three years.

	G	AB	H	2B	3B	HR	RS	RBI	BB	SB	CS	BA
1995	130	525	142	31	2	15	63	60	61	12	0	.270
Career	2261	9135	2789	503	97	211	1545	1036	948	466	119	.305
Projected	157	632	179	27	3	13	83	64	68	17	2	.283

John Olerud 1B

Age: 27   **Seasons:** 7
Height: 6' 5"   **Weight:** 218
Bats: Left   **Throws:** Left
1995 OBP: .398   **1995 SLG:** .404

Olerud is a superb professional hitter, but his 1993 batting-title season (.363) may have raised expectations to an unreasonable level. He has a perfect eye and a sweet swing, but he doesn't demolish lefties (.259). Is he the new Wally Joyner?

	G	AB	H	2B	3B	HR	RS	RBI	BB	SB	CS	BA
1995	135	492	143	32	0	8	72	54	84	0	0	.291
Career	795	2705	801	188	6	91	405	410	454	2	8	.296
Projected	157	546	173	30	0	14	81	77	90	0	1	.317

Ed Sprague 3B

Age: 28   **Seasons:** 5
Height: 6' 2"   **Weight:** 210
Bats: Right   **Throws:** Right
1995 OBP: .333   **1995 SLG:** .407

Sprague was working his way out of baseball before turning his career around last year. He set personal highs in homers, RBIs, and walks. It remains to be seen if he can maintain his 1995 performance level.

	G	AB	H	2B	3B	HR	RS	RBI	BB	SB	CS	BA
1995	144	521	127	27	2	18	77	74	58	0	0	.244
Career	486	1679	421	86	4	46	188	218	135	2	3	.251
Projected	140	516	119	17	1	12	45	48	44	0	1	.231

Mike Timlin P

Age: 30   **Seasons:** 5
Height: 6' 4"   **Weight:** 210
Bats: Right   **Throws:** Right
1995 OBA: .242   **1995 WHIP:** 1.31

A former minor-league starter whose fine stuff has been undercut by arm injuries, Timlin pitched well in a setup role last year. He blew four of nine save chances, so closing may not be in his future, but righthanders hit a pitiful .159 against him.

	G	GS	IP	ER	ERA	H	BB	SO	W	L	SV
1995	31	0	42.0	10	2.14	38	17	36	4	3	5
Career	208	3	289.2	120	3.73	281	134	243	19	14	12
Projected	36	0	54.1	16	2.65	50	24	49	3	2	10

Devon White OF

Age: 33   **Seasons:** 11
Height: 6' 2"   **Weight:** 190
Bats: Switch   **Throws:** Right
1995 OBP: .334   **1995 SLG:** .431

White is a phenomenal center fielder, but Joe Carter's assertion that Devo might be more valuable to the team than Roberto Alomar notwithstanding, White's contribution on offense, which always had holes, has declined due to age and injuries.

	G	AB	H	2B	3B	HR	RS	RBI	BB	SB	CS	BA
1995	101	427	121	23	5	10	61	53	29	11	2	.283
Career	1268	4942	1284	246	58	131	789	515	353	249	65	.260
Projected	138	584	150	19	4	13	62	49	32	15	3	.257

Willie Mays

The All-Time Team

Perhaps baseball's most attractive quality is its power to create nostalgia and inspire discussion. The choosing of an all-time all-star team encapsulates just such a double dip, so let's get to it.

NO	POS	PLAYER	OBP	SLG
33	SS	Honus Wagner	.390	.466
8	2B	Joe Morgan	.395	.427
3	RF	Babe Ruth	.474	.690
4	1B	Lou Gehrig	.447	.632
24	CF	Willie Mays	.387	.557
9	DH	Ted Williams	.483	.634
6	LF	Stan Musial	.418	.559
20	3B	Mike Schmidt	.384	.527
5	C	Johnny Bench	.345	.476

Honus Wagner, Shortstop

Hall of Fame player/manager John McGraw once called Wagner the best of the all-time greats, and whether you consider that a still-valid assertion a century after the fact, there can be no doubt that Wagner was, at the very least, the greatest all-around shortstop ever.

As a fielder his range was not the equal of an Ozzie Smith, but his hands were perhaps the best ever and his arm was strong and accurate. As a hitter, he dominated baseball in the deadball era: Wagner won eight National League batting championships and finished his career with mor than 3,400 hits and 700 steals. His 252 triples are the third-best total in history. Had the league sponsored an MVP award during his prime (1899–1909), it is reasonable to suggest that the Flying Dutchman, as the popular Wagner was called, would have won more such honors than any player ever.

As for postseason performance, he hit .333 with six RBIs and six steals in the 1909 World Series and, with the help of rookie pitcher Babe Adams, led Pittsburgh to a championship.

Joe Morgan, Second Base

Rogers Hornsby and, to an even greater extent, Eddie Collins are difficult to pass over. After all, who wouldn't want to have a .400 hitter at second base and in the two-hole. Hornsby rates the nod for offense, but his glovework was average at best. Collins was a superior fielder as well as a great hitter and basestealer. But when we consider all the facets of baseball performance, Morgan is our choice.

One of the game's most analytical players, Little Joe was the prime catalyst for perhaps the most powerful teams in modern baseball annals—the Cincinnati Reds of 1975 and 1976. He won back-to-back MVP awards in those years. In 1976 he topped the majors in both slugging and on-base percentage while swiping 60 bases at an 87-percent success rate. By the way, Morgan was also a five-time Gold Glove winner.

Willie Mays, Center Field

The choice between Mantle and Mays in center is probably the most difficult of all the positions. (Throw in Joltin' Joe DiMaggio to enhance the dilemma.)

Weighing advantages in each player's favor, Mays has better career numbers and an advantage in the field, but the Mick's package of speed, power, and star quality are unmatched. Mantle was a far better hitter in his prime years, and his solid output in World Series play gives him an edge over Mays, who slugged a miserable .282 in his four World Series appearances. Mantle slugged .535 in 12 World Series. Still, we'll take the Say Hey Kid over the Commerce Comet based on longevity and durability. Mays appeared in at least 150 games for 13 straight years, while Mantle reached 150 in just four of his 18 seasons.

Babe Ruth, Right Field

There are a couple of comparatively obvious selections on any all-time team, but none more so than the Bambino. Consider his lifetime slugging percentage of .690, the number-one all-time mark. (Ted Williams, who is second on the list in this category, comes in a distant 56 points behind.)

Lou Gehrig, First Base

Gehrig rarely had the spotlight to himself as a player, first sharing it with Ruth in his prime and then with the rising DiMaggio. The Iron Horse won the Triple Crown in 1934 (and struck out only 31 times) but finished just fifth in the MVP vote. Ultimately he stood side by side with death in his finest hour, redeeming us all with his courage. Now that Cal Ripken has broken his seemingly immortal record of consecutive games played, his name may be mentioned more often in connection with disease than with baseball, but his excellence and professionalism on the field will never be overshadowed.

Ted Williams, Designated Hitter

The Splendid Splinter's mighty bat reigned before the DH rule was adopted by the American League. But because of the gap between his talent as a batsman and his skills as a fielder, not to mention the difficulty of choosing between

Musial and Williams, we've carved out a spot for Ted as our designated hitter. Williams's legacy among all-time legends is first and foremost as the purest of hitters. He seemed to live for hitting a baseball, and no one before or since has outstripped his blend of power and contact. His all-time rankings of first in on-base percentage and second in slugging put him neck-and-neck with the Sultan of Swat for the status of history's greatest hitter.

Stan Musial, Left Field

Musial, who topped the National League in both on-base percentage and slugging in three different seasons and hit no lower than .310 in any of his first 16 years as a pro, may not have possessed the undiluted physical ability and God-given talent of Barry Bonds. (Perhaps no individual on this list, or any list God could come up with, does.) Bonds has already amassed the same number of MVP awards (three) in ten seasons as Musial won in 22. But we'll wait and see what type of career numbers Mr. Bonds compiles before we rate him over the Man.

Mike Schmidt, Third Base

This is the simplest choice other than the selection of Ruth in right field. Brooks Robinson makes a powerful visual impression on everyone who has ever seen his diving stops at the hot corner, but Schmidt flashed some leather, too (ten Gold Gloves), and his 13 seasons of 30-plus home runs are a baker's dozen more than Hoover produced. A more formidable challenge to Schmidt at this position is Eddie Mathews, an impressive slugger but nothing special with the glove.

Johnny Bench, Catcher

Catcher is the most important position on the diamond. With that in mind we need durability, brains, skill behind the plate and, for good measure, power with the lumber.

Bench either developed or perfected several modern-day techniques for handling this position. This, in part, earned him ten consecutive Gold Gloves.

Bench hit 389 career home runs and was a two-time MVP. His presence in Cincinnati helped give rise to the Big Red Machine, not only with his talent but with his leadership. As explosive as those lineups in Cincinnati were, the Reds' pitching staffs during those years were mediocre in terms of sheer ability (Gary Nolan and Don Gullett weren't exactly the 1970s' answers to Maddux and Glavine), and Bench's on-field management of the starting rotation was essential to the club's success.

There are strong arguments in support of Hall of Famers Mickey Cochrane, Buck Ewing, and Bill Dickey, all of whom make worthy candidates for the position of starting backstop.

Lefty Grove, Lefthanded Pitcher

Tops on the tally of requirements is that the greatest southpaw of them all be nicknamed Lefty. Done. Robert Moses Grove led his league in ERA an unprecedented nine times, in winning percentage five, and in strikeouts seven consecutive.

Walter Johnson, Righthanded Pitcher

Johnson is one of this list's most obvious choices. Never mind that he played in a different era; the Big Train seems to have hailed from another planet.

Johnson pitched for better than two decades and still maintained an amazing career earned run average of 2.17, leading his league five times. He's the only hurler ever to break the century mark in shutouts (110). Johnson was much more than overpowering; he endured to start 666 games and come within 85 innings of 6,000. And he did all this almost exclusively on one pitch, the sidearm fastball that many would-be hitters never actually saw.

Jackie Robinson

Ten Stars of the Negro Leagues

A "gentleman's agreement," adopted by the baseball establishment in the late 1880s and upheld until 1947 when Jackie Robinson joined the Brooklyn Dodgers, kept black ballplayers from competing in the major leagues, but it didn't keep them from playing baseball. During that sad and beautiful era, black athletes and entrepreneurs joined together to form their own teams and their own leagues, playing a style of baseball that was dramatic and highly competitive. The separation of blacks and whites in the early years of pro baseball rendered any attempt to systematically compare the true talents of players from all leagues an even more hopeless exercise than it otherwise would be. It's almost unheard of to see the names Josh Gibson or Willie Foster on a nonsegregated list of all-time greats because bigotry kept them from competing with their peers in the majors, and the lack of comprehensive records makes objective analysis impossible. There's no way of knowing which of the great black ballplayers would have earned a place on our all-time team, but the following article, researched and written by Tom Helberg, is our humble attempt to honor some of the men who were kept separate but were far from unequal.

Rube Foster

In February 1920, Andrew "Rube" Foster and several black team owners and sportsmen met in Kansas City and formed the Negro National League (NNL), the first successful Negro league. Consisting of eight teams from the Midwest, the league struggled initially, but it did have financial success in its first year. Its success prompted the formation of other Negro leagues, including the Eastern Colored League (ECL) in 1923, the American Negro League (ANL) in 1929, and the Negro American League (NAL) in 1937. The NNL disbanded in 1932, partially due to financial difficulties brought about by the Great Depression and the earlier passing away of Rube Foster. However, the following year it was re-formed and reorganized by Gus Greenlee, who also instituted the extremely popular East-West All-Star Game. Other important figures in the promotion and development of black baseball were team owners Cumberland Posey and J.L. Wilkinson, and a pitcher named Satchel Paige. But it was Rube Foster who was the guiding force in the early days, the man who held it all together and who would become known as the father of the Negro leagues.

Rube Foster began his baseball career as an outstanding pitcher. He acquired his nickname after beating Rube Waddell, one of the major leagues' best pitchers, in a 1902 exhibition game against the pennant-winning Philadelphia Athletics. Before long, Foster would become involved in every aspect of the game. He became a booker, a manager, a team owner, and a league founder and president.

Foster was one of the dominant pitchers of the early 1900s. At 6' 4" and over 200 pounds, he was an imposing figure on the mound and threw a blazing fastball, a wicked curveball, and a deceptive "fadeaway," or screwball. He used his brains and cunning, as well as his excellent stuff, to post incredible won-lost statistics. Unofficial records credit Foster with a 54–1 record pitching for the Cuban X Giants in 1903 and 51–4 for the Philadelphia Giants in 1905. He later became the ace for the Chicago American Giants, a team he also co-owned and managed.

As a manager Foster was a master strategist and a shrewd handler of men. He had an innovative approach to the game. At a time when the style of play in the major leagues was primarily power oriented, Foster's teams used the bunt, the stolen base, and the hit-and-run as their main offensive weapons. Opposing managers never knew what to expect. Foster once had his team bunt seven consecutive times. Instead of relying on the longball, Foster would use a walk, a sacrifice, a stolen base, a suicide squeeze to mount a constant offensive attack. In 1910 he managed the Chicago Leland Giants to a record of 123–6.

As a baseball executive, Foster's name could be mentioned in the same sentence with Connie Mack and Branch Rickey. He had the keen business sense, the leadership ability, and the determination that were necessary in providing a financial stability for the new league. He worked to achieve league parity and a more even schedule, and even helped struggling teams with money from his own pocket. He ruled the league with an iron hand, but his dictatorial leadership helped give it a professionalism and legitimacy that he hoped would lead to his ultimate goal: opening the doors of major-league baseball.

Rube Foster was one of the most important figures in black baseball history. He left his imprint on all areas of the game. Perhaps his biggest impact was the revolutionary brand of baseball he fostered: developing to a high art form the use of strategy, the unexpected, and speed.

Cool Papa Bell

James "Cool Papa" Bell was one of the fastest men to play in the Negro leagues, perhaps the fastest man to ever play baseball anywhere, anytime. He was so fast, it was said, that he could turn off the lights, hop into bed, pull up the covers, and be asleep before it got dark. This may be one of Satchel Paige's famous tales, but it is true that when Bell challenged Olympic gold medalist Jesse Owens to a race around the bases, Owens respectfully declined.

Bell's speed made him a constant threat to take the extra base, or two—to go from first to third on a sacrifice bunt, to score from second base on an infield single. It was for this kind of speed and daring baserunning that Bell is well remembered.

Cool Papa was involved in one of the great plays in the history of the Negro leagues. In the 1934 East-West All-Star Game, a game that became a major showcase and the most important event of the season, Bell exhibited his incredible run-scoring ability. The game was a classic pitcher's duel. After seven innings, with Satchel Paige of the East and Willie Foster of the West on the mound, the score was still deadlocked at 0–0. In the top of the eighth, Bell walked and then stole second. He was taking a good lead off second when batter Jud Wilson hit a broken-bat grounder toward shortstop. Bell flew around third base as shortstop Willie Wells fielded the ball and fired to the plate. However, before the ball arrived, Bell had slid safely across home. The East won the game 1–0.

Infielders routinely played close when Bell came to bat, as if there were a runner on third and no one out. And still, even on sharply hit ground balls, opposing fans would shout, "Hurry." On defense, his speed allowed him to play a shallow center field, so shallow that he was known to sneak in behind a runner at second base for the pickoff play.

In addition to being the league's most feared baserunner, Cool Papa was a terrific hitter and a durable star. A switch-hitter, Bell hit over .400 several times. In 1945, at the age of 42, he hit .373. He retired the following year after hitting .412. Bell was an important member of three of the league's best teams: the 1920s St. Louis Stars, the 1930s Pittsburgh Crawfords, and the Homestead Grays of the 1940s. Bell was a popular player and a perennial all-star selection.

Cool Papa Bell got his nickname when he was just 19. In tense, game situations, even at that young age, he was always able to stay composed and cool. According to people who knew him, he remained that way throughout his life. Cool Papa Bell was inducted into the Major League Baseball Hall of Fame in 1974.

Josh Gibson

The Negro leagues also featured their share of power hitters. While Babe Ruth was making a reputation as the home-run king of his era in the major leagues, Josh Gibson was doing the same thing in the NNL and the Latin American leagues. From 1930 to 1946, Gibson hit home runs about as far and as often as anyone playing the game. Some of his home runs were so awesome that legends began to grow around them.

One story goes that one afternoon in the 1930s, while playing a game in Pittsburgh, Gibson hit a shot so high and far that it never came down. That night Gibson's team drove to Philadelphia for a game scheduled the next day. In the middle of that game, a ball suddenly came down out of the sky and was caught by the center fielder. The home plate umpire, who had also umpired the previous game, turned, pointed to Gibson in the dugout and said, "You're out. Yesterday. In Pittsburgh."

But along with the legends are some real, honest-to-goodness home-run blasts. In 1930, Gibson became the first man to hit a ball over the 457-foot center-field wall at Pittsburgh's Forbes Field. He repeated the feat in 1937, clearing the wall, according to one newspaper account, by more than 100 feet. Gibson hit some of the longest home runs ever hit in Yankee Stadium. In 1930, at the age of 18, Josh hit a homer that landed against the back wall of the bullpen in left field, a blast of more than 500 feet. Another Gibson drive hit two feet from the top of the facade above the bleachers in center field, a distance of about 580 feet. It was estimated that the ball would have traveled 700 feet if it had cleared the wall.

Unlike most power hitters, who use their entire body to swing, Gibson had a short, fluid, and graceful swing. His upper-body strength and quick bat supplied such power that he didn't need a big swing. His power went to all fields and his batting average was consistently over

.300. In 1943, Gibson led the league in hits, doubles, triples, home runs, and batting average.

Gibson's home-run–to–at-bat ratio was amazing. In 1939 NNL action, he hit a home run in one out of every four and a half times at the plate. In a 550 at-bat season, that would translate to more than 120 home runs for the year. In 1937, Gibson had an unheard-of slugging average of 1.190 in league action, and in 1939 it was 1.033.

Josh Gibson was not a good defensive catcher when he first started—one teammate said Josh couldn't catch a train if one came across the plate—but over the years he made himself into one. However, no one had to teach Gibson how to throw. He had a natural throwing arm that was strong and accurate. Sometimes before the start of a game, Gibson would place a fielder's glove over each base and then from home plate would knock each glove off with three quick throws.

Many thought that Josh Gibson would be the player to finally break major-league baseball's color barrier. In the early 1940s, he did have some talks with Clark Griffith, owner of the Washington Senators, but nothing ever came of it. When Jackie Robinson first signed with the Dodgers, Gibson was already 34 years old. He gradually realized that time was against him and he would never make it to the majors. Friends and teammates said that that realization left him brokenhearted. Josh Gibson died suddenly at home in 1947 at age 36.

Gibson played several seasons of baseball in Mexico and Puerto Rico, where he achieved a great deal of fame. Fans would often hang banners in the trees outside San Juan's Escambron Stadium, marking the places where some of Gibson's out-of-the-park home runs had landed. Some of those banners remained hanging for years—a fitting tribute to the power of Josh Gibson.

Buck Leonard

Walter "Buck" Leonard was a great hitter and a teammate of Josh Gibson's on the powerful Homestead Grays teams of the 1930s and 1940s. With Gibson and Leonard batting in the three and four positions, the Grays had a one-two power threat similar to the Yankees' Ruth and Gehrig. In fact, Gibson and Leonard were often referred to as the black Ruth and the black Gehrig. And since Buck Leonard was a good-hitting, smooth-fielding, consistent first baseman who played the game with grace and style, the comparison seems a natural one.

Leonard had a long and distinguished career. He broke into professional baseball with the Brooklyn Royal Giants in 1933, joined the Homestead Grays in 1934, and played first base for the Grays for the next 17 years, rarely missing a game. After leaving the Grays he went to Mexico and played for five years there before retiring at the age of 48, hitting .312 with 13 home runs in 62 games in the Mexican Central League in his last season.

Buck Leonard helped the Homestead Grays win ten pennants and four black World Series titles. He had a lifetime batting average of .341. He didn't quite have the power of Josh Gibson, but he rarely ever struck out. Trying to sneak a fastball past Buck Leonard, one opposing pitcher said, was like trying to sneak a sunrise past a rooster. He hit a league-leading .383 in 1940 and .395 in 1948. He also hit .382 against major-league pitching in exhibition games and barnstorming tours. In one exhibition game against major-league all-stars, he hit a tremendous home run against Bob Feller. According to one player, perhaps borrowing some hyperbole from Satchel Paige, the ball flew over the fence, out of the ballpark, and over rooftops until it hit the town's water tower. It rained in that town for five days. Buck Leonard was one of the most liked and well respected players in the league, by both fans and players. He was voted to the all-star team a record eleven times. A ballplayer's ballplayer, Buck was a team player all the way, always dependable and professional. In 1972, Buck Leonard was inducted into the Major League Baseball Hall of Fame. In his acceptance speech he said that he thought that he and the other Negro leaguers had contributed something to the game of baseball and that he would do everything in his power to "take care of this induction." Buck Leonard was a first-class first baseman.

Martin Dihigo

Martin Dihigo was a premier second baseman. He was also a premier outfielder and a premier pitcher. One of the most versatile players of all time, Dihigo regularly played every position on the diamond, with precision, sometimes playing more than two positions in a single game. In the 1935 NNL All-Star Game, he started the game batting third and playing center field, then late in the game was called to the mound to pitch in relief.

Dihigo was born in Cuba and played much of his baseball there as well as in Mexico and the United States. He came to America in the early 1920s hoping to sign with one of the major-league teams. Unable to do that, he signed with the Eastern Cuban Stars in 1923 and played for several NNL and ECL clubs in the 1920s and 1930s. Dihigo played 14 years in the Negro leagues, where he starred primarily as a hitter and position player, and ten years in Latin America, where he was known more as a pitcher.

Dihigo's all-around talents included a bat that hit for power and average, a fine glove and great range in the field, good speed on the bases, and an exceptionally strong throwing arm. He once exhibited his great arm in a pregame entertainment that accompanied many of the Negro league games. In a throwing contest Dihigo was pitted against a jai alai player to see who could make the best throw from home plate to the center-field bleachers. First the jai alai player loaded a ball into his wicker basket and made a throw that went into the bleachers on one bounce. Dihigo then reared back and threw a bullet that sailed into the center field seats on the fly.

Martin Dihigo is a member of the Cuban, Mexican, and American halls of fame. His plaque at the Mexican Solon de Fame details some of his accomplishments in the Mexican leagues: he had a .317 career batting average; in 1938 he became the first player to hit six-for-six in a game; as a pitcher his won-lost record was 119–57, a .676 winning percentage that stands as the all-time best; his career earned run average of 2.84 is also a record. His overall lifetime pitching record was 261–138.

Back in America, Dihigo led the ECL in home runs in 1926 and 1927, led the ANL with a .386 batting average in 1929, and hit .393 in 1930. Hall of Famer Johnny Mize, once a teammate of Dihigo's in the Dominican Republic, said that Dihigo was the best player he'd ever played with or against.

John Henry Lloyd

John Henry "Pop" Lloyd was the best-known player of his era. Babe Ruth once called Lloyd the greatest player of all time. He was the top shortstop in the Negro leagues at the same time that Honus Wagner was the top shortstop in the major leagues, thus Lloyd was often referred to as the black Wagner. When Honus Wagner was told of this, he said he felt privileged to be compared to Lloyd.

John Lloyd established a .368 career batting average in his 26 years of play in the Negro leagues, the top recorded lifetime average. He hit .417 in 1910 and .475 in 1911, when he was in his prime, and more than a decade later was still able to top .400. He was a complete player who could hit for power, play solid defense, and come through in the clutch.

The reserve clause in the Negro-league contract was not enforced as rigidly as it was in the major leagues, so many Negro leaguers frequently moved from team to team. Lloyd played for more than a dozen teams, once joking, "I go where the money is." From 1914 to 1917, Lloyd starred and batted cleanup for the powerful Chicago American Giants. In 1923 player/manager Lloyd hit .418 and led the Hilldale Daisies to the first pennant in the new Eastern Colored League. In 1929 he hit .362 for the Lincoln Giants of the ANL.

Like many professional athletes, Lloyd was a fierce and aggressive competitor on the playing field, but off it he was good-natured and easygoing. He developed into an excellent manager and became a valued mentor to many of the younger players. He was great at instilling confidence and helping his players achieve to the best of their abilities. Considered by many to be the elder statesman of black baseball, he gradually began being affectionately referred to as Pop.

After retiring from professional baseball, Pop Lloyd continued to manage and play first base for various sandlot teams while working as a janitor in Atlantic City. He also served as the town's Little League commissioner and became extremely popular and influential with the children there. In 1949, Atlantic City dedicated its ballpark as the John Henry Lloyd Park in honor of his achievements and community service. Pop Lloyd was elected to the Baseball Hall of Fame in 1977.

Willie Wells

Whereas Lloyd was the best shortstop of the 1910s and 1920s, Willie Wells was the best during the 1930s and 1940s. Many similarities exist between Wells and Lloyd. Wells could also hit for power and average. In 1929 he led the NNL with 29 home runs and won the batting crown that year (.368) and in 1930 (.404). He was a superb defensive player, not as quick and mobile as Lloyd, but his quick release and intelligent positioning made up for it. Wells made a thorough study of opposing hitters so he knew where to best position himself. He was also a good baserunner—in 1929, Wells stole home with the winning run on consecutive days against a team of major-league all-stars.

Also like Pop Lloyd, Willie Wells was a traveling man, playing for at least ten different teams in a career of more than 20 years. He was a member of the St. Louis Stars teams that won NNL championships in 1928, 1930, and 1931. He helped the Chicago American Giants win two pennants, including the first in the new NNL in 1933. He was a member of the Newark Eagles' famous million-dollar infield and was a part of the Kansas City Monarchs' dynasty of the late 1930s and early 1940s. Pitchers back then often used the brushback pitch to intimidate good hitters, even more so than they do today. Today's "chin music" was a whole symphony back in the heyday of the Negro leagues. And it was much more dangerous back then, when batting helmets hadn't even been thought of yet. Wells was often thrown at, and once he was beaned by a Baltimore pitcher and knocked unconscious. He was advised by a doctor to take a few days off. However, the next day Wells was back at the ballpark, after stopping first at a nearby construction site to borrow a hard hat from one of the workers. People thought he looked crazy standing up there at the plate wearing that hard hat, but in a way Willie Wells was the pioneer for the modern-day batting helmet.

Wells was an eight-time all-star, posting a .438 slugging percentage in those games. Of the Negro league players not yet in the Hall of Fame, many consider Willie Wells to be the most deserving of induction.

Ray Dandridge

Ray Dandridge was one of the top players at third base. At first glance, Dandridge wouldn't strike one as a great athlete. Short, squat, with legs so bowed, one player remarked, that a train could easily pass through—but ground balls very rarely ever did. He was one of the smoothest fielders to ever patrol the hot corner, always ready to handle just about anything. When the ball took a wicked hop, Ray's glove hopped right along with it; when the batter laid down a bunt, Dandridge was able to charge the ball, field it barehanded, and get the out at first base.

Dandridge broke into the Negro leagues with the Detroit Stars in 1933, moving to the Newark Dodgers and then to the Newark Eagles in 1936, compiling a lifetime batting average of .325. With Ray Dandridge at third, Willie Wells at shortstop, Dick Seay at second, and George Suttles at first, the Eagles had what many consider to be the best infield in Negro-league history. Dandridge also played eight seasons of baseball in Mexico, where he hit .345 and became so popular that his picture was used by a local politician in his election-campaign poster. Dandridge started out wanting to be a power hitter. He used a light bat and always swung for the fences. But Detroit manager Candy Jim Taylor convinced him to change his batting style. Dandridge changed to a heavier bat, started to go with the ball rather than always trying to pull it, and learned to hit solid linedrives all over the field. Soon after that, he was a consistent .300-plus hitter.

Ray Dandridge said that he always hoped to make it to the major leagues, even if it was just to have a cup of coffee. He was, in fact, signed by the New York Giants and in 1949 was assigned to their top minor-league team, the Minneapolis Millers of the American Association. Ray was fantastic in Minneapolis. In 1949, Dandridge hit .362 and was the league's Rookie of the Year at the age of 35. In 1950 he led the league with 195 hits, batted .311, and was the American Association's Most Valuable Player. And yet, for some reason, he never got the call to go up and join the Giants.

However, in August 1987, Ray Dandridge went to Cooperstown, New York, was inducted into baseball's Hall of Fame, and had himself a cup of coffee.

Oscar Charleston

Oscar Charleston was also elected to the Hall of Fame based on his career in the Negro leagues. A great center fielder and all-around player, Charleston has often been referred to as the very best. He had a 27-year career in the Negro leagues, including ten as a player/manager. He was once described as having the power and charisma of Babe Ruth, the speed, instincts and tenacity of Ty Cobb, and the defensive prowess and range of Tris Speaker.

Charleston was a six-foot, 200-pound, powerfully built lefthanded slugger. He led the league in home runs three times, and in doubles and triples twice. In 1921, in only 60 league games, he hit 15 home runs, 14 doubles, and 11 triples, stole 35 bases, and batted .434. In one game that season, Charleston hit three home runs against the Chicago American Giants and after the last one spent about ten minutes gathering up the money that had been thrown from the stands. He had success hitting against major-league pitching in exhibition games, batting .326 overall and hitting home runs off both Walter Johnson and Lefty Grove.

Along with power, Charleston was blessed with great speed and good baserunning instincts. Like Ty Cobb, he was aggressive on the basepaths, sliding in hard with spikes high in the air. He had the speed to turn singles into doubles and drag bunts into base hits.

In the outfield, Charleston covered an unbelievable amount of ground. He played the shallowest center field this side of Tris Speaker and yet was still able to get back in time to snare long linedrives. Off at the crack of the bat, Charleston sometimes seemed to outrun the ball to make the catch. One of his teammates said that Oscar was so good he could play the whole outfield by himself and the other two outfielders could stand by the foul lines and catch the foul balls.

Along with hitting, running, and fielding, there was a fourth thing that Oscar Charleston excelled at: fighting. And it's not certain which of the four he was best at, or which one he loved the most. Charleston was never one to back down from a fight. It was said that he was tough enough to go bear hunting with a stick, fearless enough to snatch the hood off a Klansman, and strong enough to loosen a baseball's cover with one hand. His temper would sometimes get him into trouble, both on and off the field. He once got so enraged after a close call went against him that he knocked the umpire out cold, setting off a brawl that drew the police and got Charleston arrested.

Despite his fierce nature and temperamental outbursts, Charleston was idolized by his fans, especially kids, in much the same way that Babe Ruth was. After retiring from active play, he scouted the Negro leagues to help Branch Rickey find the black player to break baseball's color barrier.

Satchel Paige

There were many pitchers in the Negro leagues who had major-league quality talent. Smokey Joe Williams had an overpowering fastball and was one of the top strikeout pitchers and a dominant force on the mound for more than two decades. Cannonball Dick Redding, another fastball artist, had incredible stamina and in his prime sometimes pitched both games of a doubleheader. Bullet Joe Rogan was a quality pitcher and a superb hitter who often hit cleanup and played center field when not pitching

Satchel Paige was perhaps the best pitcher and certainly the most well known player in black baseball.

Satchel Paige was a showman, a storyteller, a comedian, a folk celebrity, and an American legend. But above all, he was a fantastic baseball pitcher. Dizzy Dean, who often pitched against Satchel in barnstorming exhibition games in the 1930s, said that Paige was the best pitcher he had ever seen, adding, "And I see myself in the mirror every morning."

Satchel loved to throw a baseball. And it didn't matter who he pitched for, where he was pitching, or what time of year it was. He started with the Chattanooga Black Lookouts in 1926 and by the time he retired he had pitched for 250 teams in the NNL, the NAL, the major and minor leagues, on barnstorming tours, and in just about every country in Latin America. By his own estimation, Satchel pitched in 2,500 games and won about 2,000 of them. And since he played both summer and winter baseball for 30 years, those numbers might not be a complete exaggeration.

Satchel Paige could throw the fastball. His fastball was so good that he didn't start throwing a curve until the late 1930s. Until then he relied on his blazing heater and pinpoint control. His fastball had the rise, the extra hop, and the late speed that separate the hard throwers from the greatest power pitchers. Satchel had names for all his pitches. He threw a "bee ball" (so called because all a hitter could do was listen to it buzz across the plate), a "be ball" (" 'cause it be wherever I want it to be"), "Little Tom" (fastball), "Long Tom" (very fast ball), the "bat dodger," and "thoughtful stuff." Later in his career he began throwing the "two-hump blooper" (changeup) and the hesitation pitch, where he would stop in middelivery, plant his foot, and then release the ball to an off-balance batter.

Of all the teams Paige pitched for, he is probably most associated with the Pittsburgh Crawfords and the

Kansas City Monarchs. Satchel was a member of the great
Crawford teams of the 1930s, posting records of 32–7 in
1932 and 31–4 in 1933, and going 10–1 in league action in
1934, including four straight shutouts, a no-hitter, and a
17-strike-out game. In 1939 he was signed by the Kansas
City Monarchs even though it was said that Satchel had
pitched himself out and that his arm strength was gone.
But miraculously Paige got his fastball back, added some
new offspeed pitches, and helped the Monarchs win four
straight NAL championships from 1939 to 1942. He
starred in the 1942 Series, winning three games as the
Monarchs swept the Homestead Grays.

Many people referred to Satchel as the Franchise.
He was the game's top drawing card, and his presence on
a team often made the difference between financial profit
and loss. When Paige pitched in Griffith Stadium, where
the Washington Senators averaged 8,000 fans, 30,000
would show up to watch Satchel pitch. In 1946 he drew
46,000 to Yankee Stadium. Even people who weren't
that interested in sports would come from miles around
to see the flamboyant pitcher with the windmill windup,
the high leg kick, and the hesitation pitch. And Satchel
rarely failed to entertain.

Satchel believed that baseball should be fun. He
would sometimes call in his outfielders and have them sit
on the infield grass while he struck out the side. He was
known to intentionally walk the bases loaded and then
announce that he was going to strike out the next three
batters. Then, while the crowd went crazy, he would do it.

Satchel loved life and was able to meet most any situation with good humor. Once while traveling across state
for a game, he was arrested for speeding. In court the
judge fined him 20 dollars and asked him if he had anything to say. Satchel took out 20 dollars, then another 20,
and said, "Your honor, here's forty dollars 'cause I'm
gonna be passing back this way again tomorrow." When

Babe Ruth hit a 500-foot home run off Paige in an exhibition game, Satchel stared at Ruth all the way around the bases. However, as Ruth crossed home plate, Satchel was there to greet him with a hand shake and congratulations.

Satchel drew crowds wherever he went. Before one game, while signing autographs for a mob of fans, he unknowingly signed his own divorce papers, which an attorney had handed him to be "autographed." Afterward, Satchel said he felt a "powerful lightness" in his hip pocket.

In 1948, Paige was signed by Bill Veeck of the Cleveland Indians, becoming a 42-year-old major-league rookie. Paige joined the team on July 7, and even though he was well past his prime, he was an important part of the Indians' pennant drive. He had a 6–1 record, including a pair of three-hit shutouts in crucial games in August. He also played for three years for the St. Louis Browns of the American League and won 12 games in 1952, the most ever by a 46-year-old.

Throughout his career, Satchel would hire himself out to pitch for other professional and semipro teams, playing with any team he could hook up with and any team that would pay. He played all over in ballparks, farm fields, sandlots, fair grounds, penitentiaries, any place where there was a baseball diamond. In looking back over his life, Satchel once said that he felt no bitterness, and that if given the chance to do it all over again, he would. In 1971, Satchel Paige became the first Negro leaguer to be inducted into the Hall of Fame.

Barry Bonds

Award Winners

MOST VALUABLE PLAYER

1931	AL	Lefty Grove, PHI	P	31–4	2.06 ERA	5 SV
	NL	Frankie Frisch, STL	2B	.311 BA	4 HR	82 RBI
1932	AL	Jimmie Foxx, PHI	1B	.364 BA	58 HR	169 RBI
	NL	Chuck Klein, PHI	OF	.348 BA	38 HR	137 RBI
1933	AL	Jimmie Foxx, PHI	1B	.356 BA	48 HR	163 RBI
	NL	Carl Hubbell, NY	P	21–12	2.30 ERA	5 SV
1934	AL	Mickey Cochrane, DET	C	.320 BA	2 HR	76 RBI
	NL	Dizzy Dean, STL	P	30–7	2.66 ERA	7 SV
1935	AL	Hank Greenberg, DET	1B	.328 BA	36 HR	170 RBI
	NL	Gabby Hartnett, CHI	C	.344 BA	13 HR	91 RBI
1936	AL	Lou Gehrig, NY	1B	.354 BA	49 HR	152 RBI
	NL	Carl Hubbell, NY	P	26–6	2.31 ERA	3 SV
1937	AL	Charley Gehringer, DET	2B	.371 BA	14 HR	96 RBI
	NL	Joe Medwick, STL	OF	.374 BA	31 HR	154 RBI
1938	AL	Jimmie Foxx, BOS	1B	.349 BA	50 HR	175 RBI
	NL	Ernie Lombardi, CIN	C	.342 BA	19 HR	95 RBI
1939	AL	Joe DiMaggio, NY	OF	.381 BA	31 HR	133 RBI
	NL	Bucky Walters, CIN	P	27–11	2.29 ERA	0 SV
1940	AL	Hank Greenberg, DET	1B	.340 BA	41 HR	150 RBI
	NL	Frank McCormick, CIN	1B	.309 BA	19 HR	127 RBI
1941	AL	Joe DiMaggio, NY	OF	.357 BA	30 HR	125 RBI
	NL	Dolph Camilli, BKN	1B	.285 BA	34 HR	120 RBI
1942	AL	Joe Gordon, NY	2B	.322 BA	18 HR	103 RBI
	NL	Mort Cooper, STL	P	22–7	1.78 ERA	0 SV
1943	AL	Spud Chandler, NY	P	20–4	1.64 ERA	0 SV
	NL	Stan Musial, STL	OF	.357 BA	13 HR	81 RBI
1944	AL	Hal Newhouser, DET	P	29–9	2.22 ERA	2 SV
	NL	Marty Marion, STL	SS	.267 BA	6 HR	63 RBI
1945	AL	Hal Newhouser, DET	P	25–9	1.81 ERA	2 SV
	NL	Phil Cavaretta, CHI	1B	.355 BA	6 HR	97 RBI
1946	AL	Ted Williams, BOS	OF	.342 BA	38 HR	123 RBI
	NL	Stan Musial, STL	1B	.365 BA	16 HR	103 RBI
1947	AL	Joe DiMaggio, NY	OF	.315 BA	20 HR	97 RBI
	NL	Bob Elliott, BOS	3B	.317 BA	22 HR	113 RBI
1948	AL	Lou Boudreau, CLE	SS	.355 BA	18 HR	106 RBI
	NL	Stan Musial, STL	OF	.376 BA	39 HR	131 RBI
1949	AL	Ted Williams, BOS	OF	.343 BA	43 HR	159 RBI
	NL	Jackie Robinson, BKN	2B	.342 BA	16 HR	124 RBI
1950	AL	Phil Rizzuto, NY	SS	.324 BA	7 HR	66 RBI
	NL	Jim Konstanty, PHI	P	16–7	2.66 ERA	22 SV
1951	AL	Yogi Berra, NY	C	.294 BA	27 HR	88 RBI
	NL	Roy Campanella, BKN	C	.325 BA	33 HR	108 RBI
1952	AL	Bobby Shantz, PHI	P	24–7	2.48 ERA	0 SV
	NL	Hank Sauer, CHI	OF	.270 BA	37 HR	121 RBI

MOST VALUABLE PLAYER (continued)

1953	AL	Al Rosen, CLE	3B	.336 BA	43 HR	145 RBI
	NL	Roy Campanella, BKN	C	.312 BA	41 HR	142 RBI
1954	AL	Yogi Berra, NY	C	.307 BA	22 HR	125 RBI
	NL	Willie Mays, NY	OF	.345 BA	41 HR	110 RBI
1955	AL	Yogi Berra, NY	C	.272 BA	27 HR	108 RBI
	NL	Roy Campanella, BKN	C	.318 BA	32 HR	107 RBI
1956	AL	Mickey Mantle, NY	OF	.353 BA	52 HR	130 RBI
	NL	Don Newcombe, BKN	P	27–7	3.06 ERA	0 SV
1957	AL	Mickey Mantle, NY	OF	.365 BA	34 HR	94 RBI
	NL	Hank Aaron, MIL	OF	.322 BA	44 HR	132 RBI
1958	AL	Jackie Jensen, BOS	OF	.286 BA	35 HR	122 RBI
	NL	Ernie Banks, CHI	SS	.313 BA	47 HR	129 RBI
1959	AL	Nellie Fox, CHI	2B	.306 BA	2 HR	70 RBI
	NL	Ernie Banks, CHI	SS	.304 BA	45 HR	143 RBI
1960	AL	Roger Maris, NY	OF	.283 BA	39 HR	112 RBI
	NL	Dick Groat, PIT	SS	.325 BA	2 HR	50 RBI
1961	AL	Roger Maris, NY	OF	.269 BA	61 HR	142 RBI
	NL	Frank Robinson, CIN	OF	.323 BA	37 HR	124 RBI
1962	AL	Mickey Mantle, NY	OF	.321 BA	30 HR	89 RBI
	NL	Maury Wills, LA	SS	.299 BA	6 HR	48 RBI
1963	AL	Elston Howard, NY	C	.287 BA	28 HR	85 RBI
	NL	Sandy Koufax, LA	P	25–5	1.88 ERA	0 SV
1964	AL	Brooks Robinson, BAL	3B	.317 BA	28 HR	118 RBI
	NL	Ken Boyer, STL	3B	.295 BA	24 HR	119 RBI
1965	NL	Willie Mays, SF	OF	.317 BA	52 HR	112 RBI
	AL	Zoilo Versalles, MIN	SS	.273 BA	19 HR	77 RBI
1966	AL	Frank Robinson, BAL	OF	.316 BA	49 HR	122 RBI
	NL	Roberto Clemente, PIT	OF	.317 BA	29 HR	119 RBI
1967	AL	Carl Yastrzemski, BOS	OF	.326 BA	44 HR	121 RBI
	NL	Orlando Cepeda, STL	1B	.325 BA	25 HR	111 RBI
1968	AL	Denny McLain, DET	P	31–6	1.96 ERA	0 SV
	NL	Bob Gibson, STL	P	22–9	1.12 ERA	0 SV
1969	AL	Harmon Killebrew, MIN	1B	.276 BA	49 HR	140 RBI
	NL	Willie McCovey, SF	1B	.320 BA	45 HR	126 RBI
1970	AL	Boog Powell, BAL	1B	.297 BA	35 HR	114 RBI
	NL	Johnny Bench, CIN	C	.293 BA	2 HR	27 RBI
1971	AL	Vida Blue, OAK	P	24–8	1.82 ERA	0 SV
	NL	Joe Torre, STL	3B	.363 BA	24 HR	137 RBI
1972	AL	Dick Allen, CHI	1B	.308 BA	37 HR	113 RB
	NL	Johnny Bench, CIN	C	.270 BA	40 HR	125 RBI
1973	A	Reggie Jackson, OAK	OF	.293 BA	32 HR	117 RBI
	NL	Pete Rose, CIN	OF	.338 BA	5 HR	64 RBI
1974	AL	Jeff Burroughs, TEX	OF	.301 BA	25 HR	118 RBI
	NL	Steve Garvey, LA	1B	.312 BA	21 HR	111 RBI
1975	AL	Fred Lynn, BOS	OF	.331 BA	21 HR	105 RBI
	NL	Joe Morgan, CIN	2B	.327 BA	17 HR	94 RBI

1976	AL	Thurman Munson, NY	C	.302 BA	17 HR	105 RBI
	NL	Joe Morgan, CIN	2B	.320 BA	27 HR	111 RBI
1977	AL	Rod Carew, MIN	1B	.388 BA	14 HR	100 RBI
	NL	George Foster, CIN	OF	.320 BA	52 HR	149 RBI
1978	AL	Jim Rice, BOS	OF	.315 BA	46 HR	139 RBI
	NL	Dave Parker, PIT	OF	.334 BA	30 HR	117 RBI
1979	AL	Don Baylor, CAL	OF	.296 BA	36 HR	139 RBI
	NL	Keith Hernandez, STL	1B	.344 BA	11 HR	105 RBI
		Willie Stargell, PIT	1B	.281 BA	32 HR	82 RBI
1980	AL	George Brett, KC	3B	.390 BA	24 HR	118 RBI
	NL	Mike Schmidt, PHI	3B	.286 BA	48 HR	121 RBI
1981	AL	Rollie Fingers, MIL	P	6–3	1.04 ERA	28 SV
	NL	Mike Schmidt, PHI	3B	.316 BA	31 HR	91 RBI
1982	AL	Robin Yount, MIL	OF	.331 BA	29 HR	114 RBI
	NL	Dale Murphy, ATL	OF	.281 BA	36 HR	109 RBI
1983	AL	Cal Ripken, BAL	SS	.318 BA	27 HR	102 RBI
	NL	Dale Murphy, ATL	OF	.302 BA	36 HR	121 RBI
1984	AL	Willie Hernandez, DET	P	9–3	1.92 ERA	32 SV
	NL	Ryne Sandberg, CHI	2B	.314 BA	19 HR	84 RBI
1985	AL	Don Mattingly, NY	1B	.324 BA	35 HR	145 RBI
	NL	Willie McGee, STL	OF	.353 BA	7 HR	48 RBI
1986	AL	Roger Clemens, BOS	P	24–4	2.48 ERA	0 SV
	NL	Mike Schmidt, PHI	3B	.290 BA	37 HR	119 RBI
1987	AL	George Bell, TOR	OF	.308 BA	47 HR	134 RBI
	NL	Andre Dawson, CHI	OF	.287 BA	49 HR	137 RBI
1988	AL	Jose Canseco, OAK	OF	.307 BA	42 HR	124 RBI
	NL	Kirk Gibson, LA	OF	.290 BA	25 HR	76 RBI
1989	AL	Robin Yount, MIL	OF	.318 BA	21 HR	103 RBI
	NL	Kevin Mitchell, SF	OF	.291 BA	47 HR	125 RBI
1990	AL	Rickey Henderson, OAK	OF	.325 BA	28 HR	61 RBI
	NL	Barry Bonds, PIT	OF	.301 BA	33 HR	114 RBI
1991	AL	Cal Ripken, BAL	SS	.323 BA	34 HR	114 RBI
	NL	Terry Pendleton, ATL	3B	.319 BA	22 HR	86 RBI
1992	AL	Dennis Eckersley, OAK	P	7–1	1.91 ERA	51 SV
	NL	Barry Bonds, PIT	OF	.311 BA	34 HR	103 RBI
1993	AL	Frank Thomas, CHI	1B	.317 BA	41 HR	128 RBI
	NL	Barry Bonds, SF	OF	.336 BA	46 HR	123 RBI
1994	AL	Frank Thomas, CHI	1B	.353 BA	38 HR	101 RBI
	NL	Jeff Bagwell, HOU	1B	.368 BA	39 HR	116 RBI
1995	AL	Mo Vaughn, BOS	1B	.300 BA	39 HR	126 RBI
	NL	Barry Larkin, CIN	SS	.319 BA	15 HR	66 RBI

David Cone

CY YOUNG

Year	Lg	Player	W–L	ERA	SV
1956		Don Newcombe, BKN	27–7	3.06 ERA	0 SV
1957		Warren Spahn, MIL	21–11	2.69 ERA	3 SV
1958		Bob Turley, NY	21–7	2.97 ERA	1 SV
1959		Early Wynn, CHI	22–10	3.17 ERA	0 SV
1960		Vernon Law, PIT	20–9	3.08 ERA	0 SV
1961		Whitey Ford, NY	25–4	3.21 ERA	0 SV
1962		Don Drysdale, LA	25–9	2.83 ERA	1 SV
1963		Sandy Koufax, LA	25–5	1.88 ERA	0 SV
1964		Dean Chance, LA	20–9	1.65 ERA	4 SV
1965		Sandy Koufax, LA	26–8	2.04 ERA	2 SV
1966		Sandy Koufax, LA	27–9	1.73 ERA	0 SV
1967	AL	Jim Lonborg, BOS	22–9	3.16 ERA	0 SV
	NL	Mike McCormick, SF	22–10	2.85 ERA	0 SV
1968	AL	Denny McLain, DET	31–6	1.96 ERA	0 SV
	NL	Bob Gibson, STL	22–9	1.12 ERA	0 SV
1969	AL	Denny McLain, DET	24–9	2.80 ERA	0 SV
		Mike Cuellar, BAL	23–11	2.38 ERA	0 SV
	NL	Tom Seaver, NY	25–7	2.21 ERA	0 SV
1970	AL	Jim Perry, MIN	24–12	3.04 ERA	0 SV
	NL	Bob Gibson, STL	23–7	3.12 ERA	0 SV
1971	AL	Vida Blue, OAK	24–8	1.82 ERA	0 SV
	NL	Fergie Jenkins, CHI	24–13	2.77 ERA	0 SV
1972	AL	Gaylord Perry, CLE	24–16	1.92 ERA	1 SV
	NL	Steve Carlton, PHI	27–10	1.97 ERA	0 SV
1973	AL	Jim Palmer, BAL	22–9	2.40 ERA	1 SV
	NL	Tom Seaver, NY	19–10	2.08 ERA	0 SV
1974	AL	Jim Hunter, OAK	25–12	2.49 ERA	0 SV
	NL	Mike Marshall, LA	15–12	2.42 ERA	21 SV
1975	AL	Jim Palmer, BAL	23–11	2.09 ERA	1 SV
	NL	Tom Seaver, NY	22–9	2.38 ERA	0 SV
1976	AL	Jim Palmer, BAL	22–13	2.51 ERA	0 SV
	NL	Randy Jones, SD	22–14	2.74 ERA	0 SV
1977	AL	Sparky Lyle, NY	13–5	2.17 ERA	26 SV
	NL	Steve Carlton, PHI	23–10	2.64 ERA	0 SV
1978	AL	Ron Guidry, NY	25–3	1.74 ERA	0 SV
	NL	Gaylord Perry, SD	21–6	2.73 ERA	0 SV
1979	AL	Mike Flanagan, BAL	23–9	3.08 ERA	0 SV
	NL	Bruce Sutter, CHI	6–6	2.22 ERA	37 SV
1980	AL	Steve Stone, BAL	25–7	3.23 ERA	0 SV
	NL	Steve Carlton, PHI	24–9	2.34 ERA	0 SV
1981	AL	Rollie Fingers, MIL	6–3	1.04 ERA	28 SV
	NL	Fernando Valenzuela, LA	13–7	2.48 ERA	0 SV
1982	AL	Pete Vuckovich, MIL	18–6	3.34 ERA	0 SV
	NL	Steve Carlton, PHI	23–11	3.10 ERA	0 SV
1983	AL	LaMarr Hoyt, CHI	24–10	3.66 ERA	0 SV
	NL	John Denny, PHI	19–6	2.37 ERA	0 SV

CY YOUNG (continued)

Year	Lg	Player	Record	ERA	SV
1984	AL	Willie Hernandez, DET	9–3	1.92 ERA	32 SV
	NL	Rick Sutcliffe, CHI	20–6	3.97 ERA	0 SV
1985	AL	Bret Saberhagen, KC	20–6	2.87 ERA	0 SV
	NL	Dwight Gooden, NY	24–4	1.53 ERA	0 SV
1986	AL	Roger Clemens, BOS	24–4	2.48 ERA	0 SV
	NL	Mike Scott, HOU	18–10	2.22 ERA	0 SV
1987	AL	Roger Clemens, BOS	20–9	2.97 ERA	0 SV
	NL	Steve Bedrosian, PHI	5–3	2.83 ERA	40 SV
1988	AL	Frank Viola, MIN	24–7	2.64 ERA	0 SV
	NL	Orel Hershiser, LA	23–8	2.26 ERA	1 SV
1989	AL	Bret Saberhagen, KC	23–6	2.16 ERA	0 SV
	NL	Mark Davis, SD	4–3	1.85 ERA	44 SV
1990	AL	Bob Welch, OAK	27–6	2.95 ERA	0 SV
	NL	Doug Drabek, PIT	22–6	2.76 ERA	0 SV
1991	AL	Roger Clemens, BOS	18–10	2.62 ERA	0 SV
	NL	Tom Glavine, ATL	20–11	2.55 ERA	0 SV
1992	AL	Dennis Eckersley, OAK	7–1	1.91 ERA	51 SV
	NL	Greg Maddux, CHI	20–11	2.18 ERA	0 SV
1993	AL	Jack McDowell, CHI	22–10	3.37 ERA	0 SV
	NL	Greg Maddux, ATL	20–10	2.36 ERA	0 SV
1994	AL	David Cone, KC	16–5	2.94 ERA	0 SV
	NL	Greg Maddux, ATL	16–6	1.56 ERA	0 SV
1995	AL	Randy Johnson, SEA	18–2	2.48 ERA	0 SV
	NL	Greg Maddux, ATL	19–2	1.63 ERA	0 SV

ROOKIE OF THE YEAR

1949	AL	Roy Sievers, STL	OF	.306 BA	16 HR	91 RBI
	NL	Don Newcombe, BKN	P	17–8	3.17 ERA	1 SV
1950	AL	Walt Dropo, BOS	1B	.322 BA	34 HR	144 RBI
	NL	Sam Jethroe, BOS	OF	.273 BA	18 HR	58 RBI
1951	AL	Gil McDougald, NY	3B	.306 BA	14 HR	63 RBI
	NL	Willie Mays, NY	OF	.274 BA	20 HR	68 RBI
1952	AL	Harry Byrd, PHI	P	15–15	3.31 ERA	2 SV
	NL	Joe Black, BKN	P	15–4	2.15	15 SV
1953	AL	Harvey Kuenn, DET	SS	.308 BA	2 HR	48 RBI
	NL	Jim Gilliam, BKN	2B	.278 BA	6 HR	63 RBI
1954	AL	Bob Grim, NY	P	20–6	3.26 ERA	0 SV
	NL	Wally Moon, STL	OF	.304 BA	12 HR	76 RBI
1955	AL	Herb Score, CLE	P	16–10	2.85 ERA	0 SV
	NL	Bill Virdon, STL	OF	.281 BA	17 HR	68 RBI
1956	AL	Luis Aparicio, CHI	SS	.266 BA	3 HR	56 RBI
	NL	Frank Robinson, CIN	OF	.290 BA	38 HR	83 RBI
1957	AL	Tony Kubek, NY	SS	.297 BA	3 HR	39 RBI
	NL	Jack Sanford, PHI	P	19–8	3.08 ERA	0 SV

1958	AL	Albie Pearson, WAS	OF	.275 BA	3 HR	33 RBI
	NL	Orlando Cepeda, SF	1B	.312 BA	25 HR	96 RBI
1959	AL	Bob Allison, WAS	OF	.261 BA	30 HR	85 RBI
	NL	Willie McCovey, SF	1B	.354 BA	13 HR	38 RBI
1960	AL	Ron Hansen, BAL	SS	.255 BA	22 HR	86 RBI
	NL	Frank Howard, LA	OF	.268 BA	23 HR	77 RBI
1961	AL	Don Schwall, BOS	P	15–7	3.22 ERA	0 SV
	NL	Billy Williams, CHI	OF	.278 BA	25 HR	86 RBI
1962	AL	Tom Tresh, NY	SS	.286 BA	20 HR	93 RBI
	NL	Ken Hubbs, CHI	2B	.260 BA	5 HR	49 RBI
1963	AL	Gary Peters, CHI	P	19–8	2.33 ERA	0 SV
	NL	Pete Rose, CIN	2B	.273 BA	6 HR	41 RBI
1964	AL	Tony Oliva, MIN	OF	.323 BA	32 HR	94 RBI
	NL	Dick Allen, PHI	3B	.318 BA	29 HR	91 RBI
1965	AL	Curt Blefary, BAL	OF	.260 BA	22 HR	70 RBI
	NL	Jim Lefebvre, LA	2B	.250 BA	12 HR	69 RBI
1966	AL	Tommie Agee, CHI	OF	.273 BA	22 HR	86 RBI
	NL	Tommy Helms, CIN	2B	.284 BA	9 HR	49 RBI
1967	AL	Rod Carew, MIN	2B	.292 BA	8 HR	51 RBI
	NL	Tom Seaver, NY	P	16–13	2.76 ERA	0 SV
1968	AL	Stan Bahnsen, NY	P	17–12	2.05 ERA	0 SV
	NL	Johnny Bench, CIN	C	.275 BA	15 HR	82 RBI
1969	AL	Lou Piniella, KC	OF	.282 BA	11 HR	68 RBI
	NL	Ted Sizemore, LA	2B	.271 BA	4 HR	46 RBI
1970	AL	Thurman Munson, NY	C	.302 BA	6 HR	53 RBI
	NL	Carl Morton, MON	P	18–11	3.60 ERA	0 SV
1971	AL	Chris Chambliss, CLE	1B	.275 BA	9 HR	48 RBI
	NL	Earl Williams, ATL	C	.260 BA	33 HR	87 RBI
1972	AL	Carlton Fisk, BOS	C	.293 BA	22 HR	61 RBI
	NL	Jon Matlack, NY	P	15–10	2.32 ERA	0 SV
1973	AL	Al Bumbry, BAL	OF	.337 BA	7 HR	34 RBI
	NL	Gary Matthews, SF	OF	.300 BA	12 HR	58 RBI
1974	AL	Mike Hargrove, TEX	1B	.323 BA	4 HR	66 RBI
	NL	Bake McBride, STL	OF	.309 BA	6 HR	56 RBI
1975	AL	Fred Lynn, BOS	OF	.331 BA	21 HR	105 RBI
	NL	John Montefusco, SF	P	15–9	2.88 ERA	0 SV
1976	AL	Mark Fidrych, DET	P	19–9	2.34 ERA	0 SV
	NL	Pat Zachry, CIN	P	14–7	2.74 ERA	0 SV
		Butch Metzger, SD	P	11–4	2.92 ERA	16 SV
1977	AL	Eddie Murray, BAL	1B	.283 BA	27 HR	88 RBI
	NL	Andre Dawson, MON	OF	.282 BA	19 HR	65 RBI
1978	AL	Lou Whitaker, DET	2B	.285 BA	3 HR	58 RBI
	NL	Bob Horner, ATL	3B	.266 BA	23 HR	63 RBI
1979	AL	Alfredo Griffin, TOR	SS	.287 BA	2 HR	31 RBI
		John Castino, MIN	3B	.285 BA	5 HR	52 RBI
	NL	Rick Sutcliffe, LA	P	17–10	3.46 ERA	0 SV
1980	AL	Joe Charboneau, CLE	OF	.289 BA	23 HR	87 RBI

Alvin Davis

	NL	Steve Howe, LA	P	7–9	2.66 ERA	17 SV
1981	AL	Dave Righetti, NY	P	8–4	2.05 ERA	0 SV
	NL	Fernando Valenzuela, LA	P	13–7	2.48 ERA	0 SV
1982	AL	Cal Ripken, BAL	SS	.264 BA	28 HR	93 RBI
	NL	Steve Sax, LA	2B	.282 BA	4 HR	47 RBI
1983	AL	Ron Kittle, CHI	OF	.254 BA	35 HR	100 RBI
	NL	Darryl Strawberry, NY	OF	.257 BA	26 HR	74 RBI
1984	AL	Alvin Davis, SEA	1B	.284 BA	27 HR	116 RBI
	NL	Dwight Gooden, NY	P	17–9	2.60 ERA	0 SV
1985	AL	Ozzie Guillen, CHI	SS	.273 BA	1 HR	33 RBI
	NL	Vince Coleman, STL	OF	.267 BA	1 HR	40 RBI
1986	AL	Jose Canseco, OAK	OF	.240 BA	33 HR	117 RBI
	NL	Todd Worrell, STL	P	9–10	2.08 ERA	36 SV
1987	AL	Mark McGwire, OAK	1B	.289 BA	49 HR	118 RBI
	NL	Benito Santiago, SD	C	.300 BA	18 HR	79 RBI
1988	AL	Walt Weiss, OAK	SS	.250 BA	3 HR	39 RBI
	NL	Chris Sabo, CIN	3B	.271 BA	11 HR	44 RBI
1989	AL	Gregg Olson, BAL	P	5–2	1.69 ERA	27 SV
	NL	Jerome Walton, CHI	OF	.293 BA	5 HR	46 RBI
1990	AL	Sandy Alomar, CLE	C	.290 BA	9 HR	66 RBI
	NL	Dave Justice, ATL	OF	.282 BA	28 HR	78 RBI
1991	AL	Chuck Knoblauch, MIN	2B	.281 BA	1 HR	50 RBI
	NL	Jeff Bagwell, HOU	1B	.294 BA	15 HR	82 RBI
1992	AL	Pat Listach, MIL	SS	.290 BA	1 HR	47 RBI
	NL	Eric Karros, LA	1B	.257 BA	20 HR	88 RBI
1993	AL	Tim Salmon, CAL	OF	.283 BA	31 HR	95 RBI
	NL	Mike Piazza, LA	C	.318 BA	35 HR	112 RBI
1994	AL	Bob Hamelin, KC	DH	.282 BA	24 HR	65 RBI
	NL	Raul Mondesi, LA	OF	.306 BA	16 HR	56 RBI
1995	AL	Marty Cordova, MIN	OF	.277 BA	24 HR	84 RBI
	NL	Hideo Nomo, LA	P	13–6 BA	2.54 ERA	0 SV

GOLD GLOVE

Pitchers

Year	NATIONAL LEAGUE	AMERICAN LEAGUE
1957	No selection	Bobby Shantz, NY
1958	Harvey Haddix, CIN	Bobby Shantz, NY
1959	Harvey Haddix, PIT	Bobby Shantz, NY
1960	Harvey Haddix, PIT	Bobby Shantz, NY
1961	Bobby Shantz, PIT	Frank Lary, DET
1962	Bobby Shantz, STL	Jim Kaat, MIN
1963	Bobby Shantz, STL	Jim Kaat, MIN
1964	Bobby Shantz, PHI	Jim Kaat, MIN
1965	Bob Gibson, STL	Jim Kaat, MIN
1966	Bob Gibson, STL	Jim Kaat, MIN
1967	Bob Gibson, STL	Jim Kaat, MIN
1968	Bob Gibson, STL	Jim Kaat, MIN
1969	Bob Gibson, STL	Jim Kaat, MIN
1970	Bob Gibson, STL	Jim Kaat, MIN
1971	Bob Gibson, STL	Jim Kaat, MIN
1972	Bob Gibson, STL	Jim Kaat, MIN
1973	Bob Gibson, STL	Jim Kaat, MIN
1974	Andy Messersmith, LA	Jim Kaat, CHI
1975	Andy Messersmith, LA	Jim Kaat, CHI
1976	Jim Kaat, PHI	Jim Palmer, BAL
1977	Jim Kaat, PHI	Jim Palmer, BAL
1978	Phil Niekro, ATL	Jim Palmer, BAL
1979	Phil Niekro, ATL	Jim Palmer, BAL
1980	Phil Niekro, ATL	Mike Norris, OAK
1981	Steve Carlton, PHI	Mike Norris, OAK
1982	Phil Niekro, ATL	Ron Guidry, NY
1983	Phil Niekro, ATL	Ron Guidry, NY
1984	Joaquin Andujar, STL	Ron Guidry, NY
1985	Rick Reuschel, PIT	Ron Guidry, NY
1986	Fernando Valenzuela, LA	Ron Guidry, NY
1987	Rick Reuschel, SF	Mark Langston, SEA
1988	Orel Hershiser, LA	Mark Langston, SEA
1989	Ron Darling, NY	Bret Saberhagen, KC
1990	Greg Maddux, CHI	Mike Boddicker, BOS
1991	Greg Maddux, CHI	Mark Langston, CAL
1992	Greg Maddux, CHI	Mark Langston, CAL
1993	Greg Maddux, ATL	Mark Langston, CAL
1994	Greg Maddux, ATL	Mark Langston, CAL
1995	Greg Maddux, ATL	Mark Langston, CAL

Catchers

Year	NATIONAL LEAGUE	AMERICAN LEAGUE
1957	No selection	Sherm Lollar, CHI
1958	Del Crandall, MIL	Sherm Lollar, CHI
1959	Del Crandall, MIL	Sherm Lollar, CHI
1960	Del Crandall, MIL	Earl Battey, WAS
1961	John Roseboro, LA	Earl Battey, MIN
1962	Del Crandall, MIL	Earl Battey, MIN
1963	Johnny Edwards, CIN	Elston Howard, NY
1964	Johnny Edwards, CIN	Elston Howard, NY
1965	Joe Torre, MIL	Bill Freehan, DET
1966	John Roseboro, LA	Bill Freehan, DET
1967	Randy Hundley, CHI	Bill Freehan, DET
1968	Johnny Bench, CIN	Bill Freehan, DET
1969	Johnny Bench, CIN	Bill Freehan, DET
1970	Johnny Bench, CIN	Ray Fosse, CLE
1971	Johnny Bench, CIN	Ray Fosse, CLE
1972	Johnny Bench, CIN	Carlton Fisk, BOS
1973	Johnny Bench, CIN	Thurman Munson, NY
1974	Johnny Bench, CIN	Thurman Munson, NY
1975	Johnny Bench, CIN	Thurman Munson, NY
1976	Johnny Bench, CIN	Jim Sundberg, TEX
1977	Johnny Bench, CIN	Jim Sundberg, TEX
1978	Bob Boone, PHI	Jim Sundberg, TEX
1979	Bob Boone, PHI	Jim Sundberg, TEX
1980	Gary Carter, MON	Jim Sundberg, TEX
1981	Gary Carter, MON	Jim Sundberg, TEX
1982	Gary Carter, MON	Bob Boone, CAL
1983	Tony Pena, PIT	Lance Parrish, DET
1984	Tony Pena, PIT	Lance Parrish, DET
1985	Tony Pena, PIT	Lance Parrish, DET
1986	Jody Davis, CHI	Bob Boone, CAL
1987	Mike LaValliere, PIT	Bob Boone, CAL
1988	Benito Santiago, SD	Bob Boone, CAL
1989	Benito Santiago, SD	Bob Boone, CAL
1990	Benito Santiago, SD	Sandy Alomar, CLE
1991	Tom Pagnozzi, STL	Tony Pena, BOS
1992	Tom Pagnozzi, STL	Ivan Rodriguez, TEX
1993	Kirt Manwaring, SF	Ivan Rodriguez, TEX
1994	Tom Pagnozzi, STL	Ivan Rodriguez, TEX
1995	Charles Johnson, FLA	Ivan Rodriguez, TEX

First Basemen

Year	NATIONAL LEAGUE	AMERICAN LEAGUE
1957	Gil Hodges, BKN	No Selection
1958	Gil Hodges, LA	Vic Power, CLE
1959	Gil Hodges, LA	Vic Power, CLE
1960	Bill White, STL	Vic Power, CLE
1961	Bill White, STL	Vic Power, CLE
1962	Bill White, STL	Vic Power, MIN
1963	Bill White, STL	Vic Power, MIN
1964	Bill White, STL	Vic Power, LA
1965	Bill White, STL	Joe Pepitone, NY
1966	Bill White, PHI	Joe Pepitone, NY
1967	Wes Parker, LA	George Scott, BOS
1968	Wes Parker, LA	George Scott, BOS
1969	Wes Parker, LA	Joe Pepitone, NY
1970	Wes Parker, LA	Jim Spencer, CAL
1971	Wes Parker, LA	George Scott, BOS
1972	Wes Parker, LA	George Scott, MIL
1973	Mike Jorgenson, MON	George Scott, MIL
1974	Steve Garvey, LA	George Scott, MIL
1975	Steve Garvey, LA	George Scott, MIL
1976	Steve Garvey, LA	George Scott, MIL
1977	Steve Garvey, LA	Jim Spencer, CHI
1978	Keith Hernandez, STL	Chris Chambliss, NY
1979	Keith Hernandez, STL	Cecil Cooper, MIL
1980	Keith Hernandez, STL	Cecil Cooper, MIL
1981	Keith Hernandez, STL	Mike Squires, CHI
1982	Keith Hernandez, STL	Eddie Murray, BAL
1983	Keith Hernandez, STL–NY	Eddie Murray, BAL
1984	Keith Hernandez, NY	Eddie Murray, BAL
1985	Keith Hernandez, NY	Don Mattingly, NY
1986	Keith Hernandez, NY	Don Mattingly, NY
1987	Keith Hernandez, NY	Don Mattingly, NY
1988	Keith Hernandez, NY	Don Mattingly, NY
1989	Andres Galarraga, MON	Don Mattingly, NY
1990	Andres Galarraga, MON	Mark McGwire, OAK
1991	Will Clark, SF	Don Mattingly, NY
1992	Mark Grace, CHI	Don Mattingly, NY
1993	Mark Grace, CHI	Don Mattingly, NY
1994	Jeff Bagwell, HOU	Don Mattingly, NY
1995	Mark Grace, CHI	J.T. Snow, CAL

Second Basemen

Year	NATIONAL LEAGUE	AMERICAN LEAGUE
1957	No selection	Nellie Fox, CHI
1958	Bill Mazeroski, PIT	Frank Bolling, DET
1959	Charlie Neal, LA	Nellie Fox, CHI
1960	Bill Mazeroski, PIT	Nellie Fox, CHI
1961	Bill Mazeroski, PIT	Bobby Richardson, NY
1962	Ken Hubbs, CHI	Bobby Richardson, NY
1963	Bill Mazeroski, PIT	Bobby Richardson, NY
1964	Bill Mazeroski, PIT	Bobby Richardson, NY
1965	Bill Mazeroski, PIT	Bobby Richardson, NY
1966	Bill Mazeroski, PIT	Bobby Knoop, CAL
1967	Bill Mazeroski, PIT	Bobby Knoop, CAL
1968	Glenn Beckert, CHI	Bobby Knoop, CAL
1969	Felix Millan, ATL	Dave Johnson, BAL
1970	Tommy Helms, CIN	Dave Johnson, BAL
1971	Tommy Helms, CIN	Dave Johnson, BAL
1972	Felix Millan, ATL	Doug Griffin, BOS
1973	Joe Morgan, CIN	Bobby Grich, BAL
1974	Joe Morgan, CIN	Bobby Grich, BAL
1975	Joe Morgan, CIN	Bobby Grich, BAL
1976	Joe Morgan, CIN	Bobby Grich, BAL
1977	Joe Morgan, CIN	Frank White, KC
1978	Davey Lopes, LA	Frank White, KC
1979	Manny Trillo, PHI	Frank White, KC
1980	Doug Flynn, NY	Frank White, KC
1981	Manny Trillo, PHI	Frank White, KC
1982	Manny Trillo, PHI	Frank White, KC
1983	Ryne Sandberg, CHI	Lou Whitaker, DET
1984	Ryne Sandberg, CHI	Lou Whitaker, DET
1985	Ryne Sandberg, CHI	Lou Whitaker, DET
1986	Ryne Sandberg, CHI	Frank White, KC
1987	Ryne Sandberg, CHI	Frank White, KC
1988	Ryne Sandberg, CHI	Harold Reynolds, SEA
1989	Ryne Sandberg, CHI	Harold Reynolds, SEA
1990	Ryne Sandberg, CHI	Harold Reynolds, SEA
1991	Ryne Sandberg, CHI	Roberto Alomar, TOR
1992	Jose Lind, PIT	Roberto Alomar, TOR
1993	Robby Thompson, SF	Roberto Alomar, TOR
1994	Craig Biggio, HOU	Roberto Alomar, TOR
1995	Craig Biggio, HOU	Roberto Alomar, TOR

Ozzie Guillen

Shortstops

Year	NATIONAL LEAGUE	AMERICAN LEAGUE
1957	Roy McMillan, CIN	No selection
1958	Roy McMillan, CIN	Luis Aparicio, CHI
1959	Roy McMillan, CIN	Luis Aparicio, CHI
1960	Ernie Banks, CHI	Luis Aparicio, CHI
1961	Maury Wills, LA	Luis Aparicio, CHI
1962	Maury Wills, LA	Luis Aparicio, CHI
1963	Bobby Wine, PHI	Zoilo Versalles, MIN
1964	Ruben Amaro, PHI	Luis Aparicio, BAL
1965	Leo Cardenas, CIN	Zoilo Versalles, MIN
1966	Gene Alley, PIT	Luis Aparicio, BAL
1967	Gene Alley, PIT	Jim Fregosi, CAL
1968	Dal Maxvill, STL	Luis Aparicio, CHI
1969	Don Kessinger, CHI	Mark Belanger, BAL
1970	Don Kessinger, CHI	Luis Aparicio, CHI
1971	Buddy Harrelson, NY	Mark Belanger, BAL
1972	Larry Bowa, PHI	Eddie Brinkman, DET
1973	Roger Metzger, HOU	Mark Belanger, BAL
1974	Dave Concepcion, CIN	Mark Belanger, BAL
1975	Dave Concepcion, CIN	Mark Belanger, BAL
1976	Dave Concepcion, CIN	Mark Belanger, BAL
1977	Dave Concepcion, CIN	Mark Belanger, BAL
1978	Larry Bowa, PHI	Mark Belanger, BAL
1979	Dave Concepcion, CIN	Rick Burleson, BOS
1980	Ozzie Smith, SD	Alan Trammell, DET
1981	Ozzie Smith, SD	Alan Trammell, DET
1982	Ozzie Smith, STL	Robin Yount, MIL
1983	Ozzie Smith, STL	Alan Trammell, DET
1984	Ozzie Smith, STL	Alan Trammell, DET
1985	Ozzie Smith, STL	Alfredo Griffin, OAK
1986	Ozzie Smith, STL	Tony Fernandez, TOR
1987	Ozzie Smith, STL	Tony Fernandez, TOR
1988	Ozzie Smith, STL	Tony Fernandez, TOR
1989	Ozzie Smith, STL	Tony Fernandez, TOR
1990	Ozzie Smith, STL	Ozzie Guillen, CHI
1991	Ozzie Smith, STL	Cal Ripken, BAL
1992	Ozzie Smith, STL	Cal Ripken, BAL
1993	Jay Bell, PIT	Omar Vizquel, SEA
1994	Barry Larkin, CIN	Omar Vizquel, CLE
1995	Barry Larkin, CIN	Omar Vizquel, CLE

Ken Caminiti

Third Basemen

Year	NATIONAL LEAGUE	AMERICAN LEAGUE
1957	No selection	Frank Malzone, BOS
1958	Ken Boyer, STL	Frank Malzone, BOS
1959	Ken Boyer, STL	Frank Malzone, BOS
1960	Ken Boyer, STL	Brooks Robinson, BAL
1961	Ken Boyer, STL	Brooks Robinson, BAL
1962	Jim Davenport, SF	Brooks Robinson, BAL
1963	Ken Boyer, STL	Brooks Robinson, BAL
1964	Ron Santo, CHI	Brooks Robinson, BAL
1965	Ron Santo, CHI	Brooks Robinson, BAL
1966	Ron Santo, CHI	Brooks Robinson, BAL
1967	Ron Santo, CHI	Brooks Robinson, BAL
1968	Ron Santo, CHI	Brooks Robinson, BAL
1969	Clete Boyer, ATL	Brooks Robinson, BAL
1970	Doug Rader, HOU	Brooks Robinson, BAL
1971	Doug Rader, HOU	Brooks Robinson, BAL
1972	Doug Rader, HOU	Brooks Robinson, BAL
1973	Doug Rader, HOU	Brooks Robinson, BAL
1974	Doug Rader, HOU	Brooks Robinson, BAL
1975	Ken Reitz, STL	Brooks Robinson, BAL
1976	Mike Schmidt, PHI	Aurelio Rodriguez, DET
1977	Mike Schmidt, PHI	Graig Nettles, NY
1978	Mike Schmidt, PHI	Graig Nettles, NY
1979	Mike Schmidt, PHI	Buddy Bell, TEX
1980	Mike Schmidt, PHI	Buddy Bell, TEX
1981	Mike Schmidt, PHI	Buddy Bell, TEX
1982	Mike Schmidt, PHI	Buddy Bell, TEX
1983	Mike Schmidt, PHI	Buddy Bell, TEX
1984	Mike Schmidt, PHI	Buddy Bell, TEX
1985	Tim Wallach, MON	George Brett, KC
1986	Mike Schmidt, PHI	Gary Gaetti, MIN
1987	Terry Pendleton, STL	Gary Gaetti, MIN
1988	Tim Wallach, MON	Gary Gaetti, MIN
1989	Terry Pendleton, STL	Gary Gaetti, MIN
1990	Tim Wallach, MON	Kelly Gruber, TOR
1991	Matt Williams, SF	Robin Ventura, CHI
1992	Terry Pendleton, STL	Robin Ventura, CHI
1993	Matt Williams, SF	Robin Ventura, CHI
1994	Matt Williams, SF	Wade Boggs, NY
1995	Ken Caminiti, SD	Wade Boggs, NY

National League Outfielders

1957	Willie Mays, NY	No other selection	
1958	Frank Robinson, CIN	Willie Mays, SF	Hank Aaron, MIL
1959	Jackie Brandt, SF	Willie Mays, SF	Hank Aaron, MIL
1960	Wally Moon, LA	Willie Mays, SF	Hank Aaron, MIL
1961	Willie Mays, SF	Roberto Clemente, PIT	Vada Pinson, CIN
1962	Willie Mays, SF	Roberto Clemente, PIT	Bill Virdon, PIT
1963	Willie Mays, SF	Roberto Clemente, PIT	Curt Flood, STL
1964	Willie Mays, SF	Roberto Clemente, PIT	Curt Flood, STL
1965	Willie Mays, SF	Roberto Clemente, PIT	Curt Flood, STL
1966	Willie Mays, SF	Curt Flood, STL	Roberto Clemente, PIT
1967	Roberto Clemente, PIT	Curt Flood, STL	Willie Mays, SF
1968	Willie Mays, SF	Roberto Clemente, PIT	Curt Flood, STL
1969	Roberto Clemente, PIT	Curt Flood, STL	Pete Rose, CIN
1970	Roberto Clemente, PIT	Tommie Agee, NY	Pete Rose, CIN
1971	Roberto Clemente, PIT	Bobby Bonds, SF	Willie Davis, LA
1972	Roberto Clemente, PIT	Cesar Cedeno, HOU	Willie Davis, LA
1973	Bobby Bonds, SF	Cesar Cedeno, HOU	Willie Davis, LA
1974	Cesar Cedeno, HOU	Cesar Geronimo, CIN	Bobby Bonds, SF
1975	Cesar Cedeno, HOU	Cesar Geronimo, CIN	Garry Maddox, PHI
1976	Cesar Cedeno, HOU	Cesar Geronimo, CIN	Garry Maddox, PHI
1977	Cesar Geronimo, CIN	Garry Maddox, PHI	Dave Parker, PIT
1978	Garry Maddox, PHI	Dave Parker, PIT	Ellis Valentine, MON
1979	Garry Maddox, PHI	Dave Parker, PIT	Dave Winfield, SD
1980	Andre Dawson, MON	Garry Maddox, PHI	Dave Winfield, SD
1981	Andre Dawson, MON	Garry Maddox, PHI	Dusty Baker, LA
1982	Andre Dawson, MON	Dale Murphy, ATL	Garry Maddox, PHI
1983	Andre Dawson, MON	Dale Murphy, ATL	Willie McGee, STL
1984	Dale Murphy, ATL	Bob Dernier, CHI	Andre Dawson, MON
1985	Willie McGee, STL	Dale Murphy, ATL	Andre Dawson, MON
1986	Tony Gwynn, SD	Dale Murphy, ATL	Willie McGee, STL
1987	Eric Davis, Cin	Tony Gwynn, SD	Andre Dawson, CHI
1988	Andy Van Slyke, PIT	Eric Davis, CIN	Andre Dawson, CHI
1989	Andy Van Slyke, PIT	Eric Davis, CIN	Tony Gwynn, SD
1990	Andy Van Slyke, PIT	Tony Gwynn, SD	Barry Bonds, PIT
1991	Barry Bonds, PIT	Tony Gwynn, SD	Andy Van Slyke, PIT
1992	Barry Bonds, SF	Larry Walker, MON	Marquis Grissom, MON
1993	Barry Bonds, SF	Larry Walker, MON	Marquis Grissom, MON
1994	Barry Bonds, SF	Darren Lewis, SF	Marquis Grissom, MON
1995	Raul Mondesi, LA	Steve Finley, SD	Marquis Grissom, ATL

American League Outfielders

1957	Minnie Minoso, CHI	Al Kaline, DET	No other selection
1958	Norm Siebern, NY	Jim Piersall, BOS	Al Kaline, DET
1959	Minnie Minoso, CLE	Al Kaline, DET	Jackie Jensen, BOS
1960	Minnie Minoso, CHI	Jim Landis, CHI	Roger Maris, NY
1961	Al Kaline, DET	Jim Piersall, CLE	Jim Landis, CHI
1962	Jim Landis, CHI	Mickey Mantle, NY	Al Kaline, DET
1963	Al Kaline, DET	Carl Yastrzemski, BOS	Jim Landis, CHI
1964	Al Kaline, DET	Jim Landis, CHI	Vic Davalillo, CLE
1965	Al Kaline, DET	Tom Tresh, NY	Carl Yastrzemski, BOS
1966	Al Kaline, DET	Tommie Agee, CHI	Tony Oliva, MIN
1967	Carl Yastrzemski, BOS	Paul Blair, BAL	Al Kaline, DET
1968	Mickey Stanley, DET	Carl Yastrzemski, BOS	Reggie Smith, BOS
1969	Paul Blair, BAL	Mickey Stanley, DET	Carl Yastrzemski, BOS
1970	Mickey Stanley, DET	Paul Blair, BAL	Ken Berry, CHI
1971	Paul Blair, BAL	Amos Otis, KC	Carl Yastrzemski, BOS
1972	Paul Blair, BAL	Bobby Murcer, NY	Ken Berry, CAL
1973	Paul Blair, BAL	Amos Otis, KC	Mickey Stanley, DET
1974	Paul Blair, BAL	Amos Otis, KC	Joe Rudi, OAK
1975	Paul Blair, BAL	Joe Rudi, OAK	Fred Lynn, BOS
1976	Joe Rudi, OAK	Dwight Evans, BOS	Rick Manning, CLE
1977	Juan Beniquez, TEX	Carl Yastrzemski, BOS	Al Cowens, KC
1978	Fred Lynn, BOS	Dwight Evans, BOS	Rick Miller, CAL
1979	Dwight Evans, BOS	Sixto Lezcano, MIL	Fred Lynn, BOS
1980	Fred Lynn, BOS	Dwayne Murphy, OAK	Willie Wilson, KC
1981	Dwayne Murphy, OAK	Dwight Evans, BOS	Rickey Henderson, OAK
1982	Dwight Evans, BOS	Dave Winfield, NY	Dwayne Murphy, OAK
1983	Dwight Evans, BOS	Dave Winfield, NY	Dwayne Murphy, OAK
1984	Dwight Evans, BOS	Dave Winfield, NY	Dwayne Murphy, OAK
1985	Gary Pettis, CAL	Dave Winfield, NY	Dwight Evans, BOS
			Dwayne Murphy, OAK
1986	Gary Pettis, CAL	Jesse Barfield, TOR	Kirby Puckett, MIN
1987	Jesse Barfield, TOR	Kirby Puckett, MIN	Dave Winfield, NY
1988	Kirby Puckett, MIN	Devon White, CAL	Gary Pettis, DET
1989	Devon White, CAL	Gary Pettis, DET	Kirby Puckett, MIN
1990	Gary Pettis, TEX	Ken Griffey, SEA	Ellis Burks, BOS
1991	Ken Griffey, SEA	Devon White, TOR	Kirby Puckett, MIN
1992	Ken Griffey, SEA	Devon White, TOR	Kirby Puckett, MIN
1993	Ken Griffey, SEA	Devon White, TOR	Kenny Lofton, CLE
1994	Ken Griffey, SEA	Devon White, TOR	Kenny Lofton, CLE
1995	Ken Griffey, SEA	Devon White, TOR	Kenny Lofton, CLE

Mickey Mantle

Career Records

Games

1. Pete Rose — 3,562
2. Carl Yastrzemski — 3,308
3. Hank Aaron — 3,298
4. Ty Cobb — 3,035
5. Stan Musial — 3,026
6. Willie Mays — 2,992
8. Dave Winfield — 2,973
8. Rusty Staub — 2,951
9. Brooks Robinson — 2,896
10. Robin Yount — 2,856

Runs

1. Ty Cobb — 2,246
2. Hank Aaron — 2,174
   Babe Ruth — 2,174
4. Pete Rose — 2,165
5. Willie Mays — 2,062
6. Stan Musial — 1,949
7. Lou Gehrig — 1,888
8. Tris Speaker — 1,882
9. Mel Ott — 1,859
10. Frank Robinson — 1,829

Hits

1. Pete Rose — 4,256
2. Ty Cobb — 4,189
3. Hank Aaron — 3,771
4. Stan Musial — 3,630
5. Tris Speaker — 3,514
6. Carl Yastrzemski — 3,419
7. Honus Wagner — 3,415
8. Eddie Collins — 3,312
9. Willie Mays — 3,283
10. Nap Lajoie — 3,242

Doubles

1. Tris Speaker — 792
2. Pete Rose — 746
3. Stan Musial — 725
4. Ty Cobb — 724
5. George Brett — 665
6. Nap Lajoie — 657
7. Carl Yastrzemski — 646
8. Honus Wagner — 640
9. Hank Aaron — 624
10. Paul Waner — 605

Triples

1. Sam Crawford — 309
2. Ty Cobb — 295
3. Honus Wagner — 252
4. Jake Beckley — 243
5. Roger Conner — 233
6. Tris Speaker — 222
7. Fred Clarke — 220
8. Dan Brouthers — 205
9. Joe Kelley — 194
10. Paul Waner — 191

Home Runs

1. Hank Aaron — 755
2. Babe Ruth — 714
3. Willie Mays — 660
4. Frank Robinson — 586
5. Harmon Killebrew — 573
6. Reggie Jackson — 563
7. Mike Schmidt — 548
8. Mickey Mantle — 536
9. Jimmie Foxx — 534
10. Willie McCovey — 521
    Ted Williams — 521

Total Bases

1.	Hank Aaron	6,856
2.	Stan Musial	6,134
3.	Willie Mays	6,066
4.	Ty Cobb	5,854
5.	Babe Ruth	5,793
6.	Pete Rose	5,752
7.	Carl Yastrzemski	5,539
8.	Frank Robinson	5,373
9.	Dave Winfield	5,221
10.	Eddie Murray	5,108

Runs Batted In

1.	Hank Aaron	2,297
2.	Babe Ruth	2,213
3.	Lou Gehrig	1,995
4.	Stan Musial	1,951
5.	Ty Cobb	1,937
6.	Jimmie Foxx	1,922
7.	Willie Mays	1,903
9.	Mel Ott	1,860
10.	Carl Yastrzemski	1,844

Walks

1.	Babe Ruth	2,056
2.	Ted Williams	2,019
3.	Joe Morgan	1,865
4.	Carl Yastrzemski	1,845
5.	Mickey Mantle	1,733
6.	Mel Ott	1,708
7.	Eddie Yost	1,614
8.	Darrell Evans	1,605
9.	Stan Musial	1,599
10.	Pete Rose	1,566

Strikeouts

1.	Reggie Jackson	2,597
2.	Willie Stargell	1,936
3.	Mike Schmidt	1,883
4.	Tony Perez	1,867
5.	Dave Kingman	1,816
6.	Bobby Bonds	1,757
7.	Dale Murphy	1,733
8.	Lou Brock	1,730
9.	Mickey Mantle	1,710
10.	Harmon Killebrew	1,699

Batting Average

1.	Ty Cobb	.366
2.	Rogers Hornsby	.358
3.	Joe Jackson	.356
4.	Ed Delahanty	.346
5.	Tris Speaker	.345
6.	Ted Williams	.344
7.	Billy Hamilton	.344
8.	Dan Brouthers	.342
	Harry Heilmann	.342
	Babe Ruth	.342

Slugging Percentage

1.	Babe Ruth	.690
2.	Ted Williams	.634
3.	Lou Gehrig	.632
4.	Jimmie Foxx	.609
5.	Hank Greenberg	.605
6.	Joe DiMaggio	.579
7.	Rogers Hornsby	.577
8.	Johnny Mize	.562
9.	Stan Musial	.559
10.	Mickey Mantle	.557
	Willie Mays	.557

On-Base Percentage

1.	Ted Williams	.483
2.	Babe Ruth	.474
3.	John McGraw	.465
4.	Billy Hamilton	.455
5.	Lou Gehrig	.447
6.	Rogers Hornsby	.434
7.	Ty Cobb	.433
8.	Jimmie Foxx	.428
9.	Tris Speaker	.428
10.	Ferris Fain	.425

Stolen Bases

1.	Rickey Henderson	1,149
2.	Lou Brock	938
3.	Billy Hamilton	912
4.	Ty Cobb	891
5.	Tim Raines	777
6.	Eddie Collins	744
7.	Vince Coleman	740
8.	Arlie Latham	739
9.	Max Carey	738
10.	Honus Wagner	722

Wins

1.	Cy Young	511
2.	Walter Johnson	417
3.	Pete Alexander	373
	Christy Mathewson	373
5.	Warren Spahn	363
6.	Kid Nichols	361
7.	Jim Galvin	360
8.	Tim Keefe	342
9.	Steve Carlton	329
10.	John Clarkson	328

Losses

1.	Cy Young	316
2.	Jim Galvin	308
3.	Nolan Ryan	292
4.	Walter Johnson	279
5.	Phil Niekro	274
6.	Gaylord Perry	265
7.	Don Sutton	256
8.	Jack Powell	254
9.	Eppa Rixey	251
10.	Bert Blyleven	250

Games Started

1.	Cy Young	815
2.	Nolan Ryan	773
3.	Don Sutton	756
4.	Phil Niekro	716
5.	Steve Carlton	709
6.	Tommy John	700
7.	Gaylord Perry	690
8.	Bert Blyleven	685
9.	Jim Galvin	682
10.	Walter Johnson	666

Innings Pitched

1.	Cy Young	7,354.2
2.	Jim Galvin	5,941.1
3.	Walter Johnson	5,923.2
4.	Phil Niekro	5,404.1
5.	Nolan Ryan	5,386.0
6.	Gaylord Perry	5,350.1
7.	Don Sutton	5,282.1
8.	Warren Spahn	5,243.2
9.	Steve Carlton	5,217.1
10.	Pete Alexander	5,189.1

Saves

1.	Lee Smith	471
2.	Jeff Reardon	367
3.	Rollie Fingers	341
4.	Dennis Eckersley	323
5.	Tom Henke	311
6.	Rich Gossage	310
7.	Bruce Sutter	300
8.	John Franco	295
9.	Dave Righetti	252
10.	Dan Quisenberry	244

Strikeouts

1.	Nolan Ryan	5,714
2.	Steve Carlton	4,136
3.	Bert Blyleven	3,701
4.	Tom Seaver	3,640
5.	Don Sutton	3,574
6.	Gaylord Perry	3,534
7.	Walter Johnson	3,509
8.	Phil Niekro	3,342
9.	Fergie Jenkins	3,192
10.	Bob Gibson	3,117

Earned Run Average

1.	Ed Walsh	1.82
2.	Addie Joss	1.89
3.	Mordecai Brown	2.06
4.	John Ward	2.10
5.	Christy Mathewson	2.13
6.	Walter Johnson	2.16
	Rube Waddell	2.16
8.	Orval Overall	2.23
9.	Tommy Bond	2.25
10.	Ed Reulbach	2.28
	Will White	2.28

Jeff Bagwell

Single-Season Records

At-Bats

1.	Willie Wilson	1980	705
2.	Juan Samuel	1984	701
3.	Dave Cash	1975	699
4.	Matty Alou	1969	698
5.	Woody Jensen	1936	696
6.	Maury Wills	1962	695
	Omar Moreno	1979	695
8.	Bobby Richardson	1962	692
9.	Kirby Puckett	1985	691
10.	Lou Brock	1967	689
	Sandy Alomar	1971	689

Runs

1.	Billy Hamilton	1894	192
2.	Tom Brown	1891	177
	Babe Ruth	1921	177
4.	Tip O'Neill	1887	167
	Lou Gehrig	1936	167
6.	Billy Hamilton	1895	166
7.	Willie Keeler	1894	165
	Joe Kelley	1894	165
9.	Arlie Latham	1887	163
	Babe Ruth	1928	163
	Lou Gehrig	1931	163

Hits

1.	George Sisler	1920	257
2.	Lefty O'Doul	1929	254
	Bill Terry	1930	254
4.	Al Simmons	1925	253
5.	Rogers Hornsby	1922	250
	Chuck Klein	1930	250
7.	Ty Cobb	1911	248
8.	George Sisler	1922	246
9.	Heinie Manush	1928	241
10.	Babe Herman	1930	241

Doubles

1.	Earl Webb	1931	67
2.	George H. Burns	1926	64
	Joe Medwick	1936	64
4.	Hank Greenberg	1934	63
5.	Paul Waner	1932	62
6.	Charlie Gehringer	1936	60
7.	Tris Speaker	1923	59
	Chuck Klein	1930	59
9.	Billy Herman	1935	57
	Billy Herman	1936	57

Triples

1.	Chief Wilson	1912	36
2.	Dave Orr	1886	31
	Heinie Reitz	1894	31
4.	Perry Werden	1893	29
5.	Harry Davis	1897	28
6.	George Davis	1893	27
	Sam Thompson	1894	27
	Jimmy Williams	1899	27
9.	John Reilly	1890	26
	George Treadway	1894	26
	Joe Jackson	1912	26
	Sam Crawford	1914	26
	Kiki Cuyler	1925	26

Home Runs

1.	Roger Maris	1961	61
2.	Babe Ruth	1927	60
3.	Babe Ruth	1921	59
4.	Jimmie Foxx	1932	58
	Hank Greenberg	1938	58
6.	Hack Wilson	1930	56
7.	Babe Ruth	1920	54
	Babe Ruth	1928	54
	Ralph Kiner	1949	54
	Mickey Mantle	1961	54

Total Bases

1. Babe Ruth	1921	457
2. Rogers Hornsby	1922	450
3. Lou Gehrig	1927	447
4. Chuck Klein	1930	445
5. Jimmie Foxx	1932	438
6. Stan Musial	1948	429
7. Hack Wilson	1930	423
8. Chuck Klein	1932	420
9. Lou Gehrig	1930	419
10. Joe DiMaggio	1937	418

Batting Average

1. Hugh Duffy	1894	.440
2. Tip O'Neill	1887	.435
3. Ross Barnes	1876	.429
4. Nap Lajoie	1901	.426
5. Willie Keeler	1897	.424
Rogers Hornsby	1924	.424
7. Ty Cobb	1911	.420
George Sisler	1922	.420
9. Fred Dunlap	1884	.412
10. Ed Delahanty	1899	.410

Runs Batted In

1. Hack Wilson	1930	190
2. Lou Gehrig	1931	184
3. Hank Greenberg	1937	183
4. Lou Gehrig	1927	175
Jimmie Foxx	1938	175
6. Lou Gehrig	1930	174
7. Babe Ruth	1921	171
8. Chuck Klein	1930	170
Hank Greenberg	1935	170
10. Jimmie Foxx	1932	169

Slugging Percentage

1. Babe Ruth	1920	.847
2. Babe Ruth	1921	.846
3. Babe Ruth	1927	.772
4. Lou Gehrig	1927	.765
5. Babe Ruth	1923	.764
6. Rogers Hornsby	1925	.756
7. Jeff Bagwell	1994	.750
8. Jimmie Foxx	1932	.749
9. Babe Ruth	1924	.739
10. Babe Ruth	1926	.737

Walks

1. Babe Ruth	1923	170
2. Ted Williams	1947	162
Ted Williams	1949	162
4. Ted Williams	1946	156
5. Eddie Yost	1956	151
6. Eddie Joost	1949	149
7. Babe Ruth	1920	148
Eddie Stanky	1945	148
Jim Wynn	1969	148
10. Jimmy Sheckard	1911	147

On-Base Percentage

1. Ted Williams	1941	.551
2. John McGraw	1899	.547
3. Babe Ruth	1923	.545
4. Babe Ruth	1920	.530
5. Ted Williams	1957	.528
6. Billy Hamilton	1894	.523
7. Babe Ruth	1926	.516
Ted Williams	1954	.516
9. Mickey Mantle	1957	.515
10. Babe Ruth	1924	.513

Strikeouts

1. Bobby Bonds	1970	189
2. Bobby Bonds	1969	187
3. Rob Deer	1987	186
4. Pete Incaviglia	1986	185
5. Cecil Fielder	1990	182
6. Mike Schmidt	1975	180
7. Rob Deer	1986	179
8. Dave Nicholson	1963	175
Gorman Thomas	1979	175
Jose Canseco	1986	175
Rob Deer	1991	175

Stolen Bases

1. Hugh Nicol	1887	138
2. Rickey Henderson	1982	130
3. Arlie Latham	1887	129
4. Lou Brock	1974	118
5. Charlie Comiskey	1887	117
6. John Ward	1887	111
Billy Hamilton	1889	111
Billy Hamilton	1891	111
9. Vince Coleman	1985	110
10. Arlie Latham	1888	109
Vince Coleman	1987	109

Wins

1.	Charley Radbourn	1884	59
2.	John Clarkson	1885	53
3.	Guy Hecker	1884	52
4.	John Clarkson	1889	49
5.	Charley Radbourn	1883	48
	Charlie Buffinton	1884	48
7.	Al Spalding	1876	47
	John Ward	1879	47
9.	Jim Galvin	1883	46
	Jim Galvin	1884	46
	Matt Kilroy	1887	46

Losses

1.	John Coleman	1883	48
2.	Will White	1880	42
3.	Larry McKeon	1884	41
4.	George Bradley	1879	40
	Jim McCormick	1879	40
6.	Henry Porter	1888	37
	Kid Carsey	1891	37
	George Cobb	1892	37
9.	Stump Weidman	1886	36
	Bill Hutchinson	1892	36

Games Started

1.	Will White	1879	75
	Jim Galvin	1883	75
3.	Jim McCormick	1880	74
4.	Charley Radbourn	1884	73
	Guy Hecker	1884	73
6.	Jim Galvin	1884	72
	John Clarkson	1889	72
8.	Bill Hutchinson	1892	71
9.	John Clarkson	1885	70
10.	Matt Kilroy	1887	69

Innings Pitched

1.	Will White	1879	680.0
2.	Charley Radbourn	1884	678.2
3.	Guy Hecker	1884	670.2
4.	Jim McCormick	1880	657.2
5.	Jim Galvin	1883	656.1
6.	Jim Galvin	1884	636.1
7.	Charley Radbourn	1883	632.1
8.	Bill Hutchinson	1892	627.0
9.	John Clarkson	1885	623.0
10.	Jim Devlin	1876	622.0

Saves

1.	Bobby Thigpen	1990	57
2.	Randy Myers	1993	53
3.	Dennis Eckersley	1990	48
	Rod Beck	1993	48
5.	Lee Smith	1991	47
6.	Dave Righetti	1986	46
	Bryan Harvey	1991	46
8.	Dan Quisenberry	1983	45
	Bruce Sutter	1984	45
	Dennis Eckersley	1988	45
	Bryan Harvey	1993	45
	Jeff Montgomery	1993	45
	Duane Ward	1993	45

Strikeouts

1.	Matt Kilroy	1886	513
2.	Toad Ramsey	1886	499
3.	Hugh Daily	1884	483
4.	Charley Radbourn	1884	441
5.	Charlie Buffinton	1884	417
6.	Guy Hecker	1884	385
7.	Nolan Ryan	1973	383
8.	Sandy Koufax	1965	382
9.	Bill Sweeney	1884	374
10.	Jim Galvin	1884	369

Earned Run Average

1.	Tim Keefe	1880	0.86
2.	Dutch Leonard	1914	0.96
3.	Mordecai Brown	1906	1.04
4.	Bob Gibson	1968	1.12
5.	Christy Mathewson	1909	1.14
6.	Walter Johnson	1913	1.14
7.	Jack Pfiester	1907	1.15
8.	Addie Joss	1908	1.16
9.	Carl Lundgren	1907	1.17
10.	Denny Driscoll	1882	1.21

George Brett

Year-by-Year Leaders

BATTING AVERAGE

Year	National League	BA	American League	BA
1901	Jesse Burkett, STL	.376	Nap Lajoie, PHI	.422
1902	Ginger Beaumont, PIT	.357	Ed Delahanty, WAS	.376
1903	Honus Wagner, PIT	.355	Nap Lajoie, CLE	.355
1904	Honus Wagner, PIT	.349	Nap Lajoie, CLE	.381
1905	Cy Seymour, CIN	.377	Elmer Flick, CLE	.306
1906	Honus Wagner, PIT	.339	George Stone, STL	.358
1907	Honus Wagner, PIT	.350	Ty Cobb, DET	.350
1908	Honus Wagner, PIT	.354	Ty Cobb, DET	.324
1909	Honus Wagner, PIT	.339	Ty Cobb, DET	.377
1910	Sherry Magee, PHI	.331	Ty Cobb, DET	.385
1911	Honus Wagner, PIT	.334	Ty Cobb, DET	.420
1912	Heinie Zimmerman, CHI	.372	Ty Cobb, DET	.410
1913	Jake Daubert, BKN	.350	Ty Cobb, DET	.390
1914	Jake Daubert, BKN	.329	Ty Cobb, DET	.368
1915	Larry Doyle, NY	.320	Ty Cobb, DET	.369
1916	Hal Chase, CIN	.339	Tris Speaker, CLE	.386
1917	Edd Roush, CIN	.341	Ty Cobb, DET	.383
1918	Zack Wheat, BKN	.335	Ty Cobb, DET	.382
1919	Edd Roush, CIN	.321	Ty Cobb, DET	.384
1920	Rogers Hornsby, STL	.370	George Sisler, STL	.407
1921	Rogers Hornsby, STL	.397	Harry Heilmann, DET	.394
1922	Rogers Hornsby, STL	.401	George Sisler, STL	.420
1923	Rogers Hornsby, STL	.384	Harry Heilmann, DET	.403
1924	Rogers Hornsby, STL	.424	Babe Ruth, NY	.378
1925	Rogers Hornsby, STL	.403	Harry Heilmann, DET	.393
1926	Bubbles Hargrave, CIN	.353	Heinie Manush, DET	.378
1927	Paul Waner, PIT	.380	Harry Heilmann, DET	.398
1928	Rogers Hornsby, STL	.387	Goose Goslin, WAS	.379
1929	Lefty O'Doul, PHI	.398	Lew Fonseca, CLE	.369
1930	Bill Terry, NY	.401	Al Simmons, PHI	.381
1931	Chick Hafey, STL	.349	Al Simmons, PHI	.390
1932	Lefty O'Doul, BKN	.368	Dale Alexander, BOS-DET	.367
1933	Chuck Klein, PHI	.368	Jimmy Foxx, PHI	.356
1934	Paul Waner, PIT	.362	Lou Gehrig, NY	.363
1935	Arky Vaughan, PIT	.385	Buddy Myer, WAS	.349
1936	Paul Waner, PIT	.373	Luke Appling, CHI	.388
1937	Joe Medwick, STL	.374	Charlie Gehringer, DET	.371
1938	Ernie Lombardi, CIN	.342	Jimmie Foxx, BOS	.349
1939	Johnny Mize, STL	.349	Joe DiMaggio, NY	.381
1940	Stan Hack, CHI	.317	Joe DiMaggio, NY	.352
1941	Pete Reiser, BKN	.343	Ted Williams, BOS	.406
1942	Enos Slaughter, STL	.318	Ted Williams, BOS	.356
1943	Stan Musial, STL	.357	Luke Appling, CHI	.328

BATTING AVERAGE (continued)

Year	National League	BA	American League	B
1944	Dixie Walker, BKN	.357	Lou Boudreau, CLE	.3
1945	Phil Cavarretta, CHI	.355	Snuffy Stirnweiss, NY	.30
1946	Stan Musial, STL	.365	Mickey Vernon, WAS	.35
1947	Harry Walker, STL-PHI	.363	Ted Williams, BOS	.3
1948	Stan Musial, STL	.376	Ted Williams, BOS	.30
1949	Jackie Robinson, BKN	.342	George Kell, DET	.34
1950	Stan Musial, STL	.346	Billy Goodman, BOS	.3
1951	Stan Musial, STL	.355	Ferris Fain, PHI	.3
1952	Stan Musial, STL	.336	Ferris Fain, PHI	.32
1953	Carl Furillo, BKN	.344	Mickey Vernon, WAS	.32
1954	Willie Mays, NY	.345	Bobby Avila, CLE	.3
1955	Richie Ashburn, PHI	.338	Al Kaline, DET	.34
1956	Hank Aaron, MIL	.328	Mickey Mantle, NY	.35
1957	Stan Musial, STL	.351	Ted Williams, BOS	.38
1958	Richie Ashburn, PHI	.350	Ted Williams, BOS	.32
1959	Hank Aaron, MIL	.355	Harvey Kuenn, DET	.35
1960	Dick Groat, PIT	.325	Pete Runnels, BOS	.3
1961	Roberto Clemente, PIT	.351	Norm Cash, DET	.36
1962	Tommy Davis, LA	.346	Pete Runnels, BOS	.32
1963	Tommy Davis, LA	.326	Carl Yastrzemski, BOS	.32
1964	Roberto Clemente, PIT	.339	Tony Oliva, MIN	.32
1965	Roberto Clemente, PIT	.329	Tony Oliva, MIN	.32
1966	Matty Alou, PIT	.342	Frank Robinson, BAL	.31
1967	Roberto Clemente, PIT	.357	Carl Yastrzemski, BOS	.32
1968	Pete Rose, CIN	.335	Carl Yastrzemski, BOS	.30
1969	Pete Rose, CIN	.348	Rod Carew, MIN	.3
1970	Rico Carty, ATL	.366	Alex Johnson, CAL	.33
1971	Joe Torre, STL	.363	Tony Oliva, MIN	.3
1972	Billy Williams, CHI	.333	Rod Carew, MIN	.3
1973	Pete Rose, CIN	.338	Rod Carew, MIN	.35
1974	Ralph Garr, ATL	.353	Rod Carew, MIN	.36
1975	Bill Madlock, CHI	.354	Rod Carew, MIN	.3
1976	Bill Madlock, CHI	.339	George Brett, KC	.3
1977	Dave Parker, PIT	.338	Rod Carew, MIN	.38
1978	Dave Parker, PIT	.334	Rod Carew, MIN	.3
1979	Keith Hernandez, STL	.344	Fred Lynn, BOS	.3
1980	Bill Buckner, CHI	.324	George Brett, KC	.39
1981	Pete Rose, PHI	.325	Carney Lansford, BOS	.3
1982	Al Oliver, MON	.331	Willie Wilson, KC	.3
1983	Bill Madlock, PHI	.323	Wade Boggs, BOS	.3
1984	Tony Gwynn, SD	.351	Don Mattingly, NY	.3
1985	Willie McGee, STL	.353	Wade Boggs, BOS	.3
1986	Tim Raines, MON	.334	Wade Boggs, BOS	.3
1987	Tony Gwynn, SD	.370	Wade Boggs, BOS	.3
1988	Tony Gwynn, SD	.313	Wade Boggs, BOS	.3

Year	National League	BA	American League	BA
1989	Tony Gwynn, SD	.336	Kirby Puckett, MIN	.339
1990	Willie McGee, STL	.335	George Brett, KC	.329
1991	Terry Pendleton, ATL	.319	Julio Franco, TEX	.341
1992	Gary Sheffield, SD	.330	Edgar Martinez, SEA	.343
1993	Andres Galarraga, COL	.370	John Olerud, TOR	.363
1994	Tony Gwynn, SD	.394	Paul O'Neill, NY	.359
1995	Tony Gwynn, SD	.368	Edgar Martinez, SEA	.356

HOME RUNS

Year	NATIONAL LEAGUE	HR	AMERICAN LEAGUE	HR
1901	Sam Crawford, CIN	16	Napoleon Lajoie, PHI	13
1902	Tommy Leach, PIT	6	Socks Seybold, PHI	16
1903	Jimmy Sheckard, BKN	9	Buck Freeman, BOS	13
1904	Harry Lumley, BKN	9	Harry Davis, PHI	10
1905	Fred Odwell, CIN	9	Harry Davis, PHI	8
1906	Tim Jordan, BKN	12	Harry Davis, PHI	12
1907	Dave Brain, BOS	10	Harry Davis, PHI	8
1908	Tim Jordan, BKN	12	Sam Crawford, DET	7
1909	Red Murray, NY	7	Ty Cobb, DET	9
1910	Fred Beck, BOS	10	Jake Stahl, BOS	10
	Frank Schulte, CHI	10		
1911	Frank Schulte, CHI	21	Frank Baker, PHI	11
1912	Heinie Zimmerman, CHI	14	Frank Baker, PHI	10
			Tris Speaker, BOS	10
1913	Gavvy Cravath, PHI	19	Frank Baker, PHI	12
1914	Gavvy Cravath, PHI	19	Frank Baker, PHI	9
1915	Gavvy Cravath, PHI	24	Braggo Roth, CHI-CLE	7
1916	Dave Robertson, NY	12	Wally Pipp, NY	12
	Cy Williams, CHI	12		
1917	Gavvy Cravath, PHI	12	Wally Pipp, NY	9
	Dave Robertson, NY	12		
1918	Gavvy Cravath, PHI	8	Babe Ruth, BOS	11
			Tilly Walker, PHI	11
1919	Gavvy Cravath, PHI	12	Babe Ruth, BOS	29
1920	Cy Williams, PHI	15	Babe Ruth, NY	54
1921	George Kelly, NY	23	Babe Ruth, NY	59
1922	Rogers Hornsby, STL	42	Ken Williams, STL	39
1923	Cy Williams, PHI	41	Babe Ruth, NY	41
1924	Jack Fournier, BKN	27	Babe Ruth, NY	46
1925	Rogers Hornsby, STL	39	Bob Meusel, NY	33
1926	Hack Wilson, CHI	21	Babe Ruth, NY	47
1927	Hack Wilson, CHI	30	Babe Ruth, NY	60
	Cy Williams, PHI	30		
1928	Jim Bottomley, STL	31	Babe Ruth, NY	54

HOME RUNS (continued)

Year	NATIONAL LEAGUE	HR	AMERICAN LEAGUE	HR
	Hack Wilson, CHI	31		
1929	Chuck Klein, PHI	43	Babe Ruth, NY	46
1930	Hack Wilson, CHI	56	Babe Ruth, NY	49
1931	Chuck Klein, PHI	31	Lou Gehrig, NY	46
			Babe Ruth, NY	46
1932	Chuck Klein, PHI	38	Jimmy Foxx, PHI	58
	Mel Ott, NY	38		
1933	Chuck Klein, PHI	28	Jimmy Foxx, PHI	48
1934	Ripper Collins, STL	35	Lou Gehrig, NY	49
	Mel Ott, NY	35		
1935	Wally Barger, BOS	34	Jimmy Foxx, PHI	36
			Hank Greenberg, DET	36
1936	Mel Ott, NY	33	Lou Gehrig, NY	49
1937	Joe Medwick, STL	31	Joe DiMaggio, NY	46
	Mel Ott, NY	31		
1938	Mel Ott, NY	36	Hank Greenberg, DET	58
1939	Johnny Mize, STL	28	Jimmie Foxx, BOS	35
1940	Johnny Mize, STL	43	Hank Greenberg, DET	41
1941	Dolph Camilli, BKN	34	Ted Williams, BOS	37
1942	Mel Ott, NY	30	Ted Williams, BOS	36
1943	Bill Nicholson, CHI	29	Rudy York, DET	34
1944	Bill Nicholson, CHI	33	Nick Etten, NY	22
1945	Tommy Holmes, BOS	28	Vern Stephens, STL	24
1946	Ralph Kiner, PIT	23	Hank Greenberg, DET	44
1947	Johnny Mize, NY	51	Ted Williams, BOS	32
	Ralph Kiner, PIT	51		
1948	Ralph Kiner, PIT	40	Joe DiMaggio, NY	39
	Johnny Mize, NY	40		
1949	Ralph Kiner, PIT	54	Ted Williams, BOS	43
1950	Ralph Kiner, PIT	47	Al Rosen, CLE	37
1951	Ralph Kiner, PIT	42	Gus Zernial, CHI-PHI	33
1952	Ralph Kiner, PIT	37	Larry Doby, CLE	32
	Hank Sauer, CHI	37		
1953	Eddie Matthews, MIL	47	Al Rosen, CLE	43
1954	Ted Kluszewski, CIN	49	Larry Doby, CLE	32
1955	Willie Mays, NY	51	Mickey Mantle, NY	37
1956	Duke Snider, BKN	43	Mickey Mantle, NY	52
1957	Hank Aaron, MIL	44	Roy Sievers, WAS	42
1958	Ernie Banks, CHI	47	Mickey Mantle, NY	42
1959	Eddie Matthews, MIL	46	Rocky Colavito, CLE	42
			Harmon Killebrew, WAS	42
1960	Ernie Banks, CHI	41	Mickey Mantle, NY	40
1961	Orlando Cepeda, SF	46	Roger Maris, NY	61
1962	Willie Mays, SF	49	Harmon Killebrew, MIN	48
1963	Hank Aaron, MIL	44	Harmon Killebrew, MIN	45

Year	NATIONAL LEAGUE	HR	AMERICAN LEAGUE	HR
	Willie McCovey, SF	44		
1964	Willie Mays, SF	47	Harmon Killebrew, MIN	49
1965	Willie Mays, SF	52	Tony Conigliaro, BOS	32
1966	Hank Aaron, ATL	44	Frank Robinson, BAL	49
1967	Hank Aaron, ATL	39	Harmon Killebrew, MIN	44
			Carl Yastrzemski, BOS	44
1968	Willie McCovey, SF	36	Frank Howard, WAS	44
1969	Willie McCovey, SF	46	Harmon Killebrew, MIN	49
1970	Johnny Bench, CIN	45	Frank Howard, WAS	44
1971	Willie Stargell, PIT	48	Bill Melton, CHI	33
1972	Johnny Bench, CIN	40	Dick Allen, CHI	37
1973	Willie Stargell, PIT	44	Reggie Jackson, OAK	32
1974	Mike Schmidt, PHI	36	Dick Allen, CHI	32
1975	Mike Schmidt, PHI	38	Reggie Jackson, OAK	36
			George Scott, MIL	36
1976	Mike Schmidt, PHI	38	Graig Nettles, NY	32
1977	George Foster, CIN	52	Jim Rice, BOS	39
1978	George Foster, CIN	40	Jim Rice, BOS	46
1979	Dave Kingman, CHI	48	Gorman Thomas, MIL	45
1980	Mike Schmidt, PHI	48	Reggie Jackson, NY	41
			Ben Oglivie, MIL	41
1981	Mike Schmidt, PHI	31	Tony Armas, OAK	22
			Dwight Evans, BOS	22
			Bobby Grich, CAL	22
			Eddie Murray, BAL	22
1982	Dave Kingman, NY	37	Reggie Jackson, CAL	39
			Gorman Thomas, MIL	39
1983	Mike Schmidt, PHI	40	Jim Rice, BOS	39
1984	Dale Murphy, ATL	36	Tony Armas, BOS	43
	Mike Schmidt, PHI	36		
1985	Dale Murphy, ATL	37	Darrell Evans, DET	40
1986	Mike Schmidt, PHI	37	Jesse Barfield, TOR	40
1987	Andre Dawson, CHI	49	Mark McGwire, OAK	49
1988	Darryl Strawberry, NY	39	Jose Canseco, OAK	42
1989	Kevin Mitchell, SF	47	Fred McGriff, TOR	36
1990	Ryne Sandberg, CHI	40	Cecil Fielder, DET	51
1991	Howard Johnson, NY	38	Jose Canseco, OAK	44
			Cecil Fielder, DET	44
1992	Fred McGriff, SD	35	Juan Gonzalez, TEX	43
1993	Barry Bonds, SF	46	Juan Gonzalez, TEX	46
1994	Matt Williams, SF	43	Ken Griffey, SEA	40
1995	Dante Bichette, COL	40	Albert Belle, CLE	50

RUNS BATTED IN

Year	National League	RBI	American League	RBI
1901	Honus Wagner, PIT	126	Nap Lajoie, PHI	125
1902	Honus Wagner, PIT	91	Buck Freeman, BOS	121
1903	Sam Mertes, NY	104	Buck Freeman, BOS	104
1904	Bill Dahlen, NY	80	Nap Lajoie, CLE	102
1905	Cy Seymour, CIN	121	Harry Davis, PHI	83
1906	Jim Nealon, PIT	83	Harry Davis, PHI	96
	Harry Steinfeldt, CHI	83		
1907	Sherry Magee, PHI	85	Ty Cobb, DET	116
1908	Honus Wagner, PIT	109	Ty Cobb, DET	108
1909	Honus Wagner, PIT	100	Ty Cobb, DET	107
1910	Sherry Magee, PHI	123	Sam Crawford, DET	120
1911	Frank Schulte, CHI	107	Ty Cobb, DET	144
	Chief Wilson, PIT	107		
1912	Honus Wagner, PIT	102	Frank Baker, PHI	133
1913	Gavvy Cravath, PHI	128	Frank Baker, PHI	126
1914	Sherry Magee, PHI	103	Sam Crawford, DET	104
1915	Gavvy Cravath, PHI	115	Sam Crawford, DET	112
			Bobby Veach, DET	112
1916	Heinie Zimmerman, CHI-NY	83	Del Pratt, STL	103
1917	Heinie Zimmerman, NY	102	Bobby Veach, DET	103
1918	Sherry Magee, CIN	76	Bobby Veach, DET	78
1919	Hy Myers, BKN	73	Babe Ruth, BOS	114
1920	Rogers Hornsby, STL	94	Babe Ruth, NY	137
	George Kelly, NY	94		
1921	Rogers Hornsby, STL	126	Babe Ruth, NY	171
1922	Rogers Hornsby, STL	152	Ken Williams, STL	155
1923	Emil Meusel, NY	125	Babe Ruth, NY	130
			Tris Speaker, CLE	130
1924	George Kelly, NY	136	Goose Goslin, WAS	129
1925	Rogers Hornsby, STL	143	Bob Meusel, NY	138
1926	Jim Bottomley, STL	120	Babe Ruth, NY	145
1927	Paul Waner, PIT	131	Lou Gehrig, NY	175
1928	Jim Bottomley, STL	136	Babe Ruth, NY	142
			Lou Gehrig, NY	142
1929	Hack Wilson, CHI	159	Al Simmons, PHI	157
1930	Hack Wilson, CHI	190	Lou Gehrig, NY	174
1931	Chuck Klein, PHI	121	Lou Gehrig, NY	184
1932	Don Hurst, PHI	143	Jimmy Foxx, PHI	169
1933	Chuck Klein, PHI	120	Jimmy Foxx, PHI	163
1934	Mel Ott, NY	135	Lou Gehrig, NY	165
1935	Wally Berger, BOS	130	Hank Greenberg, DET	170
1936	Joe Medwick, STL	138	Hal Trosky, CLE	162
1937	Joe Medwick, STL	154	Hank Greenberg, DET	183
1938	Joe Medwick, STL	122	Jimmie Foxx, BOS	175
1939	Frank McCormick, CIN	128	Ted Williams, BOS	145

Year	National League	RBI	American League	RBI
1940	Johnny Mize, STL	137	Hank Greenberg, DET	150
1941	Dolph Camilli, BKN	120	Joe DiMaggio, NY	125
1942	Johnny Mize, NY	110	Ted Williams, BOS	137
1943	Bill Nicholson, CHI	128	Rudy York, DET	118
1944	Bill Nicholson, CHI	122	Vern Stephens, STL	109
1945	Dixie Walker, BKN	124	Nick Etten, NY	111
1946	Enos Slaughter, STL	130	Hank Greenberg, DET	127
1947	Johnny Mize, NY	138	Ted Williams, BOS	114
1948	Stan Musial, STL	131	Joe DiMaggio, NY	155
1949	Ralph Kiner, PIT	127	Vern Stephens, BOS	159
			Ted Williams, BOS	159
1950	Del Ennis, PHI	126	Walt Dropo, BOS	144
			Vern Stephens, BOS	144
1951	Monte Irvin, NY	121	Gus Zernial, CHI-PHI	129
1952	Hank Sauer, CHI	121	Al Rosen, CLE	105
1953	Roy Campanella, BKN	142	Al Rosen, CLE	145
1954	Ted Kluszewski, CIN	141	Larry Doby, CLE	126
1955	Duke Snider, BKN	136	Ray Boone, DET	116
			Jackie Jensen, BOS	116
1956	Stan Musial, STL	109	Mickey Mantle, NY	130
1957	Hank Aaron, MIL	132	Roy Sievers, WAS	114
1958	Ernie Banks, CHI	129	Jackie Jensen, BOS	122
1959	Ernie Banks, CHI	143	Jackie Jensen, BOS	112
1960	Hank Aaron, MIL	126	Roger Maris, NY	112
1961	Orlando Cepeda, SF	142	Roger Maris, NY	142
1962	Tommy Davis, LA	153	Harmon Killebrew, MIN	126
1963	Hank Aaron, MIL	130	Dick Stuart, BOS	118
1964	Ken Boyer, STL	119	Brooks Robinson, BAL	118
1965	Deron Johnson, CIN	130	Rocky Colavito, CLE	108
1966	Hank Aaron, ATL	127	Frank Robinson, BAL	122
1967	Orlando Cepeda, STL	111	Carl Yastrzemski, BOS	121
1968	Willie McCovey, SF	105	Ken Harrelson, BOS	109
1969	Willie McCovey, SF	126	Harmon Killebrew, MIN	140
1970	Johnny Bench, CIN	148	Frank Howard, WAS	126
1971	Joe Torre, STL	137	Harmon Killebrew, MIN	119
1972	Johnny Bench, CIN	125	Dick Allen, CHI	113
1973	Willie Stargell, PIT	119	Reggie Jackson, OAK	117
1974	Johnny Bench, CIN	129	Jeff Burroughs, TEX	118
1975	Greg Luzinski, PHI	120	George Scott, MIL	109
1976	George Foster, CIN	121	Lee May, BAL	109
1977	George Foster, CIN	149	Larry Hisle, MIN	119
1978	George Foster, CIN	120	Jim Rice, BOS	139
1979	Dave Winfield, SD	118	Don Baylor, CAL	139
1980	Mike Schmidt, PHI	121	Cecil Cooper, MIL	122
1981	Mike Schmidt, PHI	91	Eddie Murray, BAL	78

RUNS BATTED IN (continued)

Year	National League	RBI	American League	RBI
1982	Dale Murphy, ATL	109	Hal McRae, KC	133
	Al Oliver, MON	109		
1983	Dale Murphy, ATL	121	Cecil Cooper, MIL	126
			Jim Rice, BOS	126
1984	Gary Carter, MON	106	Tony Armas, BOS	123
	Mike Schmidt, PHI	106		
1985	Dave Parker, CIN	125	Don Mattingly, NY	145
1986	Mike Schmidt, PHI	119	Joe Carter, CLE	121
1987	Andre Dawson, CHI	137	George Bell, TOR	134
1988	Will Clark, SF	109	Jose Canseco, OAK	124
1989	Kevin Mitchell, SF	125	Ruben Sierra, TEX	119
1990	Matt Williams, SF	122	Cecil Fielder, DET	132
1991	Howard Johnson, NY	117	Cecil Fielder, DET	133
1992	Darren Daulton, PHI	109	Cecil Fielder, DET	124
1993	Barry Bonds, SF	123	Albert Belle, CLE	129
1994	Jeff Bagwell, HOU	116	Kirby Puckett, MIN	112
1995	Dante Bichette, COL	128	Albert Belle, CLE	126

STOLEN BASES

Year	National League	SB	American League	SB
1901	Honus Wagner, PIT	49	Frank Isbell, CHI	52
1902	Honus Wagner, PIT	42	Topsy Hartsel, PHI	47
1903	Frank Chance, CHI	67	Harry Bay, CLE	45
	Jimmy Sheckard, BKN	67		
1904	Honus Wagner, PIT	53	Elmer Flick, CLE	42
1905	Art Devlin, NY	59	Danny Hoffman, PHI	46
	Billy Maloney, CHI	59		
1906	Frank Chance, CHI	57	John Anderson, WAS	39
			Elmer Flick, WAS	39
1907	Honus Wagner, PIT	61	Ty Cobb, DET	49
1908	Honus Wagner, PIT	53	Patsy Dougherty, CHI	47
1909	Bob Bescher, CIN	54	Ty Cobb, DET	76
1910	Bob Bescher, CIN	70	Eddie Collins, PHI	81
1911	Bob Bescher, CIN	80	Ty Cobb, DET	83
1912	Bob Bescher, CIN	67	Clyde Milan, WAS	88
1913	Max Carey, PIT	61	Clyde Milan, WAS	75
1914	George J. Burns, NY	62	Fritz Maisel, NY	74
1915	Max Carey, PIT	36	Ty Cobb, DET	96
1916	Max Carey, PIT	63	Ty Cobb, DET	68
1917	Max Carey, PIT	46	Ty Cobb, DET	55
1918	Max Carey, PIT	58	George Sisler, STL	45
1919	George J. Burns, NY	40	Eddie Collins, CHI	33
1920	Max Carey, PIT	52	Sam Rice, WAS	63
1921	Frankie Frisch, NY	49	George Sisler, STL	35

Year	National League	SB	American League	SB
1922	Max Carey, PIT	51	George Sisler, STL	51
1923	Max Carey, PIT	51	Eddie Collins, CHI	47
1924	Max Carey, PIT	49	Eddie Collins, CHI	42
1925	Max Carey, PIT	46	Johnny Mostil, CHI	43
1926	Kiki Cuyler, PIT	35	Johnny Mostil, CHI	35
1927	Frankie Frisch, STL	48	George Sisler, STL	27
1928	Kiki Cuyler, CHI	37	Buddy Myer, BOS	30
1929	Kiki Cuyler, CHI	43	Charlie Gehringer, DET	28
1930	Kiki Cuyler, CHI	37	Marty McManus, DET	23
1931	Frankie Frisch, STL	28	Ben Chapman, NY	61
1932	Chuck Klein, PHI	20	Ben Chapman, NY	38
1933	Pepper Martin, STL	26	Ben Chapman, NY	27
1934	Pepper Martin, STL	23	Billy Werber, BOS	40
1935	Augie Galan, CHI	22	Billy Werber, BOS	29
1936	Pepper Martin, STL	23	Lyn Lary, STL	37
1937	Augie Galan, CHI	23	Ben Chapman, BOS-WAS	35
			Billy Werber, PHI	35
1938	Stan Hack, CHI	16	Frank Crosetti, NY	27
1939	Stan Hack, CHI	17	George Case, WAS	51
	Lee Handley, PIT	17		
1940	Lonny Frey, CIN	22	George Case, WAS	35
1941	Danny Murtaugh, PHI	18	George Case, WAS	33
1942	Pete Reiser, BKN	20	George Case, WAS	44
1943	Arky Vaughan, BKN	20	George Case, WAS	61
1944	Johnny Barrett, PIT	28	Snuffy Stirnweiss, NY	55
1945	Red Schoendienst, STL	26	Snuffy Stirnweiss, NY	33
1946	Pete Reiser, BKN	34	George Case, CLE	28
1947	Jackie Robinson, BKN	29	Bob Dillinger, STL	34
1948	Richie Ashburn, PHI	32	Bob Dillinger, STL	28
1949	Jackie Robinson, BKN	37	Bob Dillinger, STL	20
1950	Sam Jethroe, BOS	35	Dom DiMaggio, BOS	15
1951	Sam Jethroe, BOS	35	Minnie Minoso, CHI-CLE	31
1952	Pee Wee Reese, BKN	30	Minnie Minoso, CHI	22
1953	Bill Bruton, MIL	26	Minnie Minoso, CHI	25
1954	Bill Bruton, MIL	34	Jackie Jensen, BOS	22
1955	Bill Bruton, MIL	25	Jim Rivera, CHI	25
1956	Willie Mays, NY	40	Luis Aparicio, CHI	21
1957	Willie Mays, NY	38	Luis Aparicio, CHI	28
1958	Willie Mays, SF	31	Luis Aparicio, CHI	29
1959	Willie Mays, SF	27	Luis Aparicio, CHI	56
1960	Maury Wills, LA	50	Luis Aparicio, CHI	51
1961	Maury Wills, LA	35	Luis Aparicio, CHI	53
1962	Maury Wills, LA	104	Luis Aparicio, CHI	31
1963	Maury Wills, LA	40	Luis Aparicio, BAL	40
1964	Maury Wills, LA	53	Luis Aparicio, BAL	57

STOLEN BASES (continued)

Year	National League	SB	American League	SB
1965	Maury Wills, LA	94	Bert Campaneris, KC	51
1966	Lou Brock, STL	74	Bert Campaneris, KC	52
1967	Lou Brock, STL	52	Bert Campaneris, KC	55
1968	Lou Brock, STL	62	Bert Campaneris, OAK	62
1969	Lou Brock, STL	53	Tommy Harper, SEA	73
1970	Bobby Tolan, CIN	57	Bert Campaneris, OAK	42
1971	Lou Brock, STL	64	Amos Otis, KC	52
1972	Lou Brock, STL	63	Bert Campaneris, OAK	52
1973	Lou Brock, STL	70	Tommy Harper, BOS	54
1974	Lou Brock, STL	118	Billy North, OAK	54
1975	Davey Lopes, LA	77	Mickey Rivers, CAL	70
1976	Davey Lopes, LA	63	Billy North, OAK	75
1977	Frank Taveras, PIT	70	Fred Patek, KC	53
1978	Omar Moreno, PIT	71	Ron LeFlore, DET	68
1979	Omar Moreno, PIT	77	Willie Wilson, KC	83
1980	Ron LeFlore, MON	97	Rickey Henderson, OAK	100
1981	Tim Raines, MON	71	Rickey Henderson, OAK	56
1982	Tim Raines, MON	78	Rickey Henderson, OAK	130
1983	Tim Raines, MON	90	Rickey Henderson, OAK	108
1984	Tim Raines, MON	75	Rickey Henderson, OAK	66
1985	Vince Coleman, STL	110	Rickey Henderson, NY	80
1986	Vince Coleman, STL	107	Rickey Henderson, NY	87
1987	Vince Coleman, STL	109	Harold Reynolds, SEA	60
1988	Vince Coleman, STL	81	Rickey Henderson, NY	93
1989	Vince Coleman, STL	65	Rickey Henderson, NY-OAK	77
1990	Vince Coleman, STL	77	Rickey Henderson, OAK	65
1991	Marquis Grissom, MON	76	Rickey Henderson, OAK	58
1992	Marquis Grissom, MON	78	Kenny Lofton, CLE	66
1993	Chuck Carr, FLO	58	Kenny Lofton, CLE	70
1994	Craig Biggio, HOU	39	Kenny Lofton, CLE	60
1995	Quilvio Veras, FLO	56	Kenny Lofton, CLE	54

WINS

Year	National League	Wins	American League	Wins
1901	Bill Donovan, BKN	25	Cy Young, BOS	33
1902	Jack Chesbro, PIT	28	Cy Young, BOS	32
1903	Joe McGinnity, NY	31	Cy Young, BOS	28
1904	Joe McGinnity, NY	35	Jack Chesbro, NY	41
1905	Christy Mathewson, NY	31	Rube Waddell, PHI	26
1906	Joe McGinnity, NY	27	Al Orth, NY	27
1907	Christy Mathewson, NY	24	Addie Joss, CLE	27
			Doc White, CHI	27
1908	Christy Mathewson, NY	37	Ed Walsh, CHI	40
1909	Mordecai Brown, CHI	27	George Mullin, DET	29
1910	Christy Mathewson, NY	27	Jack Coombs, PHI	31
1911	Pete Alexander, PHI	28	Jack Coombs, PHI	28
1912	Larry Cheney, CHI	26	Smokey Joe Wood, BOS	34
	Rube Marquard, NY	26		
1913	Tom Seaton, PHI	27	Walter Johnson, WAS	36
1914	Pete Alexander, PHI	27	Walter Johnson, WAS	28
	Richard Rudolph, BOS	27		
1915	Pete Alexander, PHI	31	Walter Johnson, WAS	28
1916	Pete Alexander, PHI	33	Walter Johnson, WAS	25
1917	Pete Alexander, PHI	30	Eddie Cicotte, CHI	28
1918	Hippo Vaughn, CHI	22	Walter Johnson, WAS	23
1919	Jesse Barnes, NY	25	Eddie Cicotte, CHI	29
1920	Pete Alexander, CHI	27	Jim Bagby, CLE	31
1921	Wilbur Cooper, PIT	22	Carl Mays, NY	27
	Burleigh Grimes, BKN	22	Urban Shocker, STL	27
1922	Eppa Rixey, CIN	25	Eddie Rommel, PHI	27
1923	Dolf Luque, CIN	27	George Uhle, CLE	26
1924	Dazzy Vance, BKN	28	Walter Johnson, WAS	23
1925	Dazzy Vance, BKN	22	Eddie Rommel, PHI	21
1926	Pete Donahue, CIN	20	George Uhle, CLE	27
	Ray Kremer, PIT	20		
	Lee Meadows, PIT	20		
	Flint Rhem, STL	20		
1927	Charlie Root, CHI	26	Waite Hoyt, NY	22
			Ted Lyons, CHI	22
1928	Rube Benton, NY	25	Lefty Grove, PHI	24
	Burleigh Grimes, PIT	25	George Pipgras, NY	24
1929	Pat Malone, CHI	22	George Earnshaw, PHI	24
1930	Ray Kremer, PIT	20	Lefty Grove, PHI	28
	Pat Malone, CHI	20		
1931	James Elliott, PHI	19	Lefty Grove, PHI	31
	Billy Hallahan, STL	19		
	Heinie Meine, PIT	19		
1932	Lonnie Warneke, CHI	22	General Crowder, WAS	26
1933	Carl Hubbell, NY	23	General Crowder, WAS	24

WINS (continued)

Year	National League	Wins	American League	Wins
			Lefty Grove, PHI	24
1934	Dizzy Dean, STL	30	Lefty Gomez, NY	26
1935	Dizzy Dean, STL	28	Wes Ferrell, BOS	25
1936	Carl Hubbell, NY	26	Tommy Bridges, DET	23
1937	Carl Hubbell, NY	22	Lefty Gomez, NY	21
1938	Bill Lee, CHI	22	Red Ruffing, NY	21
1939	Bucky Walters, CIN	27	Bob Feller, CLE	24
1940	Bucky Walters, CIN	22	Bob Feller, CLE	27
1941	Kirby Higbe, BKN	22	Bob Feller, CLE	25
	Whit Wyatt, BKN	22		
1942	Mort Cooper, STL	22	Tex Hughson, BOS	22
1943	Mort Cooper, STL	21	Spud Chandler, NY	20
	Elmer Riddle, CIN	21	Dizzy Trout, DET	20
	Rip Sewell, PIT	21		
1944	Bucky Walters, CIN	23	Hal Newhouser, DET	29
1945	Red Barrett, BOS-STL	23	Hal Newhouser, DET	25
1946	Howie Pollet, STL	21	Bob Feller, CLE	26
			Hal Newhouser, DET	26
1947	Ewell Blackwell, CIN	22	Bob Feller, CLE	20
1948	Johnny Sain, BOS	24	Hal Newhouser, DET	21
1949	Warren Spahn, BOS	21	Mel Parnell, BOS	25
1950	Warren Spahn, BOS	21	Bob Lemon, CLE	23
1951	Larry Jansen, NY	23	Bob Feller, CLE	22
	Sal Maglie, NY	23		
1952	Robin Roberts, PHI	28	Bobby Shantz, PHI	24
1953	Robin Roberts, PHI	23	Bob Porterfield, WAS	22
	Warren Spahn, MIL	23		
1954	Robin Roberts, PHI	23	Bob Lemon, CLE	23
			Early Wynn, CLE	23
1955	Robin Roberts, PHI	23	Whitey Ford, NY	18
			Bob Lemon, CLE	18
			Frank Sullivan, BOS	18
1956	Don Newcombe, BKN	27	Frank Lary, DET	21
1957	Warren Spahn, MIL	21	Jim Bunning, DET	20
			Billy Pierce, CHI	20
1958	Bob Friend, PIT	22	Bob Turley, NY	21
	Warren Spahn, MIL	22		
1959	Lew Burdette, MIL	21	Early Wynn, CHI	22
	Sam Jones, SF	21		
	Warren Spahn, MIL	21		
1960	Warren Spahn, MIL	21	Jim Perry, CLE	18
	Ernie Broglio, STL	21	Chuck Estrada, BAL	18
1961	Warren Spahn, MIL	21	Whitey Ford, NY	25
1962	Don Drysdale, LA	25	Ralph Terry, NY	23
1963	Sandy Koufax, LA	25	Whitey Ford, NY	24

Year	National League	Wins	American League	Wins
	Juan Marichal, SF	25		
1964	Larry Jackson, CHI	24	Dean Chance, LA	20
			Gary Peters, CHI	20
1965	Sandy Koufax, LA	26	Mudcat Grant, MIN	21
1966	Sandy Koufax, LA	27	Jim Kaat, MIN	25
1967	Mike McCormick, SF	22	Jim Lonborg, BOS	22
			Earl Wilson, DET	22
1968	Juan Marichal, SF	26	Denny McLain, DET	31
1969	Tom Seaver, NY	25	Denny McLain, DET	24
1970	Gaylord Perry, SF	23	Mike Cuellar, BAL	24
	Bob Gibson, STL	23	Dave McNally, BAL	24
			Jim Perry, MIN	24
1971	Ferguson Jenkins, CHI	24	Mickey Lolich, DET	25
1972	Steve Carlton, PHI	27	Gaylord Perry, CLE	24
			Wilbur Wood, CHI	24
1973	Ron Bryant, SF	24	Wilbur Wood, CHI	24
1974	Phil Niekro, ATL	20	Catfish Hunter, OAK	25
	Andy Messersmith, LA	20	Ferguson Jenkins, TEX	25
1975	Tom Seaver, NY	22	Catfish Hunter, NY	23
			Jim Palmer, BAL	23
1976	Randy Jones, SD	22	Jim Palmer, BAL	22
1977	Steve Carlton, PHI	23	Dave Goltz, MIN	20
			Dennis Leonard, KC	20
			Jim Palmer, BAL	20
1978	Gaylord Perry, SD	21	Ron Guidry, NY	25
1979	Joe Niekro, HOU	21	Mike Flanagan, BAL	23
	Phil Niekro, ATL	21		
1980	Steve Carlton, PHI	24	Steve Stone, BAL	25
1981	Tom Seaver, CIN	14	Dennis Martinez, BAL	14
			Steve McCatty, OAK	14
			Jack Morris, DET	14
			Pete Vuckovich, MIL	14
1982	Steve Carlton, PHI	23	LaMarr Hoyt, CHI	19
1983	John Denny, PHI	19	LaMarr Hoyt, CHI	24
1984	Joaquin Andujar, STL	20	Mike Boddicker, BAL	20
1985	Dwight Gooden, NY	24	Ron Guidry, NY	22
1986	Fernando Valenzuela, LA	21	Roger Clemens, BOS	24
1987	Rick Sutcliffe, CHI	18	Roger Clemens, BOS	20
			Dave Stewart, OAK	20
1988	Orel Hershiser, LA	23	Frank Viola, MIN	24
	Danny Jackson, CIN	23		
1989	Mike Scott, HOU	20	Bret Saberhagen, KC	23
1990	Doug Drabek, PIT	22	Bob Welch, OAK	27
1991	Tom Glavine, ATL	20	Scott Erickson, MIN	20
	John Smiley, PIT	20	Bill Gullickson, DET	20

WINS (continued)

Year	National League	Wins	American League	Wins
1992	Tom Glavine, ATL	20	Kevin Brown, TEX	21
	Greg Maddux, CHI	20	Jack Morris, TOR	21
1993	John Burkett, SF	22	Jack McDowell, CHI	22
	Tom Glavine, ATL	22		
1994	Ken Hill, MON	16	Jimmy Key, NY	17
	Greg Maddux, ATL	16		
1995	Greg Maddux, ATL	19	Mike Mussina, BAL	19

ERA

Year	National League	ERA	American League	ERA
1901	Jesse Tannehill, PIT	2.18	Cy Young, BOS	1.62
1902	Jack Taylor, CHI	1.33	Ed Siever, DET	1.91
1903	Sam Leever, PIT	2.06	Earl Moore, CLE	1.77
1904	Joe McGinnity, NY	1.61	Addie Joss, CLE	1.59
1905	Christy Mathewson, NY	1.27	Rube Waddell, PHI	1.48
1906	Mordecai Brown, CHI	1.04	Doc White, CHI	1.52
1907	Jack Pfiester, CHI	1.15	Ed Walsh, CHI	1.60
1908	Christy Mathewson, NY	1.43	Addie Joss, CLE	1.16
1909	Christy Mathewson, NY	1.14	Harry Krause, PHI	1.39
1910	King Cole, CHI	1.80	Ed Walsh, CHI	1.27
1911	Christy Mathewson, NY	1.99	Vean Gregg, CLE	1.81
1912	Jeff Tesreau, NY	1.96	Walter Johnson, WAS	1.39
1913	Christy Mathewson, NY	2.06	Walter Johnson, WAS	1.09
1914	Bill Doak, STL	1.72	Dutch Leonard, BOS	1.01
1915	Pete Alexander, PHI	1.22	Smokey Joe Wood, BOS	1.49
1916	Pete Alexander, PHI	1.55	Babe Ruth, BOS	1.75
1917	Fred Anderson, NY	1.44	Eddie Cicotte, CHI	1.53
1918	Hippo Vaughn, CHI	1.74	Walter Johnson, WAS	1.27
1919	Pete Alexander, CHI	1.72	Walter Johnson, WAS	1.49
1920	Pete Alexander, CHI	1.91	Bob Shawkey, NY	2.45
1921	Bill Doak, STL	2.59	Red Faber, CHI	2.48
1922	Phil Douglas, NY	2.63	Red Faber, CHI	2.80
1923	Dolf Luque, CIN	1.93	Stan Coveleski, CLE	2.76
1924	Dazzy Vance, BKN	2.16	Walter Johnson, WAS	2.72
1925	Dolf Luque, CIN	2.63	Stan Coveleski, WAS	2.84
1926	Ray Kremer, PIT	2.61	Lefty Grove, PHI	2.51
1927	Ray Kremer, PIT	2.47	Waite Hoyt, NY	2.63
1928	Dazzy Vance, BKN	2.09	Garland Braxton, WAS	2.51
1929	Bill Walker, NY	3.09	Lefty Grove, PHI	2.81
1930	Dazzy Vance, BKN	2.61	Lefty Grove, PHI	2.54
1931	Bill Walker, NY	2.26	Lefty Grove, PHI	2.06
1932	Lonnie Warneke, CHI	2.37	Lefty Grove, PHI	2.84
1933	Carl Hubbell, NY	1.66	Monte Pearson, CLE	2.33
1934	Carl Hubbell, NY	2.30	Lefty Gomez, NY	2.33

Year	National League	ERA	American League	ERA
1935	Cy Blanton, PIT	2.58	Lefty Grove, BOS	2.70
1936	Carl Hubbell, NY	2.31	Lefty Grove, BOS	2.81
1937	James Turner, BOS	2.38	Lefty Gomez, NY	2.33
1938	Bill Lee, CHI	2.66	Lefty Grove, BOS	3.08
1939	Bucky Walters, CIN	2.29	Lefty Grove, BOS	2.54
1940	Bucky Walters, CIN	2.48	Ernie Bonham, NY	1.90
1941	Elmer Riddle, CIN	2.24	Thornton Lee, CHI	2.37
1942	Mort Cooper, STL	1.78	Ted Lyons, CHI	2.10
1943	Max Lanier, STL	1.90	Spud Chandler, NY	1.64
1944	Ed Heusser, CIN	2.38	Dizzy Trout, DET	2.12
1945	Ray Prim, CHI	2.40	Hal Newhouser, DET	1.81
1946	Howie Pollet, STL	2.10	Hal Newhouser, DET	1.94
1947	Warren Spahn, BOS	2.33	Spud Chandler, NY	2.46
1948	Harry Brecheen, STL	2.24	Gene Bearden, CLE	2.43
1949	Dave Koslo, NY	2.50	Mel Parnell, BOS	2.77
1950	Sal Maglie, NY	2.71	Early Wynn, CLE	3.20
1951	Chet Nichols, BOS	2.88	Saul Rogovin, CHI-DET	2.78
1952	Hoyt Wilhelm, NY	2.43	Allie Reynolds, NY	2.06
1953	Warren Spahn, MIL	2.10	Ed Lopat, NY	2.42
1954	Johnny Antonelli, NY	2.30	Mike Garcia, CLE	2.64
1955	Bob Friend, PIT	2.83	Billy Pierce, CHI	1.97
1956	Lew Burdette, MIL	2.70	Whitey Ford, NY	2.47
1957	Johnny Podres, BKN	2.66	Bobby Shantz, NY	2.45
1958	Stu Miller, SF	2.47	Whitey Ford, NY	2.01
1959	Sam Jones, SF	2.83	Hoyt Wilhelm, BAL	2.19
1960	Mike McCormick, SF	2.70	Frank Baumann, CHI	2.67
1961	Warren Spahn, MIL	3.02	Dick Donovan, WAS	2.40
1962	Sandy Koufax, LA	2.54	Hank Aguirre, DET	2.21
1963	Sandy Koufax, LA	1.88	Gary Peters, CHI	2.33
1964	Sandy Koufax, LA	1.74	Dean Chance, LA	1.65
1965	Sandy Koufax, LA	2.04	Sam McDowell, CLE	2.18
1966	Sandy Koufax, LA	1.73	Gary Peters, CHI	1.98
1967	Phil Niekro, ATL	1.87	Joel Horlen, CHI	2.06
1968	Bob Gibson, STL	1.12	Luis Tiant, CLE	1.60
1969	Juan Marichal, SF	2.10	Dick Bosman, WAS	2.19
1970	Tom Seaver, NY	2.82	Diego Segui, OAK	2.56
1971	Tom Seaver, NY	1.76	Vida Blue, OAK	1.82
1972	Steve Carlton, PHI	1.97	Luis Tiant, CLE	1.91
1973	Tom Seaver, NY	2.08	Jim Palmer, BAL	2.40
1974	Buzz Capra, ATL	2.28	Catfish Hunter, OAK	2.49
1975	Randy Jones, SD	2.24	Jim Palmer, BAL	2.09
1976	John Denny, STL	2.52	Mark Fidrych, DET	2.34
1977	John Candelaria, PIT	2.34	Frank Tanana, CAL	2.54
1978	Craig Swan, NY	2.43	Ron Guidry, NY	1.74
1979	J.R. Richard, HOU	2.71	Ron Guidry, NY	2.78

ERA (continued)

Year	National League	ERA	American League	ERA
1980	Don Sutton, LA	2.20	Rudy May, NY	2.47
1981	Nolan Ryan, HOU	1.69	Steve McCatty, OAK	2.32
1982	Steve Rogers, MON	2.40	Rick Sutcliffe, CLE	2.96
1983	Atlee Hammaker, SF	2.25	Rick Honeycutt, TEX	2.42
1984	Alejandro Pena, LA	2.48	Mike Boddicker, BAL	2.79
1985	Dwight Gooden, NY	1.53	Dave Stieb, TOR	2.48
1986	Mike Scott, HOU	2.22	Roger Clemens, BOS	2.48
1987	Nolan Ryan, HOU	2.76	Jimmy Key, TOR	2.76
1988	Joe Magrane, STL	2.18	Allan Anderson, MIN	2.45
			Teddy Higuera, MIL	2.45
1989	Scott Garrelts, SF	2.28	Bret Saberhagen, KC	2.16
1990	Danny Darwin, HOU	2.21	Roger Clemens, BOS	1.93
1991	Dennis Martinez, MON	2.39	Roger Clemens, BOS	2.62
1992	Bill Swift, SF	2.08	Roger Clemens, BOS	2.41
1993	Greg Maddux, ATL	2.36	Kevin Appier, KC	2.56
1994	Greg Maddux, ATL	1.56	Steve Ontiveros, OAK	2.65
1995	Greg Maddux, ATL	1.63	Randy Johnson, SEA	2.48

STRIKEOUTS

Year	National League	SO	American League	SO
1901	Noodles Hahn, CIN	239	Cy Young, BOS	158
1902	Vic Willis, BOS	225	Rube Waddell, PHI	210
1903	Christy Mathewson, NY	267	Rube Waddell, PHI	302
1904	Christy Mathewson, NY	212	Rube Waddell, PHI	349
1905	Christy Mathewson, NY	206	Rube Waddell, PHI	287
1906	Fred Beebe, CHI-STL	171	Rube Waddell, PHI	196
1907	Christy Mathewson, NY	178	Rube Waddell, PHI	232
1908	Christy Mathewson, NY	259	Ed Walsh, CHI	269
1909	Orval Overall, CHI	205	Frank Smith, CHI	177
1910	Earl Moore, PHI	185	Walter Johnson, WAS	313
1911	Rube Marquard, NY	237	Ed Walsh, CHI	255
1912	Pete Alexander, PHI	195	Walter Johnson, WAS	303
1913	Tom Seaton, PHI	168	Walter Johnson, WAS	243
1914	Pete Alexander, PHI	214	Walter Johnson, WAS	225
1915	Pete Alexander, PHI	241	Walter Johnson, WAS	203
1916	Pete Alexander, PHI	167	Walter Johnson, WAS	228
1917	Pete Alexander, PHI	200	Walter Johnson, WAS	188
1918	Hippo Vaughn, CHI	148	Walter Johnson, WAS	162
1919	Hippo Vaughn, CHI	141	Walter Johnson, WAS	147
1920	Pete Alexander, CHI	173	Stan Coveleski, CLE	133
1921	Burleigh Grimes, BKN	136	Walter Johnson, WAS	143
1922	Dazzy Vance, BKN	134	Urban Shocker, STL	149
1923	Dazzy Vance, BKN	197	Walter Johnson, WAS	130
1924	Dazzy Vance, BKN	262	Walter Johnson, WAS	158

Year	National League	SO	American League	SO
1925	Dazzy Vance, BKN	221	Lefty Grove, PHI	116
1926	Dazzy Vance, BKN	140	Lefty Grove, PHI	194
1927	Dazzy Vance, BKN	184	Lefty Grove, PHI	174
1928	Dazzy Vance, BKN	200	Lefty Grove, PHI	183
1929	Pat Malone, CHI	166	Lefty Grove, PHI	170
1930	Bill Hallahan, STL	177	Lefty Grove, PHI	209
1931	Billy Hallahan, STL	159	Lefty Grove, PHI	209
1932	Dizzy Dean, STL	191	Red Ruffing, NY	190
1933	Dizzy Dean, STL	199	Lefty Gomez, NY	163
1934	Dizzy Dean, STL	195	Lefty Gomez, NY	158
1935	Dizzy Dean, STL	182	Tommy Bridges, DET	163
1936	Van Mungo, BKN	238	Tommy Bridges, DET	175
1937	Carl Hubbell, NY	159	Lefty Gomez, NY	194
1938	Clay Bryant, CHI	135	Bob Feller, CLE	240
1939	Claude Passeau, PHI-CIN	137	Bob Feller, CLE	246
1940	Kirby Higbe, PHI	137	Bob Feller, CLE	261
1941	Johnny Vander Meer, CIN	202	Bob Feller, CLE	260
1942	Johnny Vander Meer, CIN	186	Bobo Newsom, WAS	113
			Tex Hughson, BOS	113
1943	Johnny Vander Meer, CIN	174	Allie Reynolds, CLE	151
1944	Bill Voiselle, NY	161	Hal Newhouser, DET	187
1945	Preacher Roe, PIT	148	Hal Newhouser, DET	212
1946	Johnny Schmitz, CHI	135	Bob Feller, CLE	348
1947	Ewell Blackwell, CIN	193	Bob Feller, CLE	196
1948	Harry Brecheen, STL	149	Bob Feller, CLE	164
1949	Warren Spahn, BOS	151	Virgil Trucks, DET	153
1950	Warren Spahn, BOS	191	Bob Lemon, CLE	170
1951	Don Newcombe, BKN	164	Vic Raschi, NY	164
	Warren Spahn, BOS	164		
1952	Warren Spahn, BOS	183	Allie Reynolds, NY	160
1953	Robin Roberts, PHI	198	Billy Pierce, CHI	186
1954	Robin Roberts, PHI	185	Bob Turley, BAL	185
1955	Sam Jones, CHI	198	Herb Score, CLE	245
1956	Sam Jones, CHI	176	Herb Score, CLE	263
1957	Jack Sanford, PHI	188	Early Wynn, CLE	184
1958	Sam Jones, STL	225	Early Wynn, CHI	179
1959	Don Drysdale, LA	242	Jim Bunning, DET	201
1960	Don Drysdale, LA	246	Jim Bunning, DET	201
1961	Sandy Koufax, LA	269	Camilo Pascual, MIN	221
1962	Don Drysdale, LA	232	Camilo Pascual, MIN	206
1963	Sandy Koufax, LA	306	Camilo Pascual, MIN	202
1964	Bob Veale, PIT	250	Al Downing, NY	217
1965	Sandy Koufax, LA	382	Sam McDowell, CLE	325
1966	Sandy Koufax, LA	317	Sam McDowell, CLE	225
1967	Jim Bunning, PHI	253	Jim Lonborg, BOS	246

STRIKEOUTS (continued)

Year	National League	SO	American League	SO
1968	Bob Gibson, STL	268	Sam McDowell, CLE	283
1969	Ferguson Jenkins, CHI	273	Sam McDowell, CLE	279
1970	Tom Seaver, NY	283	Sam McDowell, CLE	304
1971	Tom Seaver, NY	289	Mickey Lolich, DET	308
1972	Steve Carlton, PHI	310	Nolan Ryan, CAL	329
1973	Tom Seaver, NY	251	Nolan Ryan, CAL	383
1974	Steve Carlton, PHI	240	Nolan Ryan, CAL	367
1975	Tom Seaver, NY	243	Frank Tanana, CAL	269
1976	Tom Seaver, NY	235	Nolan Ryan, CAL	327
1977	Phil Niekro, ATL	262	Nolan Ryan, CAL	341
1978	J.R. Richard, HOU	303	Nolan Ryan, CAL	260
1979	J.R. Richard, HOU	313	Nolan Ryan, CAL	223
1980	Steve Carlton, PHI	286	Len Barker, CLE	187
1981	Fernando Valenzuela, LA	180	Len Barker, CLE	127
1982	Steve Carlton, PHI	286	Floyd Bannister, SEA	209
1983	Steve Carlton, PHI	275	Jack Morris, DET	232
1984	Dwight Gooden, NY	276	Mark Langston, SEA	204
1985	Dwight Gooden, NY	268	Bert Blyleven, CLE-MIN	206
1986	Mike Scott, HOU	306	Mark Langston, SEA	245
1987	Nolan Ryan, HOU	270	Mark Langston, SEA	262
1988	Nolan Ryan, HOU	228	Roger Clemens, BOS	291
1989	Jose DeLeon, STL	201	Nolan Ryan, TEX	301
1990	David Cone, NY	233	Nolan Ryan, TEX	232
1991	David Cone, NY	241	Roger Clemens, BOS	241
1992	John Smoltz, ATL	215	Randy Johnson, SEA	241
1993	Jose Rijo, CIN	227	Randy Johnson, SEA	308
1994	Andy Benes, SD	189	Randy Johnson, SEA	204
1995	Hideo Nomo, LA	236	Randy Johnson, SEA	294

Tom Seaver

Barry Larkin

World Series Winners

	AL Champion	NL Champion	World Series Champion	
1903	Boston Pilgrims	Pittsburgh Pirates	Boston Pilgrims	5–3
1905	Philadelphia Athletics	New York Giants	New York Giants	4–1
1906	Chicago White Sox	Chicago Cubs	Chicago White Sox	4–2
1907	Detroit Tigers	Chicago Cubs	Chicago Cubs	4–0
1908	Detroit Tigers	Chicago Cubs	Chicago Cubs	4–1
1909	Detroit Tigers	Pittsburgh Pirates	Pittsburgh Pirates	4–3
1910	Philadelphia Athletics	Chicago Cubs	Philadelphia Athletics	4–1
1911	Philadelphia Athletics	New York Giants	Philadelphia Athletics	4–2
1912	Boston Red Sox	New York Giants	Boston Red Sox	4–3
1913	Philadelphia Athletics	New York Giants	Philadelphia Athletics	4–1
1914	Philadelphia Athletics	Boston Braves	Boston Braves	4–0
1915	Boston Red Sox	Philadelphia Phillies	Boston Red Sox	4–1
1916	Boston Red Sox	Brooklyn Robins	Boston Red Sox	4–1
1917	Chicago White Sox	New York Giants	Chicago White Sox	4–2
1918	Boston Red Sox	Chicago Cubs	Boston Red Sox	4–2
1919	Chicago White Sox	Cincinnati Reds	Cincinnati Reds	5–3
1920	Cleveland Indians	Brooklyn Robins	Cleveland Indians	5–2
1921	New York Yankees	New York Giants	New York Yankees	5–3
1922	New York Yankees	New York Giants	New York Giants	4–0
1923	New York Yankees	New York Giants	New York Yankees	4–2
1924	Washington Senators	New York Giants	Washington Senators	4–2
1925	Washington Senators	Pittsburgh Pirates	Pittsburgh Pirates	4–3
1926	New York Yankees	St. Louis Cardinals	St. Louis Cardinals	4–3
1927	New York Yankees	Pittsburgh Pirates	New York Yankees	4–0
1928	New York Yankees	St. Louis Cardinals	New York Yankees	4–0
1929	Philadelphia Athletics	Chicago Cubs	Philadelphia Athletics	4–2
1930	Philadelphia Athletics	St. Louis Cardinals	Philadelphia Athletics	4–2
1931	Philadelphia Athletics	St. Louis Cardinals	St. Louis Cardinals	4–3
1932	New York Yankees	Chicago Cubs	New York Yankees	4–0
1933	Washington Senators	New York Giants	New York Giants	4–1
1934	Detroit Tigers	St. Louis Cardinals	St. Louis Cardinals	4–3
1935	Detroit Tigers	Chicago Cubs	Detroit Tigers	4–2
1936	New York Yankees	New York Giants	New York Yankees	4–2
1937	New York Yankees	New York Giants	New York Yankees	4–1
1938	New York Yankees	Chicago Cubs	New York Yankees	4–0
1939	New York Yankees	Cincinnati Reds	New York Yankees	4–0
1940	Detroit Tigers	Cincinnati Reds	Cincinnati Reds	4–3
1941	New York Yankees	Brooklyn Dodgers	New York Yankees	4–1
1942	New York Yankees	St. Louis Cardinals	St. Louis Cardinals	4–1
1943	New York Yankees	St. Louis Cardinals	New York Yankees	4–1
1944	St. Louis Browns	St. Louis Cardinals	St. Louis Cardinals	4–2
1945	Detroit Tigers	Chicago Cubs	Detroit Tigers	4–3
1946	Boston Red Sox	St. Louis Cardinals	St. Louis Cardinals	4–3
1947	New York Yankees	Chicago Cubs	New York Yankees	4–3
1948	Cleveland Indians	Boston Braves	Cleveland Indians	4–2

	AL Champion	**NL Champion**	**World Series Champion**	
1949	New York Yankees	Brooklyn Dodgers	New York Yankees	4–1
1950	New York Yankees	Philadelphia Phillies	New York Yankees	4–0
1951	New York Yankees	New York Giants	New York Yankees	4–2
1952	New York Yankees	Brooklyn Dodgers	New York Yankees	4–3
1953	New York Yankees	Brooklyn Dodgers	New York Yankees	4–2
1954	Cleveland Indians	New York Giants	New York Giants	4–0
1955	New York Yankees	Brooklyn Dodgers	Brooklyn Dodgers	4–3
1956	New York Yankees	Brooklyn Dodgers	New York Yankees	4–3
1957	New York Yankees	Milwaukee Braves	Milwaukee Braves	4–3
1958	New York Yankees	Milwaukee Braves	New York Yankees	4–3
1959	Chicago White Sox	Los Angeles Dodgers	Los Angeles Dodgers	4–2
1960	New York Yankees	Pittsburgh Pirates	Pittsburgh Pirates	4–3
1961	New York Yankees	Cincinnati Reds	New York Yankees	4–1
1962	New York Yankees	San Francisco Giants	New York Yankees	4–3
1963	New York Yankees	Los Angeles Dodgers	Los Angeles Dodgers	4–2
1964	New York Yankees	St. Louis Cardinals	St. Louis Cardinals	4–3
1965	Minnesota Twins	Los Angeles Dodgers	Los Angeles Dodgers	4–3
1966	Baltimore Orioles	Los Angeles Dodgers	Baltimore Orioles	4–0
1967	Boston Red Sox	St. Louis Cardinals	St. Louis Cardinals	4–3
1968	Detroit Tigers	St. Louis Cardinals	Detroit Tigers	4–3
1969	Baltimore Orioles	New York Mets	New York Mets	4–1
1970	Baltimore Orioles	Cincinnati Reds	Baltimore Orioles	4–1
1971	Baltimore Orioles	Pittsburgh Pirates	Pittsburgh Pirates	4–3
1972	Oakland A's	Cincinnati Reds	Oakland A's	4–3
1973	Oakland A's	New York Mets	Oakland A's	4–3
1974	Oakland A's	Los Angeles Dodgers	Oakland A's	4–1
1975	Boston Red Sox	Cincinnati Reds	Cincinnati Reds	4–3
1976	New York Yankees	Cincinnati Reds	Cincinnati Reds	4–0
1977	New York Yankees	Los Angeles Dodgers	New York Yankees	4–2
1978	New York Yankees	Los Angeles Dodgers	New York Yankees	4–2
1979	Baltimore Orioles	Pittsburgh Pirates	Pittsburgh Pirates	4–3
1980	Kansas City Royals	Philadelphia Phillies	Philadelphia Phillies	4–2
1981	New York Yankees	Los Angeles Dodgers	Los Angeles Dodgers	4–2
1982	Milwaukee Brewers	St. Louis Cardinals	St. Louis Cardinals	4–3
1983	Baltimore Orioles	Philadelphia Phillies	Baltimore Orioles	4–1
1984	Detroit Tigers	San Diego Padres	Detroit Tigers	4–1
1985	Kansas City Royals	St. Louis Cardinals	Kansas City Royals	4–3
1986	Boston Red Sox	New York Mets	New York Mets	4–3
1987	Minnesota Twins	St. Louis Cardinals	Minnesota Twins	4–3
1988	Oakland A's	Los Angeles Dodgers	Los Angeles Dodgers	4–1
1989	Oakland A's	San Francisco Giants	Oakland A's	4–0
1990	Oakland A's	Cincinnati Reds	Cincinnati Reds	4–0
1991	Minnesota Twins	Atlanta Braves	Minnesota Twins	4–3
1992	Toronto Blue Jays	Atlanta Braves	Toronto Blue Jays	4–2
1993	Toronto Blue Jays	Philadelphia Phillies	Toronto Blue Jays	4–2
1995	Cleveland Indians	Atlanta Braves	Atlanta Braves	4–2

World Series MVPs

1995 Tom Glavine, ATL
1993 Paul Molitor, TOR
1992 Pat Borders, TOR
1991 Jack Morris, MIN
1990 Jose Rijo, CIN
1989 Dave Stewart, OAK
1988 Orel Hershiser, LA
1987 Frank Viola, MIN
1986 Ray Knight, NYM
1985 Bret Saberhagen, KC
1984 Alan Trammell, DET
1983 Rick Dempsey, BAL
1982 Darrell Porter, STL
1981 Ron Cey, LA
      Pedro Guerrero LA
      Steve Yeager, LA
1980 Mike Schmidt, PHI
1979 Willie Stargell, PIT
1978 Bucky Dent, NYY
1977 Reggie Jackson, NYY
1976 Johnny Bench, CIN
1975 Pete Rose, CIN
1974 Rollie Fingers, OAK
1973 Reggie Jackson, OAK
1972 Gene Tenace, OAK
1971 Roberto Clemente, PIT
1970 Brooks Robinson, BAL
1969 Donn Clendenon, NYM
1968 Mickey Lolich, DET
1967 Bob Gibson, STL
1966 Frank Robinson, BAL
1965 Sandy Koufax, LA
1964 Bob Gibson, STL
1963 Sandy Koufax, LA
1962 Ralph Terry, NYY
1961 Whitey Ford, NYY
1960 Bobby Richardson, NYY
1959 Larry Sherry, LA
1958 Bob Turley, NYY
1957 Lew Burdette, MIL
1956 Don Larsen, NYY
1955 Johnny Podres, BKN

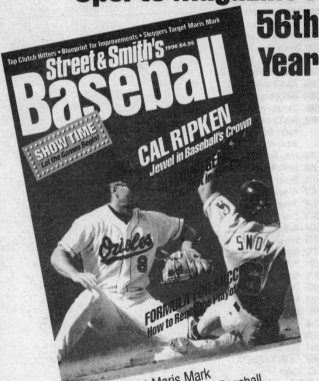